Who's Who on TV

WHO'S WHO

ON TELEVISION

FIFTH **1990-91** EDITION

Boxtree

First published 1990
Fifth edition © Boxtree Limited and
Independent Television Publications Limited

Previous editions of *Who's Who On Television*
published by Independent Television Books Limited

Design by Paterson-Jones
Typesetting and reproduction
by Rowland Phototypesetting Limited, Bury St Edmunds, Suffolk
Printed and bound in Great Britain
by Richard Clay Limited, Bungay, Suffolk

for Boxtree Limited
36 Tavistock Street
London WC2E 7PB

British Library Cataloguing in Publication Data
Who's who on television – 5th ed.
1. Television programmes. Stars – Biographies –
Collections
I. Hayward, Anthony
791.45028092

ISBN 1-85283-105-7

CONTENTS

Foreword

Welcome to *Who's Who On Television*, presenting 1000 of today's stars of the small screen. In this completely revised and updated edition, you will find actors and actresses, presenters and entertainers who have been household names for years, alongside some of the younger stars who have made an impression more recently.

Entries are listed alphabetically by surname. They include personal details and a list of credits, not necessarily comprehensive because of space restrictions, but always highlighting important work.

The *Unforgettables* section at the back of the book features 30 of TV's best-loved personalities who, sadly, are no longer with us. You will also find a directory of television companies, theatrical agents and fan clubs.

I would like to thank all the stars, agents and television companies for their help in compiling this book. Thanks are also due to Elaine Collins at Boxtree, who kept everything running smoothly during the production process, and those at *TVTimes* magazine who gave their assistance.

Anthony Hayward
Editor

ABBOT, Russ

Comedian/entertainer/actor. b. 18 September, Chester. Started in 1965 playing drums with the Black Abbots. Spent the next 15 years in summer seasons, pantomimes, theatre and cabaret. TV incl: *What's On Next?; The Comedians; Who Do You Do?* Went solo 1980. In 1984 made his West End debut in *Little Me* at the Prince of Wales. TV incl: *Russ Abbot's Madhouse; The Russ Abbot Show;* plus TV specials. Has had several hit records. Awards incl: ITV Personality of the Year; *TVTimes* Award as Funniest Man on TV, 1983–5, 1987–8; Comedian of the Decade, 1989. m. Tricia; 1 d. Erika, 3 s. Richard, Gary, Christopher. Address: c/o Mike Hughes Entertainments. **Most Cherished Possession:** 'My family.' **Favourite Memory:** 'My trips to Scotland when I was a boy.'

ACKLAND, Joss

Actor, b. 29 February 1928, London. Trained at Central School of Speech Training and Dramatic Art. Numerous West End plays and seasons at the Old Vic and Mermaid Theatre (as associate director). Opened Barbican Theatre as Falstaff in *Henry IV Parts 1 and 2.* West End musicals incl: Jorrocks in *Jorrocks; A Little Night Music; Evita;* Captain Hook in *Peter Pan – The Musical.* Films incl: *The Sicilian; White Mischief; Lethal Weapon II; To Forget Palermo; The Hunt For Red October; Six Columns In the Chronicle.* TV incl: *Shadowlands;* Sir Burton in *Queenie; First and Last; The Man Who Lived at The Ritz.* Autobiography: *I Must Be In There Somewhere.* m. Rosemary Kircaldy; 5 d. Melanie, Antonia, Penelope, Samantha, Kirsty, 2 s. Paul (dec.), Toby. Address: c/o Garrick Club, Garrick Street, London WC2. Hobbies: writing, photography. Pets: cats, when possible.

ADAMS, Tony

Actor, b. 11 December 1940, Anglesey, North Wales. Trained at Italia Conti Stage School. Theatre incl: *West Side Story; The Boy Friend; Mame; Gaslight; Cinderella.* Films incl: *Reluctant Bride; Touch and Go; Villain;* Lizard in *Woman's Skin.* Radio incl: *Lord of the Flies; Day of the Triffids; The Silver King.* TV incl: *Kiss Me Kate; Court Martial; One Pair of Eyes; The Two Ronnies; Crown Court; Doctor Who; General Hospital;* Royal Variety Show, 1982. Adam Chance in *Crossroads* (1978–88). Runs a business charter company from his yacht on the South Coast. Address: c/o Michael Ladkin. Birthsign: Sagittarius. **Most Cherished Possession:** 'My health.' **Favourite Memory:** 'Giving the eulogy in memory of Noele Gordon at St Philip's Cathedral in Birmingham.'

AGUTTER, Jenny

Actress, b. 20 December 1952, Taunton, Somerset. Trained at the Elmhurst Ballet School, Surrey. Started career in films, aged 11, in *East of Sudan,* then *Ballerina, I Start Counting, Walkabout* and *The Railway Children.* Theatre incl: *The Tempest; Betrayal* (both with the RSC, 1982–3). Other films incl: *Equus* (BAFTA Best Supporting Actress Award); *Sweet William; Secret Places; Dark Tower.* Recent TV incl: *Magnum P.I.; The Twilight Zone; Murder, She Wrote.* Book: *Snap.* Address: c/o ICM. Birthsign: Sagittarius. Hobby: photography. **Most Cherished Possession:** 'A turn-of-the-century travelling clock given to me by my parents.' **Favourite Memory:** 'Running out in the rain aged nine in Cyprus after five months of dry heat; and meeting Walt Disney while filming his feature *Ballerina.*'

AIRD, Holly

Actress, b. 18 May 1969, Aldershot, Hants. Trained at the Bush Davies Dance and Education School. At the age of 10, played Miss Polly in *The History of Mr Polly,* followed by *The Flame Trees of Thika,* both for TV. Other TV incl: *The Muse Secrets; Spider's Webb; Seal Morning; TVTimes Star Family Challenge; Affairs of the Heart; Happy Valley, Inspector Morse.* Address: c/o Hutton Management. Birthsign: Taurus. Hobbies: Fifties American cars, jogging. Pets: one dog, Toffee, one cat, Boggy. **Most Cherished Possession:** 'My car, because it gets me where I want to go and it never answers back (a black, 1964 customised VW Beetle).' **Favourite Memory:** 'My 18th birthday party, because it was an absolute riot.'

ALAN, Ray

Entertainer/ventriloquist/actor/writer, b. 18 September, Greenwich, London. Started as a call-boy at Lewisham Hippodrome, aged 13. Professional debut at Chatham's Theatre Royal. Toured Britain in variety, and with Laurel and Hardy. TV series incl: *Tich and Quackers; Ice Show; It's Your Word; Magic Circle; Cartoon Carnival; Three Little Words; The Bobby Davro Show.* Numerous other TV appearances incl: *Give Us a Clue; Starburst.* Hosted *The Impressionists* on Radio 2. Wrote and devised TV special *A Gottle of Geer.* Is an established comedy writer for TV. Wrote and presented *Starmakers*, a history of variety agents. Address: c/o Peter Prichard. Hobby: model railways. **Most Cherished Possession:** ' 'Signed photographs of all the stars with whom I've worked.' **Favourite Memory:** 'Touring with Laurel and Hardy.'

ALDRED, Sophie

Actress, b. 20 August 1962, Greenwich, London. Gained a BA Hons degree in drama from Manchester University and trained as a soprano at the Northern College of Music; plays the trumpet and piano. Theatre: *The Silver Lake; The Good Person of Sezchuan; Theatre of Thelema; Underground Man; Hansel and Gretel* (opera); *Fiddler On the Roof; Cinderella.* TV: *Knowhow; Knock-Knock; Playbus* (storyteller/singer); *Jackanory* (storyteller); a presenter in *Noel's Christmas Presents; Corners* (presenter/actress); Ace in *Doctor Who; Rainbow.* Address: c/o London Management. Hobbies: reading, singing, art galleries, football, lacrosse, sailing, swimming. **Most Cherished Possession:** 'My flat – it's the place where I can be me!' **Favourite Memory:** 'My father singing *Golden Slumbers Kiss Your Eyes* to me to get me to sleep as a child.'

ALEXANDER, Jean

Actress, b. 24 February 1926, Liverpool. Library assistant for five years, before joining the Adelphi Guild Theatre in Macclesfield and touring Lancashire, Cheshire and Staffordshire. Subsequently toured with Southport and York repertory companies. Film: *Scandal.* TV incl: *Z-Cars; Jacks and Knaves; Television Club;* Hilda Ogden in *Coronation Street* (1964–87); *Boon; Last of the Summer Wine* (Christmas specials, 1988, 1989); *Woof!* Autobiography: *The Other Side of the Street* (1989). Winner, Royal Television Society Best Performance award 1984–5, *TVTimes* Best Actress on TV award 1987. Address: c/o Joan Reddin. Hobbies: reading, sewing, gardening, classical music. Birthsign: Pisces. Pets: cats.

ALEXANDER, Maev

Actress, b. 3 February 1948, Glasgow. Trained at the Royal Scottish Academy of Music and Drama. With the RSC, 1970–71, playing Perdita in *The Winter's Tale.* Frances in *Made In Bangkok* in Coventry. TV incl: *Sutherland's Law; The Gentle Touch; Holding the Fort; Angels; A Leap In the Dark; Kids; Take the Stage; The Main Chance; This Man Craig; By the Sword Divided; Fools On the Hill; Scoop;* ex-presenter of newsdesk on *That's Life!* m. Simon Dunmore; 1 d. Alix. Address: c/o Peters Fraser & Dunlop. Birthsign: Aquarius. Hobbies: bricklaying, textile design. **Most Cherished Possession:** 'My late father's silver and mother of pearl cuff links – like him, small, discreet and much valued.' **Favourite Memory:** 'Coming to after being hit by a car, and realising I wasn't dead.'

ALEXANDER, Peter

Actor, b. 15 October 1952, Midsomer Norton, Somerset. Trained 1971–3 at Guildford School of Acting. Theatre incl: *Charley's Aunt; Twelfth Night; Joseph; Filomena; Good; Cabaret; A Christmas Carol; No Sex Please, We're British; Beyond The Rainbow.* TV incl: *Family Man; Chessgame; Travelling Man; Winning Streak; Affairs of the Heart; Minder; Coronation Street; The Practice;* Phil Pearce in *Emmerdale Farm.* m. choreographer Penny Stevenson; 1 d. Emily, 1 s. Nicholas. Address: c/o Sonny Zahl Associates. Hobbies: cricket, golf, music. Pets: dogs, cats, rabbits, geese, ducks, hens and sheep. **Most Cherished Possession:** 'The farm on which we live – nestling in the Pennines, southerly-facing, with wonderful views.' **Favourite Memory:** 'The day I was married, because it was, and is, the best thing I've ever done.'

ALEXANDER, Terence

Actor, b. 11 March 1923, London. Started with the White Rose Players, Harrogate, at 16, then wide rep experience before working in London. Theatre incl: *Two and Two Make Sex; There Goes the Bride; Fringe Benefits; Poor Bitos; Move Over, Mrs Markham.* Films incl: *The League of Gentlemen; Magic Christian; Waterloo; Run a Crooked Mile; The Day of the Jackal; Internecine Affair.* Radio incl: *Law and Disorder; The Toff.* TV incl: *The Forsyte Saga; Les Dawson; Dick Emery; Devenish; Unity; Just Liz; Terry and June; Bergerac* (nine series); *Crown Court; The New Statesman.* m. (1st) Juno, (2nd) actress Jane Downs; 2 s. Nicholas, Marcus (both from 1st m.). Hobby: wine. Address: c/o Brunskill Management. Birthsign: Pisces. **Favourite Memory:** 'Finding some Pommard '66 at £3.75 a bottle instead of £20!'

ALICIA, Ana

Actress, b. 10 December 1957, Mexico City. BA in Drama from University of Texas. Film: *Halloween II.* TV films: *Coward of the County; Happy Endings; The Ordeal of Bill Carney.* TV incl: *Ryan's Hope; Quincy; BJ and the Bear; Buck Rogers in the 25th Century; Battlestar Galactica; The Misadventures of Sheriff Lobo; The Hardy Boys; McClain's Law; The Love Boat; Hotel; The Sacketts;* Melissa Cumson in *Falcon Crest.* Address: c/o Century Artists, 9744 Wilshire Blvd, Suite 206 Beverly Hills, CA 90212. **Favourite Memory:** 'I remember wearing a nun's habit in grade school — I wanted to be a nun when I grew up.'

ALLEN, Peter

Political journalist, b. 4 February 1946, Essex. Worked on local newspapers, evening papers, then went to Australia (a £10 emigrant) where he worked as a reporter in Sydney and Melbourne. Joined LBC on return to England and became political editor of IRN. Then moved to Granada TV, and is now a political correspondent for ITN. m. Rowena; 2 d. Rebecca, Naomi, 1 s. Matthew. Address: c/o ITN. Birthsign: Aquarius. Hobbies: losing golf balls, and jogging (normally after my disobedient dog). Pets: one dog, one cat, one goldfish (dec.)! **Most Cherished Possession:** 'My company credit card.'

ALLEY, Kirstie

Actress, b. 12 January 1955, Wichita, Kansas. Studied art and literature at University of Kansas and Kansas State University. Films incl: *Runaway; Summer School; Champions; Shoot To Kill; Deadly Pursuit; Look Who's Talking; Daddy's Home; Loverboy.* TV incl: *North and South, Book II* mini series; *Masquerade; A Bunny's Tale;* Rebecca Howe in *Cheers.* m. actor Parker Stevenson. Address: c/o McCartt-Oreck Barrett. Hobbies: Swimming, painting, cooking, collecting circus memorabilia. Pets: a menagerie of 40 pets: cats, dogs, fish, birds and a chicken. **Favourite Memory:** 'The night I met my husband. I saw Parker across the room and said to myself "I would kill for that man".'

ALTMAN, John

Actor, b. 2 March 1952, Reading, Berks. Graduated in photography but took up acting. Trained at York Academy of Speech and Drama. Theatre incl: *The Balcony; Dracula; Masque of the Red Death; Woyzeck.* Films incl: *Return of the Jedi; An American Werewolf in London; The Birth of The Beatles; Quadrophenia; The First Great Train Robbery; The John Lennon Story.* TV incl: *Going To Work; Life After Death; Remembrance; Lucky Jim; The Scarlet Pimpernel; Bouncing Back; Minder; EastEnders.* m. Brigitte; 1 d. Rosanna. Address: c/o Duncan Heath Associates. Birthsign: Pisces. Hobbies: running, swimming, photography, music. **Most Cherished Possession:** 'My health and strength.' **Favourite Memory:** 'The birth of my daughter.'

ALVAREZ, Tony

Actor/singer, b. 19 December 1956, Spain. Musicals incl: *Roberta; Evita*. Films incl: *Fatty Finn; Starview; Oliver; Nicholas and Alexander*. TV incl: *Two In the Bush; The Young Doctors; Skyways; Prisoner; Carson's Law*; guest appearances on *The Don Lane Show; The Mike Walsh Show*; Ronnie Corbett specials. m. Jamie. Address: c/o Richard Kent Management, 6 Goodhope Street, Paddington, Sydney. Birthsign: Sagittarius. Hobbies: squash, swimming, eating. **Most Cherished Possession:** 'Photo of my mother, and my youth in Spain.' **Favourite Memory:** 'Meeting Barbra Streisand and talking about dogs, one of my favourite things.'

AMBROSE, Gladys

Soprano/actress, b. 28 December 1930, Liverpool. Theatre incl: musicals, revues, summer shows, pantomimes, variety. TV incl: *Who Killed Julie Wallace?; Coronation Street; Visiting Day; Gulpin; Lonesome Road; Bulman; Bread; The Les Dawson Show*; Julia Brogan in *Brookside*. Radio incl: *They Call Her Their Lilli Marlene*, a BBC Radio Merseyside special to celebrate 30 years in showbusiness. m Johannes; 2 d. Janette and Wendy (The Votel Sisters). Address: c/o Brookside Productions. Birthsign: Capricorn. Hobbies: singing for all genuine charities, visiting stately homes, museums, art galleries, walking in the country or by the sea. Pets: one budgie. **Favourite Memory:** 'An electrifying standing ovation at the Winter Gardens, Blackpool, when entertaining war veterans. I was made an honorary Desert Rat.'

ANDERSON, Andy

Actor/singer, b. 18 July, Naenae, New Zealand. Started in the rock'n'roll world, singing in New Zealand groups. Theatre incl: *Pirates of Penzance; SUS; Hair*. Films: *Robbery Under Arms; Trespasses*. TV incl: Jim Sullivan in *The Sullivans; Prisoner: Cell Block H; The Great Bookie Robbery; Roche; Dire Chicken*. m. (dis.); 1 d. Christal, 2 s. Ramanu, Jamie. Address: c/o Melbourne Artist Management, 643 St Kilda Road, Melbourne, Victoria, Australia, or Robert Bruce, PO Box 67-100, Mt Eden, Auckland, New Zealand. Hobbies: scriptwriting, music, nature. **Favourite Memory:** 'Professionally, playing the Pirate King in *Penzance*; personally, the birth of my daughter.'

ANDERSON, Jean

Actress, b. 12 December 1907, Eastbourne, Sussex. Trained at RADA and in rep. Theatre incl: with the National Theatre in *Martine* and *For Services Rendered; Lent; The Dame of Sark; Hedda Gabler; Les Liasons Dangereuses*. Films incl: *The Lady Vanishes; Half a Sixpence; A Town Like Alice; The Kidnappers*. TV incl: *This Is Your Life; Little Women; Scoop; Dr Finlay's Casebook; The Railway Children; The Brothers; Tenko; Paris; Miss Marple; John Bodkin Adams; Campion; Circles of Deceit*. m. Peter Powell (dis.); 1 d. Aude. Address: c/o Brunskill Management. Birthsign: Sagittarius. Hobbies: gardening, music, horseracing, walking. **Most Cherished Possession:** 'My grandchildren – more valuable than wordly goods.' **Favourite Memory:** 'Walking on air, having signed my first contract on leaving RADA.'

ANDREWS, Anthony

Actor, b. 12 January 1948, London. Started stage career at Chichester Festival Theatre. Theatre incl: *The Dragon Variation*. Films incl: *War of the Children; Operation Daybreak; Under the Volcano; The Holcroft Covenant*. Numerous TV incl: *A Beast With Two Backs; Doomwatch; Follyfoot; The Pallisers; Upstairs, Downstairs; The Duchess of Duke Street; Romeo and Juliet; Danger UXB; Brideshead Revisited* (BAFTA Award for Best TV Actor 1981); *Love Boat; The Black Bayu; La Ronde; Ivanhoe; The Scarlet Pimpernel; Z for Zacariah; Sparkling Cyanide; AD; The Woman He Loved*. m. former actress Georgina; 1 d. Jessica, 1 s. Joshua. Address: c/o Duncan Heath Assocs. Birthsign: Capricorn. Hobbies: horses.

ANHOLT, Tony

Actor, b. 19 January 1941, Singapore. Trained at the Royal Court Theatre in mask, mime, movement, drama and voice. Theatre incl: *The Importance of Being Earnest; Sleuth; Bedroom Farce; Amadeus; The Tempest; Boys in the Band.* TV incl: *Alice; Court Martial; Minder; Juliet Bravo; Bulman; Jason Kint; The Last Days of Pompeii; A Family at War; The Fell Sergeant; Crown Court; The Sweeney; Space 1999; The Strauss Family; Triangle; The Protectors; Howards' Way; Only Fools and Horses.* 1 s. Christen. Address: c/o Roger Carey Management. Birthsign: Capricorn. Hobbies: reading, theatre, films, music, travel, gardening, fitness, psychology. Pets: golden labrador. **Most Cherished Possession:** 'Life.' **Favourite Memory:** 'The first time my son said "I love you".'

ARCHER, Geoffrey

ITN defence and diplomatic correspondent, b. 21 May 1944, London. Formerly a solicitor's articled clerk. Worked as a researcher, reporter and producer for Southern TV 1964, Anglia TV 1965 and Tyne Tees TV before joining ITN in 1969, for which he has reported widely in Europe, Africa, the Middle East and Britain. Author of two thrillers, *Skydancer* and *Shadowhunter.* m. Eva; 1 d. Alison, 1 s. James. Address: c/o ITN, London. Birthsign: Taurus/Gemini. Hobbies: sailing, walking, gardening. **Favourite Memory:** 'Watching herons fishing in the Thames at sunrise.'

ARIS, Ben

Actor, b. 16 March, 1937, London. Trained at Arts Educational School and freelance studios. Many musicals and revues as a child and young man in the West End, incl: *Pieces of Eight; Strike a Light.* Theatre incl: *Hamlet; I, Claudius; Stepping Out.* Films incl: *If; O Lucky Man; Juggernaut; Tommy, The Ritz.* TV incl: *To the Manor Born* (two series); *By the Sword Divided; Video Stars; Shine On Harvey Moon; Chance In A Million; Paradise Postponed; Call Me Mister; Hi-De-Hi* (two series); *Executive Stress; Hold the Dream; The Comic Strip Presents . . .; Hazard of Hearts; First of the Summer Wine; Young Charlie Chaplin; Agatha Christie's Poirot; Mr Majeika.* m. Yemaiel; 1 d. Rachel, 1 s. Jonathon. Address: c/o Barry Brown. Hobbies: music, ornithology, family life. Pets: two cats.

ARMSTRONG, Fiona

Newscaster/reporter for ITN, b. 28 November 1956, Preston, Lancashire. Studied German at London University. Started as a reporter with Radio 210 in Reading. Joined BBC TV Manchester as a journalist, then worked for Border TV, Cumbria, as a reporter and presenter of the nightly magazine programme. m. Rodney Potts. Address: c/o ITN. Birthsign: Sagittarius. Hobbies: cooking, swimming, walking, fishing. Pets: one cat, Max. **Most Cherished Possession:** 'My collection of old photos.' **Favourite Memory:** 'Catching my first salmon in Scotland.'

ARMSTRONG, Pamela

Journalist, b. 25 August 1951, Borneo. Trained in media and communications. Has worked as a presenter on the commercial station Capital Radio in London and on TV, incl: *London Today; Well Being;* newscaster for ITN; *Pamela Armstrong; Breakfast Time.* Address: c/o John Willcocks, 103 Charing Cross Road, London W1. Birthsign: Virgo. Hobbies: running and swimming.

ARNOLD, Debbie

Actress, b. 14 June, Sunderland. Started career in TV and has appeared in more than 200 programmes, incl: *Coronation Street; Up the Elephant and Round the Castle; Minder On the Orient Express; Miss Marple – Body In the Library; Don't Wait Up; The Bill; Ticket To Ride; All Creatures Great and Small.* London West End theatre incl: *Last of the Red Hot Lovers; The Sleeping Prince; The Lives of the Wives; Four In a Million; Women Behind Bars.* m. actor David Janson; 1 d. Ciara. Address: c/o Mary Arnold Management, Suite 2, 12 Cambridge Park, East Twickenham, Middlesex TW1 2PF. Hobbies: reading and travelling. Pets: a King Charles spaniel and a black cat. **Most Cherished Possession:** 'My relationship with David, our daughter and the life we have together.' **Favourite Memory:** 'Getting married in Hong Kong.'

ARTHUR, Bea

Actress/comedienne, b. 13 May 1925, New York. Trained at the Dramatic Workshop of the New School for Social Research in New York. Theatre incl: *Mame; No Exit; The Taming of the Shrew.* Films incl: *Mame; Lovers and Other Strangers.* TV incl: *Maude* (received Emmy award in 1977 for her performance in the title role of this series); and as Dorothy in *Golden Girls* (1988 Best Comedy Actress Emmy). m. director Gene Saks (dis.); 2 s. Matthew and Daniel. Address: c/o William Morris Agency, California. Hobbies: tending her garden. Pets: two dogs, one cat. **Favourite Memory:** 'Aged 12, I got my driver's licence. I was so tall, no one asked for proof of my age.'

ASHCROFT, Dame Peggy, DBE

Actress, b. 22 December 1907, Croydon. Trained at Central School of Dramatic Art under Elsie Fogerty. Theatre debut Birmingham, 1926. London debut 1927. Has played all great Shakespearean heroines. Leading roles at Old Vic; Sadler's Wells; John Gielgud's Company. 1962 Ashcroft Theatre, Croydon, opened, named in her honour. 1975 joined National Theatre at Old Vic. Film: *A Passage To India* (Oscar). TV debut 1956 in *Shadow of Heroes.* Other TV incl: *Caught On a Train; Cream In My Coffee; The Jewel In the Crown; Screen 1: She's Been Away; Dame Peggy: A Portrait of Peggy Ashcroft; The Heat of the Day.* CBE 1951. DBE 1956. m. (1st) Rupert Hart-Davies (dis.), (2nd) Theodore Komsarjevsky (dis.), (3rd) Jeremy Nicholas Hutchinson (dis.); 1 d. Eliza, 1 s. Nicholas. Address: c/o ICM.

ASHER, Jane

Actress, b. 5 April 1946, London. First professional appearance, aged five, in film *Mandy.* London West End debut, 1960, *Will You Walk a Little Faster.* New York debut as Juliet in *Romeo and Juliet.* 1976 joined National Theatre. Other West End Theatre incl: *Look Back In Anger; Before the Party.* Films incl: *Greengage Summer; Runners; Alfie; Dreamchild.* TV incl: *Brideshead Revisited; The Mistress; Bright Smiles; Wish Me Luck.* Books: *Jane Asher's Party Cakes; Jane Asher's Fancy Dress; Silent Night For You and Your Baby.* m. Gerald Scarfe; 1 d. Katie, 2 s. Alexander, Rory. Address: c/o Chatto & Linnit. Birthsign: Aries. Hobbies: cookery, music **Most Cherished Possession:** 'My eternity ring, which has come to symbolise our happy family.' **Favourite Memory:** 'First steps my daughter took.'

ASHLEY, Caroline

Actress, b. 4 March 1958, Lancashire. Trained at the Scottish Academy of Music, Glasgow, and Queen Margaret Drama School, Edinburgh. Taught drama for a short time before joining the cast of *Take the High Road*, as Fiona Cunningham, when it began in 1980. Address: c/o Scottish TV. Hobbies: horse-riding, theatre, badminton.

ASHTON, Al

Actor/writer (under the name Al Hunter), b. Liverpool. Trained at Manchester Polytechnic's School of Theatre. Started as a club comedian. Theatre incl: *Much Ado About Nothing; Snow Queen; Glencoe*. Films: *Remembrance; Arthur's Hallowed Ground*. TV incl: *Angels; Juliet Bravo; Lytton's Diary; Brookside, Lost Empires; Casualty*; Ray Grice in *Crossroads; C.A.T.S. Eyes*. Has written for theatre and radio, plus *The Firm* (film), *EastEnders* and *Casualty* (TV), m. Sue Gibson. Address: c/o Murphy & Heathcote, 73 Colebrooke Row, Angel, London N1. Birthsign: Cancer. Hobby: eating out. **Most Cherished Possession:** 'Indigestion tablets – I have an annoying hiatus hernia.' **Favourite Memory:** 'Seeing the policeman's face when I took a barrister to a magistrates' court to defend a driving offence I hadn't committed.'

ASHTON, John

Actor, b. 29 November 1950, London. Trained at Bristol Old Vic Theatre School. Theatre incl: *The Beggar's Opera; A Midsummer Night's Dream; Jesus Christ Superstar; Romeo and Juliet; Animal Farm; The Merchant of Venice; Abigail's Party; The Taming of the Shrew; Macbeth; The Collector*; Willy Russell's *One for the Road*; Alan Bleasdale's *Should Old Acquaintance; Serious Money*. Film: *Possessions*. TV: *The Demolition Man; The Discovery of Animal Behaviour; Out of Court; Crimewatch; Grange Hill; Brookside*; Chief Supt Don Henderson in *Waterfront Beat*. m. actress Serretta Wilson. Address: c/o Sandra Griffin. Hobbies: snooker, swimming, badminton, cycling, 'doing up the house', eating out, games, TV movies, theatre. **Most Cherished Possession:** 'My home, because it's old, eats money, needs care, hates the Chancellor and loves us.'

ASHWORTH, Dicken

Actor, b. 18 July 1946, Todmorden, Yorkshire. A teacher of English and drama before entering acting. Extensive repertory and fringe theatre. Films: *Tess; Krull; Chariots of Fire; Force 10 From Navarone; King of the Wind; The Biggest Bank Robbery*. TV incl: *Doctor Who; Blake's Seven; Minder; C.A.T.S. Eyes; Flying Lady; The Chinese Detective; Return to Treasure Island*; Alan Partridge in *Brookside; The Two of Us; Scab* (Prix Italia Prix Futura Winner); *Making Out; Better Days; Nanny*. m. set and costume designer Jane Ripley; 1 d. Tamasin Cathy. Address: c/o Howes & Prior. Hobbies: cooking, eating, wine, bowls, gardening, cricket, riding, exploring rural France, camping. Pets: Poppins, Biscuit and Truffle (three cats), Bunny Hop (rabbit), Toffee (guinea pig).

ASKWITH, Robin

Actor/writer, b. 12 October 1950, Southport, Lancs. Has appeared in London's West End in *Run For Your Wife* and *I Love My Wife*, and wrote and directed world tours of *Casanova's Last Stand* and *Confessions From a Health Farm*. Films incl: *If . . .; Canterbury Tales; Bless This House; Carry On Girls; Confessions Of a Window Cleaner; Confessions of a Pop Performer; Confessions of a Driving Instructor; Confessions From a Holiday Camp; Stand Up Virgin Soldiers; Let's Get Laid; Britannia Hospital*. TV incl: *Menace; The Misfit; On the House; Please Sir!; Fenn Street Gang; Bless This House; Father Dear Father; Dixon Of Dock Green; Beryl's Lot; Star Games; Give Us a Clue; Play of the Month; Bottle Boys; Boon*. Winner of the London *Evening News* Most Promising Newcomer award, 1975. Address: c/o ICM. Hobbies; ocean sailing, sub aqua diving.

ASNER, Edward

Actor, b. 19 November 1926, Kansas City. Started in school productions. Films incl: *Peter Gunn; The Slender Thread; Fort Apache, The Bronx; O'Hara's Wife*. TV incl: *Slattery's People; Profiles In Courage; The Fugitive; Ironside; The FBI; Medical Center; Rich Man, Poor Man; Roots; The Gathering; A Case of Libel; Tender Is the Night*; title role in *Lou Grant*; Joe Danzig in *The Bronx Zoo*. Has won seven Emmys for his work, and received The Anne Frank Human Rights Award in 1986. m. Nancy (sep.); 2 d. Lisa, Kate, 1 s. Matthew. Address: c/o Gores Fields Agency, 10100 Santa Monica Blvd., LA, CA 90067. Hobbies: reading, animals, current events. Pets: two cats. **Favourite Memory:** 'My activist presidency of The Screen Actors' Guild. I was a real controversial creature.'

ASPEL, Michael

Broadcaster/writer, b. 12 January 1933, London. BBC TV announcer/newsreader/compere, 1957–68. Capital Radio (1979–84). TV incl: *Ask Aspel: Give Us a Clue; Child's Play; The Six O'Clock Show; Aspel & Company; This Is Your Life.* Books: *Polly Wants a Zebra; Hang On!* m. actress Elizabeth Power; 2 s. Patrick, Daniel (also 3 s. Gregory, Richard, and Edward, 1 d. Jane, from previous m's). Address: c/o Bagenal Harvey Organisation. Birthsign: Capricorn. Hobbies: writing, swimming, boating, films, learning golf, various charities. Pets: one dog, Cressie. **Most Cherished Possession:** 'A 150-year-old telescope given to me by my wife.' **Favourite Memory:** 'Seeing my youngest child born, because this time I didn't faint.'

ATKINS, Eileen

Actress, b. 16 June 1934, Clapton, London. Trained at Guildhall School of Music and Drama. Theatre incl: *The Killing of Sister George: The Cocktail Party; Vivat Vivat Regina; Suzanna Andler; Sergeant Musgrave's Dance; As You Like It; Heartbreak House; Thursday's Ladies; The Winter's Tale; Cymbeline; A Room of One's Own; Passion Play.* Films incl: *The Duchess of Malfi; The Jean Rhys Women; The Three Sisters; Electra; Sons and Lovers; Smiley's People; Titus Andronicus; Eden's End; Nellie's Version.* TV incl: *Breaking Up; The Vision; The Burston Rebellion.* m. Bill Shepherd. Address: c/o Duncan Heath. Hobbies: walking, tap dancing. Pets: cats. **Most Cherished Possession:** 'My cats.'

ATKINSON, Rowan

Actor, b. 6 January 1955, Newcastle upon Tyne. Trained as an electrical engineer, but decided on a showbusiness career while at Queen's College, Oxford. Performed a one-man show in London's West End and on tour in 1981 and 1986–87. TV incl: *Not The Nine O'Clock News (1974–82); The Black Adder; Blackadder II; Blackadder III; Blackadder Goes Forth; Mr Bean.* Numerous guest appearances incl: *The Innes Book of Records; The Lena Zavaroni Show; The Secret Policeman's Ball.* Variety Club Award: BBC Personality of the Year, 1980. Address: c/o Peter Bennett Jones, 47 Dean Street, London W1. Birthsign: Capricorn. Hobbies: motor cars, motor racing.

AYRES, Rosalind

Actress, b. 7 December 1946, Birmingham. Many theatre appearances incl: Windsor; Nottingham; Guildford; Brighton; Birmingham; and London West End in *I, Claudius* and *Dracula; Now We Are Sixty.* Films incl: *That'll Be The Day; Stardust; The Lovers; The Slipper and the Rose; Cry Wolf.* Many radio plays. Numerous TV appearances incl: *Two's Company; Rings On Their Fingers; Agony; The Gentle Touch; Only When I Laugh; The Bounder; The Weather In The Streets; Father's Day; Juliet Bravo; Nurses Do; New Worlds; Gay Lord Quex; The Cat Brought It In.* m. actor Martin Jarvis. Address: c/o Michael Whitehall. Hobby: interior decoration. **Most Cherished Possession:** 'My home. Why? See Martin Jarvis's entry.'

BAILEY, Robin

Actor, b. 5 October 1919, Hucknall, Nottingham. Joined Nottingham Theatre Royal, 1938. Rep at Newcastle upon Tyne, Birmingham, Worthing. Films incl: *Private Angelo; Catch Us If You Can; Blind Terror.* TV incl: *The 64,000 Dollar Challenge,* as compere; *The Pallisers; Upstairs, Downstairs; North and South; A Legacy; For Services Rendered; If You Go Down In the Woods; Cupid's Darts; Sorry, I'm a Stranger Here Myself; Janet; Potter; Sharing Time; Tales From a Long Room; Charters and Caldicott; Bleak House; Drummonds; Rumpole of the Bailey; Return To the Broads; Tinniswood Country; Number 27.* m. Patricia; 3 s. Nicholas, Simon, Justin. Address: c/o Michael Whitehall. Birthsign: Libra. Hobbies: gardening, cricket. **Most Cherished Possession:** 'The garden.' **Favourite Memory:** 'Making the garden.'

BAIRSTOW, Amanda

Actress, b. 12 November 1960, Bingley, West Yorkshire. Trained at the Italia Conti Stage School. Theatre incl: *Noises Off; Pride and Prejudice; Rope; The Wizard of Oz; Why Not Stay For Breakfast?; The Fantasticks; Firedragon; Lady Be Good; Borne In a Handbag; Anything Goes*. TV: *Coronation Street; Juliet Bravo; Lytton's Diary; Cockles; Tears Before Bedtime; Only Children; Salad Days*. Also in many TV commercials. Address: c/o Brownjohn and King Management. Hobbies: 'Walking my dog George and cooking.' Pet: miniature Schnauzer called George. **Most Cherished Possession:** 'My personal life, which I share with a very special person, because it keeps me sane.' **Favourite Memory:** 'Sitting with my father watching Walt Disney's *The Incredible Journey*.'

BAKER, Cheryl

Singer/presenter, b. 8 March 1955, Bethnal Green, London. Started singing as a member of the group CoCo, and then joined Bucks Fizz. They came to fame in 1981 on winning the Eurovision Song Contest with *Making Your Mind Up*. TV incl: *Top of the Pops; Razzmatazz; Tiswas*. Also working as a TV presenter for *The Six O'Clock Show; How Dare You; Saturday Picture Show; Record Breakers; The Funny Side; Eggs and Baker; My Secret Desire*. Address: c/o Razz, Crofters, East Park Lane, Newchapel, Nr Lingfield, Surrey. Hobbies: crosswords, cooking. Pets: Malcolm the dog. **Most Cherished Possession:** 'Malcolm, because he's irreplaceable.' **Favourite Memory:** 'Singing *Mary's Boy Child* at a Christmas concert in 1975 with my sister Sheila.'

BAKER, Colin

Actor, b. 8 June 1943, London. Trained at LAMDA. First performed at the Arts Theatre, Cambridge, 1969. Appeared in rep and London West End in *The Other House* and *The Price of Justice*. Films incl: *Clockwork Orange; Dangerous Davies; No Longer Alone*. TV incl: *The Edwardians – Daisy; War and Peace; Harriet's Back In Town; For Maddy With Love; Swallows and Amazons Forever*. Best known in *The Brothers* and as the sixth Doctor in *Doctor Who*. m. Marion Wyatt Baker; 1 s. Jack (dec.), 2 d. Lucy, Belinda. Address: c/o Barry Burnett. Hobbies: tennis, games, most sport (as a spectator). Pets: cats, red setter and whippet.

BAKER, Danny

Presenter, b. 22 June 1957, Deptford, London. First worked as a shop assistant, receptionist and rock journalist. Presenter of *20th Century Box; The Six O'Clock Show; Danny Baker on . . .; Six O'Clock Live; Win, Lose Or Draw*. m. Wendy Janet; 1 d. Bonnie, 1 s. Sonny. Address: c/o Noel Gay Organisation. Hobbies: Millwall supporter. Pets: a dog, Twizzle. **Most Cherished Possession:** 'A paperback, *The Most Of S J Perelman*, which is a travel companion, touchstone and a dear old pal.' **Favourite Memory:** 'Norfolk Broads when I was a kid; Florida, with Wendy, when I was most definitely an adult.'

BAKER, George

Actor/writer, b. 1 April 1931, Varna, Bulgaria. First film was *The Dambusters*. Other films incl: *Moonraker; Goodbye, Mr. Chips; On Her Majesty's Secret Service; The Thirty-Nine Steps; Hopscotch; North Sea Hijack*. TV incl: *Bowler* (his own series); *I, Claudius; Minder; Triangle; The Chinese Detective; Marjorie and Men; Dead Head; Room at the Bottom; The Charmer; Coast To Coast; Verdi – Wolf To the Slaughter*; Inspector Wexford in *The Ruth Rendell Mysteries; No Job For a Lady*. Author of many radio and TV plays, incl: *A Cook For All Seasons*. m. actress Sally Horne; 4 d. Candy, Tessa, Ellie, Sharah, 1 s. Charlie. Address: c/o ICM. Hobbies: reading, riding, cooking. Pets: cat.

BAKER, Richard, OBE, RD

Presenter, b. 15 June 1925, Willesden, London. While at Peterhouse, Cambridge, joined Cambridge ADC and Footlights. Actor 1948–9. Joined BBC 1950; radio announcer 1951–54. BBC TV newsreader 1954–82. Presenter *Omnibus* 1963. Presenter of numerous music programmes incl: *The Proms*; panellist on *Face the Music*; *New Year's Day Concert From Vienna*. Radio: *Melodies For You*; *Comparing Notes*; *Mainly For Pleasure*. m. Margaret; 2 s. Andrew, James. Address: c/o Bagenal Harvey. Hobbies: music, sailing, theatre. **Most Cherished Possession:** 'My piano, because I enjoy playing it and because it was a present from my wife.' **Favourite Memory:** 'Taking our two boys when they were young to see Chelsea play. They were ardent Chelsea fans.'

BALL, Bobby

Comedian, b. 28 January 1944, Shaw. Half of the comedy partnership Cannon and Ball. Former welders in a Lancashire factory by day and a singing duo, The Harper Brothers, at night. Changed names to Cannon and Ball for *Opportunity Knocks* appearance. Voted clubland's top comedy duo, they have also won the Variety Club Showbusiness Personalities of the Year and topped various magazine and newspaper polls. Starred in their own series, *The Cannon and Ball Show*, since 1979. Subjects of *This Is Your Life*. They have also made a film, *The Boys In Blue*. m. Yvonne; 1 d. Joanne, 2 s. Darren, Robert. Address: c/o International Artistes, Albert House, Albert Street, Chadderton, Manchester OL9 7TA. Birthsign: Aquarius. Hobbies: writing songs and poetry, music, especially rock 'n' roll.

BARBER, Glynis

Actress, b. South Africa. Theatre incl: *Hamlet*; *Ring Around the Moon*; *Rebecca*; *Once In a Lifetime*; *And Then There Were None*; *Table Manners*; *Summer Breeze*. Films incl: *The Wicked Lady*; *Tangier*; *Yesterday's Hero*; *The Hound of the Baskervilles*; *Dr Jekyll and Mr Hyde*. TV incl: *Jane at War*; *Lucky Jim*; *Blakes's Seven*; *A Fine Romance*; *History of Mr Polly*; *Sandbaggers*; *The Voysey Inheritance*; *Visitors*; *Dempsey and Makepeace*; *Tales of the Unexpected*. Address: c/o James Sharkey. Hobbies: tennis, yoga.

BARKER, Ronnie, OBE

Actor/comedian, b. 25 September 1929, Bedford. Started as an amateur; Aylesbury Rep 1948, then Manchester and Oxford. Films incl: *Futtocks End*; *Home Of Your Own*; *Robin and Marian*; *Porridge*. Radio incl: *Floggits*; *The Navy Lark*. TV incl: *I'm Not Bothered*; *Frost Report*; *Foreign Affairs*; *The Ronnie Barker Playhouse*; *Frost On Sunday*; *Hark at Barker*; *His Lordship Entertains*; *A Midsummer Night's Dream*; *Seven of One*; *The Picnic*; *The Two Ronnies*; *Porridge*; *Open All Hours*; *Going Straight*. Retired from showbusiness January 1988. m. Joy Tubb; 1 d. Charlotte, 2 s. Larry, Adam. Birthsign: Libra. Hobbies: collecting Victorian postcards, prints and books.

BARKWORTH, Peter

Actor, b. 14 January 1929, Margate, Kent. Trained at RADA. London West End theatre incl: *Roar Like a Dove*; *Crown Matrimonial* (and on TV); *Donkey's Years*; *Can You Hear Me At The Back?*; *A Coat of Varnish*. Directed *Sisterly Feelings* (tour). TV incl: *The Power Game*; *Professional Foul*; *Secret Army*; *Telford's Change*; *Winston Churchill – The Wilderness Years*; *The Price*; *Late Starter*; *The Gospel According To St Matthew*. Books: *About Acting*; *First Houses*; *More About Acting*. Address: c/o Duncan Heath Associates, London. Birthsign: Capricorn. Hobbies: the countryside and paintings, music, walking, gardening, entertaining. **Most Cherished Possession:** 'Besides health, my flat in Folkestone. It's another world.' **Favourite Memory:** 'Making *Telford's Change*, when everything was perfect.'

BARLOW, Thelma

Actress, b. 19 June, Middlesbrough, Cleveland. Secretary in Huddersfield before joining Joan Littlewood's Theatre Workshop in East London. Then appeared in London's West End and classical repertory productions before joining Granada TV's *Coronation Street* as Mavis Riley (now Wilton) in 1974. 2 s. Clive, James. Address: c/o Granada TV. Birthsign: Gemini. Hobbies: cookery, organic gardening, yoga. **Most Cherished Possession:** 'Friendship.' **Favourite Memory:** 'Discovering acting – it changed my life.'

BARNES, Carol

TV journalist, b. 13 September 1944, Norwich, Norfolk. Was a public relations officer at London's Royal Court Theatre. Before joining ITN, production manager *Time Out* magazine. Presenter of *The Channel Four Daily* since 1989. m. Nigel Thomson; 1 d. Clare, 1 s. James. Address c/o ITN. Birthsign: Virgo. Hobbies: tennis, skiing, exercise. **Most Cherished Possession:** 'A baby grand piano, bought for the kids to learn on.'

BARNES, Dominique

Actress, b. 21 June 1966, Barnet, Hertfordshire. Attended drama school as a child. First professional acting role, aged 16, as John Alderton's screen daughter in both series of the Channel Four comedy *Father's Day*. Films: *Lubo's World; Bert Rigby You're a Fool*. Other TV: *Return To Waterloo; Demons; Lytton's Diary; Queen of Hearts; Gems;* BBC play *Watching; Brat Farrar; Jessie's Place; Hannay; All Creatures Great and Small; Rockliffe's Babies; Maigret; Bergerac; William Tell; The Bill; Casualty; Young, Gifted and Broke*. Address: c/o Louis Hammond Management. Birthsign: Gemini.

BARON, Lynda

Actress, b. 24 March, Manchester. Trained in ballet at Royal Academy of Dancing. Theatre incl: *Living For Pleasure; The Bedwinner; The Real Inspector Hound; Move Over Mrs Markham; Not Now, Darling; Goodbye Charlie; Butterflies Are Free; Abigail's Party; Little Me; Stepping Out.* TV incl: *Play of the Month; Don't Forget To Write; Heartlands; Grundy; Open All Hours; Z-Cars; Minder; Wogan.* m. John M Lee; 1 d. Sarah Leanne, 1 s. Morgan Brian. Address: c/o Peter Charlesworth. Birthsign: Aries. Hobbies: sewing, brewing, baking. Pets: English bull terrier, cat. **Most Cherished Possession:** 'Drawer full of photos of several generations of my family.' **Favourite Memory:** 'The look on my children's face when I won first prize for home-made wine.'

BARRACLOUGH, Roy

Actor, b. 12 July 1935, Preston, Lancs. No formal training. Has appeared in most TV comedy shows and was best known for many years for his partnership with Les Dawson. Starred in his own children's TV series, *Pardon My Genie*. Now Alec Gilroy in *Coronation Street*, for which serial he holds the record for playing most characters, five. Address: c/o Peter Graham Assocs at Crouch Salmon Assocs. Hobbies: good food, cooking, walking the dog. Pets: West Highland white terrier, Whisky. **Most Cherished Possession:** 'Electric tea-making device for the dressing room.' **Favourite Memory:** 'Appearing as the star of a pantomime at the Grand Theatre, Blackpool. It was where I spent all my pocket money as a child, going to the theatre.'

BARRIE, Amanda

Actress, b. Shirley Ann Broadbent, 14 September 1939, Ashton-under-Lyne, Lancashire, where her grandfather owned a theatre. Started dancing in public at the age of three and later trained in ballet. Left to become a chorus girl and worked extensively on the stage. Theatre incl: *On the Brighter Side; See You Inside; A Public Mischief; Any Wednesday; Twelfth Night; Absurd Person Singular; Noises Off; Stepping Out* (all London West End); *Little By Little; The Beggar's Opera; Hobson's Choice; Cabaret; Up the Eighties;* 'The Iron Lady' in *The Cabinet Mole.* Films: *Carry On Cleo; I Gotta Horse; One of Our Dinosaurs Is Missing.* TV incl: *A Midsummer Night's Dream; Struggles; Are You Being Served?; Spooner's Patch; Sanctuary; L For Lester;* Alma Sedgewick in *Coronation Street.* m. Robin Hunter (sep.). Address: c/o Peter Charlesworth. Hobbies: watching horse racing.

BARRON, James

Actor, b. 24 December 1964, London, son of actor Keith Barron. While still at school, appeared in two episodes of the BBC's *West Country Tales.* Trained at The Drama Centre, London. Theatre incl: national tours of *King's Rhapsody* and *South Pacific.* TV: *Three Up, Two Down; Laura and Disorder; Shelley; On Her Majesty's National Service; The Endless Game; Home to Roost.* m. actress Shona Lindsay (from July 1990). Address: c/o William Morris. Hobbies: 'Walking in the wind and rain – especially near the sea in winter.' Pets: Ivor the cat, George the beagle. **Most Cherished Possession:** 'My home, with Shona and Ivor in it! The best way to relax and feel cut off from the world.' **Favourite Memory:** 'Visits to Richmond Theatre pantomimes – solely responsible for wanting to be in the business.'

BARRON, John

Actor, b. 24 December 1920, Marylebone, London. Trained at RADA. Films incl: *To Catch a King; 13 For Dinner; The Great Question.* TV incl: *Emergency–Ward 10; Softy, Softly; All Gas and Gaiters; Doomwatch; Crown Court; The Fall and Rise of Reginald Perrin; The Foundation; Potter; Bernie; Spooner's Patch; Shelley; The Glums; The Wizard of Crumm; Yes Minister; To the Manor Born; The Gentle Touch; Cowboys; Whoops Apocalypse; No Place Like Home; Me and My Girl; Duty Free; Don't Wait Up; Brush Strokes.* m. actress Jean Peart; 1 step-d. Address: c/o Green & Underwood. Hobby: collecting wine. **Most Cherished Possession:** 'A bottle of Chateau Rausan Segla 1920 – not easy to replace.' **Favourite Memory:** 'First night of my last play in London, *Lend Me a Tenor.*'

BARRON, Keith

Actor, b. 8 August 1934, Mexborough, Yorkshire. Started acting with Sheffield rep. Small parts on TV and appearances with the Bristol Old Vic led to the series *The Odd Man* and *Lucky Jim.* Other TV incl: *My Good Woman; A Family at War; Let's Get Away From It All; Nigel Barton; Telford's Change; Watching Me, Watching You; West Country Tales; Duty Free; Leaving; Room at the Bottom; Take Me Home; 1996; Haggard.* m. stage designer Mary Pickard; 1 s. Jamie. Address: c/o Michael Whitehall. Hobbies: walking, relaxing. Pet: George, a beagle. **Most Cherished Possession:** 'My present script.' **Favourite Memory:** 'My first visit to a pantomime at the Sheffield Lyceum.'

BARRYMORE, Michael

Entertainer, b. 4 May 1952, Bermondsey, London. Has appeared on various variety and chat shows and toured nationwide. TV incl: *The Royal Variety Show; 40 Years On; Barrymore Special; Strike It Lucky; Live From Her Majesty's; Get Set, Go; Russ Abbot's TV Madhouse.* Also made the BBC radio series *Barrymore Plus.* m. Cheryl St Clair. Address: c/o Thames TV. Hobbies: cooking, scriptwriting, cars. Pets: West Highland terrier, Candy. **Most Cherished Possession:** 'My dressing room mascots, a black cat and a white dog. Very faithful and lucky.' **Favourite Memory:** 'Bermondsey, where I was born, and getting a standing ovation in Glasgow.'

BATES, Ralph

Actor, b. 12 February 1940, Bristol. Made his debut at the Gate Theatre, Dublin, in 1963, then joined rep. Theatre incl: *Hedda Gabler; Run For Your Wife; Woman In Mind*. Films incl: *Dr Jekyll and Sister Hyde; Horror of Frankenstein; Letters To an Unknown Lover; Persecution; Fear In the Night*. TV incl: *Poldark; The Caesars; Penmarric; Second Chance; Dear John*. m. actress Virginia Wetherell; 1 d. Daisy, 1 s. William. Address: c/o Hatton & Baker. Birthsign: Aquarius. Hobbies: travel, watching sports, stand-up comics, reading, eating, drinking wine. Pets: Stanley, a cat, Daniel, a tortoise. **Most Cherished Possession:** 'My children and my wife, not necessarily in that order. And, anyway, they possess me!' **Favourite Memory:** 'Watching my children being born.'

BAXTER, Stanley

Actor, b. 24 May 1928, Glasgow. Spent three years with Glasgow Citizens' Theatre. Moved to London in 1959. TV revues for BBC, then LWT. London West End shows incl: *The Amorous Prawn; On the Brighter Side; What The Butler Saw; Phil The Fluter*. TV incl: *The Stanley Baxter Picture Show (Parts I–III); Stanley Baxter's Christmas Box* (1976); *Merrie Old Christmas* (1977); *Stanley Baxter On Television* (1979); *The Stanley Baxter Series* (1981); *Mr Majeika* (three series). m. Moira. Address: c/o David White Assocs. Hobbies: swimming, cycling, reading. **Most Cherished Possession:** 'A now battered suitcase that holds an unbelievable amount and won't wear out.' **Favourite Memory:** 'Making the film *Very Important Person*. It was my first proper film and my best role.'

BAYLDON, Geoffrey

Actor, b. 7 January 1924, Leeds. Trained at Old Vic Theatre School. First professional appearance in *Tough at the Top*. Films incl: *Casino Royale; A Night To Remember; To Sir With Love; The Pink Panther Strikes Again; Porridge; Bullshot; Madame Sousatzka; The Tenth Man*. TV incl: *Nicholas Nickleby; Under Western Eyes; Platonov; The Wood Demon; Catweazle* (title role); *The Avengers; The Saint; Devenish; Worzel Gummidge; All Creatures Great And Small; Bergerac; Worzel Gummidge Down Under; Juliet Bravo; Hallelujah; There Comes A Time; This Office Life; Blott On The Landscape; All Passion Spent; Star Cops; Cause Celebre; The Return of Sherlock Holmes; The Storyteller; Pisces Connection; The Chronicles of Narnia; Campion*. Address: c/o Joy Jameson. Hobbies: gardening, music, painting.

BAYNHAM, Grant

Presenter/musician, b. 3 November 1954, Haslemere, Surrey. After training for five years as a lawyer, went on to write topical songs for shows including *Start The Week With Richard Baker; Pebble Mill at One; The Tom O'Connor Show; Well, It's a Living; Pamela Armstrong*. Presented *That's Life* for four years and is musical director for the Young Shakespeare Company. m. Janet; 2 d. Emily, Maisie. Address: 4 Bridle Road, Stourbridge, West Midlands. Hobbies: music, bridge, cricket, reading. Pets: a cat, unnamed. **Most Cherished Possession:** 'My guitar, built for me by Russell Wootton.' **Favourite Memory:** 'BBC Bridge Club 1987 – bidding and making a grand slam on 27 points and no response from partner.'

BEACH, Ann

Actress/singer, b. 7 June 1938, Wolverhampton. Trained at RADA. Joined Joan Littlewood's Theatre Workshop and appeared in *The Hostage; Oh! What a Lovely War; The Dutch Courtesan; Inadmissable Evidence; Under Plain Cover*. Original Barbara in *Billy Liar; The Boy Friend; Mame; On The Twentieth Century*. Films incl: *Under Milk Wood; Oliver Twist*. TV incl: *The Government Inspector; Bouquet Of Barbed Wire; The Winslow Boy; The Vanishing Army; That Uncertain Feeling; Fresh Fields; Brookside*. m. Francis Coleman; 2 d. Charlotte, Lisa. Address: c/o Barry Brown. Birthsign: Gemini. Hobbies: music/painting. **Most Cherished Possession:** 'My old teddy bear. Treasured and loved by myself and my children.' **Favourite Memory:** 'First trip to Paris.'

BEADLE, Jeremy

Writer/broadcaster, b. 12 April, Hackney, London. Hosted radio shows incl: *Beadlebum Phone-In; Nightcap; The Odditarium; Animal, Vegetable, Mineral; Beadle's Brainbuster.* TV shows as host incl: *Game For a Laugh; Beadle's About; People Do the Funniest Things; Chain Letters; Born Lucky; Beadle's Box of Tricks.* As a writer/consultant incl: *Lucky Numbers; Ultra Quiz; Pop the Question.* Publications incl: *Today's the Day; Outlawed Inventions* (with Chris Winn); *Book of Lists; The People's Almanac; Book of Predictions;* co-editor, *Time Out.* m. Sue; 1 s. Leo, 3 d. Clare, Cassie, Bonnie. Address: c/o MPC. Hobby: work. Pets: a dog and one cat. **Most Cherished Possession:** 'Address book. It's an almanac, diary and warm memories.' **Favourite Memory:** 'Realising she loved me.'

BEASLEY, Allyce

Actress, b. Brooklyn, New York. Studied acting with Lee Strasberg and also at the State University of New York in Brockport. TV incl: *Cheers; Taxi; King's Crossing;* Agnes in *Moonlighting.* m. (2nd) actor Vincent Schiavelli. Address: c/o Progressive Artists Agency, Beverly Hills, Los Angeles, California. Hobby: aerobics. Pet: a dog, Ralph. **Most Cherished Possession:** 'My height.' **Favourite Memory:** 'The day my brother was born. My father and I took a walk on the beach, it was just the two of us.'

BEENY, Christopher

Actor, b. 7 July 1941, London. Joined Ballet Rambert, 1949, while at stage school. First role in *Peter Pan* 1951. First TV series *The Grove Family,* aged 12; *Dixon of Dock Green; Emergency—Ward 10; The Plane Makers; Armchair Theatre.* Went to RADA but gave up acting through lack of work. *Softly, Softly* brought him back to acting, followed by *Upstairs, Downstairs; Miss Jones and Son; The Rag Trade; In Loving Memory.* m. (1st) (dis.), (2nd) singer Diana Kirkwood; 1 d. Joanne, 2 s. Richard, James. Address: c/o Felix de Wolfe. Birthsign: Cancer. Hobbies: photography, sunbathing. **Most Cherished Possession:** 'A pen my wife gave me. Unfortunately, I don't get the chance to use it – it's always in her handbag!' **Favourite Memory:** 'The birth of my son, James – quite an experience.'

BEGLEY, Ed Jr

Actor, b. 16 September, Hollywood, California. Son of the late character actor Ed Begley Sr. Films incl: *Stay Hungry; Cat People; Buddy-Buddy; Private Lessons; Goin' South; Streets of Fire; Protocol; The In-Laws; Transylvania 6-5000.* TV incl: *Happy Days; Room 222; Quincy; M*A*S*H; Mary Hartman, Mary Hartman; Laverne and Shirley; The Incredible Ida Early; Confessions of a She Devil.* Received three Emmy nominations for role as Dr Victor Ehrlich in *St Elsewhere.* m. Ingrid; 1 s. Nicholas, 1 d. Amanda. Address: c/o ICM, California. Hobbies: woodwork, gardening. **Most Cherished Possession:** 'My Father's Oscar.' **Favourite Memory:** 'Being present at the births of my children.'

BELAFONTE-HARPER, Shari

Actress, b. 22 September, New York. Films incl: *If You Could See What I Hear; The Time Walker; The Midnight Hour.* TV incl: *The Night the City Screamed; Velvet.* TV incl: *Hotel; Love Boat; Hart To Hart; Sheriff Lobo; Trapper John; MD; Diff'rent Strokes; Today's FBI; Code Red; Kate's Secret.* Has released an album, *Gimme Your Pop.* m. Robert Harper. Address: c/o McCartt-Oreck, Barrett, California. Birthsign: Virgo. Hobbies: fencing, racquetball, water skiing, riding. Pets: two dogs, Res, Cause. **Most Cherished Possession:** 'My shoes, I always wear two different coloured shoes; it's a little quirk I have.' **Favourite Memory:** 'I just loved growing up around the entertainment industry.'

BELL, Ann

Actress, b. 29 April 1940, Wallasey, Cheshire. Trained at RADA, then rep at Nottingham. She then joined the Old Vic in London. Many stage appearances in London and America. Films incl: *To Sir With Love; The Reckoning; The Statue; Champions.* TV incl: *Melanie; Jane Eyre; Company of Five; Uncle Vanya; The Lost Boys; Very Like a Whale; Three Sisters; Ghost Sonata; Macbeth; Way of The World; War and Peace; For Whom the Bell Tolls; Ressurection; An Unofficial Rose; Tenko* (1980–84); *Tumbledown; Christabel; Double First.* m. Robert Lang; 1 d. Rebecca, 1 s. John. Address: c/o Julian Belfrage Assocs. Birthsign: Taurus. Hobbies: swimming, reading. Pet: dog. **Most Cherished Possession:** 'My family, although I don't own them.' **Favourite Memory:** 'Holidays in the sun because I love hot climates.'

BELL, Tom

Actor, b. 1932, Liverpool. Local rep theatre, aged 15; trained at Bradford Civic Theatre School. Spell in the Army, then rep and tours, before London debut. Theatre incl: *Progress In the Park; The Ring of Truth* (Royal Shakespeare Company); *Bent; Hedda Gabler.* Films incl: *The L-Shaped Room; He Who Rides the Tiger; Quest; The Sailor's Return; The Magic Toyshop; The Innocent; Wish You Were Here; Red King, White Knight; The Krays.* TV incl: *Hedda Gabler; The Samaritan; Death of an Informer; Play for Today: Pope Pius XII; Holocaust; Out; Play For Today: Hester For Example; Words of Love; Love Story – Sweet Nothings; Sons and Lovers; Kings Royal; Reilly, Ace of Spies; Desert of Lies; Summer Lightning; The Detective; Unfinished Business; Hidden Talents; The Rainbow, Chancer.* m. Lois Daine (dis.), 1 s. Aran. Address: c/o Hutton Management.

BELLAMY, David

Botanist/writer/broadcaster, b. 18 January 1933, London. No idea what he wanted to do until he became a lab assistant. Within five years a lecturer, then senior lecturer in botany at Durham University. Entered TV and radio with his opinions on the Torrey Canyon oil disaster, 1967. TV programmes incl: *Bellamy On Botany; Bellamy's Europe; Don't Ask Me; Botanic Man; Up a Gum Tree; Backyard Safari; Discovery; The End of The Rainbow Show; Turning the Tide; Bellamy's Bird's Eye View; Bellamy's Hidden Country; Moa's Ark.* Written numerous books, incl: *The Queen's Hidden Garden.* Also written a ballet, *Heritage.* m. marine biologist Rosemary; 3 d. Henrietta, Brighid, Iseabal, 2 s. Rufus, Eoghain (four adopted). Address: c/o Tyne Tees TV. Hobbies: children, ballet. **Most Cherished Possession:** 'My family.'

BELLINGHAM, Lynda

Actress, b. 31 May 1948, Montreal, Canada. Trained at Central School of Speech and Drama, then rep at Coventry, Crewe and Oxford. Theatre incl: *Bordell; Norman Is That You?; Noises Off; Salad Days; Norman Conquests* Oxford Playhouse tour. Films incl: *Sweeney; Waterloo Bridge Handicap; Stand Up Virgin Soldiers.* TV incl: *General Hospital; Angels; The Sweeney; Z-Cars; Hazel; Funny Man* with Jimmy Jewel; *Mackenzie; Doctor Who; All Creatures Great and Small.* Also appeared in numerous panel games. She is a familiar face in the Oxo commercials. m. Nunzio Peluso; 2 s. Michael, Robert. Address: c/o Saraband Assocs. Birthsign: Gemini. Hobby: reading. Pets: a canary and a rabbit. **Favourite Memory:** 'The birth of my sons – nothing to beat it.'

BELLMAN, Gina

Actress, b. 10 July 1966, Auckland, New Zealand. Took a theatre studies A-level before entering acting. Film: *King David.* TV: mini-series *Mussolini* for NBC of America; BBC *Screen 2* film *Sitting Targets; First Love* play for Anglia TV's arts series *Folio;* Jim Henson's Channel Four series *The Storyteller;* one episode of the BBC comedy series *Only Fools and Horses;* title role in Dennis Potter's BBC series *Blackeyes.* Address: c/o Duncan Heath Associates. Birthsign: Cancer. Hobbies: listening to music, travelling. Pet: a cat called Bobo. **Most Cherished Possession:** 'My guitar – I'm learning to play.' **Favourite Memory:** 'My open-air childhood in New Zealand. It's such a relaxed place, with beautiful countryside.'

BENEDICT, Dirk

Actor, b. 1 March 1945, Helena, Montana. Trained at the John Fernald Academy of Dramatic Arts in Rochester, Michigan. Theatre incl: *Abelard and Heloise; Butterflies Are Free; Hamlet.* Films incl: *Georgia, Georgia; SSSSSSS; W.* TV incl: *Chopper One; Battlestar Galactica;* 'Faceman' in *The A-Team; Airwolf.* m. actress Toni Hudson. Address: c/o Annett Wolf, Los Angeles. Hobbies: music, cricket, gardening. **Most Cherished Possession:** 'My life! I had cancer and cured myself of the tumor – it simply disappeared. I now feel healthier than I ever have before.' **Favourite Memory:** 'My marriage to Toni. It was a spur-of-the-moment thing and we didn't tell or invite a soul to the wedding.'

BENJAMIN, Christopher

Actor, b. 27 December 1934, Trowbridge, Wilts. Trained at RADA. London West End theatre incl: *A Severed Head; Maigret and the Lady; Arturo Ui; John Bull's Other Island; Nicholas Nickleby;* Royal Shakespeare Company, 1982–5; *How the Other Half Loves; A Midsummer Night's Dream.* Films incl: *Brief Encounter.* TV incl: *The Forsyte Saga; Poldark; Doctor Who; Dick Turpin; Donkey's Years; Therese Raquin; We the Accused; It Takes a Worried Man; Holding the Fort; Nicholas Nickleby; Blott On the Landscape; The Return of Sherlock Holmes; Dempsey and Makepeace; Boon; The Diary of Anne Frank; The Miser; The Refuge; Yes, Prime Minister; The Index Has Gone Fishing; Charlie the Kid; Anything More Would Be Greedy; Saracen; Campion; Haggard; Brass.* m. Anna Fox; 2 d. Kate, Emilia, 1 s. Sebastian. Address: c/o Scott Marshall, 44 Perryn Road, London W3 7NA.

BENJAMIN, Floella

Actress/presenter/writer, b. 23 September, Trinidad. London West End shows incl: *Hair; Jesus Christ Superstar; The Black Mikado; The Husband In Law.* Film: *Black Joy.* TV as presenter incl: *Playschool; Play Away; How Dare You; Fast Forward; Switch On To English; Lay On Five; A Houseful of Plants.* Books incl: *Floella's Fun Book; Why the Agouti Has No Tail; Fall About With Flo; Caribbean Cookery; Floella's Cardboard Box Book; Floella's Floorboard Book.* m. Keith Taylor; 1 s. Aston. Address: c/o Benjamin-Taylor Assocs, 73 Palace Road, London SW2 3LB. Hobbies: photography, golf. **Most Cherished Possession:** 'A heart within a heart given to me by my hubby when we first met.' **Favourite Memory:** 'Our visit to Disneyland, because it was a joy watching my son's face.'

BENNETT, Alan

Dramatist, b. 9 May 1934, Leeds. On stage he has appeared in two of his own works, *Beyond the Fringe* and *Forty Years On* (which won London's *Evening Standard* Award); *Single Spies.* Co-author of *Sing a Rude Song.* Author of *Habeas Corpus; The Old Country; Enjoy.* Screenplays incl: *Parson's Pleasure; A Handful of Dust; Prick Up Your Ears; A Private Function.* TV appearances incl: *Sunday Night; Plato – The Drinking Party; Famous Gossips; Alice in Wonderland; Merry Wives of Windsor; Fortunes of War.* Writing for TV incl: *A Day Out; Sunset Across the Bay; A Little Outing; Me – I'm Afraid of Virginia Woolf; Afternoon Off; All Day On the Sands; A Woman of No Importance; Rolling Home; An Englishman Abroad; The Insurance Man; Talking Heads; Dinner at Noon.* Address: c/o Chatto & Linnit.

BENNETT, Hywel

Actor/director, b. 8 April 1944, Garnant, South Wales. Joined National Youth Theatre at 14. Went to RADA. Most recent theatre incl: *Three Sisters; She Stoops To Conquer.* Most recent films incl: *Murder Elite; War Zone.* TV incl: *The Sweeney; Pennies From Heaven; Strangers; Malice Aforethought; Tinker, Tailor, Soldier, Spy; Artemis 81; The Critic; The Consultant; Absent Friends; Frankie and Johnny; Shelley; Return of Shelley; Where the Buffalo Roam; Death of a Teddy Bear.* m. Cathy McGowan (dis.); 1 d. Emma Mary. Address: c/o James Sharkey. Birthsign: Aries. Hobbies: golf, fishing, walking, rugby. Pet: Amazon Blue Front Parrot. **Most Cherished Possession:** 'My sanity. Because I nearly lost it once.' **Favourite Memory:** 'Seeing my daughter Emma for the very first time.'

BENNETT, Lennie

Comedian, b. 26 September 1938, Blackpool. A former journalist with the *West Lancashire Evening Gazette*, he became a professional entertainer in 1965. First TV was in *The Good Old Days* in 1966, and is now best associated with *Punchlines*. Other TV incl: *International Cabaret; Lennie and Jerry Show; London Night Out; Rising Stars; Starburst; The Railway Carriage Game; All Star Secrets; The Kenny Everett Show; Lucky Ladders*. m. Margaret; 1 s. Tony. Address: c/o Alan Field, 11 Arden Road, Finchley, London N3 2AB, tel 081-346 7861. Birthsign: Libra. Hobbies: golf, running, squash. **Most Cherished Possession:** 'My Five Iron.' **Favourite Memory:** 'Birth of my grandson Jack.'

BENNETT, Tracie

Actress, b. 17 June 1961, Leigh, Lancashire. Trained at the Italia Conti Stage School. Theatre incl: *Alice in Wonderland; A Midsummer Night's Dream; The Merchant of Venice; Much Ado About Nothing; Robinson Crusoe; Grease; Chicago; Educating Rita; Merrily We Roll Along; Carousel; Working Class Hero; Aladdin; Amid the Standing Corn; Blood Brothers; Cinderella; Breezeblock Park; Putting On the Ritz; Ten Tiny Fingers, Nine Tiny Toes*. Films: *Knights and Emeralds; Deep Red Instant Love; Shirley Valentine*. TV: *Going Out;* Sharon Gaskell in *Coronation Street; The Rector of Stiffkey; Shame; Knock-Knock; Relative Strangers; Boon; Black Silk; Unnatural Causes; The Refuge; The Ritz; The Bretts; Alas Smith and Jones; Brush Strokes;* Norma in *Making Out* (two series). Plus TV commercials. Address: c/o Annette Stone Associates.

BENSON, Greg

Actor, 31 July 1967, Macksville, Sydney, Australia, brought up in Umina, on the New South Wales coast. His sister, who was modelling, encouraged him to do the same and, at the age of 14, he joined Chadwick, a Sydney agency. Worked on campaigns for McDonald's, Coca-Cola, Pepsi-Cola, Wrigley and, later, Levi's 501. Went into acting after being spotted by Univision. TV incl: Matt Wilson in *Home and Away*. Pop single, with *Home and Away* actress Amanda Newman-Phillips: *We've Got Each Other*. Address: c/o Chadwick Model Agency, 32a Oxford Street, Darlinghurst, NSW 2010, Australia.

BENTINE, Michael

Writer/actor/comedian/parapsychologist, b. 26 January 1922, Watford, Hertfordshire. Radio incl: *Round the Bend; Best of Bentine*. Films incl: *The Sandwich Man; Bachelor of Arts*. TV incl: *It's a Square World: Arts Bazaar; Potty Time; Mad About; Village Auction; Golden Silents*. Books incl: *The Long Banana Skin; The Door Marked Summer* (autobiographies); *Doors of the Mind; Lords of the Levels*. m. (1st) (dis.), (2nd) ex-ballet dancer Clementina Stuart; 2 d. Elaine (from 1st m.) (dec.), Fusty, Suki (from 2nd m.), 2 s. Gus (dec.), Richard. Address: c/o Jimmy Grafton Management, 9 Orme Court, London W2. Birthsign: Aquarius. Hobbies: fencing, sailing, Egyptology, astronomy. **Most Cherished Possession:** 'My sense of humour.' **Favourite Memory:** 'My friends and those I love.'

BERNSEN, Corbin

Actor, b. 7 September 1955, Hollywood, California. Studied at UCLA for degrees in Theatre and Playwriting. Films incl: *S.O.B.; King Kong; Eat My Dust; Bert Rigby, You're a Fool; The Bank Manager; Major League*. TV incl: *Ryan's Hope; Another World; The Waltons; Police Story;* Arnie Becker in *L.A. Law*. m. 1st actress Brenda Cooper (dis.), 2nd actress Amanda Pays; 1 s. Oliver. Address: c/o Agency For The Performing Arts, Los Angeles, California. Birthsign: Virgo. Hobbies: travelling, carpentry, writing, running. **Most Cherished Possession:** 'My Corvette.' **Favourite Memory:** 'My first acting job. I played a pair of naked limbs thrashing around the back seat of a Rolls-Royce in the film *Three the Hard Way*.'

BERTISH, Suzanne

Actress, b. 7 August 1954, London. Films incl: *Hanover Street; The Hunger; Hearts of Fire.*
TV incl: *The Limbo Connection; Are You Watching the Mummy?; Wings of a Dove; The Three Sisters; Maybury; The RSC On Tour (The South Bank Show); The Making of Nicholas Nickleby; The Life and Times of Nicholas Nickleby; To the Lighthouse; Freud; A Comedy of Errors; Rainy Day Women; Shine On Harvey Moon; The Lenny Henry Show; A Day In Summer.* Address: c/o James Sharkey. Birthsign: Leo. Hobby: tennis.

BEVAN, Gillian

Actress, b. 13 February, Stockport, Cheshire. Trained at the Central School of Speech and Drama, then went into rep at Perth, Salisbury, Farnham and Bristol Old Vic. Spent three seasons with Alan Ayckbourn's theatre in Scarborough and was a founder member of The Tight Assets Theatre Company. Theatre incl: *Blood Brothers; Noel and Gertie; Ophelia; School For Scandal; Follies* (in London's West End); *The Wizard of Oz* and *As You Like It* (both Royal Shakespeare Company). TV incl: *Sharon and Elsie; Coppers; Never the Twain; Lost Empires.* Address: c/o Duncan Heath. Hobbies: gardening, tennis. **Most Cherished Possession:** 'My chums – they keep me sane.' **Favourite Memory:** 'Holidays in Wales, Spain, Scotland and Africa. They were very happy times with great friends.'

BEWES, Rodney

Actor/writer, b. 27 November 1938, Bingley, Yorkshire. Went to RADA, then did rep. Decided to concentrate on TV, which led to *The Likely Lads; Whatever Happened To the Likely Lads?* and the series he wrote and produced, *Dear Mother . . . Love Albert.* Films incl: *Billy Liar; Decline and Fall; Spring and Port Wine; Dance To Your Daddy; Whatever Happened To the Likely Lads?* TV incl: *Love Story; Z-Cars; Albert; The Camera Club;* and his own series, which he wrote, *My Friend Dennis.* m. Daphne Black; 1 d. Daisy, 3 s. Joe, Tom, Billy (triplets). Address: c/o Duncan Heath Associates. Birthsign: Sagittarius. Hobbies, antiques, children. Pets: two cats, Beryl and Percy. **Most Cherished Possession:** 'My children.' **Favourite Memory:** 'The births of my children.'

BIGGINS, Christopher

Actor/director, b. 16 December 1948, Oldham, Lancashire. Trained at Bristol Old Vic Theatre School, then did rep theatre, incl: *Winnie the Pooh; Beyond the Fringe; Touch of Spring.* Films incl: *The Rocky Horror Picture Show; The Tempest; Masada.* TV incl: *Paul Temple; The Likely Lads; Porridge; Man of Straw; Upstairs, Downstairs; Some Mothers Do 'Ave 'Em; Brendan Chase; Shoestring; I, Claudius; Poldark; On Safari; Surprise, Surprise.* Address: c/o IMG. Birthsign: Sagittarius. Hobbies: eating, cinema and theatre, travel, badminton, swimming. **Most Cherished Possession:** 'My collection of paintings, especially an oil painting of me by Lady Debra MacMillan.' **Favourite Memory:** 'Meeting the Queen in my dressing room at Regent's Park Open Air Theatre.'

BILGINER, Haluk

Actor, b. 5 June 1954, Izmir, Turkey. Studied at the Turkish State Conservatoire and at LAMDA. Theatre incl: *A Little Like Drowning; My Fair Lady;* season at Newcastle Playhouse, including *The Phantom of the Opera.* TV incl: *Bergerac; Murder of a Moderate Man;* Mehmet in *EastEnders; Glory Boys.* Films incl: *Half Moon Street, Children's Crusade; Ishtar.* Address: c/o Johnson's, 57/59 Gloucester Place, London W1H 3PE. Hobbies: cooking, fishing, diving, travel, reading. Pet: a cat. **Most Cherished Possession:** 'My moustache. If I shave it off I look like a peeled apple.' **Favourite Memory:** 'When I was a battalion singer in the Turkish Army – it's the only thing I enjoyed about National Service.'

BIRD, John

Writer/actor/director, b. 22 November 1936, Nottingham. After acting and directing while at Cambridge University, joined Royal Court Theatre, London, as assistant to the director and, later, associate artistic director. In *Habeas Corpus* in London West End, 1973. Films incl: *Take a Girl Like You; The Seven Per Cent Solution; Yellow Pages*. TV incl: *BBC3; Last Laugh; The Late Show; My Father Knew Lloyd George; A Series of Birds; With Bird Will Travel; John Bird/John Wells; Blue Remembered Hills; Shades of Greene; Timon of Athens; King Lear; The Falklands Factor; Marmalade; Blue Money; Oxbridge Blues; Travelling Man*. Address: c/o Chatto & Linnit. Birthsign: Scorpio. Hobbies: music, reading, walking, animals.

BIRDSALL, Jesse

Actor, b. 13 February 1963, London. Theatre appearances incl: *Merry Wives of Windsor; Days of the Commune* with Royal Shakespeare; *Abide With Me; On the Spot*. Films incl: *Quadrophenia; Bloody Kids; Revolution; Shadey; Minder; Wish You Were Here; Getting It Right*. TV incl: *A Sudden Wrench; Remembrance; Jangles; Walter; Who'll Be Mother?; Tales Out of School; Annika; We'll Support You Evermore; Honeymoon; Elvis;* Marty in *The Fear*. Address: c/o Kate Feast Management. Birthsign: Aquarius. Hobbies: snooker, rock 'n' roll records. **Most Cherished Possession:** 'A 1958 Buick Roadmaster.' **Favourite Memory:** 'Putting my best friend into a tumble dryer.'

BISHOP, Stuart

Actor, b. 25 February 1948, Edinburgh. Trained at Royal Scottish Academy of Music and Drama, Glasgow, then worked with Scottish Theatre Co, Borderline Theatre Co, Edinburgh Lyceum, Perth rep and Tron Theatre, Glasgow. TV incl: *Murder Not Proven; Houseman's Tale; Take the High Road*. Address: c/o Young Casting. Birthsign: Pisces. Hobbies: tennis, badminton, hill walking, gardening. **Most Cherished Possession:** 'My Equity Card. After three years at drama school many good actors still cannot work.' **Favourite Memory:** 'Skye, an enchanted island. The lessons it has taught me are too numerous to mention.'

BLACK, Cilla

Singer/TV personality, b. 27 May 1943, Liverpool. Studied at Anfield Commercial College. First job as a professional singer was at a Beatles concert in Southport, where she stood in for the Fourmost who couldn't appear. Became the first girl to capture the No 1 spot in the charts in two years, with *Anyone Who Had a Heart*, which sold 100,000 copies in one day, followed three months later by *You're My World*, another No 1. 1964 she starred at the London Palladium in the Royal Variety Show. Film debut: *Work . . . Is a Four Letter Word* in 1967. Situation comedy: *Cilla's World of Comedy*. TV incl: *Surprise, Surprise; Blind Date*. Voted *TVTimes* Favourite Female TV Personality three years running. m. manager, Bobby Willis; 3 s. Robert, Benjamin, Jack. Address: c/o LWT. **Favourite Memory:** 'Meeting the Queen at my first Royal Command Performance.'

BLACK, Isobel

Actress, b. Edinburgh. No formal training but started career with rep companies in Manchester and Edinburgh. TV incl: *The Troubleshooters; The Likely Lads; The White Bird Passes; Reid The Sheepstealer; Boswell For the Defence; Three Sisters; The Brief; Scotland's Story; The Tempest; The Hostage; Tygo Road; Pola Jones; Kate McIntyre*. m. James Gatward; 3 d. Annabel, Celia, Eloise. Address: c/o LWA. Hobbies: cooking, music, gardening, riding. Pets: five cats, two dogs, a donkey and calves. **Most Cherished Possession:** 'Homemade cards from my children – both ingenious and funny.' **Favourite Memory:** 'Seeing my husband James for the first time and believing him an imposter – he said he was a TV director.'

BLACKMAN, Honor

Actress, b. 22 August, London. West End theatre incl: *The Gleam; Blind Goddess; Wait Until Dark; Who Killed Santa Claus?; Exorcism; The Sound of Music; On Your Toes.* Films incl: *Quartet; Diamond City; Goldfinger; Life at the Top; Shalako; Something Big; The Virgin and the Gypsy;* Cathy Gale in TV's *The Avengers* from 1962–64. 1 d. Lottie, 1 s. Barnaby. Address: c/o Michael Ladkin. Birthsign: Leo. Hobbies: travelling, reading. **Most Cherished Possession:** 'My home.'

BLACKNELL, Steve

TV presenter, b. 6 September 1952, Lambeth, London. TV incl: *Riverside; Sight and Sound; Breakfast Time;* pop music slots; *Life Games; Whistle Test; Off the Record; London Plus; Punchlines; Pop the Question; New Faces; Knock Your Block Off; Live Aid; What's All This Then?;* co-hosted UK's first cable music show, which led to own *London Calling* cable show. Book: *Top of the Pops.* Address: c/o Peter Charlesworth. Birthsign: Virgo. Hobbies: The Duke of Edinburgh Award scheme, cooking, having acupuncture, Shirley MacLaine books. **Most Cherished Possession:** 'Sooty, my glove puppet. He's the second, the first I had for 24 years, and we talk.' **Favourite Memory:** 'My happy summers in Cornwall with three special mates in the Seventies.'

BLAIR, Isla

Actress, b. South India. Trained at RADA, went straight into the London West End in *A Funny Thing Happened On the Way To the Forum.* Theatre incl: *The Rivals; King Lear; What the Butler Saw; The Cherry Orchard; Hay Fever; Design For Living; The Browning Version; Black Comedy.* Films incl: *The Blood of Dracula; The Battle of Britain; Valmont; Indiana Jones and the Last Crusade; Treasure Island; The Monk.* TV incl: *The Doctors; When the Boat Comes In; Wilde Alliance; The History Man; Alexa; The Bounder; King and Castle; Hold the Back Page; C.A.T.S. Eyes; Bookie; Taggart; Off Peak; Six Centuries of Verse; Mother Love; Haggard.* m. actor Julian Glover; 1 s. Jamie. Address: c/o Hutton Management, London. Hobbies: tennis, writing. Pets: two cats.

BLAIR, Lionel

Actor/TV personality, b. 12 December 1934, Montreal, Canada. Started as a child actor. First stage performance in *Wizard of Oz,* Croydon, in 1942. With no professional training, has acted, danced, sung, choreographed and directed numerous plays, musicals, revues and appeared in several Royal Variety Performances. Many TV appearances in variety shows. Men's team captain in TV's *Give Us a Clue* and host of *Name That Tune.* Autobiography: *Stage Struck.* m. Susan; 2 s. Daniel, Matthew, 1 d. Lucy. Address: c/o Peter Charlesworth. Birthsign: Sagittarius. Hobbies: watching TV, film buff.

BLAKE, Christopher

Actor, b. 23 August 1949, London. Trained at Central School of Speech and Drama. Theatre incl: *The Trials of Oscar Wilde.* Film: *Aces High.* TV incl: *Anne of Avonlea; Death Or Glory Boy; Love For Lydia; The Lost Boys; Mill On the Floss; Mixed Blessings; Alexa; That's My Boy; Love's Labours Lost.* m. Wendy; 2 d. Charlotte, Louise, 1 s. Sean. Address: c/o Ken McReddie. Birthsign: Leo/Virgo.

BLAKISTON, Caroline

Actress, b. 13 February, London. Trained at RADA. Theatre incl: *A Midsummer Night's Dream; Look Back In Anger; King Lear; The Cocktail Party; Women All Over; Particular Friendships; Les Parents Terribles; Division Belle*. West End incl: *Everything In the Garden; The Real Inspector Hound; Murderer*. Films incl: *Sunday, Bloody Sunday; Yanks; Return of the Jedi*. TV incl: *The Avengers; The Saint; The Forsyte Saga; Crown Court; Private Schultz; Shoestring; Nanny; Brass; Charters and Caldicott; Mr Palfrey of Westminster; Miss Marple; The Refuge*. m. Russell Hunter (dis.); 1 s. Adam, 1 d. Charlotte. Address: c/o Chatto & Linnit. Hobbies: sun, opera. Pet: cat. **Most Cherished Possession:** 'A cowrie shell from Cyprus.' **Favourite Memory:** 'Finding the cowrie shell.'

BLANCH, Dennis

Actor, b, 4 February 1947, Barnet, Hertfordshire. Repertory experience at Exeter, Billingham and Newcastle. Films incl: *Permission To Kill; International Velvet*. TV incl: *The XYY Man; Strangers; Thriller; Villains; New Scotland Yard; Warship; The Sweeney; No, Honestly; General Hospital; Give Us a Break; Grange Hill; Bulman; Emmerdale Farm*. m. Carol Wilks; 1 s. David. Address: c/o AIM. Birthsign: Aquarius. Hobbies: football, cricket, snooker.

BLETHYN, Brenda

Actress, b. 20 February 1946, Ramsgate, Kent. Trained at Guildford School of Drama and joined Bubble Theatre Company, London. Joined National Theatre in 1976 and appeared in *Tamburlaine The Great; Strife; Force of Habit; The Double Dealer; The Fruits of Enlightenment; The Nativity; The Passion; Doomsday; Bedroom Farce; A Midsummer Night's Dream, The Guardsman; The Provoked Wife*. London West End incl: *Steaming; Benefactors*. TV incl: *King Lear; Henry VI; The Imitation Game; Tales of the Unexpected; Floating Off; Grown Ups; Sheppey; Alas Smith and Jones; Death of an Expert Witness; Chance In a Million; The Labours of Erica*. Address: c/o Ken McReddie. Birthsign: Pisces. Hobbies: needlework, crossword puzzles.

BLOOM, Claire

Actress, b. 15 February 1931, London. Trained at Guildhall School of Music and Drama and Central School of Speech and Drama. Won BAFTA Award for Best Actress in 1985. Theatre incl: *A Streetcar Named Desire; The Innocents*. Films incl: *The Blind Goddess; Look Back In Anger; Richard III; The Spy Who Came In From the Cold; Limelight; Sammy and Rosie Get Laid*. TV incl: *Romeo and Juliet; Anna Karenina; The Legacy; Wessex Tales; In Praise of Love; Henry VIII; Hamlet; Brideshead Revisited; Ellis Island; Shadowlands; Hold the Dream; Liberty; The Ghost Writers; Anastasia; Intimate Contact;* Emmy-winning *Women Writers: The Belle of Amherst*. Autobiography: *Limelight and After*. m. actor Rod Steiger (dis.); 1 d. Anna. Address: c/o William Morris. Hobby: yoga.

BLUMENAU, Colin

Actor, b. 7 August 1956, London. Took a degree in drama at Hull University. Theatre incl: *Altogether Now;* rep at Basingstoke, Salisbury, Exeter and Milford Haven. Also appeared at New End and Tricycle theatres in London. Film: *Mendelssohn In Wales*. TV incl: *Jockey School; Andy Robson; The Bill*. m. Deborah O'Brien; 2 s. Dan, Jack. Address: c/o London Management. Birthsign: Leo. Hobbies: horses, dogs, brass bands. Pets: horses, dogs. **Favourite Memory:** 'Dartmoor.'

BOARDMAN, Stan

Comedian, b. 7 December, Liverpool. Ran his own haulage business before winning a holiday camp competition that set him into a showbusiness career. Summer season 1982 Lowestoft; *Aladdin* panto 1982; panto Liverpool Empire 1985. TV incl: *Opportunity Knocks; Celebrity Squares; Seaside Special; Runaround; The Comedians; The Video Entertainers; Success; The Railway Carriage Game; The Fame Game*. m. Vivienne; 1 d. Andrea, 1 s. Paul. Address: c/o Bernard Lee Management. Birthsign: Sagittarius. Hobbies: football, tennis. Pet: German Shepherd, Roscoe. **Most Cherished Possession:** 'A German helmet and Liverpool war medals.' **Favourite Memory:** 'Playing at Anfield for Liverpool Boys Club.'

BOHT, Jean

Actress, b. 6 March 1936, Bebington, Cheshire. Theatre incl: *Meddle Not With Change; Eskimos Do It; Where Adam Stood; Cranford; Sons and Lovers; I Woke Up One Morning*. TV incl: *Juliet Bravo; Spyship; Funnyman; Scully; Boys From the Blackstuff*; Mrs Boswell in *Bread*. m. composer Carl Davis; 2 d. Hannah Louise, Jessie Jo. Address: c/o Peters Fraser & Dunlop. Birthsign: Pisces. Hobbies: househunting. Pets: two dogs, two cats. **Most Cherished Possession:** 'My children.' **Favourite Memory:** 'Joining Liverpool Playhouse as a student in 1962.'

BOLAM, James

Actor, b. 16 June 1938, Sunderland. Stage debut in 1959 in *The Kitchen* at Royal Court Theatre, London. Numerous theatre appearances incl: *Butley; Time and Time Again; Macbeth; Treats; King Lear; A Night In Old Peking; Run For Your Wife*. Films incl: *A Kind of Loving; Half a Sixpence*. TV incl: *The Likely Lads* (1965–69); *Whatever Happened To the Likely Lads?* (1973); *When the Boat Comes In; Only When I Laugh; The Beiderbecke Affair; The Beiderbecke Tapes; The Beiderbecke Connection; Room at the Bottom* (two series); *Andy Capp*. m. actress Sue Jameson; 1 d. Lucy. Address: c/o Barry Burnett. Birthsign: Gemini. Hobby: horses.

BOLAND, Eamon

Actor, b. 15 July 1947, Manchester. Trained at Bristol Old Vic Theatre School. Extensive rep at Manchester, Liverpool and Watford. Fringe theatre incl: *Masterpieces; Coming Clean; Progress*. West End theatre incl: *Funny Peculiar; Why Me?* Film: *Business As Usual*. TV incl: *Raging Calm; Fox; Winter Sunlight; To Have and To Hold; Crossfire; Singles; The Bill; The Chief*. 1 d. Annie. Address: c/o Barry Brown. Birthsign: Cancer. Hobbies: gardening, cards, climbing. Pets: cats.

BORGNINE, Ernest

Actor, b. 2 January 1917, Hamden, Connecticut. Trained at the Randall School of Dramatic Art. More than 40 films incl: *The Wild Bunch; The Poseidon Adventure; Bad Day at Black Rock; Marty* (Best Actor Academy Award, Cannes Film Festival Best Actor Award, New York Film Critics' Award, National Board of Review Award, 1961); *Deadly Blessing*. TV movies incl: *Treasure Island; Blood Feud; The Dirty Dozen: The Next Mission; The Dirty Dozen III*. TV incl: *McHale's Navy; Airwolf; Highway to Heaven*. m. Tova; 1 d. Nancy. Address: c/o Selected Artists, California. Birthsign: Aquarius. Hobby: stamp collecting. **Most Cherished Possession:** 'My wife Tova, my fifth and most successful venture into matrimony.' **Favourite Memory:** 'My wedding.'

BOSSON, Barbara

Actress, b. 1 November, Bellvernon, Pennsylvania. Attended drama school at Carnegie-Mellon University. Trained at the Pittsburgh Playhouse, with The Committee in San Francisco and with Herbert Berghoff. Was nominated five times for the Emmy for her role as Fay Furillo in *Hill Street Blues*. Films incl: *Bullitt; Capricorn One; The Last Starfighter*. TV films incl: *The Impatient Heart; The Calendar Girl Murders*. TV appearances incl: *Richie Brockelman; Sunshine; McMillan and Wife; Owen Marshall;* Capt C Z Stern in *Hooperman*. m. Steven Bochco, executive producer of *Hill Street Blues;* 1 s. Jesse John, 1 d. Melissa. Address: c/o Writers And Artists Agency, 11726 San Vicente Blvd, Suite 300, Los Angeles, CA 90049. Hobbies: writing, but family is most important.

BOULAYE, Patti

Singer/actress, b. 3 May, Nigeria. Trained at the London School of Dramatic Art. Numerous theatre incl: *Jesus Christ Superstar; Hair; Two Gentlemen of Verona; Black Mikado*. Film, cabaret and TV appearances. m. Stephen Komlosy; 1 d. Emma, 1 s. Sebastian. Address: c/o London Management. Birthsign: Taurus. Hobbies: dress designing, painting, cooking. **Favourite Memory:** 'The days my children were born, the moment I saw and cuddled them, and the day my marriage was blessed in church.'

BOVELL, Brian

Actor, b. 26 October 1959, London. Started with the Royal Court Youth Theatre Group. Theatre incl: *Romeo and Juliet; One Fine Day; Sink Or Swim; Strange Fruit;* at the National Theatre *Measure, For Measure; The Caretaker; Bit of Business* and *Up For None; Macbeth; Othello; A Hero's Welcome*. Awarded Best Supporting Actor for *Where There Is Darkness* by British Theatre Assoc. Films incl: *Babylon; Burning an Illusion; Up High; Real Life; Playing Away*. TV incl: *Best of British; The Gentle Touch; Strangers; Bulman; The Hard Word; Driving Ambition; Miracles Take Longer; Casualty; Prospects*. Address: c/o Hope & Lyne. Birthsign: Scorpio. Hobbies: swimming, reading, films, old comics, fencing.

BOWEN, Jim

Comedian/presenter, b. 20 August 1937, Heswall, Cheshire. Originally a teacher in Lancashire and a deputy head. An entertainer in his spare time, discovered when appearing on TV in *The Comedians*, and chose to turn professional, working in clubs and cabaret. TV incl: *Muck and Brass;* presenter of *Bullseye* since 1981. m. Phyllis; 1 d. Susan, 1 s. Peter. c/o George Bartram Assocs. Birthsign: Leo. Hobbies: horse riding, tennis, boating, driving. **Most Cherished Possession:** 'A Rolls-Royce – my one indulgence.' **Favourite Memory:** 'Seeing *Bullseye* enter the TV ratings for the first time. Knowing all those millions of viewers are watching your show is a marvellous thrill.'

BOWLER, Norman

Actor, b. 1 August 1932, London. Former deckboy on an oil tanker, he travelled the world before becoming an actor. Trained at the City Literary Drama School. Appeared in repertory theatre. Theatre incl: *The Caretaker* (New York); *Death Trap* (New Zealand). Films: *Tom Thumb; Naval Patrol; Von Ryan's Express; Julius Caesar*. TV incl: *Harpers West One; Deadline Midnight; The Ratcatchers; Letters From the Dead; Park Ranger;* Det Chief Insp Harry Hawkins in *Softly, Softly* for 11 years; *Jesus of Nazareth;* Sam Benson in *Crossroads;* Frank Tate in *Emmerdale* since 1989. m. 1st (dis.), 2nd Berjouhi (dis.), 3rd Diane; 2 d. Caroline (from 1st m.), Tamara (from 2nd m.), 2 s. Joshua (from 1st m.), Simon (from 3rd m.). Address: c/o ICM. Hobbies: walking, sailing, ceramics. Pets: a dog. **Most Cherished Possession:** 'A painting by John Minton – a friend.'

BOWLES, Peter

Actor, b. 16 October 1936, London. Trained at RADA and professional actor at 18. Break in *Happy Haven* at Bristol Old Vic, repeated London 1960. Theatre incl: *Absent Friends; Dirty Linen; Born In the Gardens; The Entertainer; Canaries Sometimes Sing; Man of the Moment.* Films incl: *The Informer; Live Now, Pay Later; The Yellow Rolls-Royce; Blow Up.* TV incl: *The Avengers; The Saint; The Prisoner; Isadora; A Thinking Man as Hero; Napoleon and Love; The Survivors; Churchill's People; Only On Sunday; The Crezz; Vice Versa; Rumpole of The Bailey; To the Manor Born; Only When I Laugh; The Bounder; The Irish RM;* creator and star of *Lytton's Diary; Executive Stress; Shadow On the Sun;* co-creator and star of *Perfect Scoundrels.* m. Susan; 1 d. Sarah, 2 s. Guy, Adam. Address: c/o London Management. Hobby: modern British art.

BOWN, Paul

Actor, b. 11 October 1957, Staffordshire. No formal training. Recent theatre incl: *The Alchemist; The Gambler.* Films incl: *Morons From Outer Space; The Assam Garden; Underworld.* TV incl: *Coast To Coast; Upline;* Malcolm in *Watching* (four series); *Reasonable Force; Mr Bean.* m. Tracy Ann, 1 s. Alfie. Address: c/o Louis Hammond Management. Birthsign: Libra. Hobbies: travel, photography, music. Pets: bullfrogs. **Most Cherished Possession:** 'My 1953 Ford Prefect car. It's simple but effective.' **Favourite Memory:** 'A holiday in Istanbul. Tracy and I went there a week after we met.'

BOXLEITNER, Bruce

Actor, b. 12 May 1950, Elgin, Illinois. Films incl: *Tron; The Baltimore Bullet.* TV movies incl: *Happily Ever After; Passion Flower; Down the Long Hills; The Gambler; Gambler II; Angel In Green.* TV incl: *The Mary Tyler Moore Show; Gunsmoke; How the West Was Won; The Macahans; Police Woman; Baretta; Bring 'Em Back Alive; Scarecrow and Mrs King; Kiss Me, Kill Me; East of Eden; Fly Away Home; The Last Convertible.* m. Kathryn Holcomb; 2 s. Sam, Lee. Address: c/o Rogers & Cowan, Los Angeles. Hobbies: tennis, jogging, keeping fit. **Favourite Memory:** 'Playing Henry Higgins in my high school's production of *My Fair Lady.* I got the part the day before the play went on when the lead fell sick – and I got a standing ovation.'

BOYD, Tommy

Children's broadcaster, b. 14 December 1952, London. Joined BBC Radio Brighton as producer/presenter, 1971–73, and was also a stand-up comic, 1972–73, at Butlin's, Bognor Regis. Dolphin trainer at Brighton Dolphinarium, 1974–75. Joined LBC in London as Producer of *AM* show, 1975–76. Independent Radio Personality of the Year 1981. TV incl: *Magpie,* presenter 1977–80; *Jigsaw; Puzzle Trail; What's Happening; The Saturday Show; Starship; Wide Awake Club.* m. Jayne; 1 s. Jack. Address: c/o John Mahoney. Birthsign: Sagittarius. Hobbies: reading, sport. **Most Cherished Possession:** 'My dad's 1948 Slazenger tennis racket. I haven't lost a game using it.' **Favourite Memory:** 'My wife – and the first time our eyes met on 4 June 1973.'

BOYLE, Katie

TV and radio presenter, b. 29 May 1926, Florence, Italy. Introduced four Eurovision Song Contests between 1961 and 1974. Other TV incl: *The Name's the Same; I've Got a Secret; Tell the Truth; The Golden Girl; Through the Keyhole; Cross Wits.* Europremio Radio and Television Personality of Europe award, 1964. Radio: own show on BBC Radio 2 from January 1990. Autobiography: *What This Katie Did.* m. Sir Peter Saunders. Address: c/o BBC. Hobbies: 'Rehabilitating and re-homing rescued dogs, embroidery, jigsaw puzzles, swimming, walking, talking . . . and listening.' Pets: four rescued dogs. **Most Cherished Possession:** 'My photograph albums.' **Favourite Memory:** 'Seeing *The Mousetrap* for the first time and realising that the man next to me was not only the producer but also my newly wed husband.'

BRACKNELL, Leah

Actress, b. 12 July 1964, London. Trained at Webber Douglas Academy of Dramatic Art. Theatre: Joanna in *All Sewn Up*; Maria in *Out of the Valley*. TV: *The Cannon and Ball Show*; *Wogan*; Zoe Tate in *Emmerdale* since 1989. Address: c/o St James's Management, 4 Bankside Drive, Thames Ditton, Surrey KT7 0AQ. Birthsign: Cancer. Hobbies: reading, embroidery, travelling, eating. Pets: two cats. **Most Cherished Possession:** 'Barnaby the cat. My father gave her to me.' **Favourite Memory:** 'Travelling round New Zealand and Fiji when I was 18 – my first taste of independence and adventure.'

BRADY, Terence

Playwright/actor, b. 13 March 1939. Probably best known as a writer with his wife. On stage in *Beyond the Fringe*; *Present From the Corporation*. Films incl: *Baby Love*; *Foreign Exchange*. Scripts for TV incl: *Upstairs, Downstairs*; *No, Honestly*; *Yes, Honestly*; *Thomas and Sarah*; *Plays of Marriage*; *Take Three Girls*; *Pig In the Middle*; *Nanny*; *Oh Madeline!*; *Love With a Perfect Stranger*; *Father Matthew's Daughter*. He played Barty in *Pig In the Middle*. m. Charlotte Bingham; 1 d. Candida, 1 s. Matthew. Address: c/o A D Peters. Birthsign: Pisces. Hobbies: music (piano), painting, riding and breeding horses. **Most Cherished Possession:** 'Charlotte Bingham.' **Favourite Memory:** 'Fredwell, our horse, winning the George Coney Challenge Cup – because nobody thought he would.'

BRAGG, Melvyn

Writer/presenter/editor, b. 6 October 1939, Carlisle, Cumbria. Producer *Monitor* (1963); editor, *New Release* (now *Arena*), *Writers' World* and *Take It Or Leave It* (1964). Presenter, *In the Picture* (1971); 1974–8, presenter and producer, *Second House*; *Read All About It*; editor/presenter of *The South Bank Show* since 1978; LWT Head of Arts since 1982; Border TV Chairman from 1990. Plays written incl: *Mardi Gras*; *The Hired Man*; *Orion*. Film scripts incl: *Isadora*; *Jesus Christ Superstar* (with Ken Russell); *Clouds of Glory*. Books incl: *The Nerve*; *Josh Lawton*; *The Silken Net*; *Kingdom Come*; *Laurence Olivier*; *The Maid of Buttermere*; *Rich – A Life of Richard Burton*. m. (1st) Marie-Elisabeth (dec.), (2nd) Catherine; 2 d. Marie Elsa (from 1st m.), Alice, 1 s. Tom (both from 2nd marriage). Address: c/o LWT. Hobbies: walking, reading.

BRANDRETH, Gyles

Writer/presenter, b. 8 March 1948, Wuppertal, West Germany. TV incl: *Panorama*; *Opportunity Knocks*; *Call My Bluff*; *Connections*; *Babble*; *Tell the Truth*; *All Star Secrets*; *The Railway Carriage Game*; *Show Me*; *Countdown*; *Good Morning Britain*. Pantomime: *Cinderella*. Author of more than 50 children's books; biographies of Sir John Gielgud, Dan Leno and Harry Houdini; *The Complete Husband*; *The Complete Public Speaker*; *Great Theatrical Disasters*; *Great Sexual Disasters*. m. Michele Brown; 1 s. Benet, 2 d. Saethryd, Aphra. Address: c/o International Artistes. Hobbies: breaking world records. Pet: cat called GB. **Most Cherished Possession:** 'My first funny jumper.' **Favourite Memory:** 'Aged 16, leaving the rugger pitch for the last time and knowing I need never be unhappy again.'

BRIERS, Richard

Actor, b. 14 January 1934, Merton, Surrey. Went to RADA 1954–56, then rep. Theatre incl: *Present Laughter*; *Arsenic and Old Lace*; *Cat Among the Pigeons*; *Butley*; *Absurd Person Singular*; *Absent Friends*; *The Wild Duck*; *Middle-age Spread*; *Arms and the Man*; *Run For Your Wife*; *Why Me?*; *Twelfth Night*. Films incl: *Fathom*; *All the Way Up*; *A Chorus of Disapproval*; *Henry V*. TV incl: *Brothers In Law*; *Marriage Lines*; Ben Travers farces; *Norman Conquests*; *The Good Life*; *The Other One*; *Goodbye Mr Kent*; *PQ17*; *Ever Decreasing Circles*; *All In Good Faith*. m. actress Ann Davies; 2 d. Katy, Lucy. Address: c/o ICM. Hobby: theatre history. Pets: dog, Fred, cat, Tigger. **Favourite Memory:** 'My first performance in the West End in *Gilt And Gingerbread*.'

BRIGGS, Johnny

Actor, b. 5 September 1935, London. Went to Italia Conti Stage School, 1947–53. Films incl: *Cosh Boy; Hue and Cry; Perfect Friday; Best Pair of Legs In the Business; HMS Defiant; Sink the Bismark; The Last Escape.* TV incl: *No Hiding Place; The Young Generation; The Saint; The Avengers; Crime of Passion; Danger Man; The Persuaders; Softly, Softly; Crossroads;* Mike Baldwin in *Coronation Street.* Male TV Personality of the Year, 1983. m. (1st) Carole, (2nd) Christine; 1 s. Mark, 1 d. Karen (from 1st m.), 2 d. Jenifer, Stephanie, 2 s. Michael, Anthony (from 2nd m.). Address: c/o Marina Martin Management. Birthsign: Virgo. Hobbies: squash, golf. Pets: a collie and two cats. **Most Cherished Possession:** 'My golf clubs.' **Favourite Memory:** 'Meeting the Queen.'

BRITTON, Tony

Actor, b. 9 June 1924, Birmingham Theatre incl: *Move Over Mrs Markham; No, No Nanette; The Dame of Sark; My Fair Lady* (London and tour), 1978–82. Film incl: *Sunday, Bloody Sunday; There's a Girl In My Soup; The Day of the Jackal.* TV incl: *Romeo and Juliet; The Six Proud Walkers; Melissa; The Nearly Man; Father, Dear Father; Robin's Nest; Strangers and Brothers; Don't Wait Up.* m. (1st) Ruth (dis.), (2nd) Danish sculptress Eva Castle (sep.); 2 d. Cherry, Fern (from 1st m.), 1 s. Jasper (from 2nd m.). Address: c/o ICM. Birthsign: Gemini. Hobbies: gardening, flying, golf, photography. Pets: cats, Tiger and Harry. **Most Cherished Possession:** 'My garden: a permanent delight. Maintaining it is a complete escape.'

BROLIN, James

Actor/writer/director. Made film debut in *Take Her, She's Mine*, then *Goodbye Charlie.* Other films incl: *Pickup On South Street; Dear Brigitte; Von Ryan's Express; The Amityville Horror; High Risk; Beverly Hills Cowgirl Blues; Skyjacked.* TV movie: *Encounters.* TV mini-series: *Hold the Dream.* TV incl: *Bus Stop; The Monroes; Twelve O'Clock High; Marcus Welby, MD; Trapped; White Water Rebels; Cowboy; Hotel.* m (1st) (dis.), (2nd) Jan Smithers; 2 s. Josh, Jess (from 1st m.). Address: c/o Triad Artists, 10100 Santa Monica Blvd, 16th Floor, Los Angeles, California 90067. Hobbies: designing homes and offices, flying, motor sports, sailing, reading. **Most Cherished Possession:** 'I love my Cessna 185 plane.' **Favourite Memory:** 'My youth was spent stealing pennies and spending them at the fun arcade near my home.'

BROOKE, Judy

Actress, b. 21 February 1970, Leeds. Began professional career while at school; trained in violin, piano and singing. Theatre: *Our Day Out; The Amazing Dancing Bear; The Little Hotel On the Side; The Crucible; The Plotters of Cabbage Patch Corner.* TV: Yvonne in *The Beiderbecke Tapes* and *The Beiderbecke Connection; Living with AIDS; How To Be Cool; Coronation Street; All Creatures Great and Small; Goodbye and I Hope We Meet Again.* Radio: *Benjamin Barrington Dancer; Derek's Destiny; Welcome Home; Coming From Together.* Address: c/o Direct Line. Hobbies: car maintenance, aerobics, sports, music. Pets: 'My RSPCA retriever-spaniel Ben and tropical fish.' **Most Cherished Possession:** 'Ben, who takes me for walks in all weathers.' **Favourite Memory:** 'Meeting the love of my young life, Christopher Timothy!'

BROOKE-TAYLOR, Tim

Actor/writer, b. 17 July 1940, Buxton, Derbyshire. Theatre incl: *The Unvarnished Truth.* Films incl: *Twelve Plus One; The Statue.* Radio incl: *I'm Sorry I Haven't A Clue.* TV incl: *At Last The 1948 Show; Marty; Broaden Your Mind; The Goodies; Hello Cheeky* (and radio); *Me and My Girl; You Must Be the Husband.* Presenter of radio shows: *Does The Team Think?; Loose Ends; The Fame Game.* Records incl: *Funky Gibbon; The New Goodies LP.* m. Christine; 2 s. Ben, Edward. Address: c/o Jill Foster. Birthsign: Cancer. Hobbies: travel, watching sport, playing golf, skiing. Pets: a cat, Muriel. **Most Cherished Possession:** 'A picture of myself with Seve Ballesteros looking as if he is my regular golf partner.' **Favourite Memory:** 'Grace Kelly in *To Catch a Thief* – I fell in love for the first time.'

BROOKS, Nikki

Actress, b. Nikki Ashton, 29 June 1968, Nottingham. Trained at the Kaleidoscope Theatre Company, Julie Beech Stage School, Nottinghamshire, Morrison's School of Dance, and Hoofers Jazz Centre. Theatre: principal dancer in *The Leslie Crowther Show; Mother Goose; Annie; Dick Whittington*. Films: *Bloody New Year; Cresta Run*. TV: *The Secret Diary of Adrian Mole Aged 13¾; The Kid; The Marlows;* Rosie Harding in *Crossroads; The Bill;* Hilandra in new BSB soap *Jupiter Moon*. Numerous TV commercials. Pop single: *Cheers to the Two of You* (EMI). Address: c/o CCA. Hobbies: cinema, theatre, motor racing, travel, fitness, reading. **Most Cherished Possession:** 'My first bra, because it's still too big!' **Favourite Memory:** 'At home after school, singing songs like *Ten Little Speckled Frogs,* while my father played the guitar.'

BROOKS, Ray

Actor, b. 20 April 1939, Brighton, Sussex. Started in rep in Nottingham in 1957. Theatre incl: *Backbone*. Films incl: *HMS Defiant; Play It Cool; Some People: The Knack; The Last Grenade*. TV incl: *Taxi; Cathy Come Home; The Raging Moon; That Woman Is Wrecking Our Marriage; Death of an Expert Witness; Office Romances; Pennywise; Big Deal; Running Wild*. m. Sadie; 1 d. Emma, 2 s. William, Tom. Address: c/o Marmont Management. Birthsign: Aries. Hobbies: supporting Fulham FC, writing songs.

BROWN, Duggie

Actor/comedian, b. 7 August, Rotherham, South Yorks. Theatre incl: *The Price of Coal*. Light entertainment on TV incl: *The Wheeltappers and Shunters Social Club; 3-2-1; Square One; Pro-Celebrity Snooker*. Part in film *Kes* led to acting roles on TV incl: *The House That Jack Built; Days of Hope; Leeds United; Take My Wife; The Glamour Girls; The Cuckoo Waltz; The Zodiac Game; The Hard Word; The Enigma Files; All Creatures Great and Small*. m. Jackie Ann; 1 d. Jacqueline. Address: c/o ATS Casting. Hobbies: golf, darts, snooker. Pets: golden cocker spaniel, Sam. **Most Cherished Possession:** 'Waltham fob watch from my late father.' **Favourite Memory:** 'Interviewing Bob Hope in America along with George Burns – they are my favourite comics.'

BROWN, Faith

Singer/impressionist/actress, b. 28 May 1944, Liverpool. Entered showbusiness through local talent shows and starting singing with a Liverpool-based band at 16. TV incl: *Who Do You Do?; For My Next Trick; Celebrity Squares; The Faith Brown Awards; Blankety Blank; The Faith Brown Chat Show; Golden Gala; Starburst*. Speciality Act of the Year 1980; *TVTimes* Award for Funniest Woman on TV 1980. m. Len Wady; 1 d. Danielle. Address: c/o Tony Lewis Entertainments. Birthsign: Gemini. Hobbies: fishing, cooking. Pet: dog, Usef. **Most Cherished Possession:** 'My daughter. Her birth, after waiting for many years, was the best thing that has happened in my life.' **Favourite Memory:** 'Seeing Eamonn Andrews jump out and say "Faith Brown, This Is Your Life".'

BROWN, Janet

Actress/comedienne, b. Rutherglen, Glasgow. Films incl: *Floodtide; Folly To Be Wise; For Your Eyes Only*. Has appeared in two Command Performances, 1975 and 1979. TV incl: *Who Do You Do?; The Mike Yarwood Show;* own special *Meet Janet Brown;* two series of *Janet & Co,* 1981, won her the *TVTimes* Award for Funniest Woman on TV, Personality of the Year in TV and Radio, and the Pye Colour TV Award. Has written her autobiography, *Prime Mimicker*. m. Peter Butterworth (dec.); 1 d. Emma, 1 s. Tyler. Address: c/o Bernard Lee Management. Birthsign: Sagittarius. Hobbies: antiques, travel. **Most Cherished Possession:** 'My family.' **Favourite Memory:** 'My son and daughter being in the audience at Drury Lane for the Command Performance.'

BROWN, Susan

Actress, b. 6 May 1946, Manchester. Trained at Rose Bruford College. Extensive theatre incl: *Road* at Royal Court. Film: *Hope and Glory*. TV incl: *The Kids From 47A; The Duchess of Duke Street; Fanny By Gaslight;* Connie Clayton in *Coronation Street;* Ruby in *Andy Capp;* Helen in *Road* (Prix Italia winner); Tracy in *Loving Hazel; Murder Weekend;* Avril in *Making Out.* Address: c/o Barry Brown. Hobbies: cooking, horse-riding, travel. Pets: cat called Lucy. **Most Cherished Possession:** 'A huge ring made of Irish silver that I wear every day.' **Favourite Memory:** 'Sitting in an open air "hot tub" in California, at night, listening to the crickets and tree frogs.'

BROWNING, Michael

Actor, b. 15 May 1930, Ongar, Essex. Trained at RADA, then did rep at Windsor, Farnham, Oxford, Bromley, Leatherhead, Worthing and Northampton. Season at Regent's Park Open Air Theatre. Other theatre incl: *Twelfth Night; Love's Labours Lost.* London West End incl: *The Visit.* TV incl: *Airline; Take Three Women; Minder; The Bill; Emmerdale Farm; Crossroads; Murder at the Vicarage* in the *Miss Marples* series; *Coronation Street; Take the High Road.* Address: c/o Sue Hammer Management, Otterbourne House, Chobham Road, Ottershaw, Chertsey, Surrey KT16 0QF. Hobbies: tennis, jogging, painting, music, writing. **Most Cherished Possession:** 'A country cottage in Suffolk, where I can go to lick the wounds.'

BRUNSON, Michael

Journalist, b. 12 August 1940, Norwich, Norfolk. After Queen's College, Oxford, worked for BBC Radio and TV; joined ITN 1968. US correspondent 1973–77, covering Watergate, US Presidential election; Diplomatic Editor, 1978–86, attending every major international summit meeting around the world; Political Editor since 1986, covering events in Government and at Westminster. m. Susan; 2 s. Jonathan, Robin. Address: c/o ITN, London. Birthsign: Leo. Hobbies: 'Gardening and escaping to Norfolk.'

BRYAN, Dora

Actress, b. 7 February 1923, Southport. Stage debut as a child in pantomime 1935. Numerous theatre appearances incl: *The Merry Wives of Windsor; She Stoops To Conquer.* Films incl: *The Blue Lamp; A Taste of Honey; The Great St Trinian's Train Robbery; Apartment Zero.* TV incl: *Both Ends Meet; Triangles; Foxy Lady; Dora; Rookery Nook.* Has written a book: *According To Dora.* m. William Lawton; 1 d. Georgina, 2 s. Daniel, William. Address: c/o James Sharkey. Hobbies: learning new things. Pets: Old English Sheep Dog, Alsatian, two cats. **Most Cherished Possession:** 'My husband.' **Favourite Memory:** 'Seeing my book *According To Dora* in a shop.'

BUCHANAN, Neil

Presenter/writer, b. 11 October 1961, Liverpool. Background as a musician and songwriter. TV: *Number 73* (eight series); *Motormouth; Motormouth 2;* co-deviser and presenter, children's art programme *Art Attack.* Records: two LPs with rock group Marseille, *Marseille* and *Red, White and Slightly Blue* (Phonogram). m. Niki Woodcock. Address: c/o Peter Plant, Severn Management Services, 36 Chadbrook Crest, Richmond Hill Road, Edgbaston, Birmingham B15 2RJ. Birthsign: Libra. Hobbies: wildlife, TV production, music production. Pets: cocker spaniel Looby Loo. **Most Cherished Possession:** 'A 1960 "antique" electric guitar that has toured the world with me.' **Favourite Memory:** 'Performing to 20,000 people in American ice hockey stadiums every night for two months.'

BULLOCH, Jeremy

Actor, b. 16 February 1945, Market Harborough, Leicestershire. Trained at the Corona Academy, 1957–62. Theatre incl: *Dangerous Obsession; I Love You, Mrs Patterson; What Every Woman Knows; Every Other Evening*. Films incl: *The Virgin and the Gypsy; For Your Eyes Only; Octopussy; Summer Holiday; The Spy Who Loved Me; Mary Queen of Scots; The Empire Strikes Back; Return of the Jedi*. TV incl: *The Newcomers; Billy Bunter; The Professionals; George and Mildred; Agony; Robin of Sherwood; Boon; After Henry; Casualty*. m. Maureen Patricia; 3 s. Christian, Jamie, Robbie. Address: c/o Barry Brown. Hobbies: cricket, football, golf. Pets: four cats. **Most Cherished Possession:** 'My wine cellar!' **Favourite Memory:** 'A family trip to Florida without the children knowing we were going to Disneyworld. The look on their faces was unforgettable.'

BURDIS, Ray

Actor, b. 23 August 1958, London. Trained at the Anna Scher Theatre and has been a member of that theatre since July 1970. Films incl: *Scum; Music Machine; Ghandi*. Most recent TV incl: *Three Up, Two Down; Now and Then*. Other TV incl: *Dream Stuffing; Minder; The Professionals; West; The Gentle Touch; Going Out; Triangle; Ain't Many Angles; Mary's Wife*. m. Jacqui. Address: c/o Anna Scher Theatre Management. Birthsign: Leo/Virgo. Hobby: flying. Pet: Sherbert the cat. **Most Cherished Possession:** 'Sherbert the cat – it's mad.' **Favourite Memory:** 'When I had a £1000 bet on a sure winner . . . it lost.'

BURGESS, Mark

Actor, b. 9 April 1959, Kingston-upon-Thames, Surrey. Trained at Guilford School of Acting. Theatre incl: *Deathtrap; Another Country*. TV incl: *Knights of God*; Gordon Collins in *Brookside*. m. Elizabeth; 1 d. Romy, 1 s. Alex. Address: c/o John Mahoney Management. Birthsign: Aries. Hobbies: doing work on the house and garden, watching sport, playing snooker. **Most Cherished Possession:** 'A specially commissioned drawing of me playing snooker with Alex Higgins.' **Favourite Memory:** 'Family holiday in Brittany in 1989, after the birth of Alex.'

BURKE, Alfred

Actor, b. 28 January 1918, Peckham, London. Trained at RADA and started career at the Barn Theatre, Shere, Surrey, 1939. Rep at Birmingham, Leeds and Manchester. First London West End appearance in *Desire Caught By the Tail*; also in *Sailor Beware; The Seagull* with the RSC. Films incl: *The Angry Silence; Yangtse Incident; Interpol; Bitter Victory; The House On Garibaldi Street; One Day In the Life of Ivan Denisovich; John Paul II; Kim*. Was Frank Marker in TV's *Public Eye*. Other TV incl: *The Exiles; The Brontes; The Tip; Treasure Island; Enemy at the Door; Mary Blandy; The Rod of Iron; No 10; The Glory Boys; Ladies Night; Bergerac; Sophia and Constance*. m. Barbara, former stage manager; two sets of twins, Jacob and Harriet, Kelly and Louisa. Address: c/o Joy Jameson. Hobbies: football, music, historic houses.

BURNET, Sir Alastair

Newscaster, b. 12 July 1928, Sheffield. Worked on *The Glasgow Herald* and *The Economist* before joining ITN in 1963 as political editor. TV incl: *News at Ten; News at 5.45; TV Eye*; with the BBC from 1972–74, *Panorama*. Anchorman for major programmes incl: Apollo space missions, General Elections, Budgets, royal weddings, the visit of Pope John Paul II to Britain. Three-times winner of the Richard Dimbleby Award; Royal Television Society Judges' Prize, 1982; Political Broadcaster of the Year, 1970. Editor of *The Economist*, 1965–74; and of the *Daily Express*, 1974–76. Independent national director of *The Times*. m. Maureen Sinclair. Address: c/o ITN. Birthsign: Cancer.

BURNS, Gordon

TV producer/presenter, b. 10 June 1942, Belfast. Trained in newspaper journalism and radio on *East Antrim Times, Belfast Telegraph* and BBC London. TV incl: reporter, *World In Action;* reporter/presenter *Reports Politics;* presenter *Granada 500; The Gordon Burns Hour;* presenter *UTV Reports* (1969–73); sports editor UTV (1967–73); Granada Reports presenter; presenter *The Krypton Factor; Irish Angle; A Way of Life; Password; Surprise, Surprise.* m. Sheelagh; 1 s. Tristun, 1 d. Anna. Address: c/o Granada TV. Birthsign: Gemini. Hobbies; Liverpool Football Club, watching cricket, Irish politics. Pet: cat. **Most Cherished Possession:** 'My home, because it's where I most like to be.' **Favourite Memory:** 'Seeing the birth of my daughter.'

BURROWS, Malandra

Actress/singer, b. 4 November 1965, Woolton, Liverpool. She trained at the Mabel Fletcher Drama College in Liverpool, but began her career at the age of seven in YTV's *Junior Showtime* and appeared and won *New Faces* at the age of nine. Has performed in fringe theatre and pantomimes. TV incl: *Brookside;* Kathy Merrick in *Emmerdale.* Address: c/o Yorkshire Television. Birthsign: Scorpio. Hobbies: horse riding, walking. Pets: Bonkers, a mongrel dog. **Most Cherished Possession:** 'My grandmum Nelly's music box, reminding me of her beautiful singing voice and enthusiastic encouragement.' **Favourite Memory:** 'Liverpool, which has the loveliest, most talented, colourful and humorous people anywhere.'

BYATT, Michelle

Actress, b. 3 November 1970, Liverpool. Trained first at the Merseyside Dance and Drama Centre, then at the London Studio Centre (finishing July 1990). Theatre: *All Flesh Is Grass; Yer Dancing?; Innocent Mistress; Katie Krackernuts; The Piper of Hamelin.* Film: Jude in *Business as Usual.* TV: Nikki in *Brookside;* Judith in *Watching;* appeared in a scene reconstructing classroom violence for *World In Action.* TV commercials: Allied Carpets; Clearasil. Agent: Nigel Martin-Smith. Hobbies: 'Swimming, walking, listening to good music, astrology, having a good time.' Pet: a cat called Benji. **Most Cherished Possession:** 'My family, because they're my best friends and they make me laugh.' **Favourite Memory:** 'Passing my driving test, because I became totally independent and able to go anywhere I pleased.'

BYGRAVES, Max, OBE

Entertainer, b. 16 October 1922, Rotherhithe, London. West End debut at London Palladium, 1949. Films incl: *Charlie Moon; A Cry From the Streets; Spare the Rod.* Radio incl: *Educating Archie.* TV incl: *Max Bygraves; Max; Singalongamax; Max Rolls On; Side by Side; Family Fortunes.* Has made more Royal Variety Performances than any other artist. Has three platinum, 31 gold and 15 silver discs, all for his *Singalong* LPs. Books: *I Wanna Tell You a Story* (autobiog); *The Milkman's On His Way* (novel); *After Thoughts* (second volume of autobiog). m. Gladys (Blossom); 2 d. Christine, Maxine, 1 s. Anthony. Address: c/o Jennifer Maffini, Roebuck House, Castle Street, London SW1 5BE. Birthsign: Libra. Hobbies: golf, vintage cars, reading, travel. **Most Cherished Possession:** 'My address book – I only enter the names of friends I appreciate.'

BYRNE, Patsy

Actress b. 13 July, Ashford, Kent. Diploma in theatre arts, taught speech and drama. Five years in weekly and fortnightly rep during the Fifties; two years with the English Stage Company at the Royal Court Theatre, performances including *Sergeant Musgrave's Dance* and *One Way Pendulum;* six years with the Royal Shakespeare Company at Stratford-upon-Avon and Aldwych, including *The Caucasian Chalk Circle, The Cherry Orchard* and *As You Like It.* TV includes many situation comedies and recently: *Inspector Morse; A Taste For Death; Blackadder II;* Mrs Stoneway in *Watching* (four series). m. Patrick Seccombe. Address: c/o Crouch Salmon Associates. Hobbies: reading, travelling, gardening. **Favourite Memory:** 'Family summer holidays in Finland: glorious sun and heat, a wooden house by the lake, feasting, swimming, Midsummer Night fireworks.'

BYRNE, Peter

Actor/director, b. 29 January 1928, London. Trained at Italia Conti Stage School. Director productions Bournemouth Theatre Co, 1965–66. Theatre incl: *There's a Girl In My Soup; Underground: Boeing Boeing; The Blue Lamp; Cats; Deadly Nightcap; Move Over Mrs Markham; Run For Your Wife; The Business of Murder; Wait Until Dark*. Films incl: *Large Rope; Reach For the Sky; Carry On Cabbie*. TV incl: *Dixon of Dock Green; Mutiny at Spithead; The New Canadians; Looks Familiar; Blake's Seven; The Pattern of Marriage; Cinderella; Bluebirds; Bread*. m. Renee Helen. Address: c/o Spotlight, London. Birthsign: Aquarius. Hobbies: squash, swimming, riding, golf, travel. **Most Cherished Possession:** 'My Equity card.' **Favourite Memory:** 'I've forgotten!'

BYRON, Kathleen

Actress, b. 11 January 1923, London. Trained at the Old Vic Theatre School. After the war came her acclaimed part of a mad mum in the film *Black Narcissus*. Theatre incl: *Pygmalion; Crown Matrimonial*. Other films incl: *Small Black Room; Prelude To Fame; Madness of the Heart; The Elephant Man; From a Far Country*. TV incl: *The Avengers; Who Is Sylvia?; Countercrime; Emmerdale Farm; The Golden Bowl; Portrait of a Lady; Moonstone; Heidi; Tales of the Supernatural; The Professionals; Minder; General Hospital; Hedda Gabler; Together; Unity; Nancy Astor; Angels; Dearly Beloved; Gentlemen and Players; Casualty; Portrait of a Marriage*. m. writer Alaric Jacob; 1 d. Harriet, 1 s. Jasper. Address: c/o Rolf Kruger. Birthsign: Capricorn. Hobbies: pottery, gardening. Pets: cats. **Most Cherished Possession:** 'Family and friends.' **Favourite Memory:** 'Surviving any first night.'

CADELL, Simon

Actor, b. 19 July 1950, London. Trained at Bristol Old Vic Theatre School then joined the *company* itself. TV incl: *Hadleigh; Hine; Love Story; A Man From Haven; Love School; Glittering Prizes; Wings; She Fell Among Thieves; Enemy at the Door; Edward and Mrs Simpson; Minder; Bergerac; Hi-de-Hi; Blott On the Landscape; Life Without George; The Dog It Was That Died; A Wanted Man; Pride and Extreme Prejudice*. Address: c/o MLR. Birthsign: Cancer. Hobby: travel.

CAINE, Marti

Comedian, b. 26 January 1945, Sheffield. A former model, entered showbusiness at the age of 19 as a singer and then compère. Since appearing on and winning *New Faces*, 1975, she has worked extensively in cabaret, concerts and theatre seasons throughout Britain and in Australia, New Zealand and America. Stage incl: *Funny Girl*. Films incl: *Birds of Paradise*. TV incl: *This Is Your Life; Des O'Connor Tonight; Parkinson; The Marti Caine Show; Marti Caine; Hilary; New Faces* presenter. m. Malcolm Stringer (dis.), (2nd) Kenneth Ives, 2 s. Lee, Max (both from 1st m.). Address: c/o ICM. Birthsign: Aquarius. Hobbies: gardening, music, films, interior decor. **Most Cherished Possession:** 'Home – it's a refuge.' **Favourite Memory:** 'Watching my kids ripping the wrapping from their Christmas presents.'

CAINE, Michael

Actor, b. 14 March 1933, Bermondsey, South London. Films incl: *Zulu; The Ipcress File; Alfie; Funeral In Berlin; Billion Dollar Brain; The Italian Job; Too Late the Hero; Get Carter; Kidnapped; The Black Windmill; Harry and Walter Go To New York; The Eagle Has Landed; A Bridge Too Far; Ashanti; Beyond the Poseidon Adventure; Escape To Victory; Educating Rita; The Honorary Consul; Blame It On Rio; Hannah and Her Sisters; Mona Lisa; The Fourth Protocol; Jaws – The Revenge; Dirty Rotten Scoundrels; A Shock To the System; Bullseye*. TV: *The Compartment; The Playmates; Hobson's Choice; Funny Noises With Their Mouths; The Way With Reggie; Luck of the Draw; Hamlet; The Other Man; Jack The Ripper; Jekyll & Hyde*. m. 1st Patricia Haines, 2nd Shakira; 2 d. Dominique (from 1st m.), Natasha. Address: c/o ICM. Hobbies: gardening. Pets: two dogs.

CALLOW, Simon

Actor, b. 15 June 1949, London. Trained at The Dance Centre before rep. West End performances incl: *Total Eclipse; Beastly Beatitudes of Balthazar B; The Relapse; On the Spot; Faust.* At the National Theatre he has been in *As You Like It; Galileo; Amadeus; Sisterly Feelings; Single Spies.* Films incl: *Amadeus; The Good Father; A Room With a View.* Films as director: *At Freddy's; Ballad of the Sad Café.* TV incl: *Wings of Song; Instant Englishment Plus VAT; Man of Destiny; Deadhead; Chance In a Million.* Address: c/o Marina Martin Management. Hobby: spending money pointlessly. Pet: Boxer named Brunge. **Most Cherished Possession:** 'Toy bear called Bruin.'

CAMPBELL, Gavin

Actor/presenter/journalist/broadcaster. b. 17 March 1946, Letchworth, Hertfordshire. Trained at Central School of Speech and Drama; worked with Joan Littlewood Theatre Workshop. In British premiere *When One Is Somebody* (York). TV incl: *Department S; Vendetta; Armchair Theatre.* BBC Radio as newsreader/announcer, then producer until joined TV's *That's Life* as reporter/presenter. Also reported for *Breakfast Time; Nationwide; London Plus; South-East at Six.* m. Liz Hendry; 2 d. Holly, Hannah. Address: c/o Jon Roseman Assocs. Birthsign: Pisces. Hobbies incl: scuba-diving, mountaineering. **Most Cherished Possession:** 'My father's war medals which he left to me.' **Favourite Memory:** 'Holding both my new-born daughters.'

CAMPBELL, Joanne

Actress, b. 8 February 1964, Northampton. Has made numerous stage appearances. TV incl: BBC's *Parents and Teenagers* for *Open University; Night Kids; Copperfield Comedy And Co; All Electric Amusement Arcade; Dramarama; Me and My Girl; Home James!.* Address: c/o Evans & Reiss. Birthsign: Aquarius. Hobbies: horse riding, playing tennis, dancing, swimming. **Most Cherished Possession:** 'A little rag doll because she has been with me since I was 10, so she has seen all.' **Favourite Memory:** 'Visiting Jamaica as a child because it is the birthplace of my father.'

CAMPBELL, Nicky

Presenter, b. 10 April 1961, Edinburgh. Disc jockey and jingles writer for ILR station Northsound Radio in Aberdeen, before moving to Capital Radio in London. Joined Radio 1 in 1987. TV incl: *Top of the Pops; Video Juke Box;* a scriptwriter for *Spitting Image;* host of the game show *Wheel of Fortune; The New Year Show.* m. Linda. Address: c/o BBC Radio 1, Broadcasting House, Portland Place, London W1A 1AA. Birthsign: Aries.

CANNON, Tommy

Comedian, b. 27 June 1938, Oldham. Half of the comedy partnership Cannon and Ball. Former welders in a Lancashire factory by day and a singing duo, The Harper Brothers, at night. Changed names to Cannon and Ball for *Opportunity Knocks* appearance. Voted clubland's top comedy duo, they have also won The Variety Club Showbusiness Personalities of the Year and topped various magazine and newspaper popularity polls. Starred in their own series, *The Cannon and Ball Show* (1979–88); *Casino.* Subjects of *This Is Your Life.* They have also made a film *The Boys In Blue.* m. Margaret (sep.); 2 d. Janette, Julie. Address: c/o International Artistes, Albert House, Albert Street, Chadderton, Manchester OL9 7TA. Birthsign: Cancer. Hobbies: golf, keep-fit and most sports.

CAPRON, Brian

Actor, b. 11 February 1949, Woodbridge, Suffolk. Trained at LAMDA, followed by over three years at Northcott Theatre, Exeter. Has also spent time at other theatres countrywide incl: Welsh National; Gardner Centre; Bush; King's Head; and recently did a national tour in David Hare's *Knuckle*. TV incl: *A Place To Hide; The Sweeney; Coronation Street; Bergerac; Grange Hill; The Gentle Touch; Minder; Up The Elephant . . .; Full House; Never Say Die; Jack the Ripper; Never Come Back; The Bill*. m. Janette Legge; 2 d. Lucy Jane, Ellen Louise. Address: c/o Markham & Froggatt, London. Birthsign: Aquarius. Hobbies: reading, riding, camping. Pets: three goldfish. **Most Cherished Possession:** 'My car keys, for the freedom they give me.' **Favourite Memory:** 'Being around at the birth of my two daughters.'

CARBY, Fanny

Actress, b. 2 February, Sutton Coldfield, Warwicks. Spent eight years at Joan Littlewood's Theatre Workshop, where she was in *Ned Kelly; Oh! What A Lovely War*. Films incl: *The Elephant Man; Loophole; The Nightingale Saga*. Extensive TV incl: *The Good Companions; Forgive Our Foolish Ways; Angels; The Cost of Loving; Cockles; Juliet Bravo; The Good Dr Booker Adams; David Copperfield; The Little Matchgirl*; three series with Spike Milligan; *Coronation Street; Till Death Us Do Part; House Plant*. Address: c/o Barry Burnett. Hobbies: gardening, antiques. Pets: cat called Mrs Tiggy. **Most Cherished Possession:** 'My cottage and garden in the country. My cat lives there and I can get away from everything and find peace.' **Favourite Memory:** 'The first night of *Oh! What A Lovely War*.'

CAROLGEES, Bob

Comedy entertainer, b. 12 May 1948, Birmingham. Considerable experience in cabaret and theatre, including four Royal Gala performances, entertainment trips to the Falkland Islands. TV incl: *Tiswas; 3-2-1; Russell Harty; OTT; Saturday Stayback; Aspel & Company; Wogan; Live From Her Majesty's; Look Who's Talking; Live From The Palladium; Seaside Special; Sunday Sunday; Surprise, Surprise; Concentration* (presenter). Plus TV commercials. m. Alison; 1 d. Natalie, 1 s. Richard. Address: c/o Tony West Entertainments, 158 College Road, Crosby, Liverpool L23 3DP. Hobbies: swimming, windsurfing, gardening. **Most Cherished Possession:** 'My house, because I never thought I would own such a grand place.' **Favourite Memory:** 'Holding my daughter for the first time.'

CARPENTER, Harry

Sports commentator, b. 17 October 1925, London. Former Fleet Street journalist. Commentator at world heavyweight title fights since 1956 and every Olympic Games since 1956. Joined BBC full-time in 1962. Also presenter of Wimbledon Lawn Tennis; Open Golf Championships; Oxford–Cambridge boat race. Author of three books on boxing. Winner of American Sportscasters' Association International Award, 1989. m. Phyllis; 1 s. Clive. Hobbies: golf, classical music. Address: c/o BBC TV, London. Birthsign: Libra. **Favourite Possession:** 'The house in Sandwich where I look out on to the graveyard of St Clement's, which has an 11th-century Norman tower. Peace, perfect peace.'

CARPENTER, Sue

Presenter/journalist, b. 17 May 1956, London. Started out in TV in the Middle East, before becoming a presenter on BBC's *Breakfast Time* and *News Afternoon; Channel 4 News; News at 5.40; ITN News*. Address: c/o Jon Roseman Associates, 103 Charing Cross Road, London WC2. Birthsign: Taurus. Hobbies: 'Watching motor racing, walking, aerobics. Pet: dog. **Favourite Memory:** 'Buying a turkey from Smithfield on Christmas Eve. As a small child it meant staying up late, eating roast chestnuts and then seeing the lights in Oxford Street.'

CARROTT, Jasper

Comedian, b. 14 March 1945, Birmingham, as Robert Davies. Started his career in 1969 in a club where he was host and compere. Became an all-round entertainer in clubs, universities and at concerts. Film: *Jane and the Lost City*. Made his TV debut with his own BBC special. Other TV incl: *An Audience With Jasper Carrott; Half Hour With Jasper Carrott; The Unrecorded Jasper Carrott; Carrott De Sol; Carrott's Lib*, which won a BAFTA award in 1984; and *Carrott Confidential*. His records have earned him three gold and three silver discs. m. Hazel; 3 d. Lucy, Jennifer, Hannah, 1 s. Jake. Address: c/o BBC TV. Birthsign: Pisces. Hobbies: golf, squash.

CARSON, Frank, KSF

Comedian, b. 6 November 1926, Belfast. Knight of the Grand Cross of St Gregory. Was a TV favourite in Ireland before coming to England to try his luck in clubland. After *The Good Old Days, Opportunity Knocks* and *The Comedians*, he has become one of the country's leading performers and is much in demand and much televised. Other TV incl: *The Melting Pot; Celebrity Squares; The Ballyskillen Opera House;* a regular on *Tiswas;* subject of *This Is Your Life*. m. Ruth; 1 d. Majella, 2 s. Tony, Aidan. Address: c/o Dorothy Solmon, Roebuck House, Castle Street, London SW1 5BE. Birthsign: Scorpio. Hobbies: golf, collecting money.

CARTER, Lynda

Actress/singer/dancer, b. 24 July 1951, Phoenix, Arizona. Former Miss USA is best known for her portrayal of Diana Prince, *Wonder Woman*. TV film: *Rita Hayworth – The Love Goddess*. Other TV incl: *Stillwatch; Partners In Crime; Body and Soul; Born To Be Sold; Muppets*. m. (1st) Ron Samuels (dis.), (2nd) Robert Altman; 1 s. James. Address: c/o William Morris, 151 El Camino Drive, Beverly Hills, CA 90212. Birthsign: Leo. Hobbies: tennis, riding, swimming, music, ballet. Pets: two Dobermans. **Favourite Memory:** 'My five years as Wonder Woman.'

CARTERET, Anna

Actress, b. 11 December 1942, Bangalore, India. Spent six years in rep and 12 years as a leading actress at the National Theatre. Recent stage incl: *The Beaux Stratagem* at the Lyric, Hammersmith; *A Piece of My Mind* at the Apollo, Shaftesbury Avenue; *A Doll's House* at Riverside Studios. Inspector Kate Longton in the BBC TV series *Juliet Bravo*. Other recent TV includes the plays: *Change Partners; Being Normal; Tickets For the Titanic; The Shell Seekers*. m. Christopher Morahan; 2 d. Rebecca, Hattie. Address: c/o Peters Fraser & Dunlop. Hobbies: music, jogging, gardening. Pets: black cat called Michael Jackson. **Most Cherished Possession:** 'My Filofax and my typewriter, because they are my means of communicating with the rest of the world!'

CASHMAN, Michael

Actor/writer, b. 17 December 1950, London. Holder of Special Service Award from the American Association of Physicians For Human Rights. Started as a child actor. Theatre incl: *Oliver; Peter Pan; Zigger Zagger; Before Your Very Eyes; Bricks 'n' Mortar; The Chairs;* National Theatre player 1989–90, in *Bent*. Films incl: *The Virgin Soldiers; Zee & Co.; Unman*. TV incl: *Angels; Waste; The Sandbaggers; Nobody's Perfect; The Gentle Touch; Seven Deadly Virtues; Game For a Laugh; Bird of Prey; Dempsey and Makepeace; The Winning Streak; Season's Greetings; EastEnders*. Address: c/o Barry Burnett. Hobbies: Walking, gardening, music, travel, photography. **Most Cherished Possession:** 'A sense of humour to cope with the world and prevent too much self-importance.' **Favourite Memory:** 'First trip to the seaside – Southend – as a child.'

CASS, David

News presenter, b. 4 April, Huddersfield, Yorkshire. Worked his way up through newspapers, local radio and regional television to presenting the news on national television; sports correspondent, 1978–84; Britain's first networked night-time newscaster, 1988; Washington correspondent for ITN's *World News* on *The Channel Four Daily* since 1989. m. Buddug Rhiannon; 2 s. Russell, William. Address: c/o ITN, Washington. Birthsign: Aries. Hobbies: playing cricket, mostly for charity; gardening. Pets: Collie bitch, Breeze; Sheltie bitch, Honey. **Favourite Memory:** 'The Moscow Olympics, where I met my wife.'

CASTLE, Roy

Entertainer/actor, b. 31 August 1932, Scholes, near Huddersfield. Turned pro. 1953. Stooge for Jimmy James and Jimmy Clitheroe. Stage incl: *Singing In the Rain*. Films incl: *Dr Who and the Daleks; Carry On Up the Khyber*. Radio incl: *Castle's On the Air*. TV incl: *The Roy Castle Show; Roy Castle Beats Time;* 16 series presenting *The Record Breakers*. m. Fiona; 2 d. Julia, Antonia, 2 s. Daniel, Benjamin. Address: c/o London Management. Birthsign: Virgo. Hobbies: gardening, squash, golf, charity cricket, sleep. **Most Cherished Possession:** 'Good health. Without it you can't enjoy even the most expensive of possessions.' **Favourite Memory:** 'The 1958 Royal Variety Show. I had finally made it into the well-known brigade.'

CAZENOVE, Christopher

Actor, b. 17 December 1945, Winchester. Trained at Bristol Old Vic Theatre School and rep in Leicester, Leatherhead, Windsor and Pitlochry before London's West End. Theatre incl: *My Darling Daisy; Winslow Boy; Joking Apart; Goodbye Fidel* on Broadway. Films incl: *Royal Flash; East of Elephant Rock; The Girls In Blue Velvet; Zulu Dawn; Eye of the Needle; From a Far Country; Heat and Dust; Mata Hari; The Fantasist; Souvenir; Hold My Hand, I'm Dying; The Lady and The Highwayman*. TV incl: *The Regiment; The Duchess of Duke Street; The Rivals of Sherlock Holmes; Affairs of the Heart; Jennie; Lady Randolph Churchill; Lady Killers; The Red Signal; Jenny's War; Lace 2; Cain and Abel; Dynasty; Windmills of the Gods; Shades of Love; Tears In the Rain; Ticket To Ride*. m. actress Angharad Rees; 2 s. Linford, Rhys William. Address: c/o Michael Whitehall.

CHADBON, Tom

Actor, b. 27 February 1946, Luton. Trained for the stage at RADA and followed this with work in rep. He has extensive theatre work to his credit, has appeared in more than 150 television plays and series, a dozen feature films and been on the radio and in commercials. m. Jane; 2 s. Dominic, Nicholas, 2 d. Amelia, Felicity. Address: c/o Michael Ladkin. Birthsign: Pisces. Hobbies: birds, garden, guitar. Pets: Bull Terrier. **Favourite Memory:** 'Chelsea in the spring of 1964. It was a great time to be alive.'

CHADWICK, Cy

Actor, b. 2 June 1969, Leeds. Trained at the Intake Theatre Arts School, Leeds. TV incl: *Book Tower; How We Used To Live; On The Boat; Television Bremen; Go-Getters; The Funny Side*. Nick Bates in *Emmerdale*. Address: c/o 766 Wilmslow Road, Didsbury, Manchester. Birthsign: Gemini. Hobbies: photography, music, keeping busy, driving alone. Pet: a dog called Timmy. **Most Cherished Possession:** 'My diary, photo collection and contents of my top drawer.' **Favourite Memory:** 'One wonderful winter's evening by the sea in Morecambe!'

CHALMERS, Judith

Broadcaster, b. 10 October, Manchester. Started broadcasting at BBC Manchester at the age of 13, in *Children's Hour*. Then BBC TV announcing in London. TV incl: *Wish You Were Here . . .?* since its launch in 1973 and *The Home Service*, which she devised. Commentator for ITV coverage of Derby and royal and state occasions. Travel editor of *Woman's Realm* magazine. Chairman of the Appeals Committee for Women's National Cancer Control Campaign. m. Neil Durden-Smith; 1 d. Emma, 1 s. Mark. Address: c/o IMG. Birthsign: Libra. Hobbies: walking, birdwatching, rugby, cricket, photography. **Most Cherished Possession:** 'China figure bought for me by my parents.' **Favourite Memory:** 'The births of my children.'

CHEGWIN, Keith

TV broadcaster, b. 17 January 1957, Liverpool. Attended stage school in London for six years and took a degree in English Literature at Oxford University. Stage incl: *The Good Old Bad Old Days; Tom Brown's Schooldays; Wally Scott Live*. Films incl: Polanski's *Macbeth* and, for the Children's Film Foundation, *Eggheads Robot; Robin Hood Junior*. Has broadcast on Radios 1, 2 and 4. TV incl: *Swap Shop; Saturday Superstore; Cheggers Plays Pop; Wackers; Cheggers' Action Reports; Chegwin Checks It Out; Sky Star Search*. m. Maggie Philbin of BBC's *Tomorrow's World;* 1 d. Rose Elizabeth. Address: c/o Dave Winslett. Birthsign: Capricorn. Hobbies: horse riding, playing the piano, reading, writing. Pets: two dogs, Hollie and Muffin, three horses, four cats. **Favourite Memory:** 'Eating a mint humbug in 1982 because it lasted so long.'

CHERITON, Shirley

Actress, b. 28 June 1955, London. Trained at the Italia Conti Stage School. Theatre incl: *Goldilocks and the Three Bears; Pyjama Tops; Dick Whittington; The Monkey Walk;* Willy Russell's *One For the Road; Robin Hood*. TV incl: *Crown Court; Within These Walls; The Cuckoo Waltz; Z-Cars; Bless This House; General Hospital; Angels; Hazell; Secombe With Music; The Final Frontier; EastEnders; Three Up, Two Down*. 2 s. Mark, Adam. Hobbies: swimming, keep fit. Address: c/o St James's Management, London. Birthsign: Cancer. **Most Cherished Possession:** 'A St Christopher my son bought for me to keep me safe.'

CHILD, Jeremy

Actor, b 20 September 1944, Woking, Surrey. Attended the Bristol Old Vic Theatre School. Theatre incl: *Conduct Unbecoming; Twelfth Night; Donkey's Years; Hay Fever; An Ideal Husband*. Films incl: *The Stud; Winston Churchill; Give My Regards To Broad Street*. Extensive TV incl: *Robin's Nest; Edward and Mrs Simpson; When the Boat Comes In; Minder; Bergerac; The Jewel In the Crown; First Among Equals; Game, Set & Match*. m. (1st) Deborah Grant (dis.), (2nd) Jan Todd (dis.), (3rd) Libby Morgan; 3 d. Melissa, Lenora, Eliza, 1 s. Alexander. Address: c/o Richard Stone. Birthsign: Virgo. Hobbies: cooking, gardening, flying, laughing. **Favourite Memory:** 'The births of my three children.'

CHILDS, Tracey

Actress, b. 30 May 1963, Chiswick. Five years at Elmhurst Ballet School, followed by Guildhall. Her first job was a two-minute part in *Upstairs, Downstairs*. Theatre incl: *The Hunchback of Nôtre Dame; Great Expectations – The Musical*. TV incl: *The Prime of Miss Jean Brodie; Sense and Sensibility; Baal; The Scarlet Pimpernel; A Married Man; Morgan's Boy; The Victoria Wood Show; Deceptions; The Happy Autumn Fields; Shades; A Talent For Murder; Flesh and Blood; The Devil's Crown; Prometheus; Cold Warrior; Dempsey and Makepeace; Howards' Way; Gems; The Shell Seekers*. Address: c/o Evans & Reiss. Birthsign: Gemini. Hobbies incl: dancing, walking, reading. Pets: Flat-coated retriever, Harvey. **Most Cherished Possession:** 'My health.' **Favourite Memory:** 'When I was too young to know how difficult acting was!'

CHURCHILL, Donald

Writer/actor, b. 6 November 1930, Southall, Middlesex. Output includes 40 plays for TV. Theatre incl: *Under My Skin; Fringe Benefits* (with Peter Yeldham). Films incl: *My Family and Other Animals.* TV incl: *The Cherry On the Top; Feeling the Pinch; You Don't Know Me, But; Hearts and Flowers; Moody and Peg* (with Julia Jones); *Feeling His Way; Spooner's Patch; Good Night – God Bless* (with Joe McGrath); *Mr Pye.* m. Pauline Yates; 2 d. Jemma, Polly. Address: c/o Marina Martin Management. Birthsign: Scorpio. Hobby: trying to learn French.

CLARKE, Jacqueline

Actress, b. 13 February 1942, Buckinghamshire. Trained at RADA, rep at York, Harrogate and Bournemouth. Theatre incl: *The Boy Friend; Oh Mr Porter; Gingerbread Man; Woman In Mind.* Radio incl: Roy Castle, Les Dawson and Mike Yarwood shows. Light entertainment shows for TV incl: *Dave Allen at Large* (for seven years); and with Mike Yarwood, Mike Reid, Les Dawson, Kelly Monteith, Terry Scott, Kenny Everett and Jasper Carrott; *A Sharp Intake of Breath; Second Time Around; The Critic; Eureka; Chish 'n' Fips.* m. Barrie Gosney; 1 d. Catherine Ann. Address: c/o Barry Burnett. Birthsign: Aquarius. Hobbies: gardening, pastel painting, walking. **Most Cherished Possession:** 'My mother's violin in its velvet case. Sweet music of the soul plays on.'

CLARKE, Justine

Actress. Appeared in TV commercials from the age of seven. Film: *Mad Max: Beyond Thunderdome.* TV: *Professor Poopsnaggle; Maestro's Company; Willing and Abel;* Princess Kate in *Touch the Sun* series; *A Country Practice;* Ruth 'Roo' Stewart in *Home and Away.* Address: c/o International Casting Services, 147a King Street, Sydney, NSW 2000, Australia.

CLAYTON, Edward

Actor/singer, b. 9 October 1940, Shelfield, Staffordshire. Theatre incl: Beadle in *Sweeney Todd – The Demon Barber of Fleet Street;* Turner in *Destiny; Comedians;* Obadiah Upward in *Poppy;* Dad in *Trafford Tanzi.* Films: *Wilt; Paris By Night.* TV incl: Stan Harvey in *Crossroads; Tucker's Luck;* Brian in *Eh Brian, It's a Whopper; Whoops Apocalypse;* Robson in *First Among Equals;* Tom Bridges in *A Sort of Innocence;* Vince Roper in *The Bell Run;* Charlie Davis in *The Contract;* Arthur Parkinson in *Brookside;* Tom Casey in *Coronation Street;* Brummie in *The Bill.* m. Caroline; 3 d. Ella, Joby, Rosalie. Address: c/o Sandra Griffin. Hobbies: 'Finding work!' Pets: a donkey, dogs and cats. **Most Cherished Possession:** 'My wife.' **Favourite Memory:** 'Winning £200 on the Pools.'

CLEESE, John

Writer/actor, b. 27 October 1939, Weston-super-Mare. Started in Cambridge Footlights Revue. Travelled to America with the Revue and stayed on to play in *Half a Sixpence.* Returned to make *The Frost Report; I'm Sorry I'll Read That Again; At Last The 1948 Show; Monty Python's Flying Circus; Fawlty Towers,* for which he won *TVTimes* Award for Funniest Man on TV (1978–9). Films incl: *Privates On Parade; Silverado; Clockwise; A Fish Called Wanda.* m. (1st) Connie Booth (dis.), (2nd) film director Barbara Trentham; 2 d. Cynthia, Camilla. Address: c/o David Wilkinson. **Most Cherished Possession:** 'Four fossilised nasal hairs from Alexander the Great.' **Favourite Memory:** 'Scoring England's winning goal in the 1966 World Cup Final.'

CLIFTON, Bernie

Actor/comedian/entertainer, b. 22 April, St Helens, Lancashire. Started working as one half of a vocal/comedy duo, The Two Terry's, then two years in RAF. Solo singer before becoming a comedian. TV debut 1971 in *The Good Old Days*. TV incl: *The Comedians; Crackerjack* (host for three series); *Theatre Royal; The Marti Caine Show; Des O'Connor Tonight; All Star Secrets; 3-2-1; The Jim Davidson Show; Bernie Clifton On Stage;* 1979 Royal Variety Show. Radio series incl: *Three In a Row; Bernie Clifton's Comedy Shop.* Theatre tours, cabaret, summer season and panto engagements. Address: c/o Michael Vine Assocs, 43 Cunliffe Road, Blackpool. Hobbies: running, has competed in London Marathon six times, flying micro-lite aircraft. **Most Cherished Possession:** 'My Derbyshire farm.'

CLIVE, John

Writer/actor, b. 6 January 1938, London. Started as a child actor. After RAF, stage incl: *Absurd Person Singular; The Real Inspector Hound; The Happy Apple; Wizard of Oz.* Films incl: *The Italian Job; Clockwork Orange; Carry On Abroad; Great Expectations.* TV incl: *How Green Was My Valley; The History of Mr Polly; A Dream of Alice; Lady Windermere's Fan; One Way Out; A Christmas Carol.* Screenplays: *Barricade: Broken Wings; Shutdown.* Produced documentary *Some Of Our Airmen Are No Longer Missing.* Books incl: *KG 200; The Last Liberator; Ark; Barossa; Broken Wings; The Lions Cage.* m. Carole Ann (dis.); 1 d. Hannah, 1 s. Alexander. Address: c/o CCA. Hobbies: exercising dog and myself. Pets: a Weimeraner dog and a Burmese blue cat.

COBURN, Norman

Actor, b. 6 March 1937, Sydney, Australia. Started acting at the age of 14, working in radio and theatre in Sydney. Toured for two years with the newly formed Elizabethan Theatre Trust in the mid-Fifties. Moved to Britain and worked in weekly repertory theatre. British TV incl: *No Hiding Place; The Professionals; Coronation Street.* In 1981, returned to Australia, where TV incl: *A Country Practice; 1915; Peach's Gold; Land of Hope; Five Mile Creek; Rafferty's Rules; Coral Island;* Donald Fisher in *Home and Away.* Theatre incl: plays with the Northern Territory Theatre Company; *Hamlet,* with the Phillip Street Theatre. Address: c/o Australian Creative Management, 169 Phillip Road, Sydney, NSW 2000, Australia.

COLE, George

Actor, b. 22 April 1925, London. Discovered in 1940 by Alastair Sim to play a cockney evacuee in *Cottage To Let* and became a star overnight. Theatre incl: *Flare Path; Mr Bolfy; Too True To Be Good; The Philanthropist; Brimstone and Treacle; The Pirate of Penzance; A Month of Sundays; A Piece of My Mind.* Films incl: *Cottage To Let; My Brother's Keeper; Laughter In Paradise; Top Secret; The Belles of St Trinian's; Blue Murder at St Trinian's; One Way Pendulum.* On radio, household name in *A Life of Bliss.* TV incl: *Sex Game; Murder; Don't Forget To Write; Minder* (six series); *The Bounder; Blott On the Landscape; Comrade Dad; A Man of Our Times; A Day To Remember; Natural Causes; Single Voices.* m. (2nd) Penny Morrell; 1 d. Tara, 1 s. Toby. Address: c/o Joy Jameson. Hobby: doing nothing. **Most Cherished Possession:** 'My *TVTimes* Award!'

COLE, Julie Dawn

Actress, b. 26 October 1957, Guildford, Surrey. London West End theatre incl: *Dry Rot; The Browning Version; A Friend Indeed; Easy Virtue.* Films: *Willy Wonka and the Chocolate Factory; That Lucky Touch; Camille.* TV incl: *Angels; Poldark; Mill On the Floss; Bergerac; Casualty; Tandoori Nights; Up the Elephant.* m. Nick Wilton; 1 d. Holly India. Address: c/o Barry Burnett. Birthsign: Scorpio. Hobbies: a standard Schnauzer called Shambles. **Most Cherished Possession:** 'A 2ft granite elephant weighing 55st, an impulse buy on holiday in India.' **Favourite Memory:** 'Trying to catch eels with my grandad in the River Usk, South Wales.'

COLE, Simon

ITN reporter, b. 19 March 1951, Tidworth. Gained his reporting experience on newspapers and radio. m. Magda. Address: c/o ITN, London. Birthsign: Pisces. Hobbies: reading, crosswords, guitar. Pets: aggressive tomcat. **Most Cherished Possession:** 'Hand-made electric guitar.' **Favourite Memory:** 'Wedding in Las Vegas. I married Magda and won at blackjack.'

COLEMAN, David

Reporter/interviewer, b. 26 April 1926, Alderley Edge, Cheshire. Started as newspaper journalist; editor of *Cheshire Country Express* at 23. Freelance radio contributor before joining BBC in Birmingham and later in London. Many years of TV experience incl: *Match of the Day; Grandstand; Sportsnight With Coleman; A Question of Sport.* m. Barbara; 3 d. Anne, Mandy, Samantha, 3 s. David, Dean (twins), Michael. Address: c/o Bagenal Harvey Organisation. Birthsign: Taurus. Hobby: golf.

COLEMAN, Jack

Actor, b. 21 February 1958, Philadelphia, USA. Studied drama at Duke University, North Carolina, and then attended the National Theatre Institute, Waterford, Connecticut. Theatre incl: *Grease; The Common Pursuit; Bouncers* (for which he won the Drama Critics' Circle Award for Best Actor in 1987). Steven Carrington in TV soap *Dynasty.* Address: c/o John Zaring Film Associates, Beverly Hills. Birthsign: Pisces. **Most Cherished Possession:** 'My home in New England. Every man's got to relax now and then.'

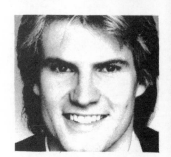

COLLINS, Joan

Actress, b. 23 May 1936, London. Studied at RADA. Made her debut in *Lady Godivia Rides Again.* Other films incl: *The Girl On the Red Velvet Swings; Island In the Sun; Rally Round the Flag, Boys; The Road To Hong Kong; The Big Sleep; The Day of the Fox; The Stud; The Bitch.* TV incl: *Tales of the Unexpected; The Money Changers; Dynasty; Sins.* Books: *Past Imperfect; Joan Collins' Beauty Book; Katy – A Fight For Life;* novel *Prime Time.* m. (1st) actor Maxwell Reed (dis.), (2nd) actor Anthony Newley (dis.), (3rd) film producer Ron Kass (dis.), (4th) Peter Holm (dis.); 3 d. Tara, Sacha (from 2nd m.), Katyana (from 3rd m.). Address: c/o Peter Charlesworth. Birthsign: Gemini. Hobbies: photography, collecting antiques, designing clothes.

COLLINS, John D

Actor, b. 2 December 1942, London. Trained at RADA. Stage experience has included Noel Coward's *Tonight at 8.30,* and *Time and Time Again* in Vienna and Sweden respectively. TV incl: *Chance In a Million; Hammer House of Horror; Only Fools and Horses; Yes Minister; 'Allo 'Allo; Rude Health.* m. Caryll; 1 d. Philippa, 1 s. Christopher. Address: c/o Evans & Reiss. Birthsign: Sagittarius. Hobbies: music, computing. Pets: cat, hamster. **Most Cherished Possession:** 'My health – with it I don't do much, without it nothing.' **Favourite Memory:** 'Passing the audition to drama school.'

COLLINS, Lewis

Actor, b. 27 May, Birkenhead. Trained at LAMDA then three years in rep. Theatre incl: *City Sugar; The Threepenny Opera; Babes In the Wood; Cinderella; Troilus and Cressida; King Lear*. Films incl: *Who Dares Wins; Commando Leopard*. TV incl: *Warship; The New Avengers; The Cuckoo Waltz; The Professionals; Must Wear Tights; A Night On the Town; Jack the Ripper*. Address: c/o ICM. Hobbies: writing, photography, flying. **Most Cherished Possession:** 'Paul McCartney's leather jacket – on permanent loan from Mike McCartney since 1962! (When we were both ladies' hairdressers)' **Favourite Memory:** 'Improvised bedtime stories from my mum. She was a brilliant comic.'

COLLINS, Matthew

Writer/TV presenter, b. 13 December 1960. Studied French at Manchester University (also speaks Spanish) and journalism at Cardiff. Special assignments and independent traveller for *The Travel Show*. Writes for many publications and is preparing a guide to Spain for publishers Simon & Schuster. Address: c/o Jacque Evans Management. Birthsign: Sagittarius. Hobbies: talking, listening, eating, drinking, running, horse-riding, weight training. **Most Cherished Possession:** 'My tiny short-wave radio. I can sometimes find Britain in some far-off land.' **Favourite Memory:** 'Being alone in a French nudist camp, where single men and photography were banned, with three Nikon cameras round my neck!'

CONDON, James

Actor, b. 27 September 1923, Fremantle, Western Australia. Started out as a radio actor in Australia in 1942. Worked for BBC radio and TV between 1949 and 1951 then returned to Australia to make numerous plays and TV series. Films incl: *The Stowaway; Tim; Hoodwink; The Boy Who Had Everything; Backstage*. Recent TV incl: *1915; Bellamy; The Young Doctors; Sons and Daughters; Prisoner: Cell Block H; Neighbours; Flying Doctors; Luke's Kingdom*. m. actress Anne Haddy; 4 d. from first marriage Elizabeth, Susan, Catherine, Mary Anne. Address: c/o International Casting, Sydney, Australia. Birthsign: Libra. Hobbies: walking, reading, fan of Australian Rules football and cricket. **Most Cherished Possession:** 'My beloved wife, though it would be truer to say she possesses me.'

CONNERY, Jason

Actor, b. 11 January 1963, London. Started career in Perth rep. Theatre incl: *Journey's End; The Three Musketeers*. Films incl: *Lords of Discipline; Dream One; The Boy Who Had Everything; Puss In Boots; La Venexiana; The Train; Bye Bye Baby; Casablanca Express; The Secret Life of Ian Fleming*. TV incl: *The First Modern Olympics; Doctor Who; Robin Hood in Robin of Sherwood; Serenade For Dead Lovers; The Train*. Address: c/o Joy Jameson. Birthsign: Capricorn. Hobbies: sports, writing music, going to the theatre, cooking. Pets: tropical fish. **Most Cherished Possession:** 'My motorbike – because it's so much fun to drive, carefully of course!'

CONWELL, Nula

Actress, b. 24 May 1959, London. Trained at the Anna Scher Theatre School. Theatre incl: *Obsession*. Films: *Fords On Water; The Elephant Man; Red Saturday*. TV: *Magpie; Eric Sykes; Dinner at the Sporting Club; Out; Vanishing Army; Telford's Change; Only a Game; The Police; If Only; Going Out; Shoestring; Playhouse: A Silly Little Habit; Stars of the Roller State Disco; Roll Over Beethoven*; WPC Viv Martella in *The Bill; Eyes; Only Fools and Horses* (two series); *The Laughter Show; Home Cooking; You In Mind; Give Us a Clue*. Address: c/o Anna Scher Theatre Management. Hobbies: circuit training, swimming, walking, cooking. **Most Cherished Possession:** 'My VW Beetle. She's just had her 18th birthday and is still going strong.' **Favourite Memory:** 'Me and my three sisters living at home. We had some great times together.'

CONTI, Tom

Actor, b. 22 November 1941, Paisley, Scotland. Theatre incl: *Savages* (debut); *Other People; The Black and White Minstrels; Don Juan; The Devil's Disciple; Whose Life Is It Anyway?* (played the lead, both in the West End and on Broadway, and received a Tony Award for his performance); *They're Playing Our Song; Romantic Comedy.* Films incl: *Flame; Full Circle; Eclipse; Galileo; Merry Christmas Mr Lawrence; American Dreamer; Saving Grace; Miracles; Reuben, Reuben; Heavenly Pursuits; Roman Holiday; Shirley Valentine.* TV incl: *Madame Bovary; Treats; The Norman Conquests; Blade On the Feather; The Glittering Prizes.* Work as a director incl: *Before the Party; The Housekeeper; Last Licks.* m. Kara Wilson; 1 d. Nina. Address: c/o Markham & Froggatt.

CONWAY, Nick

Actor, b. 25 December 1962, Shrewsbury. Member of Manchester Youth Theatre for five years. Theatre incl: *Roll On Four O'Clock; Johnny Oil; Arriverderci Millwall; A Common Woman; Dressing Up; Pied Piper; Breezeblock Park.* TV incl: *Keep On Running; Thank You Mrs Clinkscales;* Billy Boswell in *Bread; Bluebell; Starting Out; Sea View; Juliet Bravo; Going To Work; Miracles Take Longer; The Brief; The Practice.* Address: c/o Hamper-Neafsey Associates. Birthsign: Capricorn. Hobbies: football, running, song writing, reading. **Favourite Memory:** 'Manchester City 5 Manchester United 1.'

COOK, Sue

Broadcaster, b. 30 March 1949, Ruislip, Middlesex. Started broadcasting in 1972 and has worked for Capital Radio, BBC Radios 1 and 4, BBC TV and Thames TV on a wide variety of programmes, from documentaries to quiz shows. TV incl: *Out of Court; Nationwide; Crimewatch UK.* m. John Williams; 1 s. Charlie, 1 d. Megan. Address: c/o Michael Ladkin. Birthsign: Aries. Hobbies: music – making it and listening to it, learning the piano, driving, relaxing at home. **Most Cherished Possession:** 'My faithful, threadbare teddybear who has been with me in sickness and health since I was two.' **Favourite Memory:** 'The day my son Charlie was born – the best thing that ever happened to me!'

COOMBS, Pat

Actress, b. 27 August, London. After a scholarship to LAMDA, in rep with companies all over England. First came to fore in *Hello Playmates*, with Irene Handl. More recently, films incl: *Oooh . . . You Are Awful; Adolf Hitler – My Part In His Downfall.* TV incl: *Beggar My Neighbour; Celebrity Squares; Blankety Blank; 3-2-1; This Is Your Life* (as a subject); two series of *The Lady Is a Tramp;* four series of *You're Only Young Twice;* for Children's ITV, *Ragdolly Anna; And There's More; Mr Majeika; EastEnders.* Address: c/o Barry Burnett Organisation. Hobbies: writing letters, driving, reading, 'Puss-cats!' Pets: cats Persil and Rudy. **Most Cherished Possession:** 'A shirt bought in the early Sixties and still going strong!' **Favourite Memory:** 'My mum – who was funny, friendly and altogether smashing!'

COPLEY, Paul

Actor/writer, b. 25 November 1944, Denby Dale, Yorkshire. Trained as an English and drama teacher. Joined Leeds Playhouse Theatre as actor/teacher. Theatre incl: *For King and Country; Making Noise Quietly; King Lear; Twelfth Night; Prin.* Films incl: *A Bridge Too Far; Zulu Dawn; War and Remembrance.* Radio incl: *Jesus; King Street Junior.* TV incl: *Days of Hope; Trinity Tales; Death of a Princess; The Bright Side; Silas Marner; Oedipus at Colonus; The Mistress; Our Geoff; Gruey; Testimony of a Child.* Work as a writer has included six full-length stage plays including *Calling.* Most recent work for radio: *Shakespeare In Africa.* m. Natasha Pyne. Address: c/o Kate Feast. Hobbies: swimming, motor-cycling. **Most Cherished Possession:** 'My ageing Peugeot motor car.'

CORBETT, Matthew

Entertainer, b. 28 March 1948, Yorkshire. Trained as an actor at Central School of Speech and Drama, and in rep at Bristol, York, Chelmsford, Dundee and Richmond. TV incl: *Magpie; Rainbow; Matt and Gerry Ltd; The Sooty Show*, which he took over from his father Harry. Has recently taken Sooty on tour to Hong Kong and Australia. m. Sallie; 1 d. Tamsin, 2 s. Benjamin, Joe. Address: c/o Vincent Shaw Assocs, 20 Jay Mews, Kensington Gore, London SW7 2EP. Birthsign: Aries. Hobbies: music (writing and recording), travel, being on his narrowboat. **Favourite Memory:** 'Holiday in the Himalayas – perfect peace and tranquility.'

CORBETT, Ronnie

Actor/comedian, b. 4 December 1930, Edinburgh. Started amateur dramatics at 16. Many TV shows incl: *Crackerjack; The Dickie Henderson Show; Frost Report*, after being spotted by David Frost in Danny La Rue's nightclub; *No That's Me Over Here; Frost On Sunday; The Corbett Follies; The Two Ronnies; Sorry; Bruce and Ronnie*. m. Anne Hart; 2 d. Emma, Sophie. Address: c/o Sonny Zahl Associates. Birthsign: Sagittarius. Hobbies: golf, football, horse racing. **Most Cherished Possession:** 'My home – our house – a source of untold peace and pleasure.' **Favourite Memory:** 'Moving into above.'

CORKE, Fiona

Actress, b. 1961, Melbourne. Became involved in local drama and music groups as a child. After leaving school, did various jobs, including waitressing and working in a clothes shop. Trained at various theatre workshops. Theatre: *Hotel Bonegilla; Jolly Jumbuck; The Journey; Cafe Misto; Stop Laughing, This Could Be Serious; On the Line; Revel Without a Cause*. Films: *War Story/I Live With My Dad/Karma Oblivious* (shown at the Melbourne Film Festival); films for Swinburne Film and TV School. TV: *Zoo Family; Special Squad; Whose Baby?; Sword of Honour; The Great Bookie Robbery; The Fast Lane;* Gail Robinson in *Neighbours*, 1986–9. Address: c/o London Management.

CORNWELL, Judy

Actress/author, b. 22 February, London. Trained as a dancer and singer. London debut in *Oh! What a Lovely War*. Stage also incl: *Mr Whatnot; Don't Let Summer Come*. Films incl: *Every Home Should Have One; Wuthering Heights; Devil's Lieutenant; Asking For Trouble*. TV incl: *Call Me Daddy* (Emmy award, 1967); *Moody and Peg; Good Companions; Cakes and Ale* (nominated Best Actress by SFTA 1974); *December Rose; Paying Guests; Bergerac; Rumpole of the Bailey; Strong Poison; Farrington of the F.O.; Doctor Who*. Novel: *Cow and Cow Parsley*. m. John Parry; 1 s. Edward. Address: c/o Michael Ladkin. Hobbies: writing, cooking, psychology, gardening, swimming, collecting stones. **Favourite Memory:** 'My wedding day, 26 years ago. The best contract I ever signed.'

COSBY, Bill

Actor/director/writer, b. 12 July 1937, Philadelphia night club. Has made many successful comedy records. Films incl: *Hickey and Boggs; Uptown Saturday Night; Let's Do It Again; A Piece of Action; California Suite; Leonard Part 6*. Books: *Fatherhood; Love and Marriage*. Became well-known in Britain when he starred with Robert Culp in *I Spy*; then went on to his own television series *The Cosby Show*. m. Camille; 1 s. Ennis, 4 d. Erika, Erinn, Ensa, Evin. Address: c/o Willaim Morris, 151 El Camino Drv, Beverly Hills, CA 90212. Birthsign: Cancer. Hobby: tennis. Pets: one show dog. **Most Cherished Possession:** 'My family.' **Favourite Memory:** 'Ripples on my stomach – like Sly Stallone.'

COSSINS, James

Actor, b. 4 December 1933, Beckenham, Kent. Trained for the stage at RADA and was awarded the Silver Medal in 1952. After serving in the RAF, spent several years in rep. London West End appearances incl: *Bonne Soupe; Celebration; She Stoops To Conquer; The Beggar's Opera; The Anniversary; Man and Superman; Stage Struck*. Films incl: *How I Won the War; Otley; A Dandy In Aspic; Scrooge; Privilege; The Lost Continent; Melody; Wuthering Heights; Villain; Young Winston; Hitler – The Last Ten Days; The Man With the Golden Gun; The Great Train Robbery; Sphinx; Gandhi; The Confessions of Felix Krull; A Fish Called Wanda*. TV incl: *Mad Jack; A Day Out; Dombey and Son; The Pickwick Papers, Marjorie and Men; Rude Health; Miss Marple at Bertram's Hotel; Bergerac; Chelworth*. Address: c/o Julian Belfrage Associates. Hobbies: gardening, cooking.

COUNSELL, Elizabeth

Actress, b. 7 June 1942, Windsor, Berkshire. Parents, John Counsell and Mary Kerridge, ran the Theatre Royal, Windsor. Theatre incl: *As You Like It; Much Ado About Nothing; Dear Liar; Shakespeare's People; Jean Seberg; Present Laughter*. TV incl: *Top Secret Life of Edgar Briggs; Song By Song By Hart; Partners; Executive Stress; Brush Strokes*. m. actor David Simeon; 1 s. Leo. Address: c/o Daly Gagan Associates. Birthsign: Gemini. Hobbies: bird watching, songwriting, guitar playing. **Most Cherished Possession:** 'Book of Shakespeare's sonnets signed by John Gielgud.' **Favourite Memory:** 'The Congregation at our wedding breaking into spontaneous applause after the ceremony.'

COURTENAY, Margaret

Actress, b. 14 November 1923, Cardiff. Trained at LAMDA and did rep, incl: Stratford, Bristol Old Vic, Oxford, Regent's Park, Welsh National Theatre, Chichester, and many foreign tours. Theatre incl: *Ring Round the Moon; Alfie; The Killing of Sister George; 13 Rue de L'Amour; The Rivals; 42nd Street; Follies; The Admirable Crichton; Romeo and Juliet*. Films incl: *Isadora; Under Milk Wood; The Mirror Crack'd; Duet For One*. TV incl: *It Ain't Half Hot Mum; Good Companions; Never the Twain; Fresh Fields; Executive Stress; Don't Wait Up; Paradise Postponed*. m. (dis.); 1 s. Julian. Address: c/o Duncan Heath Assocs. Birthsign: Scorpio. Hobbies: reading, painting, talking, gardening. **Most Cherished Possession:** 'Great-grandmother's gold locket and chain containing first cut curl of son and grandson.'

COWPER, Nicola

Actress, b. 21 December 1967, Chelsea, London. Modelled and appeared in TV commercials up to the age of nine. Two years later, begain training full-time at the Corona Stage School. Films: Angie in *Winter Flight;* Lucy in Dennis Potter's *Dreamchild;* Nicole in *Underworld; Lionheart; Journey To the Centre I; Journey To the Centre II*. TV: *Break In the Sun* (aged 12); *Minder; Home Video; The Burston Rebellion; S.W.A.L.K.;* Heather Golding in *The Practice; Night Voices;* Gina in *Streetwise*. Address: c/o Brunskill Management. Pets: a dog called Sidney and two terrapins. **Most Cherished Possession:** 'A blue patchwork jumper knitted by my mum. I just love it.' **Favourite Memory:** 'Winning a tennis racket at school as Sports Girl of the Year. I never could play tennis, though. Maybe that's why I got a racket!'

COX, Doc

Presenter/singer, b. 1 July 1946, Sheffield, Yorkshire. Started out as BBC sound backroom boy. TV incl: *Nationwide; Look Stranger; Grapevine; Forty Minutes' Skiffle; Children In Need; Names & Games; Blankety Blank; Jim'll Fix It;* presenter/film director on *That's Life!* Address: c/o Arlington Enterprises. Birthsign: Cancer. Hobbies: blues, rhythm and blues, rock'n'roll, DIY, cycling, collecting vintage records, playing in the band Ivors Jivers. Pets: cat, Watkins. **Most Cherished Possession:** 'Either the ukelele I make my Ivor Biggun records with . . . or my genuine 1958 juke box!' **Favourite Memory:** 'Being kissed, in Disneyworld, by Minnie Mouse (because she squeaked!)'

CRAIG, Andy

Presenter/journalist/producer, b. 5 December 1954, Cumbria. Gained an Honours degree in agriculture from Newcastle upon Tyne University. Joined Tyne Tees TV in 1978, presenting the weekday magazine *Northern Life*, after working for Metro Radio. Went to *Central News*, hosted TV-am's *Good Morning Britain* briefly, then *Central Weekend Live*. In 1986, produced ITV's first networked AIDS programme, *Everyone's Problem*. Hosted Channel Four's *The Home Service* and its sequel, *Hot Property*, ITV's *The Time . . . The Place . . .* and TVS's *Head To Head*. Co-presented LWT's live *Searchline Special*, was guest host of ITV's *This Morning* and, since 1989, has hosted the ITV quiz *Sporting Triangles*. Also presenter of ITV cartoon series *Coconuts*. Address: c/o Orbi-Tel, 3 The Coppice, Seer Green, Beaconsfield, Buckinghamshire HP9 2SH.

CRAIG, Michael

Actor, b. 27 January 1929, Poona, India. Started career in rep. From 1954–61, film contract with the Rank Organisation. Theatre incl: season at Stratford, 1963–64; *A Whistle In the Dark; Funny Girl*. Films incl: *Passage Home; Yield To the Night; The Angry Silence* (also the writer); *Doctor In Love; The Killing In Angel Street*. More than 40 TV appearances incl: *Tiger Trap* (also the writer); *Husbands and Lovers; Second Time Around; The Foundation; Triangle*. m. Susan; 1 d. Jessica, 2 s. Stephen, Michael. Address: c/o Chatto & Linnit. Birthsign: Aquarius. Hobbies: golf, reading, writing. **Most Cherished Possession:** 'Academy Award Nomination for Best Story and Screenplay, 1960.' **Favourite Memory:** 'Seeing my daughter born.'

CRAIG, Wendy

Actress, b. 20 June 1934, Sacriston, Co Durham. Won first acting award at the age of three. Trained at London's Central School of Dramatic Art before going to Ipswich Rep. Leading theatre appearances incl: *Mr Kettle and Mrs Moon; Ride a Cock Horse; Peter Pan; The Taming of The Shrew; The Constant Wife; Beyond Reasonable Doubt*. Films incl: *Room at the Top; I'll Never Forget What's His Name*. TV incl: *Not In Front of the Children; And Mother Makes Three; Butterflies; Nanny*. TVTimes readers' Funniest Woman on TV, 1972/73/74. Woman of the Year, BBC, 1984. m. musician/writer Jack Bentley; 2 s. Alastair, Ross. Address: c/o Hatton & Baker. Birthsign: Gemini. Hobbies: music, horticulture.

CRANE, Andy

Presenter, b. 24 February 1964, Morecambe, Lancashire. Trained as a technical operator at Piccadilly Radio in Manchester and became a presenter, also for Capital Radio, London; *History Lost and Found* presenter for BBC radio for schools and presenter for *Children's BBC*, TV. Address: c/o PVA. Birthsign: Pisces. Hobbies: sailing, basketball. **Most Cherished Possession:** 'A silver chain given to me by my mother.' **Favourite Memory:** 'Twelve months spent in America as an exchange student 1980–81.'

CRANHAM, Kenneth

Actor, b. 12 December 1944, Dunfermline, Scotland. Trained at RADA and with the National Youth Theatre. Wide TV appearances incl: *Coronation Street; Danger UXB; Sound of the Guns; Butterflies Don't Count; 'Tis Pity She's a Whore; Cribb; Caretaker; The Bell; The Merchant of Venice; La Ronde; Shine On Harvey Moon; Reilly Ace of Spies; The Dumb Waiter; Inspector Morse; The Birthday Party; Oranges Are Not The Only Fruit*. m. Charlotte Cornwell (sep.); 1 d. Nancy Grace. Address: c/o Markham & Froggatt. Birthsign: Sagittarius. Hobbies: photography, music. **Most Cherished Possession:** 'A collection of wedding photos of both sets of parents.' **Favourite Memory:** 'Seeing and hearing pipe band at night when young.'

CRAVEN, John

Broadcaster and writer, b. 16 August, Leeds. Newspaper journalist in Yorkshire before joining the BBC as news scriptwriter. TV incl: *Look North; Points West; Search Breakthrough; Swap Shop; Saturday SuperStore; Newsround*, 1972–9, presenter and, later, editor; *Country File*. Also many guest appearances on TV and radio, corporate videos and writer of a weekly Green column in *Woman's Realm*. Book: *Wildlife In the News*. m. Marilyn; 2 d. Emma, Victoria. Pets: two cats, hamster. Hobbies: aviation, swimming, gold, wildlife. Address: c/o Noel Gay Artists. Birthsign: Leo. **Most Cherished Possession:** 'My first "byline", on an article written for a works magazine in Leeds.' **Favourite Memory:** 'Being here when my daughters were born.'

CRIBBINS, Bernard

Actor, b. 29 December 1928, Oldham, Lancashire. First appeared on stage at Oldham Rep in 1942. Theatre incl: *Not Now Darling; The Love Game; There Goes the Bride; Run For Your Wife; Guys and Dolls*. Films incl: *Casino Royale; The Railway Children; The Water Babies*. TV incl: two series of his own show, *Cribbins; Comedy Playhouse; Get the Drift; Jackanory; The Wombles; You Must Be Joking; Fawlty Towers; Star Turn* (presenter); *Shillingbury Tales; Langley Bottom; High and Dry; When We Are Married*. m. Gillian McBarnet. Address: c/o Crouch Salmon Assoc. Birthsign: Capricorn. Hobbies: fly fishing, golf, sleeping. Pets: Cavalier King Charles Spaniel. **Most Cherished Possession:** 'My pen-knife. Because I'm always losing it.' **Favourite Memory:** 'First parachute jump. Because I did it!'

CRICK, Michael

ITN television journalist, b. 21 May 1958. Educated Manchester Grammar School. Gained First Class Honours degree in Philosophy, Politics and Economics at New College, Oxford. President of Oxford Union 1979. Joined ITN as graduate trainee in 1980. Writer for *Channel 4 News*, 1983–84. Reporter for *Channel 4 News*, 1984–8. Washington correspondent since 1988. Founder Editor of *The Oxford Handbook*. Author of books: *Militant; Scargill and the Miners; The March of Militant; Manchester United: The Betrayal of a Legend*. m. TV journalist Margaret Hounsell; 1 d. Catherine. Address: c/o ITN. Birthsign: Taurus. Pets: tench called Terry.

CRICKET, Jimmy

Comedian, b. 17 October 1945, Cookstown, County Tyrone. Started as camp entertainer for Butlins and Pontins and worked on club circuits. TV incl: Children's Royal Variety Show; The Royal Variety Show; four series of *And There's More* for Central TV; plus pantomimes, cabaret, concert tours and summer seasons. m. May; 2 s. Dale, Frank, 2 d. Jamie May, Katie. Address: c/o International Artistes, London. Birthsign: Libra. Hobbies: jogging, playing football with the kids, listening to music, watching old Hollywood musicals. **Most Cherished Possession:** 'My character hat given me by BBC to wear on TV's *Good Old Days* show.' **Favourite Memory:** 'My wedding day. Having lent our car, we walked home two miles from evening party in our wedding clothes.'

CRONIN, Paul

Actor, b. 8 July 1938, Jamestown, Australia. Has 20 years' experience in the television industry and has won five awards for Most Popular Lead Actor for his work in *The Sullivans*. Other TV incl: *Solo One; Matlock Police; Matthew & Son; A Place To Call Home*. m. Helen; 4 d. Jane, Katherine, Susanne, Juliana. Address: 197 Cotham Road, Kew, 3103 Victoria, Australia. Birthsign: Cancer. Hobby: Executive Chairman of Australian football team, Brisbane Bears. Pets: dog.

CROSBIE, Anette

Actress, b. 12 February, Edinburgh. Trained at Bristol Old Vic Theatre School and has worked extensively in the theatre, incl: *Tramway Road; A Collier's Friday Night; Talk of the Devil; The Trojan War.* TV incl: *Edward VII* (*TVTimes* Best Actress Award, also BAFTA Actress of the Year, 1975); *The Six Wives of Henry VIII; Lillie; Family Dance* (and theatre); *Northern Lights; The Disappearance Of Harry; Off Peak; Paradise Postponed; Beyond the Pale.* Recent radio: *Clayhanger.* m. Michael Griffith; 1 s. Owen, 1 d. Selina. Address: c/o Julian Belfrage Assocs.

CROWTHER, Leslie

Actor/comedian, b. 6 February 1933, Nottingham. While studying drama appeared in school broadcasts for BBC, then rep at Regent's Park Open Air Theatre. Theatre incl: *High Spirits; Underneath the Arches;* Royal Variety Performance. TV incl: *Crackerjack; The Saturday Crowd; Crowther's In Town; Leslie Crowther's Scrap Book; The Crowther Collection; Whose Baby?; The Price Is Right; Time Of Your Life* (as subject); *Spotlight On Leslie Crowther.* m. Jean; 4 d. Lindsay and Elizabeth (twins), Caroline, Charlotte, 1 s. Nicholas. Birthsign: Aquarius. Hobbies: cricket, collecting pot lids. **Most Cherished Possession:** 'My wife Jean – because I love her.' **Favourite Memory:** 'Everything connected with our lives together.'

CRYER, Barry

Writer, b. 23 March 1935, Leeds, Yorkshire. Writing, performing since 1957, incl: Les Dawson; David Frost; Kenny Everett; Rory Bremner; Russ Abbott; Mike Yarwood; Jasper Carrott; Les Dennis; Bob Hope; George Burns. Other TV incl: *The Two Ronnies; Morecambe and Wise; Tommy Cooper.* Awards incl: BAFTA, Golden Rose of Montreux. m. Terry; 3 s. Anthony, David, Robert, 1 d. Jacqueline. Address: c/o Roger Hancock. Hobbies: walking (non-driver), intensive study of public transport, reading. Pets: four dogs, four cats, rabbit, terrapin. **Most Cherished Possession:** 'Bottle opener.' **Favourite Memory:** 'The birth of my first son at 5am while I was working in a nightclub.'

CUKA, Frances

Actress, b. London. Trained at Guildhall School. London theatre incl: *A Taste of Honey; Under Milk Wood; Beggar's Opera; Sweet Bird of Youth.* RSC: *Twelfth Night; The Merchant of Venice; Troilus and Cressida; Silver Tassle; Silence; Travesties; Nicholas Nickleby.* Films incl: *Henry VIII and His Six Wives; Scrooge; Watcher In the Woods.* TV incl: *Member of the Wedding; Day of the Tortoise; Days In the Trees; Within These Walls; Point of Departure; The Beggar's Opera; The Old Wives' Tale; One Day at a Time; Miss Nightingale; Henry IV Part II;* Mary Lancaster in *Crossroads.* Address: c/o Lou Coulson. Hobbies incl: theatre, opera and watching ballet; exploring old churches.

CUNLIFFE, Jane

Actress, b. 1 June 1962, Oldham, Lancashire. Undertook training at the Manchester Polytechnic School of Theatre. TV incl: Laura Gordon-Davies in *Brookside; Emmerdale Farm; Chateauvallon* (working on the voice dubbing); *Bulman; The Practice; Strike It Rich;* lead role of Francesca in *Hollywood Sports; The Irish Project.* Address: c/o Green & Underwood. Birthsign: Gemini. Hobbies: reading, shopping, eating out. **Most Cherished Possession:** 'Anything given to me by my family or my boyfriend.'

CURRY, Mark

Actor/presenter, b. 27 August 1961, Stafford. No theatrical training. Has appeared in pantomime in Bridlington, Darlington, Bath, Cambridge and Manchester. Was with Harrogate Theatre Company for two years, where he played Billy in *Billy Liar*. Recent Theatre incl: *Mover Over Mrs Markham*. TV incl: *Junior Showtime* for six years from the age of seven. At the age of nine co-starred with Eartha Kitt. Other TV incl: *Sounding Brass; Stop-Watch; Get Set For Summer; Saturday Picture Show; Make 'Em Laugh; Treasure Houses; All Star Record Breakers; Blue Peter; Blankety Blank; Bread*. Address: c/o Arlington Enterprise. Birthsign: Virgo. Hobby: tennis. **Favourite Memory:** 'Singing *New York, New York* in Red Square.'

CUTHBERTSON, Iain

Actor, b. 4 January 1930, Glasgow. Began as radio actor, then radio journalist, with the BBC in Glasgow. Started acting at Glasgow Citizens' Theatre, of which he became General Manager and Director of Productions in 1962. In 1965 Associate Director of London's Royal Court. Films incl: *The Railway Children; Up the Chastity Belt*. TV incl: *The Borderers; The Onedin Line; Scotch On the Rocks; Black Beauty; The Ghosts of Motley Hall; Charlie Endell; Vice Versa; The Assam Garden; Supergran; A Venus De Milo Instead; A Perfect Spy; Twist In the Tale; Minder*. m. actress Anne Kirsten. Address: c/o French's. Birthsign: Capricorn. Hobbies: sailing, fishing. **Most Cherished Possession:** 'A grey bicycle.' **Favourite Memory:** 'A trip to New Zealand.'

DALY, Tyne

Actress, b. 21 February 1947, Madison, Wisconsin. Daughter of actor James Daly. Attended Musical and Dramatic Academy. Films incl: *The Enforcer; John and Mary*. Numerous guest TV roles incl: *The Virginian; General Hospital; Quincy*. TV movies: *The Women's Room; Cagney and Lacey*, which led to TV series. Her role as Mary Beth Lacey won her four Emmys. Other TV incl: *The Entertainer; Larry; The Man Who Could Talk To Kids*. m. Georg Stanford Brown; 3 d. Elisabeth, Kathryne, Alyxandra Beatris. Address: c/o CBS, Los Angeles, CA 90036. Hobbies: reading, knitting. **Most Cherished Possession:** 'My role as Mary Beth Lacey. There is so much of me in her.' **Favourite Memory:** 'Watching my parents perform. That's how I developed a fascination for acting.'

DANCE, Charles

Actor, b. 10 October 1946, Rednal, Worcestershire. Theatre incl: *The Beggar's Opera; The Taming of the Shrew; Saint Joan; Sleeping Beauty; The Three Sisters*. Joined Royal Shakespeare Company 1975 and appeared in many productions incl: title role in *Henry V*, New York tour, 1975; title role *Coriolanus*, 1979 and 1989. Films incl: *For Your Eyes Only; Plenty; Good Morning Babylon; Hidden City; White Mischief; The Golden Child*. TV incl: *Edward VII; Dreams of Leaving; Nancy Astor; The Last Day; The Jewel In the Crown; Goldeneye; Phantom of the Opera* (mini-series).m. Joanna; 1 s. Oliver, 1 d. Rebecca. Address: c/o CDA. Hobbies: tennis, music, polo, photography. **Most Cherished Possession:** 'A Victorian music box, an anniversary present from my wife.'

DANEMAN, Paul

Actor, b. 26 October 1925, London. Trained at RADA, then did rep and joined Old Vic. First stage appearance as front legs of a horse in *Alice in Wonderland*. Original Vladimir in *Waiting For Godot* at the Arts Theatre, London. Theatre incl: *Camelot; Hadrian VII; Don't Start Without Me; Double Edge; Pygmalion; Shut Your Eyes and Think of England; The Jeweller's Shop*. TV incl: *Our Mutal Friend; Emma; Persuasion; An Age of Kings; Not In Front of the Children; Spy Trap; Waste; Arnold; Partners; Stay With Me Till Morning; Tishoo; Two Gentlemen of Verona; Antigone; Hold The Dream; The Little Matchgirl; Tears In the Rain; Ffizz; Blore MP; Till We Meet Again*. m. (1st) Susan (dis.), (2nd) Meredith; 2 d. Sophie, Flora. Address: c/o Chatto & Linnit. Birthsign: Scorpio. Hobby: painting.

DANIELS, Martin

Entertainer, b. 19 August 1963, South Bank, nr Middlesbrough. Began in clubs and cabaret. Summer seasons incl: Margate, Blackpool. UK tour. Pantomimes in Liverpool, Poole, Leeds, Southport. TV incl: three Junior Royal Variety Shows; *Saturday Superstore; Swap Shop; The Little and Large Show; 3-2-1; Sooty; The Paul Daniels Magic Show; Russell Harty; Freetime; The Generation Game; Game For a Laugh; Les Dennis's Laughter Show.* Address: c/o Mike Hughes Entertainments. Birthsign: Leo. Hobbies: tap dancing, playing guitar. Pets: cat Chaplin. **Most Cherished Possession:** 'My first flat, which I am very proud of.' **Favourite Memory:** 'When I took my mum on a tour across America. It had been her lifelong ambition to visit the country.'

DANIELS, Paul

Comedian/magician, b. 6 April 1938, Middlesbrough. Became interested in magic at 11. First job was junior clerk, and after a spell in the Army returned to office work but did part-time entertaining. Ran a grocer's shop before becoming an entertainer full-time. TV debut on *Opportunity Knocks.* TV incl: *Be My Guest; Wheeltappers and Shunters Social Club; The Paul Daniels Show; Fall In the Stars; Blackpool Bonanza; The Paul Daniels Magic Show* (won Montreux Golden Rose, 1985); *Odd One Out; Every Second Counts.* m. (dis.); (2nd) Debbie McGee; 3 s. Paul, Martin, Gary (from 1st m.). Address: c/o BBC TV. Birthsign: Aries. Hobby: photography.

DANIELS, William

Actor, b. 31 March 1927, Brooklyn, New York. Studied acting with Lee Strasberg in New York. Films incl: *Family Honeymoon; Ladybug; Marlow; 1776; A Thousand Clowns; The Graduate; Black Sunday; Two For the Road; The Parallax View; The One and Only; Oh God; Blue Lagoon; Reds.* TV films incl: *A Case of Rape; The Francis Gary Powers Story; Rehearsal For Murder; Blind Ambition; The Adams Chronicles; The Little Match Girl.* TV incl: *Captain Nice; The Nancy Walker Show; Freebee and the Been; Knightrider.* Two Emmy awards for his role as Dr Mark Craig in *St Elsewhere.* m. actress Bonnie Bartlett; 2 s. Address: c/o The Artists Agency, 10000 Santa Monica Blvd, L.A., California 90067. Hobbies: classical guitar, chess, tennis, reading, cooking.

DANSON, Ted

Actor, b. 29 December, San Diego, California. Graduated from Carnegie-Mellon University with a drama degree. Films incl: *The Onion Field; Body Heat; Creepshow; A Fine Mess; Three Men and a Baby; Cousins.* Barman Sam Malone in TV's *Cheers,* for which he was nominated for an Emmy. Other TV incl: *Somerset; Family; Magnum PI; The Women's Room; When the Bough Breaks; Something About Amelia,* for which he won Golden Globe Best Actor Award 1984. m. Casey; 2 d. Kate, Alexis. Address: c/o Bauman Hiller Agency, 9200 Sunset Blvd, Suite 202, Los Angles, CA 90069. Hobbies: American Indian artifacts, racquetball. **Favourite Memory:** 'Playing a lemon chiffon pie mix in a commercial.'

DANVERS, Ivor

Actor, b. Westcliffe-on-Sea, Essex. Started career aged 13 in rep and films until National Service, then trained at the Central School of Speech and Drama. Theatre (West End) incl: *Journey's End; The Mousetrap; The Norman Conquests.* Has directed many plays incl: *The Man Who Came To Dinner; Plaza Suite.* TV incl: *Minder; Terry and June; No Place Like Home; Tenko; We're Going To Be All Right; Howards' Way* (six series). m. Henrietta Holmes; 1 d. Lindsey (singer), 1 s. Tom (musician). Address: c/o April Young. Birthsign: Cancer. Hobbies: golf, bridge, chess, poker. Pets: one cat, Mog. **Most Cherished Possession:** 'After my wife and family, I suppose my golf clubs.' **Favourite Memory:** 'Being accepted by Central School and knowing I was to be an actor again.'

DARREN, James

Actor, b. 8 June, Philadelphia. Trained by drama coach Stella Adler. Films incl: *Rumble On the Docks; Gidget; All the Young Men; The Lively Set; Diamond Head; The Guns of Navarone; Operation Madball; The Boss's Son.* TV incl: *Time Tunnel; City Beneath the Sea; The Lives of Jenny Dolan;* Officer Jim Corrigan in *T J Hooker.* m. (1st) Gloria Terlitxky (dis.), (2nd) Evy; 1 s. James (from 1st m.), 2 s. Christian, Anthony (from 2nd m.). Address: c/o The Chasin Agency, 190 Canyon Drive, Beverly Hills, California 90210. Hobbies: racquetball, dirt biking riding. **Favourite Memory:** 'Locking a nun in a closet when she tried to keep me after school. I drove the teachers crazy!'

DAVENPORT, Nigel

Actor, b. 23 May 1928, Shelford, Cambridge. Was a member of the Oxford University Dramatic Society while a student there. After military service worked as a DJ. Theatre incl: *Three Sisters; Murder Among Friends; Cowardice; King Lear; The Old Country.* Recent films incl: *Zulu Dawn; The London Affair; Greystoke; Chariots of Fire; Nighthawks; Without a Clue.* TV incl: *South Riding; The Applecart; Oil Strike North; Romance; The Prince Regent; Much Ado About Nothing; The Biko Inquest; Howards' Way.* m. (1st) Helena (dis.), (2nd) actress Maria Aitken; 1 d. Laura, 1 s. Hugo (from 1st m.), 1 s. Jack (from 2nd m.). Address: c/o Green and Underwood. Birthsign: Gemini. Hobbies: gardening. **Most Cherished Possession:** 'My gardening gloves.' **Favourite Memory:** 'Waking up this morning.'

DAVEY, Bernard

Weather forecaster/presenter, b. 29 March 1943, Belfast. Worked for Meteorological Office since leaving school in 1962, serving in Libya, Germany and several UK locations. m. Teresa; 1 s. Cormac, 2 d. Mica, Shauna. Address: c/o BBC TV. Birthsign: Aries. Hobbies: sport, football, coaching, wildlife, gardening, Indian ink drawing. Pets: cat (Tess). **Most Cherished Possession:** 'Collection of stories written by my mother, compiled by my wife, illustrated by me.' **Favourite Memory:** 'My first pair of football boots. I quickly outgrew them, but wore them for years.'

DAVIDSON, Jim

Actor/comedian/entertainer, b. 13 December 1953, London. A member of Ralph Reader's Gang Show aged 12. Later played drums with a local pub band, before breaking into comedy and turning professional. TV debut on *New Faces* in 1976. Other TV incl: *What's On Next?; Night Out; Tiswas; Make 'Em Laugh; The Jim Davidson Show; Home James!; Wednesday at Eight; Stand Up Jim Davidson.* Subject of *This Is Your Life.* Books: *Too Risky; Jim Davidson Gets Hooked; Too Frisky.* LPs: *The Jim Davidson Album; A Dirty Weekend With Jim Davidson; Another Dirty Weekend With Jim Davidson.* m. 1st Susan (dis.), 2nd Julie (dis.), 3rd TV presenter Alison Holloway (dis.); 1 d. Sarah (from 1st m.), 2 s. Cameron (from 2nd), Charlie (by Tracie Hilton). Address: c/o International Artistes. Hobbies: fishing, football.

DAVIDSON, Ross

Actor, 25 August 1949, Airdrie, Scotland. Ex-PE teacher and water polo internationalist. Went into acting. Theatre incl: *Rosencrantz and Guildenstern Are Dead; The Importance of Being Earnest; Royal Hunt of the Sun; Animal Farm; Joseph; Godspell; Piaf; Robin Hood.* London Theatre: *Guys and Dolls* at the National Theatre; *The Merchant of Venice* and *Robin Hood* at Young Vic; *Layers* at ICA. Films incl: *The Pirates of Penzance; The Meaning of Life; Paracelus.* TV incl: *Stanley Baxter; Marco Baccer; Songs of Britain; Thingumyjig; EastEnders; Rivals; Monkey Walk; Daytime Live* presenter; *Run the Gauntler* presenter. Address: c/o Hall Management, 26 Star Street, London W2. Hobbies: snooker, all sports, football, tennis.

DAVIES, Ann

Actress, b. London. Trained with Liverpool rep as a student. Stage appearances at Liverpool, Windsor, Leatherhead, Guildford, Coventry; London. TV incl: *Doctor Who; Poldark; Equal Terms; The Nation's Health; Happy; A Voyage Round My Father; Windows; Shine On Harvey Moon; Paradise Postponed; Ever Decreasing Circles.* m. Richard Briers, 2 d. Kate, Lucy. Address: c/o Langford Assocs, Garden Studios, Betterton Street, London WC2H 9PB. Hobbies: swimming, reading, music. Pets: dog called Fred, cat called Tiger. **Most Cherished Possession:** 'Toyota car. It's a wonderful car and suits me perfectly.' **Favourite Memory:** 'Family holiday in Sussex. A great combination of everyone together, wonderful weather and a pool in the garden.'

DAVIES, Deddie

Actress, b. 2 March 1938, Bridgend, South Wales. Trained at RADA. TV incl: *You're Only Young Twice; The Gentle Touch; Father Charlie; Wentworth BA;* Agatha Christie's *Partners In Crime* and *Murder at the Vicarage; Grange Hill; Metal Mickey; The Pickwick Papers; Solo; That's My Boy; Titus Andronicus; Chance In a Million; The Canterville Ghost; C.A.T.S. Eyes; My Husband and I.* m. actor Paddy Ward. Address: c/o Culbertson Reeves, The Studio, 7a North Cross Road, London SE22, tel 081-693 9318. Birthsign: Pisces. Hobbies: travel, music, reading, the Victorian era, having adventures. **Most Cherished Possession:** 'My husband.' **Favourite Memory:** 'Too many to list.'

DAVIES, Dickie

TV presenter, b. 30 April 1933, Cheshire. Started career as entertainments purser on *Queen Mary* and *Queen Elizabeth* before joining Southern TV as announcer/newcaster. Joined *World of Sport* as presenter in 1968. Presented major sports events, including Olympic Games. Has also hosted awards and games shows. Presenter and producer of quiz show *Sportsmasters.* m. Liz; 2 s. Daniel, Peter (twins). Address: c/o LWT. Birthsign: Taurus. Hobbies: horse riding, golf. **Most Cherished Possession:** 'My 16th-century home in the middle of the country, which allows for complete relaxation.' **Favourite Memory:** 'Interviewing Muhammad Ali before he whacked Joe Bugner.'

DAVIES, Geoffrey

Actor, b. 15 December 1941, Leeds, Yorkshire. Trained at Royal Academy of Dramatic Art. Started as an ASM at Harrogate Rep. Theatre incl: *The Importance Of Being Earnest; The Odd Couple; The Living Room; The Ghost Train; The Luck of The Bodkins; No Sex Please, We're British; Outside Edge; Murder In Mind; Blythe Spirit; The Secretary Bird; Romantic Comedy; Run For Your Wife; Season's Greetings; Private Lives; And Then There Were None.* Films incl: *Oh What a Lovely War!; The Gap; Tales From the Crypt; Doctor In Trouble.* TV incl: *Kindly Leave the Raj; The Doctor* series; *The Other 'Arf; Bergerac; The Bretts; The Labours of Erica* (two series). m. Ann; 1 d. Emma. Address: c/o Barry Burnett. Birthsign: Sagittarius. Hobbies: reading, music, travel, working. Pets: two dogs, one cat.

DAVIES, Windsor

Actor, b. 28 August 1930, Canning Town, London. Worked as a miner, then completed National Service, before working in a factory and becoming a school teacher. Theatre incl: *Run For Your Wife; Roll On Four O'Clock; Baron Hardup.* TV incl: *It Ain't Half Hot Mum; Never the Twain; Sporting Chance.* m. Lynne; 4 d. Jane, Sarah, Nancy, Beth, 1 s. Daniel. Address: c/o Peter Prichard. Birthsign: Virgo. Hobbies: rugby football, reading, walking, bird watching.

DAVISON, Peter

Actor, b. 13 April 1951, London. After school plays and amateur dramatics, trained at Central School of Speech and Drama. Season at Nottingham Playhouse and then Edinburgh Festival before TV in *The Tomorrow People*. Big break was in *Love For Lydia*, then *All Creatures Great and Small*. Other TV incl: *Holding the Fort; Sink Or Swim; Hitch Hiker's Guide to the Galaxy; Doctor Who; Anna of the Five Towns; A Very Peculiar Practice; Miss Marple; Campion*. Wrote TV theme music for *Mixed Blessings*. Singing debut on *Pebble Mill at One*. m. actress Sandra Dickinson; 1 d. Georgia. Address: c/o Jeremy Conway. Birthsign: Aries. Hobbies: driving, reading, cricket. Pets: two dogs, four cats. **Most Cherished Possession:** 'My towel.'

DAVRO, Bobby

Comedian/impressionist, b. 13 September 1959, Ashford, Middlesex. Started in amateur musicals, talent contests, then working men's clubs. Many TV appearances incl: *Up For the Cup; Starburst; Night of 100 Stars; Punchline; Blankety Blank; Copycats*. Then signed exclusive ITV contract for own specials and series: *Bobby Davro TV Annual* (Christmas specials); *Bobby Davro On the Box; Bobby Davro's TV Weekly; Davro's Sketch Pad*. Address: c/o Mike Smith, 21 Fairmile Avenue, Cobham, Surrey KT11 2JA. Birthsign: Virgo. Hobbies: snooker, golf, fishing. **Most Cherished Possession:** 'A gold cross given to me by my mum and dad when I was twelve years old.' **Favourite Memory:** 'I'm privileged to be in the mad world of showbusiness – each week contains a favourite memory.'

DAWN, Elizabeth

Actress, b. 8 November 1939, Leeds. Vera Duckworth in *Coronation Street* since 1976. Other TV incl: *Play For Today; Kisses at Fifty; Speech Day; Daft As a Brush; Sunset Across the Bay; Z-Cars; Leeds United; Larry Grayson Special; All Day On the Sands; Crown Court; Sam; Raging Calm*. m. Donald Ibbetson; 3 d. Dawn, Ann-Marie, Julie, 1 s. Graham. Address: c/o Granada TV. Birthsign: Scorpio. Hobby: charity work. Pets: one dog. **Most Cherished Possession:** 'Sorry – I do not cherish possessions, only the people I love.' **Favourite Memory:** 'Seeing and holding my children for the first time.'

DAWSON, Anna

Comedy actress, b. 27 July, Bolton, Lancs. Trained at Elmhurst Ballet School and Central School of Speech and Drama. Theatre incl: Brian Rix Company; Theatre of Laughter revue. TV incl: *The Benny Hill Show; Morecambe and Wise; Life Begins at Forty*; with Bob Monkhouse; *3-2-1*; many panel games. m. Black and White minstrel John Boulter. Address: c/o CDA. Birthsign: Leo. Hobbies: Loch Ness monster cooking. Pets: three cats. **Most Cherished Possession:** 'My darling husband.' **Favourite Memory:** 'Capri, looking out to sea on an Easter Evening.'

DAWSON, Drew

Actor, b. 22 October 1943, Bridgeton, Glasgow. Trained with Glasgow RADA. Roles he is especially proud of are as Tim Cooper in *Cousin Philis*, Jimmy in *The Game*, and Jock in *Emmerdale Farm*. Divorced; 3 d. Jacqueline, Angie, Kate, 1 s. Myles. Address: c/o Ruth Boyle Management, Willow Dene, New Lane, Nun Monkton, York, North Yorkshire YO5 8EP. Birthsign: Libra. Hobbies: music, writing unused scripts, walking, painting, buying paintings, cooking for friends. **Most Cherished Possession:** 'A watch chain given to me by a very special person.' **Favourite Memory:** 'A beach, a lady, wine. Man wades into sea, plays Vivaldi on violin . . . beautiful.'

DAWSON, Les

Comedian, b. 2 February 1934, Manchester. Worked in pubs and clubs as solo comic before success on *Opportunity Knocks*, 1967. TV appearances in *Big Night Out; Sunday Night at The London Palladium* before own series, *Sez Les*. Other TV incl: *Dawson Watch; Blankety Blank;* Dawson TV Specials; *This Is Your Life; Opportunity Knocks*. Writer of *A Card For the Clubs; The Spy Who Came; Smallpiece Guide To Male Liberation; British Book of Humour; A Time Before Genesis; Dawson Gives Up*. m. 1st Margaret (dec.), 2nd Tracey; 2 d. Julie, Pamela, 1 s. Stuart (all from 1st m.). Address: c/o Regent House, 235/241 Regent Street, London W1. Birthsign: Aquarius. Hobbies: golf, swimming, music. Pets: rabbits, dog, cat. **Most Cherished Possession:** 'An elegant E Type Jaguar.' **Favourite Memory:** 'My first Royal Variety Show, 1971.'

DAY, Sir Robin

Interviewer/presenter, b. 24 October 1923, London. Started as a barrister, 1952. With British Information Services, Washington 1953–54. Freelance journalist, 1954–55, and BBC Radio talks producer before becoming ITN newscaster and parliamentary correspondent, 1955–59. Joined *Panorama* 1959 and introduced the programme 1967–72. Other TV incl: *Roving Report; The Parliamentarian; Question Time*. Books: *Television; A Personal Report; The Case For Televising Parliament; Day By Day; A Dose of My Own Hemlock*. BAFTA Award 1974; Royal TV Society Judges' Award for 30 years' outstanding contribution to TV journalism. Divorced 1986; 2 s. Alexander, Daniel. Address: c/o BBC TV. Birthsign: Scorpio. Hobbies: reading, talking, skiing.

DAYMAN, Leslie

Actor/director, b. 19 January 1938, Footscray, Victoria, Australia. Trained with the Adelaide Theatre Group. Worked as actor/director for State Theatre Company of South Australia (1968–79), Melbourne Theatre Company, Nimrod Theatre, Sydney. Theatre incl: *Macbeth; Twelfth Night; Measure For Measure*. Theatre direction incl: *A Streetcar Named Desire; The Caretaker*. Films incl: *Gallipoli; Weekend of Shadows; Molly*. TV incl: *Homicide; Sons and Daughters; A Country Practice; Prisoner: Cell Block H; Rafferty's Rules; Last Frontier*. m. to an actress; 2 s. Nicholas, Timothy. Address: c/o International Casting Service, Sydney. Birthsign: Capricorn. Hobbies: cricket, piano, music (Bach to Bartok), history, linguistics. **Favourite Memory:** 'The wonderful Peloponnese, Greece.'

DE LA TOUR, Frances

Actress, b. 30 July 1944, Bovingdon, Hertfordshire. Trained at The Drama Centre. With the RSC, 1965–71, roles incl: *The Relapse;* Peter Brook's production *A Midsummer Night's Dream*. Other theatre incl: *Duet For One*, for which she won SWET Award for Best Actress 1981, also *Evening Standard Award* and Critics' Award for Best Actress; *A Moon For the Misbegotten*, for which she won SWET Award for Best Actress 1983; *St Joan;* Lillian Hellman in *Lillian; The Three Sisters; King Lear*. Film: *Rising Damp (Standard* film award for Best Actress). TV incl: Miss Jones in *Rising Damp* (four series); *Skirmishes; Duet For One; Flickers; Clem; A King of Loving*. 1 d. Tamasin, 1 s. Josh. Address: c/o James Sharkey. Pets: cats. **Favourite Memory:** 'Lillian in *Lillian*.'

DEACON, Brian

Actor, b. 13 February 1949, Oxford. Member of Oxford Youth Theatre, then trained at Webber Douglas School in London. Rep seasons at Bristol, Coventry, Leicester, Soho Poly, Leeds, Edinburgh, Exeter, Ludlow Festival. Other theatre incl: *Antony and Cleopatra; Great and Small; As I Lay Dying; Madame Bovary; Exclusive Yarns*. Films incl: *Triple Echo; Il Bacio; Vampires; Jesus, His Life and Times*. TV films: *Inappropriate Behaviour; A Zed And Two Noughts*. TV incl: *First Sight; Ghosts; Lillie; Henry VI Parts I, II and III; Richard III; Bleak House; Separate Tables*. 1 d. Lara. Address: c/o Kate Feast Management. Birthsign: Aquarius. Hobbies: tennis, squash, football, bridge, reading, cinema, gardening, entertaining friends. **Favourite Memory:** 'The birth of my daughter.'

DEACON, Eric

Actor, b. 25 May 1960, Oxford. Trained at Webber Douglas Academy of Dramatic Art, then rep at York, Lancaster, Coventry, Birmingham, incl: *Hamlet; Equus; Caretaker; Flashpoint; Relent.* Other theatre incl: *The Alchemist Revisited; Brotherhood.* Films: *A Nous Le Petit Anglais; One of the Lads; It Could Happen To You; Bitter; Yesterday's Hero; A Zed and Two Noughts.* TV incl: *A Place Like Home; The Survivors; Penmarric; Minder; Secret Army; Spearhead; Contract; Kings Royal; Jackanory; Operation Julie; Doctor Who; Dempsey and Makepeace; C.A.T.S. Eyes; London's Burning; Hard Cases; Casualty; The Bill.* m. Laraine Joy; 2 s. Sam, Max. Address: c/o Louis Hammond Management. Birthsign: Gemini. Hobbies: writing, tennis, snooker, various sports. Pets: one dog Flynn, three cats.

DEAN, Bill

Actor, b. 3 September, Liverpool. Worked in local government before becoming a comedian in clubs and pubs in Lancashire. First role as an actor in the film *Gumshoe.* Theatre incl: *Runway* and *Touched* at the Royal Court Theatre in London; and worked with the RSC. Films incl: *Kes; Family Life; Nightwatcher.* TV incl: *Oh No It's Selwyn Froggitt; Emmerdale Farm; Good Companions; When the Boat Comes In;* Harry Cross in *Brookside.* m. (dec.); 2 s. Peter, David, 1 d. Diane. Address: c/o Crouch Salmon Assocs, London. Birthsign: Virgo. Hobbies: snooker, bowls, golf, watching soccer. **Most Cherished Possession:** 'My wallet.' **Favourite Memory:** 'Arriving in Liverpool on a troopship from Italy on VE Day.'

DEAN, Peter

Actor, b. 2 May 1939, London. Trained at Mount View Theatre School. Films incl: *Rock 'n Roll Sunville; The Great Question.* TV incl: *Sweeney; Big Deal; Coronation Street; The Bill; Give Us A Break; Minder;* Pete Beale in *EastEnders.* m. Jean. Address: c/o Howes & Prior, London. Birthsign: Taurus. Hobby: fishing. Pets: canaries. **Most Cherished Possession:** 'Gift of life: talks for itself.' **Favourite Memory:** 'Hope it's still to come.'

DELANEY, Delvene

Actress, b. 26 August 1951, Mackay, Australia. Trained at National Theatre of Australia. Started on TV as a weather girl in Brisbane 1970. TV incl: *The Paul Hogan Show; The Box; The Young Doctors; The Love Boat.* Film: *End Play.* Video: *The Beauty Cassette.* Book: *The Nine Month Calendar.* m. John Cornell; 1 d. Allira. Address: c/o Cornell Holdings. Birthsign: Virgo. Hobbies: sewing, photography, bush-walking, photo-collage. Pets: 1 dog, 1 cat, 9 chooks, 2 ducks, 2 guinea-pigs, 1 one-legged magpie. **Most Cherished Possession:** 'A 200 million-year-old anthracite fossil. The longevity of existence never ceases to humble me.' **Favourite Memory:** 'My marriage at midnight, New Year's Eve, under a century-old pear tree in rural NSW.'

DELANY, Pauline

Actress, b. 8 June, Dublin. Trained at the Brendan Smith Academy of Acting, Dublin, and then English rep. West End Theatre incl: *The Poker Session* and *The Hostage.* Other theatre incl: *Richard III; The Saxon Shore; Juno And The Paycock.* Films incl: *The Young Cassidy; Percy; Brannigan; Rooney; Trenchcoat.* TV incl: *The Seagull; The Expert; The Avengers; Z-Cars; Fallen Hero; Mixed Blessings; Maybury; Shoestring; Dangerous Davies; The Mourning Thief; Late Starter; Bergerac; Beckett at 80.* m. Gerald Simpson; 1 d. Sarah Jane. Address: c/o Daly Gagan Assocs. Birthsign: Gemini. Hobbies: history, architecture. **Most Cherished Possession:** 'My specs.' **Favourite Memory:** 'Being presented with my pretty daughter, post-Caesarean.'

DENCH, Dame Judi, OBE

Actress, b. 9 December 1934, York. Attended art school before training at Central School of Speech and Drama. Debut as Ophelia in *Hamlet* at Liverpool in 1957. Seasons at the Old Vic and RSC. Other Theatre incl: *Cabaret; Pack Of Lies; Mr And Mrs Nobody;* Cleopatra in *Antony And Cleopatra; The Cherry Orchard.* TV incl: *The Teachers; Z-Cars; Love Story; Love In A Cold Climate; A Fine Romance* (co-starring with her husband); *Saigon – Year Of The Cat; The Browning Version; Ghosts; Behaving Badly; Birthday.* Won BAFTA Award for Best Actress in a Comedy Series 1985 and for Best Support Actress 1987 (for *A Room With a View*). Voted Funniest Female on TV 1981–82 by *TVTimes* readers. m. actor Michael Williams; 1 d. Tara. Address: c/o Julian Belfrage Assocs. Birthsign: Sagittarius. Hobbies: sewing, painting, tapestry.

DENISON, Michael, CBE

Actor, b. 1 November 1915, Doncaster. Trained at Webber Douglas School, London. Acting debut in *Charley's Aunt,* Frinton-on-Sea 1938. More than 100 subsequent stage appearances, incl: *The Fourposter; Candida; On Approval; School For Scandal.* Films incl: *My Brother Jonathan; The Glass Mountain; The Franchise Affair; The Importance of Being Earnest.* Numerous TV appearances, incl: *Marco Millions; Then Milestones; The Second Man; What's My Line?; Waiting For Gillian; Olympia; Rain On the Just; Who Goes Home; Boyd QC* (first 80 episodes); *Funeral Games; Unexpectedly Vacant; The Provincial Lady;* subject of *This Is Your Life; Private Schultz; Bedroom Farce; Good Behaviour; Rumpole; Cold Warrior.* m. actress and novelist Dulcie Gray. Address: c/o ICM, London. Hobbies: golf, gardening, painting, motoring.

DENNIS, Les

Comedy impressionist, b. 12 October 1954, Liverpool. Started career at 14 in clubs. TV debut in *New Faces,* then *All Winners Show.* Other TV incl: *Who Do You Do?; Seaside Special; Russ Abbot's Madhouse.* Formed a double act with Dustin Gee in 1982, followed by three series of *The Laughter Show,* plus *Live From Her Majesty's; Go For It* and *Royal Variety Show.* After Gee's death in 1986, resumed solo career with TV series incl: *The Russ Abbot Show; Les Dennis's Laughter Show; Family Fortunes.* m. Lynne; 1 s. Philip. Address: c/o Mike Hughes Entertainments. Birthsign: Libra. Hobbies: running, cinema, theatre. **Most Cherished Possession:** 'A swimming medal won by my late father when he was a champion swimmer in Liverpool.' **Favourite Memory:** 'When my son was born.'

DERBYSHIRE, Eileen

Actress, b. 6 October 1930, Urmston, Manchester. Trained at the Northern School of Music, after teaching speech and drama. Assistant stage manager with Chorlton Rep, then joined the Century Theatre mobile theatre group, performing all over the country for two years. She first broadcast at the age of 17 and has been in many radio plays. Joined *Coronation Street* as Emily Nugent in Episode 3, in 1961. The character married Ernest Bishop in 1972, to be widowed six years later, when he was fatally shot in a wages snatch. m. Thomas Holt; 1 s. Oliver. Address: c/o Granada TV. Birthsign: Libra. Hobbies: 'No leisure!' Pets: one dog. **Most Cherished Possession:** 'My engagement ring.' **Favourite Memory:** 'The birth of my son.'

DESMOND, Lorrae, MBE

Actress/entertainer, b. 2 October 1934, Mittagong, NSW, Australia. Trained as a singer. Has done radio, TV, cabaret and summer seasons. TV and cabaret in the USA (including three months at The Tropicana, Las Vegas); and, in Australia, the Lorrae Desmond TV Show, guest spots on most drama series, and her one-woman show in theatres throughout the country. Has won three Logie awards, incl. one as Woman of the Year, and another for her role as Shirley in *A Country Practice.* m. (dis.). Address: c/o Showcast Publications, 23 Chandos Street, St. Leonards, Sydney, NWS, Australia 1065. Pets: a black cross Labrador named Boris. **Most Cherished Possession:** 'My independence, health and current airline ticket.' **Favourite Memory:** 'Being in my own garden in spring.'

DEV, Amerjit

Actor, b. 5 September 1960, Punjab, India. Trained at Webber Douglas Academy of Dramatic Art. Has worked with the Channel Theatre Company, Ramsgate, and at the Less Pavilion, Folkestone, Phoenix Theatre, Leicester, and Dokes Playhouse, Ramsgate. Film: lead role in *Caught; Terminal Eye;* Dr Singh in *EastEnders.* Address: 2 Carlton Road, London W4 5DY. Birthsign: Virgo. Hobbies: swimming, fencing, basketball, most other sports, theatre, travelling, eating, dancing. **Most Cherished Possession:** 'A ring and a chain given to me by my mother for my 21st birthday.' **Favourite Memory:** 'When everything was going right for myself, my brothers and parents a few years ago.'

DEVANEY, Sue

Actress/singer/comedienne/dancer, b. 2 July 1967, Ashton-under-Lyne, Lancashire. Trained at Oldham Theatre Workshop. London West End theatre: Ruby Birtles in *When We Are Married.* TV: Debbie Webster in *Coronation Street;* Rita Briggs in *Jonny Briggs; Exclusive Yarns;* Mad Bastard in *The Real Eddy English; About Face: Mrs Worthington's Daughter; Haggard; Spatz.* Performs in the funk band Dunky Dobbers, with actress Michelle Holmes. Address: c/o Marmont Management. Birthsign: Cancer. Hobbies: gym, travelling, making people laugh. Pets: tropical fish. **Most Cherished Possession:** 'My phone – it's my lifeline!' **Favourite Memory:** 'Performing in the bush to a small village of children in West Africa.'

DEY, Susan

Actress, b. 10 December 1952, Pekin, Illinois (raised in New York). Former top New York fashion model. Films incl: *Looker; Echo Park; Skyjacked.* TV incl: *The Partridge Family; Emerald Point N.A.S.; Circle of Fear; Malibu; Loves Me, Loves Me Not;* Grace Van Owen in *L.A. Law.* m. talent agent Lenny Hirshan (dis.), 2nd TV executive Bernard Sofronski; 1 d. Sarah. Address: William Morris Agency Los Angeles. Hobbies: gardening, camping, cooking, reading. Pets: two dogs, Bruce and Molly. **Most Cherished Possession:** 'My daughter Sarah. Nothing is more precious to me.' **Favourite Memory:** 'I loved filming *Echo Park.* It was the most creative work I've done.'

DIAMOND, Anne

TV presenter/journalist, b. 8 September 1954, Birmingham. 1975 joined the *Bridgwater Mercury* in Somerset and was art and music correspondent. 1977 joined the *Bournemouth Evening Echo;* 1979 joined ATV as reporter and presenter of *ATV Today.* When ATV was succeeded by Central TV became presenter *Central News.* 1982 became presenter BBC's *Nationwide* and lunchtime newsreader. In May 1983 joined TV-am as presenter of *Good Morning Britain;* also presenter *Anne Diamond on Sunday; TV Weekly.* m. TV executive Mike Hollingsworth; 2 s. Oliver, Jamie. Address: c/o TV-am. Birthsign: Virgo. Hobby: music.

DIBLEY, Janet

Actress, b. 13 December 1958, Doncaster. Graduated from the Rose Bruford College of Speech and Drama with B.A. Hons degree in Theatre Arts. Rep at Leeds, Perth and Exeter. Other theatre incl: *Mr. Cinders; Carousel; Twelfth Night; Figaro; Guys And Dolls; Cinderella* (at the National Theatre). TV incl: *A Brother's Tale; Foxy Lady; Lytton's Diary; The Two Of Us.* Address: c/o Kate Feast. Birthsign: Sagittarius. Hobbies: music, reading, swimming, visiting graveyards.

DICKINSON, Sandra

Actress, b. 20 October, Washington DC. After studying at University of Wisconsin and Boston University, trained at the Central School of Speech and Drama. First became known in TV commercials, but has done much theatre work, including *Legend*, in which she played Marilyn Monroe, and *Barefoot In The Park*. TV incl: *Cover; Hitch-Hiker's Guide To The Galaxy; Triangle; What Mad Pursuit; The Two Ronnies; What's On Next?; The Clairvoyant;* US series *Eisenhower and Lutz*. m. actor Peter Davison; 1 d. Georgia. Address: c/o Howes & Prior. Birthsign: Libra. Pets: 2 dogs, 4 cats. **Most Cherished Possession:** 'My sanity.' **Favourite Memory:** 'Too many.'

DICKSON, Nicolle

Actress, b. 1 January 1969, Sydney, Australia. Trained at the Keane Kids Studios. After completing her HSC at school, she took a visual arts degree at the Sydney College of Arts, where she majored in photography. That year, she broke her jaw in a car accident. Two weeks after having the wire removed from her jaw, her agent told her about an audition for the role of Bobby Simpson in *Home and Away*, which she landed. Subsequently won the Logie Award for Best New Talent. Other TV: *Jess; That's Democracy; ABC Passwords; Willing and Abel*. Plus voice-overs for TV commercials. Address: c/o Keane Management, 1246 Pittwater Road, Narrabeen 2101, Australia. Hobbies: aerobics. Pets: 'Men.' **Most Cherished Possession:** 'My best friend.' **Favourite Memory:** 'School and the time I grew up.'

DIMBLEBY, David

Interviewer/presenter, b. 28 October 1938, London. Joined BBC as a reporter in 1961, reporting for *Enquiry*. On the death of his father, Richard Dimbleby, became Managing Director, now Chairman, of family newspaper group *Richmond & Twickenham Times*. After six months in America for CBS, joined *Panorama* in 1967 as a freelance, then *24 Hours* (1969). Other TV incl: *Yesterday's Men; Reporter at Large; Dimbleby Talk-In; Panorama* 1980–82; *The White Tribe of Africa* (winner of the Royal Television Society's Supreme Documentary award 1979); *Person To Person; People and Power;* General Election results programmes, 1983 and 1987; *This Week, Next Week*, 1984–6; *An Ocean Apart*. m. cookery writer Josceline; 2 d. Liza, Kata, 1 s. Henry. Address: c/o BBC. Hobby: sailing.

DIMBLEBY, Jonathan

Broadcaster, b. 31 July 1944, Aylesbury. Son of the late Richard Dimbleby and brother of David. TV and radio reporter for BBC Bristol 1969–70; BBC radio *World at One*, 1970–71; *This Week*, 1972–9; *TV Eye*, 1979; *Jonathan Dimbleby In South America*, 1979; *Jonathan Dimbleby In Evidence; First Tuesday* (associate editor/presenter); *Jonathan Dimbleby On Sunday* (presenter/editor); *This Week* (presenter, 1986–8); *Witness* (series editor); *On the Record* (presenter since 1988). Also chairman of Radio 4's *Any Questions* and *Any Answers*. Books: *Richard Dimbleby; The Palestinians*. m. Bel Mooney; 1 d. Kitty, 1 s. Daniel. Address: c/o David Higham Associates. Hobbies: tennis, sailing. Pets: one cat.

DINSDALE, Reece

Actor, b. 6 August 1959, Normanton, West Yorkshire. Trained at the Guildhall School of Music and Drama 1977–80. Theatre: *Chips With Everything; As You Like It; Hobson's Choice; Beethoven's Tenth; Red Saturday; Observe the Sons of Ulster; Marching Towards The Somme; Woundings; Don Carlos; Old Year's Eve; Rhinoceros; Boys Means Business*. Films incl: *Winter Flight; A Private Function*. TV: *Knife Edge; Out On the Floor; The Secret Adversary; Partners In Crime; Minder; Threads; Glamour Night; Home To Roost; Robin of Sherwood; Bergerac; Coppers; The Storyteller; Take Me Home; The Attractions; Haggard*. Address: c/o Louis Hammond. Birthsign: Leo. **Favourite Memory:** 'Fronting the Huddersfield Town Football Club video – I'm their biggest fan.'

DOBSON, Anita

Actress, b. 29 April 1949, London. Trained at the Webber Douglas Academy. Stage appearances incl: *Ardele; A Night In Old Peking; Dick Whittington* (title role); *Charley's Aunt.* TV incl: *What's Your Poison?; Play Away; Nanny; Partners In Crime; Up The Elephant And Round The Castle;* Angie Watts in *EastEnders.* Address: c/o London Management. Birthsign: Taurus. Hobbies: reading, watching old black and white movies.

DOBSON, Kevin

Actor, b. 18 March, Queens, New York. Started in commercials and first acting part in the stage play *The Impossible Years,* starring Tom Ewell. He then studied at the Neighbourhood Playhouse, New York, and appeared in off-off Broadway plays. Films incl: *Love Story; Midway; Klute; The French Connection.* TV films incl: *Transplant; Orphan Train; Hardhat and Legs; Reunion; Mark, I Love You.* TV incl: *The Mod Squad;* Det Crocker in *Kojak* for five years; *Shannon; Tales of the Unexpected; Knots Landing.* m. Susan; 1 d. Miriah, 2 s. Patrick, Shawn Kevin. Address: c/o Freeman & Sutton, 8961 Sunset Blvd, Los Angeles, CA 90069. Birthsign: Pisces. Hobbies: sports – golf, baseball, swimming, football.

DODD, Ken, OBE

Comedian/singer/actor, b. 8 November 1927, Liverpool. Professional comedian since 1954. Inventor of 'The Diddymen'. Many summer and variety shows and own TV and radio programmes. Theatre incl: *Twelfth Night; Ha Ha – A Celebration Of Laughter; Ken Dodd's Laughter Show* at London Palladium and provinces. TV incl: *Ken Dodd Show; Doddy's Music Box; The Good Old Days; Super Trouper; Funny You Should Say That; Look Who's Talking; Ken Dodd's World Of Laughter; Stars On Sunday; Ken Dodd's Showbiz; The Railway Carriage Game.* Records incl: *Love Is Like A Violin; Tears; Happiness.* Address: c/o Knotty Ash, Liverpool. Birthsign: Scorpio. Hobbies: watching racing, reading science fiction and psychology.

DODWELL, Grant

Actor, b. 2 July 1952, Sydney, Australia. Trained at National Institute of Dramatic Arts 1971–73. Theatre: *You're A Good Man, Charley Brown; Godspell;* Casino tour in 1986 with *Everybody Makes Misteaks.* TV incl: *Willing & Abel; A Country Practice* (won four Logie Awards); *Homocide; Glenview High; Young Doctors; Patrol Boat.* Film: *Goodbye Paradise.* m. Sian; 1 d. Imogen. Address: c/o Harry M Miller & Company Management, 153 Dowling Street, Kings Cross, NSW 2011. Birthsign: Cancer. Hobbies: sailing, fishing. **Most Cherished Possession:** 'My boat.' **Favourite Memory:** 'Fishing on my boat.'

DOONICAN, Val

Singer/entertainer, b. 3 February 1929, Waterford, Ireland. First professional engagement in 1947 at Courtown Harbour, Co Wexford. Joined Dublin vocal quartet The Four Ramblers in 1951. Later hosted own BBC radio show, followed by first TV solo appearance. Voted BBC Personality of the Year in 1966. Has since been Show Business and Radio Personality of the Year. Hosted many seasons of his own TV show. Appeared in four Royal Variety Shows. Sales of records amount to 11 million. Hits include: *The Special Years; Walk Tall; What Would I Be.* Books: *The Special Years; Walking Tall.* m. Lynn; 2 d. Fiona, Sarah. Address: c/o Bernard Lee Management. Birthsign: Aquarius. Hobbies: golf, sketching, archery. Pets: three cats.

DOUGLAS, Angela

Actress/writer, b. 29 October 1940, Gerrards Cross, Buckinghamshire. Started acting as a teenager, then rep in Worthing until West End break in *Anniversary Waltz*. Theatre incl: *The Birthday Party; The First Mrs Frazer; The Scenario; Seven Year Itch; Killing Jessica*. Films incl: *Feet of Clay; Cleopatra; Some People; It's All Happening; The Comedy Man; John Goldfarb, Please Come Home; Carry On Cowboy; Digby, the Biggest Dog In The World*. TV incl: *The Hard Knock; A Smashing Day; Wuthering Heights; Rosemary; The Dragon's Opponent; The Gentle Touch*. Autobiographies: *Swings And Roundabouts; Angela Douglas's Present Affairs*. Regular contributor to newspapers and magazines. m. actor Kenneth More (dec.). Address: c/o ICM, London. Birthsign: Scorpio. Hobbies: design, music, cooking.

DOUGLAS, Su

Actress, b. 8 November 1942, Nottingham. Attended Aida Foster School and the Pauline Grant Ballet. Stage incl: *A Dead Secret; Houseguest; Don't Just Lie There, Say Something; Sleeping Beauty; Whodunnit; Piaf; Candida; The Elephant Man; Oliver*. Films incl: *Ghost Train Murder; Funny Money; Boys In Blue*. TV incl: *Within These Walls; Triangle; Spotlight; Prospects; Mike Yarwood Spectacular; Snow White And The Seven Dwarfs; Rude Health; Chance In a Million; Glenys Kinnock Campaign 87; Michael Barrymore Spectacular; Executive Stress; The Ruth Rendell Mysteries*. m. actor Jack Douglas; 1 d. Sarah, 1 step-d. Deborah, 1 step-s. Craig. Address: c/o AM Artists, 9a Connaught Place, London W2 2ET, tel 071-262 4218. Hobbies: keep-fit, squash, tennis, cooking. Pets: one cat. **Favourite Memory:** 'My childhood in the countryside in Kent at my Auntie Connie's cottage.'

DOWNING, Vanessa

Actress. Joined the newly formed Australian Theatre For Young People, aged 14, and was an active member of Sydney University's dramatic society while studying for a Masters degree in English literature. Then tutored at the university while attending acting night classes at the Nimrod Theatre. Theatre incl: South Australian Theatre Company; Sydney Theatre Company; *Madrigirls*, at the Sydney Opera House. Film: *The Everlasting Secret Family*. TV movie: *Double Sculls*. TV incl: *Melba;* Pippa Fletcher in *Home and Away*. m. theatre director Rodney Fisher. Address: c/o Barbara Leane and Assocs, 261 Miller Street, North Sydney, NSW 2060, Australia.

DRAKE, Gabrielle

Actress, b. Lahore, Pakistan. Trained for the stage at RADA. Theatre incl: seasons at Manchester's Royal Exchange, Bristol Old Vic, the New Shakespeare Company, and the Young Vic; *Tea Party; Jeeves; Noises Off; Court In The Act*. TV incl: *The Brothers; The Kelly Monteith Show; Crossroads;* and the TV plays *The Importance Of Being Earnest*, and *No 10; Wellington*. m. Louis De Wet. Address: c/o Peters Fraser & Dunlop. Birthsign: Aries. **Most Cherished Possession:** 'My husband, his work and his life.'

DRINKWATER, Carol

Actress/writer, b. 22 April 1948, London. Trained at Drama Centre, London, then rep, incl: Birmingham and Leeds; National Theatre; Dublin, Edinburgh and Malvern Festivals. Toured South East Asia 1981. Films incl: *Clockwork Orange; Queen Kong; Joseph Andrews; The Shout*. TV incl: *Public Eye; Bill Brand; The Sweeney; Raffles; Sam; All Creatures Great And Small* (shared 1979 Variety Club Award BBC TV Personality); *The Lady Killers; Take The Stage; Chocky; The Haunted School; Captain James Cook*. Address: c/o London Management. Birthsign: Taurus. Hobbies: scuba diving, writing, maps and atlases, travel music. **Most Cherished Possession:** 'The home I share with Michel.' **Favourite Memory:** 'Having my first novel published.' (*The Haunted School*, 1986.)

DRIVER, Betty

Actress, b. 20 May 1920, Leicester. Trained in variety and rep before moving into film and television. Joined *Coronation Street* in 1968 as Betty Turpin. Address: c/o Granada TV. Birthsign: Taurus. Hobbies: collecting antiques and paintings. Pets: one cat. **Most Cherished Possession:** 'Friendships in my profession.' **Favourite Memory:** 'All our lovely pets over the years.'

DRYER, Fred

Actor, b. 6 June 1946, Los Angeles, California. Trained for his acting career with coach Nina Foch. Films incl: *Cannonball Run II; Death Before Dishonour*. TV films incl: *Starmaker; Girl's Life; Force Seven; Something So Right; Kid From Nowhere*. Other TV incl: commentary for *CBS Sport; Cheers; Lou Grant; Laverne And Shirley; Hunter*. m. actress Tracy Vaccaro; 1 d. Caitlin. Address: c/o William Morris Agency, 151 El Camino Drive, Beverly Hills, CA 90212. Birthsign: Gemini. Hobbies: managing his Californian real estate investments, weightlifting and family. **Most Cherished Possession:** 'What else? My football.' **Favourite Memory:** 'My pro-football days with the New York Giants and LA Rams. I was more content being a sportsman than an actor.'

DU SAUTOY, Carmen

Actress, b. 26 February 1952, London. Trained in rep at Nottingham, Crewe and Oxford. From 1976–80 was a leading player with the RSC where plays incl: *Love's Labours Lost; A Midsummer Night's Dream; Wary of the World; Once In a Lifetime* (1980 London Critics' Award). Other stage incl: *Antony and Cleopatra; Macbeth; Candy Kisses*; a tour of America with the Old Vic; *Salome*. Films incl: *The Man With The Golden Gun; Our Miss Fred; You're A Fool, Bert Rigby*. TV incl: *The Citadel; The Barretts of Wimpole Street; Chessgame; Praying Mantis; South Bank Show; Lost Empires; Poor Little Rich Girl; Intercom Conspiracy; Bergerac; La Ronde*. m. Charles Savage. Address: c/o Duncan Heath. Hobbies: reading, tennis, skiing, computers. Pets: one cat (Lucky). **Favourite Memory:** 'Looking through a glass-bottomed boat at tropical fish in the sea as a small child in Pakistan.'

DUCE, Sharon

Actress, b. 17 January 1950, Sheffield. Trained at drama school and rep at York, Scarborough and Bristol Old Vic. Theatre incl: *The Foursome*; with the Actors Company 1974–76; *Touched; Tibetan Inroads; The Changeling; When I Was A Girl I Used To Scream And Shout*. Numerous TV appearances incl: *Renoir My Father; Helen, Woman For Today; Minder; The House That Jack Built; Funny Man; The Hard Word; Big Deal*. m. 1st David Munro (dis.), 2nd Dominic Guard; 1 s. William. Address: c/o Marmont Management. Birthsign: Capricorn. Hobbies: football, photography.

DUFFY, Patrick

Actor, b. Townsend, Montana. Did drama program at University of Washington. Was a member of San Diego's Shakespearen Globe Theatre. TV incl: *Hotel; Man From Atlantis; Charlie's Angels; Switch; Enola Gay; Hurricane; Dallas; Too Good To Be True*. m. Carlyn; 2 s. Padraic, Conor. Address: c/o Writers and Artists, 11726 San Vicente Blvd, LA, CA 90049. Hobbies: physical fitness, classical music, theatre, ballet. Pets: Rottweiler guard dog. **Most Cherished Possession:** 'When I left *Dallas* Larry Hagman presented me with the most beautiful hand-engraved Colt 45.' **Favourite Memory:** 'Pam Ewing's dream.'

DUNCAN, Peter

Actor/presenter, b. 3 May 1954, London. First major role as Jim Hawkins in *Treasure Island* at the Mermaid Theatre, London, then two years with the National Theatre. Recent theatre incl: *Barnum*. Films: *Lifetaker; Quilp; Stardust; Flash Gordon.* TV incl: *Oranges and Lemons; Sam; Fathers And Families; Renoir My Father; King Cinder; Flockton Flyer; Space 1999; Fallen Hero; Family Affair; Sons And Lovers;* presenter *Blue Peter,* 1980–86; two series of *Duncan Dares.* m. Annie; 3 d. Lucy, Katie, Georgia. Address: c/o Markham & Froggatt. Birthsign: Taurus. Hobbies: skiing, hang-gliding, football, building, singing, tightrope walking. **Most Cherished Possession:** 'My organic fruit 'n' veg garden. **Favourite Memory:** 'Backstage, as a child.'

DUTTINE, John

Actor, b. 15 March 1949, Barnsley. Trained at Drama Centre, London, then rep at Glasgow Citizens' Theatre, Watford and Nottingham. Films incl: *Who Dares Wins.* TV incl: *Z-Cars; Holding On; Warship; Coronation Street; Spend, Spend, Spend; Jesus Of Nazareth; Beryl's Lot; Angels; Law Centre; Wuthering Heights; Strangers; The Mallens; The Day Of The Triffids; The Outsider; Family Man; Woman Of Substance; Lame Ducks; Long Live The King; Lost Property; A Killing On The Exchange; Imaginary Friends.* Won *TV Times* Best Actor award 1980/81. 1 s. Oscar. Address: c/o Marmont Management. Birthsign: Pisces. Hobbies: walking the dog Rufus. **Most Cherished Possession:** 'Rufus!' **Favourite Memory:** 'Meeting Ernest Borgnine in his underpants!'

DYSART, Richard

Actor, b. Boston, Mass. Attended Emerson College. Films incl: *Being There; Pale Rider; Mask; The Falcon and the Snowman; The Hospital.* TV incl: *Blood and Orchids; Malice In Wonderland; The Autobiography of Miss Jane Pittman; Bitter Harvest; Last Days of Patton; Sandburg's Lincoln; First You Cry;* Leland McKenzie in *L.A. Law.* Theatre incl (Broadway): *All In Good Time; That Championship Season; The Little Town.* Address: c/o Writers and Artists Agency, 11726 San Vicente Blvd, Los Angeles, California, 90049. Hobbies: open-water diving, swimming, writing, cooking, art.

EDDINGTON, Paul, CBE

Actor, b. 18 June 1927, London. First stage appearance with ENSA 1944. Rep at Birmingham and Sheffield before RADA, 1951. Then Ipswich rep and TV (incl: *The Adventures of Robin Hood*). London stage debut 1961. Joined Bristol Old Vic following year, leaving 1963 to appear in *A Severed Head* in US. Bristol Old Vic 1965. Theatre incl: *Absurd Person Singular; Donkey's Years; Ten Times Table; Middle-Age Spread; Who's Afraid of Virginia Woolf?; Noises Off; Lovers Dancing; Forty Years On; Jumpers; HMS Pinafore* tour of Australia; *The Browning Version; Harlequinade; London Assurance.* TV incl: *Special Branch; The Good Life; Yes Minister; Yes, Prime Minister; Let There Be Love; Outside Edge; Miss Marple.* m. actress Patricia Scott; 1 d. Gemma, 3 s. Toby, Hugo, Dominic. Address: c/o ICM, London. Birthsign: Gemini. Hobbies: music, reading, art.

EDMONDS, Noel

'TV worker', b. 22 December 1948, London. Started his broadcasting career with Radio Luxembourg before moving to Radio 1, where he presented early morning show. TV shows incl: *Swap Shop; The Late, Late Breakfast Show; Time of Your Life; Christmas With Noel; Telly Addicts; Whatever Next; Saturday Roadshow.* Also *Foul Ups, Bleeps and Blunders,* for ABC in America. Voted 1989 *TVTimes* Favourite Male TV Personality. m. Helen; 2 d. Lorna, Charlotte. Address: c/o BBC TV, London. Birthsign: Capricorn. Hobbies: gardening, photography, helicopters.

EDWARDS, Glynn

Actor, b. 2 February 1931, Malaya. Trained at Central School and Joan Littlewood's Theatre Workshop. Stage incl: *Quare Fellow; Macbeth; The Glass Managerie.* Films incl: *Zulu; The Ipcress File; Under Milk Wood; Shaft In Africa; Get Carter; Minder On the Orient Express.* TV incl: *Madame Bovary; Softly, Softly; Steptoe and Son; The Main Chance; Sweet Sixteen; Minder.* m. (1st) actress Yootha Joyce (dis.), (2nd) Christine Pilgrim (dis.), (3rd) Valerie; 1 s. Tom (from 2nd m.). Address: c/o Joyce Edwards. Birthsign: Aquarius. Hobby: messing about in boats. **Most Cherished Possession:** 'My family's and friends' affection. I am no good on my own.' **Favourite Memory:** 'Hot sun, warm sea, cold drinks. Can't wait to get back to it.'

EGAN, Peter

Actor, b. 28 September 1946, London. Trained at RADA. Joined the Chichester Festival Theatre Company, followed by the RSC and National Theatre. Theatre incl: *The Rivals; Journey's End; What Every Woman Knows; Rolls Hyphen Royce; Arms and the Man.* Also directed *Battle of a Simple Man, Landmarks* and *A Midsummer Night's Dream.* Films incl: *The Hireling* (BAFTA Award for Best Actor 1972); *Chariots of Fire.* TV incl: *Lillie Langtry; Reilly Ace of Spies; The Dark Side of the Sun; Ever Decreasing Circles; Woman of Substance; Paradise Postponed; A Perfect Spy.* Won *TV Times* Best Actor Award 1986/7. m. Myra Frances; 1 d. Rebecca. Address: c/o James Sharkey Associates. Birthsign: Libra. Hobbies: travel, swimming, poker, good wine. Pets: dogs and cats.

EIKENBERRY, Jill

Actress, b. New Haven, Connecticut, raised in Maidson, Winconsin. Trained at Yale Drama School. Has appeared at Washington DC's Arena Stage. Broadway stage incl: *All Over Town; Summer Brave; Picnic.* Won OBIE award for her role in *Lemon Sky.* Films incl: *Between the Lines; Hide In Plain Sight; Butch and Sundance: The Early Days; Arthur; Rich Kids; The Manhattan Project.* TV movies incl: *Orphan Train; Swan Song; Family Sins; Assault and Matrimony; My Boyfriend's Back.* Other TV incl: Ann Kelsey in *L.A. Law; Kane and Abel; Hill Street Blues.* m. *L.A. Law* co-star Michael Tucker; 1 s. Max, 1 step-d. Alison. Address: c/o STE Agency, 211 South Beverly Drive, Beverly Hills, California 90212. Hobbies: piano, tennis, skiing, yoga, oil painting. **Favourite Memory:** 'The birth of my son.'

ELDER, Michael

Actor/writer, b. 30 April 1931, London. Trained at RADA, then worked at Byre Theatre, Citizens' Theatre, Edinburgh Gateway Company, Pitlochry Festival Theatre, Lyceum Company, and the Scottish Theatre Company. TV incl: *Sam; Edward The Seventh; Five Red Herrings; The Prime of Miss Jean Brodie; Take the High Road.* Author of over 150 radio scripts and 27 novels. TV scripts incl: *The Walls of Jericho; Kings Royal; Murder Not Proven.* Script editor, *Take the High Road.* m. Sheila Donald; 2 s. David, Simon. Address: c/o Young Casting Agency, 7 Beaumont Gate, Glasgow. Birthsign: Taurus. Hobbies: cricket, reading, Scottish history. Pets two cats. **Favourite Memory:** 'A Mediterranean cruise for our silver wedding.'

ELLIOTT, Denholm

Actor, b. 31 May 1922, London. Although he spent one term at RADA, his acting career really began in a POW camp after being shot down in 1942. First stage appearance at the Amersham playhouse, *The Guinea Pig* in the West End. Many plays followed in London, Manchester, Stratford and with the Royal Shakespeare Company, plus many tours. Films incl: *The Cruel Sea; The Seagull; A Bridge Too Far; Zulu Dawn; Trading Places; A Private Function; Razor's Edge; Room With A View.* TV incl: *Gentle Folk; Donkey's Years; Sextet; Bleak House; Codename Kyril.* BAFTA Award for Best Actor of the Year 1980. m. Susan Robinson; 1 d. Jennifer, 1 s. Mark. Address: c/o Garrick Club, Garrick Street, London WC2. Hobbies: gardening. Pets: one dog.

ELLIS, Janet

Actress/presenter, b. 16 September 1955, Kent. Trained at the Central School of Speech and Drama. Started her career in *Princess Griselda*, a BBC *Jackanory Playhouse*, followed by rep at Harrogate and Manchester's Royal Exchange. After various TV plays, appeared in four series of *Jigsaw*. Other TV incl: *Doctor Who; The Sweeney;* presenter of *Blue Peter* and Chelsea Flower Show and Motor Show programmes. m. 1st Robin (dis.), 2nd John Leach; 1 d. Sophie (from 1st m.), 1 s. Jackson (from 2nd m.). Address: c/o Arlington Enterprises. Birthsign: Virgo. Hobbies: changing her mind, shopping, writing. **Most Cherished Possession:** 'My photograph album – absolutely irreplaceable!' **Favourite Memory:** 'Getting my first ring that joined up and didn't adjust to fit!'

ELLIS, Peter

Actor, b. 30 May 1936, Bristol. After training at the Central School, he entered rep in Leeds, Sheffield, Nottingham and Birmingham. He spent three years with the Old Vic Company and then three years with the Royal Shakespeare Company. Also worked at Chichester and with Theatre Workshop and Belt and Braces Co. Theatre incl: *The Beggar's Opera; Trafford Tanzi; The Tulip Tree; Julius Caesar*. Films incl: *An American Werewolf in London; Agatha; Remembrance*. TV incl: Chief Supt Brownlow in *The Bill; Lytton's Diary; The Victoria Wood Show; Coronation Street; Edward and Mrs Simpson; In Two Minds; How We Used To Live; The Outsider; First Among Equals*. m. (dis.); 3 s. Hugh, Charlie, Christopher. Address: c/o Lou Coulson. Hobbies: gliding, walking, sailing.

ELLISON, Christopher

Actor, b. 16 December 1946, London. Trained as an artist at Camberwell School of Art, then as an actor at Studio '68. Has worked with the RSC, and at Manchester's Library Theatre and Canterbury. Also, in West End: *Once a Catholic; Oliver* (played Bill Sykes). TV incl: Det Insp Frank Burnside in *The Bill; The Professionals; Dempsey and Makepeace; The Gentle Touch; Strangers; Brond; Three Up Two Down*. m. actress Anita Joannou; 1 s. Louis. Address: c/o Barry Brown. Birthsign: Sagittarius. Hobbies: painting and illustrating, boats. **Most Cherished Possession:** 'A letter from Lillie Langtry – unfortunately, not to me personally!' **Favourite Memory:** 'Catching mackerel off the south west coast on a rare fine evening, or any Greek taverna on a hot summer's night.'

ELPHICK, Michael

Actor, b. 19 September 1946, Chichester, Sussex. Worked as an electrician before training at the Central School of Speech and Drama. Worked extensively in rep, toured in *Hamlet* and was in *The Winter's Tale* at Ludlow Festival. Other theatre incl: *Measure For Measure; Ticket of Leave Man* (National Theatre). Films incl: *Quadrophenia; The Elephant Man; The Curse of the Pink Panther; Withnail & I; Little Dorrit*. TV incl: *Holding On; The Nearly Man; The Sweeney; The Knowledge; Private Schultz; Chains; Bloomfield; Chish'n'Fips; Don't Write To Mother; Supergran; Three Up, Two Down;* and the lead role in *Boon*. m. Julia; 1 d. Kate. Address: c/o Crouch Salmon Associates. Birthsign: Virgo. Hobby: sailing. **Most Cherished Possession:** 'Old cruiser called Roja Minha moored in Portugal.'

ELTON, Ben

Comedy writer/performer. Has written for Rowan Atkinson, Rik Mayall, Lenny Henry, French and Saunders, and Adrian Edmondson. TV as writer: *The Young Ones* (BAFTA Best Comedy award 1984); *Happy Families; Filthy Rich and Catflap;* four *Blackadder* series, with Richard Curtis (BAFTA Best Comedy award 1987). Presenter and co-writer of LWT arts and entertainment series *South of Watford* (award-winner at Chicago, New York and San Francisco festivals). TV as presenter/performer: *Saturday Live; Friday Live; Wogan With Ben Elton; Ben Elton – The Man From Auntie* (also writer). Books: *Bachelor Boys* (*Young Ones* book); *Stark* (novel). Record: *Motormouth* (LP).

EMBERG, Bella

Actress/comedienne, b. 16 September 1937, Brighton. Started in rep before breaking into TV. Played *Macbeth* at Ludlow Festival. Film: *History of the World Part One*. TV incl: *Take Three Girls; Softly, Softly; Pennies From Heaven; Testament of Youth; Les Dennis's Laughter Show; Robin's Nest*. Appeared with Russ Abbot in *Russ Abbot's Madhouse* and Madhouse specials, and *The Russ Abbot Show*. Stooged for Benny Hill, Frankie Howerd, Stanley Baxter, Les Dawson. Address: c/o Mike Hughes Entertainments. Birthsign: Virgo. Hobbies: opera, driving, old films, reading biographies. **Most Cherished Possession:** 'My home.' **Favourite Memory:** 'The first time I met Russ Abbot and he invited me to appear with him. It changed my life completely.'

ENFIELD, Harry

Comedian/writer, b. 31 May 1961, Sussex. Formed a double-act, Dusty and Dick, with friend Brian Elsley while studying politics at York University. Became a *Spitting Image* scriptwriter and voice impersonator in 1983. Has since become known for his character creations Stavros and Loadsamoney. Other TV appearances include: *French and Saunders; Don't Miss Wax; The Tube; Filthy Rich and Catflap; The Lenny Henry Show; Girls On Top; Frocks on the Box; Comic Relief* (1988 and 1989); *Friday Live; Saturday Live*. Also starred, with Melvyn Bragg, in *Norbert Smith – A Life*, which he co-wrote with Geoffrey Perkins. Radio incl: *The Million Pound Show*, Steve Wright's Radio 1 show and *Loose Ends*. Other writing incl: *Saturday Live; Friday Live; Naked Video; In One Ear; Week Ending; News Huddlines*. Address: c/o PBJ Management. Birthsign: Gemini. Hobby: swimming.

ENGLISH, Arthur

Actor, b. 9 May 1919, Aldershot, Hampshire. Began in variety. Stage incl: Royal Variety Performance (twice); revues; pantomimes; Chichester Festival; *On the Rocks; Die Fleder-maus*. Book: *Through the Mill and Beyond*. TV incl: *Follyfoot; Cooper's End; Doctor In the House; The Ghosts of Motley Hall; Are You Being Served?; Funny Man; Pygmalion; In Sickness and In Health*. m. (1st) Ivy (dec.), (2nd) dancer Teresa Mann (dis.); 1 d. Ann, 1 s. Anthony (from 1st m.), 1 d. Clare Louise (from 2nd m.). Address: c/o Patrick Freeman, 4 Cromwell Grove, London W6 7RG. Hobbies: DIY, oil painting. **Favourite Memory:** 'Being at the birth of Clare Louise; being made a Freeman of the City of London in 1986; being made a Freeman of the Borough of Rushmoor, at Aldershot in January 1990.'

ENRIQUEZ, Rene

Actor, b. 24 November, San Francisco. Given the Ruben Salazar Award 1985 (an Hispanic achievement award). Attended the American Academy of Dramatic Arts, then the Lincoln Centre Repertory Company. Films incl: *Harry and Tonto; Under Fire; The Evil That Men Do; Bullet Proof*. TV films: *Choices of the Heart; Dream West*. TV incl: *Police Story; Charlie's Angels; Quincy; Benson; Hill Street Blues*. Awarded the Golden Eagle Award for Consistent Outstanding Achievement. m. (dis.). Address: c/o Tom Korman, APA, 9000 Sunset Blvd., LA, CA 90069. Birthsign: Sagittarius. Hobby: tennis. Pets: two dogs, Gordo, Flaco. **Most Cherished Possession:** 'My health and my friends.' **Favourite Memory:** 'I treasure all my memories.'

ESHLEY, Norman

Actor, b. 30 May 1945, Bristol. Trained at the Bristol Old Vic Theatre School. Stage incl: *Hamlet; Arms and the Man; Lady Chatterley's Lover; Way Upstream; The Exorcism*. His first professional appearance was in Orson Welles' film *The Immortal Story*. Other films incl: *Blind Terror; The Disappearance; Yanks*. Has appeared in many TV plays and series incl: *I, Claudius; Secret Army; The Sweeney; The Professionals; Man About the House; George and Mildred; Late Expectations; Maybury*. m. (1st) actress/singer Millicent Martin (dis.), (2nd) Lynette Braid. Address: c/o David White Associates. Birthsign: Gemini. Hobbies: football, cricket, horse racing, sailing. **Most Cherished Possession:** 'A gold watch made by my great-great grandfather.'

EVERAGE, Dame Edna, DBE

Megastar, b. Wagga-Wagga, Australia. Learned her trade with the Moonee Ponds Players, and as a guest on Barry Humphries' shows. Films incl: *Adventures of Barry McKenzie; Barry McKenzie Holds His Own; Les Patterson Saves The World*. TV incl: *An Audience With Dame Edna; The Dame Edna Experience;* numerous other BBC and ITV specials. m. Norman Stoddart Everage (dec.); 1 d. Valmai, 2 s. Bruce, Kenneth. Address: c/o Banque de Suisse, Geneva. Birthsign: Aquarius. Hobbies: caring and sharing. Pets: one bridesmaid. **Most Cherished Possession:** 'A silk scarf (gift of the Queen).' **Favourite Memory:** 'Being thanked by Mother Theresa.'

EVERETT, Kenny

Disc jockey/presenter, b. 25 December 1944, Seaforth, Liverpool. Originally wanted to become a priest and had various jobs before making his name as a DJ with Radio London. Subsequently with Capital Radio and BBC Radio. TV incl: *Nice Time; The Kenny Everett Explosion; Making Whoopee; Ev; The Kenny Everett Video Show; The Kenny Everett Television Show.* Created Captain Kremmen, Cupid Stunt and many other comical characters. Address: c/o Jo Gurnett Management. Birthsign: Capricorn. Hobby: squash.

EWART, Tim

ITN Moscow correspondent, b. 6 February 1949. Worked on newspapers in UK and Bermuda. Joined BBC World Service as a sub-editor, then news editor. Also worked for Radio Orwell. Was a BBC TV reporter 1976–79, and with Thames TV 1979–80. Joined ITN in 1980. Warsaw correspondent 1983–5; Washington correspondent 1986–9; Moscow correspondent since January 1990. m. (dis.); 1 d. Alice, 1 s. Ben. Address: c/o ITN. Hobbies: shopping at Ralph Lauren.

FANCY, Brett

Actor, b. 4 January 1964, Portsmouth. Trained at the Guildhall School of Music and Drama, London, 1982–85, where he was awarded their gold medal. Started his acting career at Chichester Festival Theatre in *The Scarlet Pimpernel; Cavalcade; Antony and Cleopatra.* Plays incl: one-man Shakespeare show *The Spirit of Jack Cade; Single Spies; Oliver Twist.* Film: *Treasure Island.* TV incl: Steve Hood in *Rockliffe's Babies;* Sean Hooper in *Square Deal.* Address: c/o Jeremy Conway. Hobbies: volleyball, swimming, ceramics, taking things apart and not being able to put them back together. **Most Cherished Possession:** 'My surname, because people always ask if it's true. It is!' **Favourite Memory:** 'A piece of advice: "Try not to make an impression but an expression."'

FISH, Michael

Weatherman, b. 27 April 1944, Eastbourne, East Sussex. Has been with the Meteorological Office for 28 years and is the BBC's longest-serving weather presenter, having started in 1974. Scripted and appeared with Patrick Moore in *The Sky at Night.* Other TV incl: *Surprise, Surprise; Record Breakers; Through the Keyhole; Growbiz Quiz; Simon and the Witch; The Clothes Show; Ghost Train; Kazuko's Karaoke Klub.* Frequent personal appearances and after-dinner speaking. m. Susan; 2 d. Alison, Nicola. Address: c/o BBC TV Weather Unit, Wood Lane, London W12. Hobbies: travel, genealogy, good food. Pets: two cats. **Most Cherished Possession:** 'My old banger – it provides me with the only way I can get to work at 4am.' **Favourite Memory:** 'The great October storm of 1987! Especially the hundreds of letters of support.'

FISHER, Jeannie

Actress, b. Glasgow. Trained at the Royal Scottish Academy of Music and Drama. Started her career as an understudy at the Royal Court, London, and appeared in *The Double Dealer; The Three Musketeers; Slag;* world premiere of *Yardsale* at Edinburgh Festival, 1985; *Macbeth* tour of India; *Whose Life Is It Anyway?;* Madame Arcati in *Blithe Spirit.* TV incl: *Canterbury Tales; The Silver Sword; Adam Smith; Arthur of the Britons;* Morag Stewart in *Take the High Road.* Numerous radio broadcasts. Address: c/o Pat Lovett Agency, 14 Broughton Place, Edinburgh E1, tel 031-557 5565. Hobbies: reading, music, swimming, eating with friends. Pets: cat. **Most Cherished Possession:** 'My cat, as she makes me laugh.' **Favourite Memory:** 'Being on holiday on an Hebridean island with an old friend.'

FITZALAN, Marsha

Actress, b. Bonn, West Germany. Trained at the Webber Douglas Academy in London and theatre incl: *84 Charing Cross Road.* Films incl: *International Velvet; Anna Karenina; A Handful of Dust.* Many TV appearances incl: *The Duchess of Duke Street; Shelley; Diamonds; Pride and Prejudice; Nancy Astor; The Wife's Revenge; Pygmalion; By the Sword Divided; A Comedy of Errors; Three Up, Two Down; Paradise Postponed; Brush Strokes; Inside Story; Hedgehog Wedding; The New Statesman; Goldeneye.* m. actor Patrick Ryecart; 2 d. Mariella, Jemima, 1 s. Frederick. Address: c/o Peters Fraser & Dunlop. Birthsign: Pisces. Hobbies: riding, hunting, gardening, and walking in the Hambledon Valley. Pets: mongrel puppy called Socks. **Most Cherished Possession:** 'A sense of humour!' **Favourite Memory:** 'Time spent as a child in Nanyuki, Kenya.'

FLANDERS, Ed

Actor, b. 29 December, Minneapolis, Minnesota. Films incl: *Grasshopper; MacArthur; Pursuit of D B Cooper; True Confessions; Killer Kane.* TV incl: *Lizzie Borden; Backstairs at the White House; The Amazing Howard Hughes; Blind Ambition; Mary White; Things In Their Season;* six episodes of *Hawaii Five-O;* Dr Westphall in *St Elsewhere.* Emmy awards for the TV film *Harry Truman: Plain Speaking, Moon of the Misbegotten* and *St Elsewhere.* m. Cody; four children. Address: c/o The Artists Agency, 10000 Santa Monica Blvd, Los Angeles, CA 90067. Hobbies: fishing, listening to music. **Most Cherished Possession:** 'My Emmy award for *St Elsewhere.*' **Favourite Memory:** 'The births of my four children.'

FINNIGAN, Judy

Presenter, b. 16 May 1948, Manchester. Gained an Honours degree at Bristol University, before joining Granada TV as a researcher. Subsequently a news reporter for Anglia TV and news reporter and presenter for Granada TV. Other TV: *Reports Action; Flying Start; Scramble; Chalkface; ITV Telethon.* Co-presenter of *This Morning* since 1988. m. 1st (dis.), 2nd co-presenter Richard Madeley; 3 s. twins Tom and Dan (from 1st m.), Jack, 1 d. Chloe. Address: c/o Granada TV. Birthsign: Taurus. Hobbies: 'Reading and desperate attempts to get the kids to shut up.' **Most Cherished Possession:** 'My family.'

FLEESHMAN, David

Actor, b. 11 July 1952, Glasgow. Educated and trained in Birmingham. Theatre incl: *Hedda Gabler; Milk and Honey; Serious Money; A Month In the Country; Guys and Dolls.* Films: *The Wall; The Nature of the Beast.* TV incl: *Boys From the Blackstuff; Edge of Darkness; Coronation Street; Dear Enemy; The Practice; Emmerdale Farm; The Outsider; Victorian Values; Bulman; One By One; Truckers; Soldier and Death; The Luddites; Blind Justice; After the War; Children's Ward; Capstick's Law; Ruth Rendell Mystery Movie; A Bit of a Do.* Extensive radio drama and *Morning Story* readings. m. actress Sue Jenkins; 1 d. Emily, 1 s. Richard. Address: c/o Rolf Kruger. Hobbies: 'Photography, swimming and dieting!' Pets: two cats, Whiskey and Charlie. **Most Cherished Possession:** 'I cherish none of my material possessions – there seems little point with two toddlers at home.'

FLETCHER, Cyril

Comedian/TV gardener, b. 25 June 1913, Watford. First made his name on radio and TV broadcasting his Odd Odes in 1936. Starred in West End revues and at the London Palladium during the Second World War. Presented his own pantomimes and summer shows for 25 years. TV incl: *What's My Line?; That's Life; Gardening Time; Cyril Fletcher's TV Garden.* President of the Pantomime Society, and author of 12 books. m. actress Betty Astell; 1 d. actress/comedienne Jill Fletcher. Address: Fort George, St Peter Port, Guernsey. Birthsign: Cancer. Hobbies: gardening and the countryside. Pets: dogs. **Most Cherished Possession:** 'My wife – we have only been married 49 years!' **Favourite Memory:** 'Marrying at St Martin-in-the-Fields, with my scottie dog as a bridesmaid.'

FLYNN, Barbara

Actress, b. 5 August 1948, Hastings, Sussex. Trained at the Guildhall School of Music and Drama (Gold Medal winner). London West End theatre: *A Murder Has Been Announced; Two and Two Make Sex; The Millionairess.* National Theatre appearances: *The Philanderer; Early Days; Tales From Hollywood; Antigone.* Plus a North American and Canadian tour of Noël Coward's *The Marquise.* TV: Freda Ashton in *A Family at War;* Dr Sheila Cassidy in *No Visible Scar; Barchester Chronicles; Open All Hours;* Jill Swinburne in *The Beiderbecke Affair; The Beiderbecke Tapes* and *The Beiderbecke Connection;* Dr Rose Marie in *A Very Peculiar Practice* (two series); *Season's Greetings; Inspector Morse; Benefactors; The Justice Game II.* m. Jeremy Taylor. Address: c/o Markham & Froggatt. Hobbies: cooking, writing, gardening. Pets: vizslas.

FORBES, Natalie

Actress, b. 1 November, Doncaster, Yorks. She began her acting career in summer season and pantomimes. Her first West End appearance was in *Beyond The Rainbow.* Other stage incl: *Outside Edge; The Best Little Whorehouse In Texas; The Collector; Insignificance.* Films incl: *Loss Adjustor, Napoleon and Josephine.* TV incl: *The Other 'Arf; Nanny; The Kelly Monteith Show; The Incredible Mr Tanner; Blood Money; The Gentle Touch; A Ferry Ride Away; Out on The Floor; Full House; Shadow of the Noose.* Address: c/o Susan Angel Associates. Birthsign: Scorpio. Hobbies: reading, gardening, opera, football. Pets: cat called Alan. **Most Cherished Possession:** 'My car, because of the freedom it gives me.'

FORD, Anna

Journalist, b. 2 October 1943, Tewkesbury, Gloucestershire, but brought up in Wigton and Eskdale, in Cumbria. Manchester University economics graduate and Open University staff tutor in Belfast, before joining Granada TV as researcher/reporter on *Reports Action* and presenter of schools programmes. Went to the BBC in 1977 as reporter on *Man Alive* and presenter of *Tomorrow's World.* Became an ITN newscaster in 1978. *TVTimes* Most Popular Female TV Personality, 1978–9. Founder member of TV-am, where she was a presenter of *Good Morning Britain.* After freelancing, returned to the BBC to host *Network* and the *Six O'Clock News.* m. (1st) Dr Alan Bittles (dis.), (2nd) cartoonist and *Tatler* editor Mark Boxer (dec.); 2 d. Claire, Kate. Address: c/o Jo Gurnett. Hobbies: opera, gardening, walking, reading. Pets: two cats.

FORSYTH, Brigit

Actress, b. 28 July, Edinburgh. Trained at RADA, followed by rep. Stage incl: *My Fat Friend; The Norman Conquests; Dusa, Fish, Stas and Vi; Effie's Burning.* Film: *The Crystal Stone.* Radio work has included many plays. TV incl: *Adam Smith; Holly; Glamour Girls; The Master of Ballantrae; The Likely Lads; Holding the Fort; Tom, Dick and Harriet; Sharon and Elsie; Bazaar and Rummage* (Play For Today); *The Practice; Poirot; Running Wild; Stanley's Vision; Cross Wits; Boon.* m. TV director Brian Mills; 1 d. Zoe, 1 s. Ben. Address: c/o Jeremy Conway. Hobbies: eating (particularly chocolate), swimming, jogging. Pets: Great Dane called Charlie, hamster, gerbils. **Most Cherished Possession:** 'The children.' **Favourite Memory:** 'Going for long walks, with a picnic, on the few really hot days we get.'

FORSYTH, Bruce

Entertainer/comedian/singer, b. 22 February 1928, Edmonton, London. Started as Boy Bruce, The Mighty Atom. In 1958 was asked to compere *Sunday Night At The London Palladium*. Films incl: *Bedknobs and Broomsticks*. TV incl: own shows; *The Generation Game; Play Your Cards Right; Hollywood Or Bust; Slinger's Day; You Bet; Bruce and Ronnie;* new *Generation Game* series, starting 1990. m. (1st) Penny Calvert (dis.), (2nd) Anthea Redfern (dis.), (3rd) Wilnelia; 5 d. Deborah, Julie, Laura (from 1st m.), Charlotte, Louisa (from 2nd m.), 1 s. Jonathan. Address: c/o Billy Marsh Assocs. Hobbies: golf, tennis. Pets: two King Charles Cavalier dogs. **Most Cherished Possession:** 'My grand piano with a set of golf clubs inside.' **Favourite Memory:** 'My first one-man show at the Palladium'

FORSYTHE, John

Actor, b. 29 January 1918, New Jersey. Began career as a sports announcer, then went on to radio acting. Studied at the New York Actors Studio. Theatre incl: *Mister Roberts; The Teahouse of the August Moon*. Films incl: *Destination Tokyo* (film debut); *And Justice For All; Goodbye and Amen; Madame X; In Cold Blood; Topaz; The Happy Endings; The Trouble With Harry*. TV incl: host/narrator of *World of Survival; Bachelor Father* (1957–62); *Charlie's Angels;* Blake Carrington in *Dynasty*. Golden Globe Award for Best Performance in a TV Drama, 1983 and 1984 for *Dynasty*. m. Julie Warren; 1 s. Dall, 2 d. Page, Brooke. Address: c/o Charter Management, 9000 Sunset Blvd, Los Angeles, CA 90069. Birthsign: Aquarius. Hobbies: tennis, racehorses. **Most Cherished Possession:** 'My art and antiques collection.'

FOWLDS, Derek

Actor, b. 2 September 1937, Balham, London. Trained at RADA, leaving with honours diploma, and has since worked mainly in TV. First became well known in *The Basil Brush Show* (1969–73). Other TV incl: *Francis Durbridge's The Doll; After That This; Miss Jones and Son; Clayhanger; Edward the Seventh; Robin's Nest; Cribb; Give Us a Clue; Strangers; Triangle; Yes Minister; Yes, Prime Minister; Rules of Engagement; Chancer; Die Kinoler*. m. (dis.); 2 s. James, Jeremy. Address: c/o CDA. Hobby: sport. **Most Cherished Possession:** 'My number three wood ever since I hit a hole-in-one.' **Favourite Memory:** 'I shall never forget watching the birth of my first son. He is now 25, but I can see him arriving into the world as if it were yesterday.'

FOWLER, Harry, MBE

Actor, b. 10 December 1926, Lambeth Walk, London. After being interviewed on *In Town Tonight* he was always being asked to play Cockney parts in British films. Has since been in more than 100 films, incl: *The Longest Day; Ladies Who Do; The Prince and the Pauper; The Pickwick Papers; Chicago Joe*. Entered TV as Corporal Flogger Hoskins in *The Army Game* in 1957. Recent TV incl: *Stalingrad; World's End; Dead Ernest; Entertainment Express; Dramarama; Me and the Girls; Scarecrow and Mrs King; Supergran; A Roller Next Year; Body Contact; Davro's Sketch Pad; The Bill*. MBE 1970. m. Catherine. Address: c/o Essanay, at Green & Underwood. Birthsign: Sagittarius. Hobbies: tennis, model railways. **Most Cherished Possession:** 'My wife Catherine – for 28 great years (so far!)' **Favourite Memory:** 'Seeing Fulham reach the 1975 FA Cup Final.'

FOXWORTH, Robert

Actor, b. Houston, Texas. Trained at Stratford University Contemporary Theatre Workshop. Theatre incl: *The Crucible* (won Theatre World Award); *Antony and Cleopatra*. Films incl: *Damien – Omen II; Airport '77; Treasure of Matecumba; The Black Marble; Prophecy*. TV incl: *Sadbird; The Storefront Lawyers; Hogan's Goat; Another Part of the Forest*. Chase Gioberti in *Falcon Crest*. TV movies: *The Questor Tapes; The FBI Versus Alvin Karpis; Mrs Sundance; The Devil's Daughter; The Memory of Eva Ryker; Act of Love; The Acts of Peter and Paul; Frankenstein; James Dean; It Happened at Lake Wood Manor; Death Moon*. Lives with actress Elizabeth Montgomery; 1 s., 1 d. Address: c/o ICM, Los Angeles. Hobbies: carpentry, gardening.

FOY, Julie

Actress, b. 5 May 1970, Bolton, Lancashire. Trained at the College of Performing Arts, Salford. Theatre: *Our Day Out*, at the Octagon Theatre, Bolton; *A Taste of Honey*, at the Theatre Royal, York. TV: *Forever Young*; Gina Seddon in *Coronation Street*; Deirdre in *How To Be Cool*; *Missing Persons*; *Dawn and the Candidate*; *Press Gang*. Address: c/o Louis Hammond Management. Hobbies: eating, singing. Pets: a cat called Ambrose. **Most Cherished Possession:** 'A china plate I got off Mum and Dad after my first job.' **Favourite Memory:** 'When an actor I worked with had to undress on stage down to his underwear, but he forgot to put on his underpants and stood there naked. I didn't know where to look or what to direct my next lines at!'

FRANKAU, Nicholas

Actor, b. 16 July 1954, Stockport, Cheshire. Trained at the Webber Douglas Academy, after graduating from St Catherine's College, Cambridge, with maths degree. Started his acting career at Southwold season in 1977. Played in *Peter Pan* at Shaftesbury Theatre. Recent films: *Plenty*; *Gunbus*. TV incl: *'Allo 'Allo!*; *The Last Term* (Play For Today); *I Remember Nelson*; *C.A.T.S. Eyes*; *Paradise Postponed*. Address: c/o Jim Thompson, Rivington House, 82 Great Eastern Street, London EC2A 3JL. Hobbies: cycle touring, repairing things. Pets: cat called Arch. **Most Cherished Possession:** 'My cat Arch – it's the only possession I have which breathes.' **Favourite Memory:** 'Aged 13 and arriving by bicycle at my grandparents' home in Sussex, having come from London. It was a long, hard journey and it was over!'

FRANKLIN, Gretchen

Actress, b. 7 July 1911, Covent Garden, London. Has been in showbusiness for more than 50 years, starting as a chorus girl. Theatre incl: *Sweet and Low*; *Hedda Gabler*; *Hay Fever*; *Logan*; *Little and Large*. TV incl: *Danger UXB*; *George and Mildred*; *Quatermass*; *Quincey's Quest*; *Some Mothers Do 'Ave 'Em*; *The Other One*; *Fox*; *The Casebook of Dr Jekyll*; *Potter*; *The Dick Emery Show*; *You're Only Young Twice*; *The Other 'Arf*; *Dead Ernest*; *Kelly Monteith*; *Maybury*; *Blackadder*; *In Loving Memory*; *The Victoria Wood Show*; *Hallelujah*; Ethel Skinner in *EastEnders*. m. writer Caswell Garth. c/o Barry Burnett. Hobbies: gardening, needlework, animals. Pets: one old cat. **Most Cherished Possession:** 'My front door keys.' **Favourite Memory:** 'You've done well today – you can go home!'

FRANKLYN, Sabina

Actress, b. 15 September, London. Began in weekly rep in Southwold, followed by tours incl: *The Man Most Likely To . . .*; *Charley's Aunt*; *Move Over Mrs Markham*; *Duty Free* in West End; and at the National Theatre, *The Moving Finger*; *The Rivals*. TV incl: *Pride and Prejudice*; *Fawlty Towers*; *Blake's Seven*; *Strangers*; *Terry and June*; *When the Boat Comes In*; *Keep It In the Family* (three series); *Byron: A Personal Tour*; *Full House* (three series); *Miss Marple*; *The Worst Witch*. m. John Challis. Address: c/o Michael Ladkin. Birthsign: Virgo. Hobbies: antiques, films, travel. **Most Cherished Possession:** 'My first piece of art deco – a tiny toast rack.' **Favourite Memory:** 'The first time I met my husband, when he walked on to the Olivier stage for rehearsals of *The Rivals*.'

FRANKLYN, William

Actor, b. 22 September 1925, Kensington, London. At the age of 15 appeared in *My Sister Eileen* at the Savoy Theatre. After the war, *Arsenic and Old Lace* followed by rep at Ryde and Margate and *The Love of Four Colonels*. Many West End plays and has directed in London and Rome. Theatre incl: *Deathtrap*; *In Praise of Love*; *Dead Ringer*; *Springtime For Henry*; *Guilty Conscience*. Has been in more than 50 films. TV incl: *Paradise Island*; *Masterspy*; *The Purple Twilight*; *The Stream Video Company*. Nine years of Schweppes commercials. m. (1st) actress Margot Johns (dis.), (2nd) actress Susanna Carroll; 3 d. Sabina (from 1st m.), Francesca, Melissa. Address: c/o John Redway & Assocs. Birthsign: Virgo. Hobbies: Italy, cricket, squash, travel writing. Pets: a schnauzer.

FRANZ, Dennis

Actor, b. 28 October, Chicago, Illinois. Attended Southern Illinois University and was a member of the Organic Theatre Company. Theatre incl: *Bleacher Bums* (for which he received an Emmy). Films incl: *Body Double; The Fury; Popeye; Blowout; Psycho II; Dressed To Kill; Remember My Name; A Fine Mess; A Perfect Couple.* TV incl: *Simon & Simon; Hunter; The A-Team; Hardcastle and McCormick; Riptide; T J Hooker; MacGruder and Loud; E.R.; Chicago Story; Bay City Blues; Deadly Messages;* Lt Norman Buntz in *Hill Street Blues.* Address: c/o Gores-Fields Agency, 10100 Santa Monica Blvd, Los Angeles, CA 90067. Hobbies: motorcycle riding, swimming, tennis, golf, music.

FRAZER, Liz

Actress, b. 14 August 1935, London. Trained at the London School of Dramatic Art, since when she has worked extensively. Stage incl: *Too True To Be Good; Next Time I'll Sing To You; Black Comedy; Bedful of Foreigners; Donkey's Years; Sweeney Todd; Annie; Oliver.* Films incl: *I'm All Right, Jack; Two Way Stretch; Live Now, Pay Later; Chicago Joe and the Showgirl;* and in many of the Carry On and Confessions films. TV incl: *Shroud For a Nightingale; Fairly Secret Army; Hardwick House; Rude Health; Miss Marple; Streetwise; Eskimos Do It;* and numerous panel games. Address: c/o Roger Carey. Birthsign: Leo. Hobby: bridge. Pets: basset hound. **Most Cherished Possession:** 'Good health, because it helps you live longer.'

FREEMAN, Paul

Actor, b. 18 January 1943, Barnet, Hertfordshire. Attended New College of Speech and Drama, Hampstead. Stage experience incl: National Theatre, Royal Shakespeare Company and Royal Court. Films incl: *Dogs of War; The Long Good Friday; Flight to Berlin; Raiders of the Lost Ark; Shanghai Surprise; The Sender; Prisoner of Rio; Without a Clue; New Wine; Eminent Domain; A World Apart.* TV incl: *Death of a Princess; Yesterday's Dreams; Falcon Crest; Winston Churchill: The Wilderness Years; Sins; Cagney and Lacey; Sakharov; Willie's Last Stand; The Index Goes Fishing; The Paris Paradox.* m. Maggie Scott; 1 d. Lucy. Address: c/o Ken McReddie, London. Birthsign: Capricorn. Hobbies: travel, reading, bird watching, gardening. **Favourite Memory:** 'Meeting Maggie in Belize.'

FRENCH, Dawn

Comedienne/actress. Trained at the Central School of Speech and Drama, London, where she met Jennifer Saunders. Dawn became a teacher briefly, before teaming up with Jennifer. French and Saunders have appeared in many *Comic Strips Presents . . .* films, mostly made for TV, incl: *Five Go Mad In Dorset; Five Go Mad On Mescalin; Consuela; Mr Jolly Lives Next Door; Strike* (winner 1981 Golden Globe); *Spaghetti Hoops; Le Kiss; Supergrass* (feature film). Other TV incl: *Girls On Top; Happy Families; French and Saunders* (three series); *Sapsorrow;* presented two Channel Four series, *Swank* about fashion and *Scoff* about food. Theatre incl: *When I Was a Girl I Used To Scream and Shout; An Evening With French and Saunders; The Secret Policeman's Biggest Ball* (also shown on TV). m. comedian and actor Lenny Henry. Address: c/o Peters Fraser & Dunlop.

FREUD, Emma

TV presenter, b. 25 January 1962, London. Obtained a BA Honours in drama from Bristol and London Universities. After leaving college worked as a journalist, composer, actress, singing telegram courier, magician's assistant and co-director of the Open Air Theatre, Regent's Park. 1st TV job in 1985 presenting *Roundabout.* Presenter of Radio 4's *Loose Ends;* LWTs *Six O'Clock Show; Night Network's Pillowtalk; Plunder; The Media Show.* Has written for *Daily Mirror, Sunday Mirror, Sunday Telegraph, Observer, Independent.* Address: c/o Noel Gay. Hobbies: parachute jumping, Cresta Run, hang-gliding. Pets: cats. **Most Cherished Possession:** 'My tenor saxophone.' **Favourite Memory:** 'The day I received my private pilot's licence.'

FROST, David, OBE

Author/interviewer/presenter/tycoon, b. 7 April 1939, Tenterden, Kent. Began TV as reporter for *This Week*, but achieved overnight success as host of *That Was The Week That Was*. Other TV incl: *A Degree of Frost; Not So Much a Programme, More a Way of Life; The Frost Report; The Frost Programme; Frost Over America; We British; The Wilson Interviews; The Nixon Interviews; The Shah Speaks; The Falklands; Where Will It End?; The Guinness Book of Records Specials; Through the Keyhole; The President and Mrs Bush Talking With David Frost* for *David Frost On Sunday*. Founder of LWT; founder and director of TV-am. m. Lady Carina Fitzalan-Howard; 3 s. Miles, Wilfred, George. Address: c/o David Paradine, London. Birthsign: Aries. Hobbies: football, cricket.

FRY, Stephen

Actor/writer/comedian, b. 24 August 1957, Hampstead, London. Was a member of the Cambridge Footlights. Radio incl: *Loose Ends; Delve Special*. Films: *The Good Father; A Handful of Dust; A Fish Called Wanda; The Secret Policeman's Second Ball*. TV incl: *Alfresco; The Young Ones; Alas Smith & Jones; Filthy Rich & Catflap; Blackadder 2; The Crystal Cube; The Tube; Saturday Live; Whose Line Is It Anyway?; Blackadder Goes Forth; A Bit of Fry and Laurie; Jeeves and Wooster; Old Flames; This Is David Lander*. He wrote the script for the stage musical *Me and My Girl*, and the plays *Latin* and *Bulldog Drummond*. Address: c/o Lorraine Hamilton, 24 Denmark St, London WC2 8NJ. Hobbies: chess, P G Wodehouse, computing, cricket, books, eating. **Most Cherished Possession:** 'My thighs, particularly the left one.'

FULLERTON, Fiona

Actress, b. 10 October 1956, Kaduna, Nigeria. Her first appearance was in the film *Run Wild, Run Free* at the age of 11. She has since worked extensively on stage, film and TV. Theatre incl: *Gypsy; The Boy Friend; Camelot; Something's Afoot; Cinderella*. Films incl: *Nicholas and Alexandra; The Human Factor; A View To a Kill*. TV incl: *A Friend Indeed; Angels; Gaugin – The Savage; Lev Tolstoy; A Question of Faith; Strange But True; Shaka Zulu; The Charmer; A Hazard of Hearts; Hemingway*. Address: c/o London Management. Birthsign: Libra. Hobbies: travel, antiques, auctions. **Most Cherished Possession:** 'My teddy bear, because I've had him since I was three.' **Favourite Memory:** 'Kissing Roger Moore in *A View To a Kill*, which was a childhood fantasy of mine.'

FURST, Stephen

Actor, b. 8 May, Norfolk, Virginia. Film appearances incl: *Scavenger Hunt; Take Down; National Lampoon's Animal House; Midnight Madness; Silent Rages; Up the Creek; Class Reunion*. TV incl: *The Day After; The Bastard; Delta House*; Dr Elliot Axelrod in *St Elsewhere; Off Sides; If It's Tuesday It Still Must Be Belgium*. m. Lorraine; 2 s. Nathan, Griffith. Address: c/o The Artists Agency, 10000 Santa Monica Blvd, Los Angeles, CA 90067. Birthsign: Taurus. Hobbies: antiques, cooking Italian cuisine, coaching a small league T-ball team. Pets: two Golden Retrievers. **Most Cherished Possession:** 'My family.' **Favourite Memory:** 'When my children were born.'

GALL, Sandy, CBE

TV journalist, b. 1 October 1927, Penang, Malaya. Started career on *Aberdeen Press and Journal*. Worked for Reuters 1953–63 and ITN since 1963. Documentaries for ITV incl: *Behind Russian Lines* (1982); *Allah Against The Gunships* (1984); *The Cresta Run* (1984); *Agony of a Nation* (1986); *Lord of the Lions* (1989). Books: *Gold Scoop; Chasing the Dragon; Don't Worry About the Money Now*, his memoirs; *Behind Russian Lines; An Afghan Journal; Afghanistan: Agony of a Nation; Salang*. m. Eleanor; 3 d. Fiona, Carlotta, Michaela, 1 s. Alexander. Address: c/o ITN, London. Birthsign: Libra. Hobbies: golf, writing thrillers. Pets: dogs, cat, ponies. **Most Cherished Possession:** 'Solomon, the family's black Labrador, for his enthusiasm.' **Favourite Memory:** 'Winning the Waldron Bowls at Rye.'

GARDEN, Graeme

Actor/writer, b. 18 February 1943, Aberdeen. Cambridge Footlights while at university. Studied medicine at King's College Hospital, London, but entered showbusiness after writing for radio, incl: *I'm Sorry, I'll Read That Again; I'm Sorry I Haven't a Clue*. With Bill Oddie wrote some of the *Doctor* TV series and *Astronauts*. Other TV incl: *Broaden Your Mind; The Goodies; Tell the Truth; A Sense of the Past; Bodymatters*. Records incl: *Funky Gibbon; The In-Betweenies*. Books: *The Seventh Man; Skylighters; Very Silly Games*. m. Emma; 1 d. Sally, 2 s. John, Tom. Address: c/o Roger Hancock. Birthsign: Aquarius. Hobbies: fishing, drawing, music, books. **Favourite Memory:** 'Family holidays.'

GARNER, James

Actor, b. 7 April 1928, Oklahoma. Had 50 jobs before becoming an actor, offered a part in *The Caine Mutiny Court Martial*. Started in TV in *Cheyenne*, followed by the successful *Maverick*. Films incl: *Darby's Rangers; Marlowe; Support Your Local Sheriff; Duel at Diablo; Grand Prix; Victor/Victoria; The Fan; Murphy's Romance; Sunset*. Nominated for Oscar for *Murphy's Romance*. TV incl: Jim Rockford in *The Rockford Files* (1974–80); *Bret Maverick; Heart Sounds; Space; Promise*. Served in US army in Korea and was awarded the Purple Heart. m. actress Lois Clarke; 1 d. Greta, 1 step-d. Kimberly. Address: c/o ICM. Pets: one dog. **Most Cherished Possession:** 'My golf clubs.' **Favourite Memory:** 'Working on my favourite film, *The Americanization of Emily*, with Julie Andrews.'

GARWOOD, Patricia

Actress, b. 28 January 1941, Paignton, Devon. Her first part was in the film *The Lavender Hill Mob*, aged nine. Trained at RADA. Member of MENSA. Stage incl: *Woman In Mind; Letters Home; Come Back to the Five and Dime Jimmy Dean, Jimmy Dean; The Watcher; Sauce For the Goose; Steel Magnolias*. Has appeared in more than 100 television plays. TV incl: *No Place Like Home; The Brack Report; Sherlock Holmes; C.A.T.S. Eyes; Lytton's Diary; Love and Marriage*. m. playwright Jeremy Paul; 4 d. Amanda, Tara, Sasha, Sophie. Address: c/o William Morris. Hobbies: sunbathing and swimming. Pets: Cassie (cocker spaniel), Josie (tabby-cat). **Most Cherished Possession:** 'My front door key.' **Favourite Memory:** 'When I met my husband.'

GASCOIGNE, Bamber

Much-travelled question master, b. 24 January 1935, London. Scholarship to Yale School of Drama. Educated at Cambridge. Later drama critic *The Spectator* and *The Observer*. Chairman of TV's *University Challenge*, 1962–87, and of *Connoissuer* since 1988. Wrote and presented *The Christians; Victorian Values; Man and Music; The Great Moghuls*. Books: *World Theatre; The Great Moghuls; Treasures And Dynasties of China; Murgatreud's Empire; The Heyday; The Christians; Quest For the Golden Hare; How to Identify Prints*. m. Christina Ditchburn. Address: c/o Curtis Brown. **Most Cherished Possession:** 'Our house – and to wake up and see the Thames at the bottom of the garden.' **Favourite Memory:** 'Arriving home in one piece after driving to India and back.'

GASCOINE, Jill

Actress, b. 11 April 1937, Lambeth, London. Trained at the Italia Conti Stage School, then rep. Theatre incl: *42nd Street*. TV incl: *Rooms; Plays For Britain; General Hospital; Three Kisses; Balzac; Z-Cars; Softly, Softly; Dixon of Dock Green; Within These Walls; Holding On; Six Days of Justice; Raffles; Beryl's Lot; Peter Pan; Oranges and Lemons; The Onedin Line; The Gentle Touch; C.A.T.S. Eyes*. Voted Best Actress by *TVTimes* readers 1984. m. (2nd) actor Alfred Molina; 2 s. Sean, Adam. Address: c/o Marina Martin Management. Birthsign: Aries. Hobbies: gardening, cooking, writing. Pets: Ella (Labrador) and two cats (Dodger and Liz). **Most Cherished Possession:** 'My home and garden.' **Favourite Memory:** 'My second wedding day.'

GAUNT, William

Actor, b. 3 April 1937, Pudsey, Yorkshire. Trained at RADA, but had already started as a child actor in the Otley Little Theatre. After RADA, worked in Dallas Theater Center, Texas, then rep *in* UK. West End stage incl: *Boys In the Band; The Flip Side; When Did You Last See Your Trousers?; Run For Your Wife.* Films incl: *The Revolutionary.* TV incl: more than 100 plays; *The Foundation; Crown Court; Love and Marriage; No Place Like Home; Capstick's Law.* Was also artistic director Liverpool Playhouse 1979–81. m. actress Carolyn Lyster; 1 d. Matilda (Tilly), 1 s. Albert (Albie). Address: c/o Julia Macdermot, London. Birthsign: Aries. Hobbies: fell walking and gardening. Pets: cocker spaniel called Rupert. **Most Cherished Possession:** 'Tilly, Albie and Carolyn.'

GETTY, Estelle

Actress, b. 25 July 1923, New York. Broadway actress trained at the Herbert Berghof Studios. Received Golden Globe award for Best Actress in a Comedy for *Golden Girls.* Also, the Helen Hayes award as Best Supporting Performer for *Torch Song Trilogy.* Films incl: *Mask; Mannequin.* TV incl: *Cagney and Lacey; Fantasy Island;* and two TVMs: *CopaCabana; Victims For Victims.* m. 40 years to Arthur Gettleman; 2 s. Barry, Carl. Address: c/o Abrams, Harris and Goldberg, 9220 Sunset Blvd, Los Angeles, CA 90069. Birthsign: Leo. Hobbies: exercise and keeping fit. Pets: couple of stuffed cats! **Most Cherished Possession:** 'My husband, he's shorter than me.' **Favourite Memory:** 'Fifty years as an actress. All my roles have been originals – mothers are my favourite characters.'

GIBBES, Robyn

Actress, b. 2 January 1957, Goroka, New Guinea. Spent three years with Ensemble Theatre. Films incl: *Gone To Ground; Letters To a Friend; Jackson High; Alison's Birthday; Wild Horses; Marie Clare; I Live With Me Dad.* Australian TV incl: *Emerging; The Young Wife; Ben Hall; Certain Women; Home; Class of '75; Glenview High; The Young Doctors; Restless Years; Cop Shop; Carson's Law.* m. Greg Apps; 1 s. Matthew. Address: c/o 3 Talbot St, Hampton 3188, Victoria, Australia. Birthsign: Capricorn. Hobbies: reading, writing and renovating their Edwardian home. Pets: Jake the Border Collie dog and Puss the cat. **Most Cherished Possession:** 'My son – he is my life support system and my sanity.' **Favourite Memory:** 'Filming in New Zealand.'

GIBSON, Richard

Actor, b. 1 January 1954, Kampala, Uganda. Trained at Central School of Speech and Drama, London. Began acting as Marcus in the film *The Go-Between,* then in *Tom Brown's Schooldays* on TV. Theatre incl: *The Winslow Boy; Love's Labours Lost; Allo! Allo!* TV incl: *Secret Diaries; Hadleigh; The Children of the New Forest; The Gate of Eden; Poldark; Penmarric; 'Allo! 'Allo!* Address: c/o Annette Stone. Birthsign: Capricorn. Hobbies: picture-framing, song-writing, cycling, carpentry. Pets: two 'killer' cats, Bill and Nine. **Most Cherished Possession:** 'My violin, given to me by my grandmother.' **Favourite Memory:** 'Hearing Yehudi Menuhin play Elgar's violin concerto from eight feet away in St. Paul's Cathedral.'

GIELGUD, Sir John, CH

Actor/director, b. 14 April 1904, London. A great-nephew of Dame Ellen Terry, he trained at Lady Benson's School and RADA. First stage appearance at the Old Vic in 1921. Theatre incl: one-man show, *Ages of Man; The Importance of Being Earnest; No Man's Land.* Films incl: *The Good Companions; Gold; Chariots of Fire; Arthur* (for which he won an Oscar); *Wagner; The Wicked Lady; Arthur 2 – On the Rocks; Getting It Right.* TV incl: *A Day By The Sea; The Cherry Orchard; Ivanov; Edward the Seventh; Why Didn't They Ask Evans?; Brideshead Revisited; Parson's Pleasure; Summer's Lease.* Books: *Early Stages* (autobiog); *Stage Directions; Distinguished Company; An Actor and His Time.* Address: c/o ICM. Hobbies: reading, walking, puzzles, travel. **Most Cherished Possession:** 'Health and memory.'

GILLESPIE, Robert

Actor/director/writer, b. 9 November 1933, Lille, France. Mother Hungarian, father Canadian of Scottish descent. Arrived Plymouth 1940 unable to speak English. Became amateur actor, then semi-pro in 1951 and, after RADA, spent two years at Old Vic. Also a director, playwright and contributor to BBC's *That Was The Week That Was*. Films incl: *A Severed Head; The National Health; The Thirty-Nine Steps; The Prisoner of Zenda*. Radio incl: *Whatever Happened To The Likely Lads?; Lord Peter Wimsey*. Numerous TV appearances incl: *The Good Life; Couples; Rising Damp; Agony; Mary's Wife;* five series of *Keep It In The Family; Blind Justice*. Address: c/o William Morris. Birthsign: Scorpio. Hobbies: reading, cinema, travel, archaeology.

GILMORE, Susan

Actress, b. 24 November 1954, London. Studied at Bristol University followed by Bristol Old Vic Theatre School. Theatre incl: *Beastly Beatitudes of Balthazar B*. TV incl: *Angels; Maelstrom; Howards' Way*. m. Daniel Topolski; 1 d. Emma Sheridan. Address: c/o Joy Jameson. Birthsign: Sagittarius. Hobbies: travel, piano, looking through junk shops. **Most Cherished Possession:** 'My daughter.' **Favourite Memory:** 'My daughter's birth.'

GLEN, Iain

Actor, b. 24 June 1961, Edinburgh. Trained at RADA, won the Bancroft Gold Medal. Films: Wallace in *Paris By Night;* John Hanning Speke in *Mountains of the Moon;* Larry Winters in *Silent Scream;* Willie Quinton in *Fools of Fortune*. TV: Allen Innes in *Blood Hunt;* 'Sailor' in *Will You Love Me Tomorrow;* Ray in *The Picnic;* Carl Galton in *The Fear*. Address: c/o Duncan Heath Associates. Birthsign: Cancer. Hobbies: guitar, piano, sports. Pets: cats.

GLOVER, Brian

Actor, b. 2 April 1934, Sheffield, South Yorkshire. Was a teacher and professional wrestler before becoming an actor. Debut in 1968 in the film *Kes* when he played a schoolmaster. Theatre incl: National Theatre and RSC; *Cage Aux Folles; Arturo Ui*. Films incl: *Brannigan; O Lucky Man; Quilp; Trial By Combat; The Great Train Robbery; An American Werewolf In London*. TV incl: *Porridge; Minder; Campion;* the voice for the Tetley Tea Folk commercials. Also a playwright. m. (dis.); 1 d. Maxine, 1 s. Gus. Address: c/o Felix de Wolfe. Birthsign: Aries. Hobby: auctions. **Most Cherished Possession:** 'My bald head. If I grew hair I'd never work again.' **Favourite Memory:** 'My 1952 M G TD – a great motor.'

GLOVER, Julian

Actor, b. 27 March 1935, London. Trained at RADA and began career as a spear carrier for the RSC 1957. Recent theatre incl: *Habeas Corpus; Educating Rita; The Aspern Papers;* also, his own adaptation of *Beowulf;* one-man show on the life and works of Robert Graves. Films incl: *Kim; Heat and Dust; For Your Eyes Only; The Fourth Protocol; Anastasia; Cry Freedom; Mandela; Hearts of Fire; Indiana Jones and the Last Crusade; Treasure Island*. TV incl: *An Age of Kings; Dombey and Son; By the Sword Divided; Wish Me Luck*. m. actress Isla Blair; 1 s. Jamie. Address: c/o Jeremy Conway. Pets: two cats. **Most Cherished Possession:** 'Robert Graves's chair in which he sat to write the Claudius books.' **Favourite Memory:** 'My wife's face at the front door when she told me she was pregnant.'

GODDARD, Liza

Actress, b. 20 January 1950, Smethwick. Trained with the Arts Educational Trust. Started career in Australia. Returned to UK in 1969 and theatre incl: *Signs of the Times; One Fair Daughter; The Three Sisters; See How They Run; Wife Begins At Forty*. Film: *Testimony*. TV incl: *Take Three Girls; Yes, Honestly; The Brothers; Roll Over Beethoven; Take Three Women; Bergerac; That's Love*. m. (dis.) Alvin Stardust; 1 s. Thorn, 1 d. Sophie. Address: c/o Barry Burnett. Birthsign: Aquarius. Hobbies: riding, reading, chicken, mucking out. Pets: five horses, five dogs, two cats, two chickens, two bullocks. **Most Cherished Possession:** 'Apart from my children, my horse Olive.' **Favourite Memory:** 'Alone with the family on a desert island in Fiji.'

GODWIN, Christopher

Actor, b. 5 August 1943, Loughborough, Leicestershire. Started career in stage management with no drama school training. Played the lead in *Ten Times Table*. Other theatre incl: *School For Scandal; Noises Off*. Films: *Porridge; Charlie Muffin; A Handful of Dust*. TV incl: *Astronauts; The Other 'Arf; Nearly a Happy Ending; A Foggy Outlook; Return to Waterloo; Roll Over Beethoven; Return to Treasure Island; Fizz; My Family and Other Animals; To Have and To Hold; Roger Doesn't Live Here Any More; Boon; Nice Work; Snakes and Ladders; The Chronicles of Narnia*. m. Christine; 2 s. Ben, Tom. Address: c/o ICM. Hobbies: cycling, cricket, carpentry, squash. Pets: two Burmese cats, Rosie and Romana. **Most Cherished Possession:** 'Books, because they're always there.' **Favourite Memory:** 'Watching the sun rise on the Alps when hitch-hiking in France.'

GONSHAW, Francesca

Actresss, b. London. Trained at Academy of Live and Recorded Arts and the Actor Centre. Theatre incl: *You Should See Us Now; Sailors' Dreams; Monty Cliff; Dear Janet Rosenberg; Dear Mr Kooning; A Midsummer Night's Dream*. Films incl: *Biggles; A Ghost In Monte Carlo*. TV incl: *Shades; The Cleopatras; Gesualdo; Crossroads; Sidni; 'Allo 'Allo!; Cold Warrior; Howards' Way; Farrington of the FO*. Address: c/o Gregg Millard, Second Floor, 12 D'Arblay Street, London W1V 3FP, tel 071-287 4700. Hobbies: piano, theatre, travel, scuba-diving, tennis, dance, books. **Most Cherished Possession:** 'John Brinsmead piano, black, shiny, sleek and constant pleasure, impossible to ignore.' **Favourite Memory:** 'Being offered Hermia and travelling to Middle East with the New Shakespeare Company.'

GOODALL, Caroline

Actress, b. 13 November 1959, London. Studied drama and English at Bristol University. Theatre incl: *Time and Time Again; Romeo and Juliet; Twelfth Night; While the Sun Shines; Daisy Pulls It Off* (original cast member); *Tons of Money* (Scarborough); *Susan's Breasts* (Royal Court); *The Dare Kiss* and *Command Or Promise* (NT); *Richard III; Misalliance and Heresies* (RSC). Film: *Every Time We Say Goodbye*. TV incl: *The Moon Stallion; Gems; Remington Steele; Tales of the Unexpected; After the War*. Address: c/o James Sharkey. Birthsign: Scorpio. Hobbies: swimming, eating out, talking, travelling. **Most Cherished Possession:** 'My old Edwardian fireplace.' **Favourite Memory:** 'Seeing a tree kangaroo in the Australian rain forest. They live in the tops of trees – crazy!'

GOODWIN, Harold

Actor, b. 22 October 1917, Wombwell, Yorkshire. Trained at RADA and was three years at Liverpool rep. First stage appearance in London's West End in *Venus Observed*. Many stage productions since and 150 films incl: *The Dam Busters; Bridge On the River Kwai; The Longest Day; All Creatures Great and Small*. Numerous TV appearances incl: *Love Story; The Crucible; That's My Boy; The Gentle Touch; Juliet Bravo; Never Too Late; Shoreline; Bulman; Casualty; Our Geoff; Brush Strokes; Woof*. m. Beatrice. Address: c/o Hilda Physick Agency, 78 Temple Sheen Road, London SW14 7RR, tel 081-876 0073. Birthsign: Libra. Hobbies: reading, cricket. **Most Cherished Possession:** 'My tent.' **Favourite Memory:** 'Acting with Lord Olivier.'

GOODWIN, Trudie

Actress, b. 13 November 1951, London. First professional work with the Theatre Centre, London, acting in two tours and directing another. Then rep at Nottingham, Worcester, Leicester Phoenix Theatre. Return to London with the Young Vic. London theatre also incl: *The Beggar's Opera; Woomberang; Godspell.* TV incl: *Fox; The Gentle Touch; The Law Machine; Woodentop; The Bill.* m. actor Kit Jackson; 1 d. Jessica. Address: c/o Ellison Combe Associates. Birthsign: Scorpio. Hobbies: painting and drawing, gardening, bridge. Pets: a huge mongrel and two cats. **Most Cherished Possession:** 'Our photograph albums, especially the photos of Jessica.' **Favourite Memory:** 'Our first holiday with the baby, on a houseboat in Salcombe – truly idyllic.'

GOODYEAR, Julie

Actress, b. 29 March 1945, Bury, Lancashire. Started career in repertory theatre in Oldham. Joined *Coronation Street* in 1966 as Bet Lynch, one of the girls in the raincoat factory. Left to return to rep and do other TV work. Returned as barmaid in 1970, later to become landlady of the Rovers Return and wife of Alec Gilroy. Other TV: *The Dustbinmen; City '68; The War of Darkie Pilbeam; Nearest and Dearest; A Family at War;* the subject of a *This Is Your Life* programme. m. 1st Ray Sutcliff (dis.), 2nd Tony Rudman (dis.), 3rd Richard Skrob (dis.); 1 s. Gary (from 1st m.). Address: c/o Granada TV.

GORDON, Hannah

Actress, b. 9 April 1941, Edinburgh. Trained at Glasgow College of Dramatic Art then rep. West End theatre incl: *Can You Hear Me At the Back?; The Killing Game; Baggage; The Jewellers Shop; The Country Girl.* Films incl: *Spring and Port Wine; The Elephant Man; Shirley Valentine.* Radio incl: *Macbeth; Hedda Gabler; Candida; St Joan; A Winter's Tale.* TV incl: *What Every Woman Knows; Middlemarch; Abelard and Heloise; My Wife Next Door; Dear Octopus; Upstairs, Downstairs; Telford's Change; Waste; Miss Morrison's Ghosts; Goodbye Mr Kent; Good Behaviour; The Day After the Fair; My Family and Other Animals; Joint Account.* m. lighting cameraman Norman Warwick; 1 s. Ben. Address: c/o Hutton Management. Birthsign: Aries. Hobbies: reading, cooking, gardening.

GORMAN, Reg

Comic actor, b. 2 August 1937, Sydney, Australia. Theatre incl: *New Faces; How to Succeed; The Odd Couple; Sweet Charity; Summer of the 17th Doll.* Films incl: *Caddie; Dusty; Drifting Avenger; Inn of the Damned.* TV incl: *I Can Jump Puddles; All the Rivers Run; The Henderson Kids; Carson's Law; Neighbours;* and six years as Jack in *The Sullivans.* m. actress Judith Roberts; 2 d. Kate, Charmaine, 1 s. Karl. Address: c/o Banksia Productions, 11th Floor, 65 York St, Sydney, New South Wales, Australia. Birthsign: Leo. Hobbies: reading, movies, archery. Pets: dog. **Most Cherished Possession:** 'My books – they helped me complete my education after I left school at 14.' **Favourite Memory:** 'Getting a standing ovation (my only one!) in my first revue, with my own sketch.'

GOUGH, Michael

Actor, b. 1917, Malaya. Theatre incl: *A Month In the Country; Don Juan; Sergeant Musgrave's Dance* (all National Theatre); *The Biko Inquest; The Cherry Orchard.* Films incl: *Anna Karenina; The Sword and the Rose; Dracula; Henry VIII; The Go-Between; The Boys From Brazil; The Dresser; Top Secret; Oxford Blues; A Christmas Carol; Out of Africa; Caravaggio; The Fourth Protocol; Batman.* TV incl: *Smiley's People; The Rivals of Sherlock Holmes; To the Lighthouse; The Citadel; Heartbreak Hotel; A Killing On the Exchange; Inspector Morse; After the War; Campion; Blackeyes; The Shell Seekers; The Mountain and the Molehill; The Case of the Late Pig.* Address: c/o Peters Fraser & Dunlop.

GRACE, Nickolas

Actor, b. 21 November 1949, West Kirby. Trained at Central School of Speech and Drama, London. Theatre incl: *Richard II* at the Young Vic; *Cabaret; Dracula; Amadeus; The Mikado; HMS Pinafore; Jenkin's Ear*. Films incl: *Heat and Dust; Sleepwalker; Europe After the Rain; Lorca; Dream Demon; Salome's Last Dance; Just Ask For Diamond*. TV incl: *The Love School; Comedy of Errors; Brideshead Revisited; Robin of Sherwood; Lace; Master of Ballantrae; The Last Place On Earth; Max Headroom; The Man In the Brown Suit; Pursuit; Birds of a Feather*. Address: c/o Hutton Management. Hobbies: cinema, swimming, running, riding travel. **Favourite Memory:** 'The first night of *Comedy of Errors* at Stratford in 1976. The audience didn't want to leave.'

GRANT, Deborah

Actress, b. 22 February 1947, London. Trained at Joyce Butler School of Dancing and Central School of Speech and Drama. Theatre incl: *Barnum; Bedroom Farce; Watch On the Rhine* at the National Theatre. TV incl: *Bergerac; Bouquet of Barbed Wire; Outside Edge; Mr Palfrey of Westminster; Victoria Wood As Seen On TV; Bulman; Room At the Bottom; Pulaski*. m. actor Gregory Floy; 2 d. Melissa and Miranda. Address: c/o Larry Dalzell Associates. Birthsign: Pisces. Hobbies: dog-walking. Pets: two goldfish, four guinea pigs, one cat and one dog. **Most Cherished Possession:** 'My children.' **Favourite Memory:** 'The most exciting moment of my career – when I was told I was to play Mrs Barnum opposite Michael Crawford at the London Palladium.'

GRANT, Russell

TV and radio astrologer, b. 5 February 1952, Hillingdon, Middlesex. Largest syndicated astrology column in Europe. TV-am's astrologer on *Good Morning Britain*. Own series for TV and radio, as well as guest appearances. Books incl: *Your Sun Signs; TVTimes* special *Your Year Ahead*. Address: c/o Jacque Evans Management. Birthsign: Sun and Moon Aquarius, Libra rising. Hobbies: collecting maps of Britain, plus Middlesex memorabilia. Pets: three cats (Tinker, Tamarisk, Archie) and labrador dog (Amber). **Most Cherished Possession:** 'My encyclopaedia of geography given to me when seven.' **Favourite Memory:** 'Meeting the Queen Mother in 1978 and presenting her with her astrological chart.'

GRAY, Dulcie, CBE

Actress, b. 20 November 1920, Kuala Lumpur, Malaysia. Trained at the Webber-Douglas Academy. First stage part as Sorel in *Hay Fever* in rep in Aberdeen 1939. Has starred in 41 plays in London's West End. Most recent stage part Teresa Browne in *The Living Room*. Made many films in the Forties and Fifties, and numerous radio plays. Most recent TV incl: Kate Harvey in BBC's *Howards' Way*. Has written 21 novels, a book of short stories and an award winning book on the conservation of British butterflies. m. actor Michael Denison. Hobbies: butterflies.

GRAY, Linda

Actress, b. 12 September 1942, Santa Monica, California. Trained with Charles Conrad's Acting Class. TV debut was as a guest on TV's *Marcus Welby, MD* and then starred in the series *All That Glitters*. Films incl: *Haywire; The Two Worlds of Jenny Logan;* Sue Ellen in *Dallas*. TV movies incl: *Chimps; Not In Front of the Children;* and *The Gambler;* She also hosted *The Body Human; The Loving Process*. TV guest appearances incl: *McCloud; Big Hawaii; Emergency; Switch*. m. director Ed Thrasher (dis.); 1 d. Kehly, 1 s. Jeff. Address: c/o ICM, 8899 Beverly Blvd, Los Angeles CA 90048. Hobbies: skiing, exercising. Pets: horses. **Most Cherished Possession:** 'My polo mallet – I've fallen in love with the game.' **Favourite Memory:** 'The birth of my children.'

GRAY, Muriel

TV presenter/writer, b. 30 August, Glasgow, Scotland. Trained as an illustrator at Glasgow School of Art. TV incl: *The Tube; The Works; Casebook Scotland; Acropolis Now; The Hogmanay Show; Bliss; The Media Show; Frocks On the Box; Walkie Talkie.* Has written for national newspapers and magazines. Address: c/o Gallus Benson Productions, Greenside House, 25 Greenside Place, Edinburgh EH1 3AA, tel 031-556 2429. Birthsign: Virgo. Hobbies: hill climbing, drinking beer, shouting at TV adverts. Pets: 'I am the house pet.' **Most Cherished Possession:** 'My Walkman. It saves me from deep conversations about cars with dull businessmen when I travel.' **Favourite Memory:** 'My first holiday in the Highlands with my boyfriend. Young, in love, and in Scotland. Heaven!'

GRAYSON, Larry

Comedian, b. 31 August 1923, Banbury. He learned his profession in summer shows and touring revues. Unknown until an appearance on Saturday Variety 1972. His *Shut That Door!* series followed and other TV incl: *The Good Old Days;* his own shows; *The Generation Game; Sweethearts.* Hobbies: winkle-picking with Everard and Slack Alice in Brixham. Pets: a very boisterious poodle called William. **Most Cherished Possession:** 'Slack Alice's secret recipe for elderberry wine.' **Favourite Memory:** 'Brenda Alcock's birthday party on November 5, 1944, when she stood on the kitchen table singing *Daddy Wouldn't Buy Me a Bow-Wow,* wearing nothing but a small Union Jack and two catherine wheels!'

GREAVES, Jimmy

TV presenter, b. 20 February 1940, East Ham, London. Former Chelsea, West Ham, Tottenham, AC Milan and England footballer who joined TV-am as presenter 1983. *TVTimes* Top 10 Awards Favourite Sports Personality On TV, 1982, 1986, 1987. Other TV incl: *Sporting Triangles;* co-presenter of *Saint & Greavsie; The Match.* m. Irene; 2 d. Lynn, Mitzi, 2 s. Daniel, Andrew. Address: c/o TV-am, London. Birthsign: Pisces. Hobbies: TV, gardening, golf.

GREENE, Michele

Actress, b. 13 February 1962, Los Angeles. After leaving school she enrolled in the University of Southern California Theatre Arts Department. Stage incl: *Dames at Sea; Once upon a Mattress; The Shadow Box.* TV incl: *Laverne and Shirley; Highway To Heaven; Simon and Simon; Bay City Blue; Seduced* (TVM); *Matlock; Perry Mason Returns;* as Abby Perkins in *L.A. Law.* Address: c/o McCartt-Oreck, Barrett, 9200 Sunset Blvd, Los Angeles, CA 90069. Birthsign: Aquarius. Hobbies. swimming, horseback riding, ballet, cooking, jewellery making. Pets: one dog.

GREENE, Sarah

Presenter/actress, b. 24 October, London. Started career in films and commercials as a child and after studying drama at Hull University. Played the lead role in *The Swish of the Curtain* in London. Then as presenter on BBC TV's *Blue Peter* for three years. Left in 1983 to join *Eureka* and *Saturday Superstore.* Many TV guest appearances. Won BBC's Top Lady On TV 1987. Presenter of *Going Live!; Posh Frocks and New Trousers.* Books incl: *We Can Say No!; The Multifacial Make-Up Book.* m. TV presenter Mike Smith. Address: c/o Michael Ladkin. Birthsign: Scorpio. Hobbies: motor racing, gardening, crosswords, Scrabble. **Most Cherished Possession:** 'My five senses, perhaps a sixth . . . all in working order . . . not forgetting the seventh – a sense of humour . . .' **Favourite Memory:** 'The London Marathon 1981 – when I met my best friend.'

GREGG, Anne

Journalist/travel writer, b. 11 February 1940, Belfast. Presenter of BBC 1's *Holiday* programme. Also travel editor for *Radio Times, Living* and *Catalyst* magazines. Has worked in news and current affairs television for Ulster TV and Anglia TV, and presented *Folio,* an arts series for Anglia. Written and presented many programmes for BBC Radio 4, from *Woman's Hour* to *In the Air.* Address: c/o Ken Wright, Quad Productions, 107 Nelson House, Dolphin Square, London SW1. Hobbies: painting, gardening, cookery. **Most Cherished Possession:** "Good health – nothing else matters very much.' **Favourite Memory:** 'Spending a night under canvas in the foothills of the Himalayas on the very spot where Prince Charles had camped!'

GRIER, Sheila

Actress, b. 11 February 1959, Glasgow. Trained at the Royal Scottish Academy of Music and Drama. Theatre incl: *Pals; Foodstuff; Babes In the Wood; Cinderella; Dick Whittington.* TV incl: *Take the High Road; The Odd Job Man; The End of the Line; Scotch and Wry; The United Shoelaces Show; Brookside; Bookie; Shadow On the Earth; Taggart; Making Out.* Address: c/o Felix de Wolfe. Birthsign: Aquarius. Hobbies: designer knitwear business, dancing, swimming. **Most Cherished Possession:** 'My family and friends.' **Favourite Memory:** 'The times I spent with my grandma.'

GRIFFITH, Andy

Actor, b. 1 June 1926, Mt Airy, North Carolina. Films incl: *No Time For Sergeants; A Face In the Crowd; Onionhead; Hearts of the West.* TV incl: *The Andy Griffith Show; Washington Behind Closed Doors; Winter Kill; Savages; Eagle One; Return to Mayberry; Fatal Vision; Centennial; From Here to Eternity; Salvage; Crime of Innocence; Under the Influence; Diary of a Perfect Murder;* Ben Matlock in *Matlock.* m. (1st) Barbara Edwards (dis.), (2nd) Solcia (dis.), (3rd) Cindi Knight; two children (from 1st m.). Address: c/o William Morris Agency, 151 El Camino Dr, Beverly Hills, CA 90212. Birthsign: Gemini. Hobbies: swimming, skeet and trap shooting, guitar-playing. **Most Cherished Possession:** 'My health. I'm now fully recovered from a rare disease that paralysed me up to my knees.'

GROOM, Simon

TV presenter, b. 12 August 1950, Derby. After University of Birmingham and a post graduate teacher training course worked as a teacher and night club disc jockey before joining BBC TV's *Blue Peter* as a presenter, which he has done for eight years. Presents TVS community programme *Action.* Appeared in *Aladdin* panto at Bournemouth during Christmas 1986. m. Ann. Address: c/o Michael Ladkin. Birthsign: Leo. Hobbies: classic cars, Derby County FC, playing drums, tennis, farming, Richard III Society. **Most Cherished Possession:** 'My *Bridge Over Troubled Water* album. It brings back happy memories of university.' **Favourite Memory:** 'Leading the Derby football team out on to the pitch in their centenary season in 1985 – I've supported them since I was a boy.'

GROTH, Michael

Presenter/musician/singer, b. 28 October, Ilkley, West Yorkshire. From 1972–82 was a solo guitarist/singer/songwriter, recorded with Blue Mink in 1976, formed the group Valentino in 1977, joined Trickster in 1979. Toured Europe with the group Boston. Wrote a hit single released in Germany and which reached No 35 in the charts. Joined BBC TV's *That's Life!* in 1982 as a presenter and stayed until 1985, when he became presenter of ITV's *Splash;* co-presenter *Hearts of Gold.* Address: c/o Fox, Concorde House, 1 Barb Mews, Brook Green, London W6 7PA. Birthsign: Scorpio. Hobbies: writing and recording music, tennis. **Most Cherished Possession:** 'Picture of my parents before they were married – they looked so happy before I came along!' **Favourite Memory:** 'Being young!'

GROUT, James

Actor, b. 22 October 1927, London. Trained at RADA and made his professional debut at the Old Vic 1950 in *Twelfth Night*. Theatre incl: three seasons at Stratford Memorial Theatre; *The Mousetrap; Ross; Half a Sixpence* (and on Broadway); *Flint; Straight Up; Lloyd George Knew My Father; 13 Rue de L'Amour; Make and Break; Sweet Bird of Youth; Way of the World; When We Are Married; The Mask of Moriarty.* TV incl: *The First Lady; Turtle's Progress; Diary of a Nobody; A Fine Romance; Reith; Cockles; Box of Delights; The Beiderbecke Affair; Yes Minister; No Place Like Home; Murder of a Moderate Man; Bust; Inspector Morse; Late Expectations.* m. Noreen. Address: c/o Crouch Salmon Assocs. Birthsign: Libra. Hobby: music. **Favourite Memory:** 'Working with Sir Ralph Richardson.'

GUARD, Christopher

Actor, b. 5 December 1953, London. No formal training but comes from a theatrical family. Theatre incl: National; RSC; and *Filumena* in London's West End. Films incl: *A Little Night Music; Memoirs of a Survivor; Loophole; Lord of the Rings.* TV incl: *David Copperfield* (title role); *Tom Brown's Schooldays; Vienna 1900; Wilfred and Eileen; My Cousin Rachel; A Woman of Substance; Return to Treasure Island; Blackeyes.* m. actress Lesley Dunlop; 2 d. Daisy, Rosie. Address: c/o Duncan Heath Associates. Birthsign: Sagittarius. Hobbies: watching Fulham FC, playing football, arranging and performing songs. Pets: three cats called Cat, Mouse and Baboon. **Most Cherished Possession:** 'My piano – it puts up with all my moods without complaint.' **Favourite Memory:** 'The birth of our first daughter!'

GUBBA, Tony

Sports commentator/broadcaster, b. 23 September 1943, Manchester. Started his career as a national newspaper journalist and then joined the BBC as correspondent in the north west. Has presented BBC sports programmes incl: *Grandstand; Sportsnight.* Commentator on *Match of the Day* and at both summer and winter Olympic Games and World Cups since 1974. m. (dis.); 2 d. Claire, Libby. Address: c/o *Sportsnight*, BBC TV, Kensington House, London. Birthsign: Libra/Virgo. Hobbies: squash, golf, all sport, DIY. **Most Cherished Possession:** 'My health.' **Favourite Memory:** 'Watching my children grow up.'

GUILLAUME, Robert

Actor/producer, b. 30 November, St Louis, Missouri. From choirboy at his local church he went on to study classical singing at Washington University. Sang in shows and festivals before appearing in *Porgy and Bess* and *Guys and Dolls* on Broadway. On TV played the wise-cracking butler in the comedy series *Soap* which led to his own spin-off series, *Benson*. Film: *Wanted: Dead Or Alive*. TV also incl: *The Kid With the 200 IQ; John Grin's Christmas; North and South*. m. (dis.); 3 children. Address: c/o William Morris Agency, 151 El Camino Drive, Beverly Hills, California 90212. Birthsign: Sagittarius. Hobbies: reading, piano, guitar, tennis. **Most Cherished Possession:** 'My BMW – we never had one in the ghetto.; **Favourite Memory:** 'Benson getting his own series.'

GUINNESS, Sir Alec, CBE

Actor, b. 2 April 1914, London. Advertising copy writer until scholarship to Fay Compton School of Dramatic Art. More than 60 stage plays, incl: *The Brothers Karamazov* (his own adaptation); *A Voyage Round My Father; The Old Country; The Merchant of Venice*. Films incl: *Great Expectations; Oliver Twist; Kind Hearts and Coronets; The Lavender Hill Mob; The Lady Killers; The Horse's Mouth; The Bridge On the River Kwai* (British Film Academy and Oscar awards); *Lawrence of Arabia; Doctor Zhivago; Scrooge; Star Wars; The Empire Strikes Back; A Passage To India; Little Dorrit*. TV incl: *Tinker, Tailor, Soldier, Spy; Smiley's People; Edwin; Monsignor Quixote*. m. Merula Salaman; 1 s. Matthew. Address: c/o London Management.

GUTHRIE, Gwyneth

Actress, b. 28 April 1936. Ayr, Scotland. Trained at the Royal Scottish Academy of Music and Drama, Glasgow. Theatre incl: *For Love Or For Money* (tour with Jimmy Logan); poetry readings at the Edinburgh Festival. Films incl: *Privilege; Years Ahead*. Played Mary Queen of Scots in radio serial. TV incl: *Sutherland's Law; Hill O' the Red Fox; Degree of Uncertainty; The Lost Tribe; The Reunion; The Prime of Miss Jean Brodie; Something's Got To Give;* Mrs Mack in *Take the High Road*. m. John Borland; 3 d. Karen, Debbie, Olwen. Address: c/o Scottish TV. Birthsign: Taurus. Hobbies: writing, music, gardening. Pets: three cats, one pony, one tortoise. **Most Cherished Possession:** 'A china Victorian doll given to me by my Auntie Daisy after my first stage appearance, aged four.'

GUTTERIDGE, Lucy

Actress, b. 28 November 1956, London. Trained at Central School of Speech and Drama, London. Theatre incl: *The Real Thing; A King of Alaska* (Los Angeles); *King Arthur* (opera, Buxton Theatre Festival). Films incl: *The Greek Tycoon; Merlin and the Sword; Trouble With Spies; Fire In Eden*. TV incl: *The Hitchhiker; The Devil's Crown; The Marrying Kind; End of Season; Love In a Cold Climate; Seven Dials Mystery; Nicholas Nickleby; Edge of the Wind; Till We Meet Again.* m. Andrew Hawkins (dis.); 1 d. Isabella. Address: c/o William Morris. Birthsign: Sagittarius. Hobbies: reading, walking, drawing, physical activities, people. Pets: three cats, one goldfish. **Most Cherished Possession:** 'Photographs or paintings – they instantly remind me of what, and who, I love.'

HADDY, Anne

Actress, b. 5 October, Quorn, South Australia. Nearly 40 years' broadcasting experience in Australia and has appeared in many Sydney theatres plus the occasional film. One of the first *Playschool* presenters. TV incl: Helen Daniels in *Neighbours*. m. 1st Max Dimmitt, 2nd actor James Condon; 1 s. Tony, 1 d. Jane (from 1st m.). Address: c/o Channel 10, Nunawading, Melbourne 3131, Victoria, Australia. Birthsign: Libra. Hobbies: walking, cooking. **Most Cherished Possession:** 'My husband and life, but not necessarily in that order.' **Favourite Memory:** 'My second wedding, which pleased the grandchildren.'

HAGMAN, Larry

Actor, b. 21 September 1930, Fort Worth, Texas. Trained at the Margo Jones Theatre, Dallas. Made professional debut in *The Taming of the Shrew*. Films incl: *Three In the Cellar; Harry and Tonto; The Eagle Has Landed; S.O.B.* TV incl: *Edge of Night; I Dream of Jeannie;* J R Ewing in *Dallas* (and executive producer since 1988). m. designer Maj Axelsson; 1 d. Kristina Mary, 1 s. Preston. Address: c/o Richard Grant, Beverly Hills, California. Hobbies: skiing, backpacking, fishing, sailing, touring, collecting hats and flags. **Most Cherished Possession:** 'The hot tub my wife designed. Life should be filled with sensual pleasures.' **Favourite Memory:** 'Seeing car bumper stickers J R For President outnumbering those for Carter and Reagan.'

HAID, Charles

Actor/producer, b. 2 June, Palo Alto, California. Directed plays in repertory before becoming an actor. Stage incl: *Elizabeth The First*. Films incl: *The Choirboys; Who'll Stop the Train; Oliver's Story; Altered States; The House of God;* exec. producer of *Square Dance*. TV incl: *A Death in Canaan; Divorce Wars; Hill Street Blues*. Co-produced the Emmy-winning *Who Are the Debolts and Where Did They Get 19 Kids?* Two Emmy nominations for *Hill Street Blues*. m. (1st) Penny, (2nd) actress Debi Richter; 2 d. Arcadia, Brittany (from 1st m.). Address: c/o Writers and Artists Agency, 11726 San Vicente Blvd, Los Angeles 90049. Birthsign: Gemini. Hobbies: surfing, sailing, horse riding. **Most Cherished Possession:** 'My two children.' **Favourite Memory:** 'My grandfather's flower garden.'

HAILES, Gary

Actor, b. 4 November 1965, North London. Trained at the Anna Scher Theatre. Theatre incl: *Doctor On the Boil; Aladdin; Jack and the Beanstalk.* Films incl: *Murder With Mirrors; Revolution.* TV incl: *Pinnochio; Nobody's Hero; Grange Hill; Contact; Born and Bred; The Other One; EastEnders.* Address: c/o Spotlight. Birthsign: Scorpio. Hobbies: swimming, reading, listening and dancing to rock'n'roll, running five to 10 miles a day. Pet: miniature Yorkshire terrier called Benji.

HALE, Gareth

Comedian/'creative force', b. 15 January 1953, London. Previously a teacher. Formed a double act with Norman Pace. TV: *Pushing Up Daisies; Coming Next; The Young Ones; Live From The Palladium;* host of *Saturday Live; Just For Laughs; The Saturday Gang; The Management;* 1987 Royal Variety Performance; *Hale & Pace* (1989 Golden Rose of Montreux winner). Books (with Norman Pace): *Falsies; The Hale & Pace Book of Writes and Rons.* LP: *Hale & Pace Live In Concert.* m. Deborah; 2 d. Sian, Cara. Address: c/o International Artistes. Birthsign: Capricorn. Hobbies: 'Too damn busy.' Pets: 'As often as possible.' **Most Cherished Possession:** 'Nothing in particular.' **Favourite Memory:** 'Waking up this morning.'

HAMEL, Veronica

Actress, b. Philadelphia. Worked as a model before becoming an actress. She has been nominated five times for an Emmy as an outstanding lead actress in a drama series. Stage incl: *The Big Knife; The Ballad of Boris K; Cactus Flower; The Miracle Worker.* Films incl: *Beyond the Poseidon Adventure; When Time Ran Out; Cannonball.* TV incl: *The Rockford Files; Kojak; Dallas; Starsky and Hutch; The Gathering; 79 Park Avenue; Hill Street Blues; Valley of the Dolls; Kane and Abel; Twist of Fate.* m. (dis.) to actor Michael Irving. Address: c/o ICM, Los Angeles. Hobbies: tennis, cooking, gardening. Pets: cat named Black. **Favourite Memory:** 'I loved fashion modelling. It was wonderful, lucrative and I kept my anonymity.'

HAMILTON, Linda

Actress, b. 26 September 1957, Salisbury, Maryland, USA. Studied acting in New York, attending workshops at the Lee Strasberg Theater Institute, then worked with a children's theatre group. Films: *King Kong Lives; T.A.G. – The Assassination Game; The Terminator; Children of the Corn; Black Moon Rising.* TV movies: *Rape and Marriage; The Rideout Case; Country Gold; Towards the Light; Secret Weapons.* TV: *Search For Tomorrow; King's Crossing; Hill Street Blues;* Catherine in *Beauty and the Beast.* m. actor Bruce Abbott; 1 s. Dalton. Address: c/o Triad Artists, 10100 Santa Monica Blvd, 16th Floor, Los Angeles, California 90067. Birthsign: Libra. Hobbies: scrabble, horse riding, relaxing, interior decorating. Pet: one dog, a German shepherd–St Bernard crossbreed.

HAMILTON, Suzanna

Actress, b. 1960. Trained at the Anna Scher Theatre School and the Central School of Music and Drama. Theatre incl: *The Real Thing; The Oven Glove; My Sister In This House; Siblings.* Films: *Swallows and Amazons* (aged 12); *Wild Cats of St Trinian's; Tess; Brimstone and Treacle;* Julia in *Nineteen Eighty-Four; Wetherby; Out of Africa.* TV incl: *Wish Me Luck; Streetwise; Small Zones; Murder East, Murder West.* Address: c/o Markham & Froggatt.

HAMLIN, Harry

Actor, b. 1951, Pasenda, California. Trained at the University of California at Berkeley, Yale Drama School and the American Conservatory Theatre. Stage incl: *Equus; Hamlet.* Films incl: *Movie Movie; Clash of the Titans; Making Love; King of the Mountains.* TV incl: *Studs Lonigan; Master of the Game; Space; L.A. Law.* Won People Magazine's Sexiest Man Alive title for 1987. m. former *Falcon Crest* actress Laura Johnson (sep.); 1 s. Dimitri (from relationship with Ursula Andress). Address: c/o William Morris Agency, Beverly Hills. Pets: cat named Meno. **Most Cherished Possession:** 'My black 911 Porsche.' **Favourite Memory:** 'The birth of my son Dimitri.'

HAMPSHIRE, Susan

Actress, b. 12 May 1942, London. Has been in over 50 plays and 30 films. TV incl: *What Katy Did; The Pallisers; The Forsyte Saga; Barchester Chronicles; Leaving; Going To Pot.* Books: *Susan's Story: The Maternal Instinct; Lucy Jane On Television; Trouble Free Gardening; Every Letter Counts.* m. Eddie Kulukundis; 1 s. Christopher, 1 d. Victoria (dec.). Address: c/o Chatto & Linnit. Birthsign: Taurus. Hobbies: gardening, writing.

HAMPTON, Meryl

Actress, b. 26 August 1952, Chester. Trained at Guildhall School of Music and Drama, followed by two years at Sheffield's Crucible Theatre where she appeared in *Charley's Aunt; Equus; Joseph and the Technicolor Dreamcoat.* Other rep stage incl: *Lucy; Harry Mixture; Lock Up Your Daughters; The Rivals; Love On the Dole; Under Milk Wood; Having a Ball; Season's Greetings; Breaking and Entering; In Dreams.* TV incl: *Softly, Softly; Knock For Knock; Letty; The GP's; Death of the Heart; Crossroads; Brookside; Casualty; First and Last; Listen To Me.* Address: c/o Sue Hammer Management, Otterbourne House, Chobham Road, Ottershaw, Chertsey, Surrey KT16 0QF, tel (0932) 874111. Hobbies: horse racing, walking. Pets: two cats. **Most Cherished Possession:** 'My friends.'

HANN, Judith

Writer/presenter, b. 8 September 1942, Littleover, Derby. BSc. in zoology at Durham University. Trained as a journalist with Westminster Press. Freelance for BBC TV incl: *Tomorrow's World.* Books incl: *But What About the Children?; Family Scientist; The Perfect Baby?; Judith Hann's Total Health Plan; The Food of Love.* Twice winner of Glaxo Award for science writers. m. TV news editor John Exelby; 2 s. Jake, Daniel. Address: c/o BBC TV, London, or Dave Winslett Entertainments. Birthsign: Virgo. Hobbies: cooking, walking. Pets: two dogs, one cat. **Most Cherished Possession:** 'My family.'

HARDY, Robert, CBE

Actor, b. 29 October 1925, Cheltenham. Began career with the Royal Shakespeare Company. First TV as *David Copperfield,* and in *The Troubleshooters.* Theatre incl: *Dear Liar,* musical *Winnie.* Films incl: *The Spy Who Came In From the Cold; Ten Rillington Place; Young Winston; The Shooting Party.* TV incl: *Elizabeth R.; Upstairs, Downstairs; The Duchess of Duke Street; Horses and Blood; All Creatures Great and Small; Twelfth Night; Fothergill; Winston Churchill – The Wilderness Years; The Demon Lover; The Cleopatras; The Death of the Heart; Hot Metal.* m. (1st) (dis.), (2nd) Sally Cooper (dis.); 2 d. Emma, Justine, 1 s. Paul. Address: c/o Chatto & Linnit, London. Birthsign: Scorpio. Hobbies: horses, archery.

HARRIS, Rolf

Entertainer/singer/songwriter/musician/artist/cartoonist, b. 30 March 1930, Perth, Australia. Started career by winning radio talent competition in 1949. Came to Britain in 1952. First stage appearance was in *One Under The Eight;* then *Talk of the Town; Royal Variety Performance.* TV incl: *Rolf's Walkabout; Hey Presto, It's Rolf; The Rolf Harris Show; Rolf On Saturday, OK?; Cartoon Time; Rolf's Cartoon Club.* Records incl: *Tie Me Kangaroo Down Sport; Sun Arise; Jake the Peg; Two Little Boys.* m. sculptress Alwen Hughes; 1 d. Bindi. Address: c/o Billy Marsh Assocs. Birthsign: Aries. Hobbies: painting, making jewellery, collecting rocks, woodwork, photography. **Most Cherished Possession:** 'The oil paintings of my family.' **Favourite Memory:** 'The happiest childhood imaginable.'

HART, Tony

Artist, b. 15 October 1925, Maidstone, Kent. After the Second World War, he finished his art training and worked as a display designer in London. Since going freelance, he has worked as a graphic artist and TV presenter of *Saturday Special; Playbox; In Town Tonight; Vision On; Take Hart* (BAFTA award, 1983), *Hartbeat.* m. Jean; 1 d. Carolyn. Hobbies: garden stonework, cooking, wine. Address: c/o Roc Renals, 10 Heatherway, Crowthorne, Berkshire RG11 6HG, tel (0344) 77638. Birthsign: Libra.

HARTMAN, Kim

Actress, b. 11 January 1955, London. Training: ASM at Belgrade Theatre, Coventry, for a year before going to the Webber Douglas Academy. Then rep. Stage incl: *The Cherry Orchard; Billy Liar; Hobson's Choice; Hay Fever; 'Allo 'Allo!;* toured Far and Middle East twice with *Move Over Mrs Markham.* Radio incl: *Lord Sky; Jamaica Inn.* TV incl: *The Peddlar* (Play For Today); *Kelly Monteith Show; 'Allo 'Allo!.* m. John Nolan; 1 s. Tom, 1 d. Miranda. Address: c/o Lou Coulson. Birthsign: Capricorn. Hobbies: antiques, painting, gardening, walking the dogs. Pets: two dogs, three cats. **Most Cherished Possession:** 'My springer spaniel, Junkyard, because he's always happy.' **Favourite Memory:** 'Going to the zoo with my grandfather in a London taxi when I was four.'

HARVEY, Jan

Actress, b. Penzance, Cornwall. Product of Homerton College, Cambridge. TV incl: *Sam; Bill Brand; A Family Affair; Second Chance; Edward VII; Old Men at the Zoo; Fell Tiger;* Jan Howard in *Howards' Way* (six series). Address: c/o Brunskill Management. Birthsign: Gemini.

HARVEY-WRIGHT, Peter

Actor, b. 4 December 1946, Melbourne, Australia. Trained at Victoria College. Stage incl: *HMS Pinafore; The Pearl Fishers; Return of Ulysees; Romeo and Juliet; Mother Courage;* plus pantomime and revues. Films incl: *Ground Zero; Ready Or Not; Below the Belt; Son of Alvin.* TV incl: *The Sullivans; Whose Baby?; Anzacs; Flying Doctors; Special Squad; Carson's Law; Neighbours; Prisoner: Cell Block H; The Henderson Kids.* Radio incl: *Don't Get Off Your Bike.* m. Marijke; 1 d. Nicole, 1 s. Luke. Address: c/o Barry Michael Artists, 14a Nelson St, Balaclava. Birthsign: Sagittarius. Hobbies: piano, tennis. **Most Cherished Possession:** 'Life – I wouldn't be dead for quids!' **Favourite Memory:** 'All of them – because I was younger then!'

HASSELHOFF, David

Actor, b. 17 July 1953, Baltimore. Trained at the Academy of Dramatic Arts, New York, and California Institute of the Arts. Films incl: *Starcrash*. TV incl: Michael Knight in *Knightrider; Griffin & Phoenix;* Lt Mitch Bucannon in *Baywatch*. Albums: *Lovin' Feelings; Knight Rocker; Looking For Freedom*. Awards incl: People's Choice, 1983; US Magazine's Teen Idol, 1984; Hispanic Award for Best TV Actor, 1985. m. 1st Catherine Hickland (dis.), 2nd Pamela Bach. Address: c/o Jan McCormack, 11342 Dona Lisa Drive, Studio City, California 91604. Hobbies: singing, deep-sea diving, tennis, water-skiing, car racing, pumping iron. Pets: six dogs, six birds and three cats. **Favourite Memory:** 'My Hawaiian honeymoon.'

HAVERS, Nigel

Actor, b. 6 November 1949, London. Broke family tradition of going into law (father was the Attorney General). Trained at Arts Educational Trust. Was Billy Owen in *The Dales* on radio, researcher on *Jimmy Young Show* before TV in *Comet Among the Stars*. Title role *Nicholas Nickleby*. Theatre incl: *Man and Superman; Season's Greetings*. Films incl: *Chariots of Fire; A Passage To India; The Whistle Blower; Empire of the Sun; Burke and Wills; Farewell to the King*. TV incl: *Goodbye Darling; Unity; Winston Churchill – The Wilderness Years; Nancy Astor; After the Party; Strangers and Brothers; The Death of the Heart; Don't Wait Up; The Charmer; Hold the Dream.* m. 1st Carolyn (dis.), 2nd Polly; 1 d. Kate. Address: c/o Michael Whitehall. Birthsign: Scorpio. Hobbies: golf, sport, reading.

HAWKINS, Carol

Actress, b. 31 January 1949, Barnet, Herts. Trained at Corona Stage School. London stage incl: *Sextet; Run For Your Wife; See How They Run; Wife Begins At Forty; The Undertaking;* and incl tours *Time and Time Again; Bedroom Farce; Wait Until Dark; Dirty Linen*. Films incl: *Please Sir; Bless This House; Not Now Comrade;* plus the *Carry On* films. TV incl: *The Fenn Street Gang; The Two Ronnies; Please Sir; Mr Big; My Husband and I; All At No 20; Carry On Laughing; Porridge; Blake's Seven; Bloomfield; See How They Run; C.A.T.S. Eyes.* m. Martyn Padbury. Address: c/o Joan Reddin. Birthsign: Aquarius. Hobbies: painting, gardening, reading, writing. Pets: two cats.

HAWTHORNE, Nigel

Actor, b. 5 April 1929, Coventry. First professional appearance in London in 1951. Stage incl: *Privates On Parade; Uncle Vanya; Otherwise Engaged; Tartuffe; The Magistrate; Across From the Garden of Allah; Hapgood; Shadowlands.* Films incl: *Gandhi; Firefox; The Chain; King of the Wind.* TV incl: *Yes Minister; Mapp and Lucia; Jenny's War; The House; Marie Curie; The Knowledge; Tartuffe; Yes, Prime Minister; The Miser; The Shawl; Relatively Speaking*. Awards incl: Clarence Derwent and SWET for *Privates On Parade;* Broadcasting Press Guild Award and BAFTA (1981 and 1982) for *Yes Minister; Yes, Prime Minister* (1986 and 1987). Address: c/o Ken McReddie. Hobbies: writing, painting, gardening, photography, sport. **Most Cherished Possession:** 'Health.' **Favourite Memory:** 'My first visit to Venice.'

HAYES, Leila

Actress/entertainer, b. Victoria, Australia. Trained at the Natalie Raine School of Drama. TV incl: *20 Good Years; Power Without Glory; Through the Looking Glass Darkly; Red Riding Hood; Sons and Daughters* (won a Penguin award for her role as Beryl Palmer); *A Country Practice*. 1 d. Melissa Jane. Hobbies: oil painting, writing, reading, sketching, needlework, swimming. Pets: one dog, one cat. Address: c/o Bedford & Pearce, 2 Portman Place, 263–269 Alfred Street North, North Sydney 2060, Australia. **Most Cherished Possession:** 'My collection of family photos and mementoes – I'm a compulsive hoarder.' **Favourite Memory:** 'The first time I held my baby daughter – a feeling of total wonder and closeness to God.'

HAYES, Melvyn

Actor, b. 11 January 1935, London. Started doing the Indian rope trick at the Comedy Theatre, London. London stage incl: *Apple of Eve; South; Change For the Angel; Spring and Port Wine*. Recent work incl: *Run For Your Wife* (tour); *Wind In the Willows* (Sadlers Wells); *The Dresser* (tour). Films incl: *Violent Background; No Trees In the Street; The Young Ones; Summer Holiday; Wonderful Life; King of the Wind*. TV incl: *Oliver Twist; The Unloved; The Silver Sword; It Ain't Half Hot Mum;* resident judge, *Sky Star Search;* voice of Skeleton in *SuperTed*. m. actress Wendy Padbury; 4 d. Sacha, Talla, Joanna, Charlotte, 1 s. Damian. Address: c/o Spotlight. Hobbies: breathing, meeting people in the street who ask questions like 'Didn't you used to be Melvyn Hayes?'

HAYES, Patricia

Actress, b. 22 December, London. Trained at RADA. Has probably worked with more comics than any other British actress. Theatre incl: *Twelfth Night; Habeas Corpus; Liza of Lambeth; Filumena; True West; Major Barbara; When We Are Married; House of Bernarda Alba*. Films incl: *Love Thy Neighbour; The Never Ending Story; Little Dorrit; Willow; A Fish Called Wanda; The Last Island; The Fool*. TV incl: *Edna, The Inebriate Woman; Tea Ladies; Till Death Us Do Part; Spooner's Patch; The Lady Is a Tramp; Winter Sunlight; Marjorie and Men; Mr Pye; Mrs Capper's Birthday; Our Lady Blue*. m. actor Valentine Brooke (dis.); 2 d. Teresa, Gemma, 1 s. actor Richard O'Callaghan. Address: c/o Hazel De Leon. Birthsign: Sagittarius. Hobbies: housework, gardening.

HAYTON, Philip

Reporter/presenter, b. 2 November 1947, Keighley, Yorkshire. Began his broadcasting career as pirate radio DJ before moving to BBC Radio Leeds. Since 1974 he has been a reporter for BBC TV News, covering the Iran Revolution; Rhodesia; Cod War; in Argentina during Falklands War; Beirut; Northern Ireland; African Famine; Seychelles Attempted Coup; and Southern Africa correspondent 1980–83. Since 1988, he has presented BBC TV's *One O'Clock News*, as well as the *Six O'Clock News* and *Nine O'Clock News*. m. Thelma; 1 s. James, 1 d. Julia. Address: c/o BBC TV News, London. Birthsign: Scorpio. Hobbies: walking, sailing, theatre. **Favourite Memory:** 'Too busy with today and tomorrow to think about the past.'

HAZLEGROVE, Jane

Actress, b. 17 July 1968, Manchester. Theatre incl: *The Crucible; Soapbox; To Kill a Mockingbird; All In Good Time; Fangs*. TV: *Picture Friend; Lovebirds; Threads; Travelling Man;* Sue Clayton in *Coronation Street;* Debbie Taylor in *Albion Market; Made In Heaven; Who's Our Little Jenny Lind; The Book Tower; How We Used To Live;* WPC Madeline Forest in *Waterfront Beat;* Rosie in *Making Out;* Alison Gibson in Channel Four film *Shooting Stars*. Also, numerous BBC radio plays. Address: c/o Inter-City Casting. Hobbies: reading, photography, travel. **Most Cherished Possession:** 'My ragdoll, Jemima! I've owned her for years and she knows all my secrets!' **Favourite Memory:** 'Christmas 1973. It's the first one I remember and it was magical!'

HEALY, Tim

Actor/comedian, b. 29 January 1952, Newcastle-upon-Tyne. Recent TV incl: *A Perfect Spy; Highway; Tickle On the Tum; A Kind of Living; Auf Wiedersehen, Pet*. Address: c/o Duncan Heath. Birthsign: Aquarius. Hobbies: golf, snooker. **Most Cherished Possession:** 'A special guitar.' **Favourite Memory:** 'Santa Claus.'

HEINEY, Paul

Writer/broadcaster, b. 20 April 1949, Sheffield. Film: *Water*. Radio: appearances on BBC Radios 2, 4. Books: three. TV; *That's Life; The Big Time; In at the Deep End; The Travel Show; What On Earth Is Going On?*m. Libby Purves; 1 s. Nicholas, 1 d. Rose. Address: c/o Jo Gurnett. Birthsign: Aries. Hobbies: sailing, horse driving, vegetable growing. **Most Cherished Possession:** 'My old wooden wheelbarrow because it has seen better plants than I will probably ever grow.' **Favourite Memory:** 'The first foreign landfall seen from the deck of my own yacht.'

HELVIN, Marie

Fashion model/TV personality, b. 13 August, Tokyo, Japan. Grew up in Hawaii. Father American of French/Danish descent, mother Japanese. Started modelling in Tokyo. Worked all over the world for leading designers and photographers. Film: *The Children*. TV presenter of *Frocks On the Box*. Book: *Catwalk – The Art of Model Style*. Regularly comments for press, radio and TV on fashion, beauty and style. Address: c/o IMG. Birthsign: Leo. Hobbies: going home to Hawaii. Pets: two cats, Sheba Lee, Susu. **Most Cherished Possession:** 'Memories of my late sister, Suzon Lee Helvin.' **Favourite Memory:** 'My first glimpse of Moorea, sailing in Cook Bay from Papeete, Tahiti – one of the most beautiful sights in the world.'

HENDERSON, Don

Actor/author/programme deviser/producer/director, b. 10 November 1932, London. An amateur actor until the age of 38, when he joined the Royal Shakespeare Company (1966–72). Films incl: *A Midsummer Night's Dream; Brazil; Squaring the Circle; Billy the Kid and the Green Baize Vampire; Baron Munchausen; Outlaws*. TV incl: *The Protectors; Crown Court; Warship; Poldark; New Scotland Yard; Softly, Softly; Dixon of Dock Green; The XYY Man; Van Der Valk; Crossroads; Angels; Strangers; The Enigma Files; The Onedin Line; Jemima Shore Investigates; Bottle Boys; Annika; Bulman; Knights of God; Dead Head; Dempsey and Makepeace; Doctor Who; Hot Metal; Minder; Last of the Summer Wine; Making Out; Maigret; The Paradise Club*. m. 1st Hilary (dec.), 2nd actress Shirley Stelfox; 1 d. Louise, 1 s. Ian (from 1st m.), 1 step-d. Helena. Address: c/o AIM.

HENRY, Lenny

Stand-up comedian/character actor, b. 29 August 1958, Dudley, Worcs. TV debut on *New Faces* in 1975 when he was 16. Has since appeared in venues all over the country. Films: *Lenny Henry Live and Unleashed; Double Take*. TV incl: *The Fosters; Tiswas;* award-winning *Three of a Kind; OTT;* first British host of *Saturday Live; Royal Variety Performances; Lenny Henry Tonite; Coast To Coast; The Suicide Club; Just Like That!; The Comic Strip Presents . . . Oxford*. m. comedienne Dawn French. Address: c/o Robert Luff, 294 Earls Court Road, London SW5 9BB. Birthsign: Virgo. Hobbies: music and reading. **Favourite Memory:** 'Winning on *New Faces*.'

HENSON, Nicky

Actor, b. 12 May 1945, London. Trained at RADA as a stage manager. First London appearance was in a revue, *All Square*, followed by *Camelot* at Drury Lane. Has since played a variety of parts in revue, musicals and as a member of the Young Vic. Other theatre incl: *She Stoops To Conquer; Measure For Measure; Look Back In Anger; Man and Superman; Noises Off; Seasons* with RSC. Films incl: *There's a Girl in My Soup; The Bawdy Adventures of Tom Jones*. TV incl: *Prometheus* series; *Seagull Island; Chains; Absurd Person Singular; Tropical Moon Over Dorking; Season's Greetings; Love After Lunch; Thin Air; Inspector Morse; Startrap*. m. (1st) actress Una Stubbs (dis.), (2nd) Marguerite Porter; 3 s. Christian, Joe, Keaton. Address: c/o Richard Stone. Hobby: motorcycling. **Most Cherished Possession:** 'Bed.'

HERRIMAN, Damon

Actor, b. 31 March 1970, Adelaide, South Australia. He started his acting career at the age of nine in the stage play *Auntie Mame*, and a year later landed a part in TV's *The Sullivans*. He has also made various documentaries and radio plays for the Australian Broadcasting Corporation. Film: *Call Me Mr Brown*. Other TV incl: *The Patchwork Hero; Sara Dane; For The Term Of His Natural Life; Taurus Rising*. Address: c/o Stacey Testro Management, South Melbourne. Birthsign: Aries. Hobbies: playing cricket, watching television. Pets: German Shepherd dog, Sheeba. **Most Cherished Possession:** 'My photo albums because they are irreplaceable.' **Favourite Memory:** 'Working in my first television series, *The Sullivans*, in 1980.'

HESKETH-HARVEY, Kit

Writer/musical performer, b. 30 April 1957, Malawi, Cent. Africa. Was a Canterbury Cathedral chorister and member of Cambridge University Footlights. In 1980 became a BBC music and arts researcher, while appearing in cabaret, *Kit and the Widow*. TV incl: *Royal Variety Performance; Live From The Palladium; Des O'Connor Live; Bob Monkhouse Show; Wogan; 3-2-1*. Was screenwriter for film *Maurice* (1987) and also lyricist for *Orlando* (1987). m. to actress Katie Rabett; 1 d. Augusta. Address: c/o London Management. Birthsign: Taurus. Hobbies: gardening, riding, cooking. Pets: Tibetan Terrier named Throwback. **Most Cherished Possession:** 'My grandmother's Bechstein piano, carried by 20 coolies through the Chinese jungle after she eloped to Shanghai.'

HEYLAND, Rob

Actor, b. 2 April 1954, London. Trained at the Central School of Speech and Drama. After appearing in *Trafford Tanzi* at the Manchester Contact Theatre, he landed the part of Donald in BBC's *One By One*. Theatre incl: *A Man For All Seasons; Funny Peculiar; Three Sisters; Romeo and Juliet* with the RSC. TV incl: *Murphy's Mob; Reilly – Ace of Spies; The Professionals; Charles & Diana: A Royal Love Story* (TVM). m. Victoria; 3 d. Florence, Lily, Clemency, 1 s. Alfred. Address: c/o Fergus Dillon Management, Middle Littleton Manor, Worcestershire WR11 5LN. Hobby: landscape design. Pets: dog, cats, ducks, peacocks, hens, horses. **Most Cherished Possession:** 'A landscape in oils by George Charlton.' **Favourite Memory:** 'A beach in the west of Ireland, at spring-time, with my wife and children.'

HICKSON, Joan

Actress, b. 5 August 1906, Kingsthorpe, Northampton. Stage debut 1927 in *His Wife's Children;* West End debut 1928 in *The Tragic Muse*. Since then has worked consistently in theatre, film and TV and is one of Britain's most distinguished character actresses. Recent theatre incl: *A Day In the Death of Joe Egg; Forget Me Not Lane; The Card; Bedroom Farce* (also New York); *On the Razzle* (National Theatre). Films incl: *The Guinea Pig; Seven Days To Noon; Yanks; The Wicked Lady*. Numerous TV credits incl: *Nanny; Good Girl; Great Expectations; Poor Little Rich Girls; Time For Murder;* as Miss Marple in BBC Agatha Christie series. Address: c/o Plunkett Greene, 4 Ovington Gardens, London SW3 1LS, tel 071-584 0688. Birthsign: Leo.

HIGHMORE, Edward

Actor, b. 3 April 1961, Kingston-upon-Thames. Went into acting after failing to make the grade for his chosen career, in forestry. After brief stints and in rep, he went straight into television work. TV incl: *Tripods; Lame Ducks; Doctor Who; Howards' Way*. Address: c/o Spotlight. Birthsign: Aries. **Most Cherished Possession:** 'I'm not particularly possessive. I cherish my partner, Sue Latimer, most.

HILL, Benny

Comedian, b. 21 January 1925, Southampton. Started in working men's clubs and in variety and summer shows. Stage debut in 1941 in *Stars In Battledress*. Also *Paris By Night; Fine Fettle*. Films incl: *The Italian Job; Chitty Chitty Bang Bang; Those Magnificent Men in Their Flying Machines*. TV: own shows for which he writes all his own scripts and music. Elected to TV Hall of Fame, *TVTimes*, 1978–79. Voted Funniest Man on TV 1981–82 by *TVTimes* readers. Address: c/o Richard Stone. Birthsign: Aquarius. Hobby: travel. **Most Cherished Possession:** 'My British passport.' **Favourite Memory:** 'Being taken at the age of 10 to a local variety theatre by my grandfather.'

HILL, Jimmy

Presenter, b. 22 July 1928, Balham, London. Professional footballer with Brentford and Fulham; PFA chairman, 1957; manager of Coventry City, 1961; became head of London Weekend's sports unit, 1967; joined BBC in 1973; Chairman of Fulham FC 1987. TV incl: *World of Sport; The Big Match; Grandstand; Match of the Day*. m. (1st) Gloria (dis.), (2nd) Heather (dis.); 2 d. Alison, Joanna (one from each marriage), 3 s. Duncan, Graham, Jamie (2 from 1st m., 1 from 2nd m.). Address: c/o BBC TV, London. Birthsign: Leo. Hobbies: golf, tennis, riding, bridge. Pets: Yellow Labrador called George. **Most Cherished Possession:** 'My own home in Sussex.' **Favourite Memory:** 'The day in 1966 when England won the World Cup.'

HILL, Rose

Actress/singer, b. 5 June 1914, London. Studied at the Guildhall School of Music and Drama. Theatre incl: *The Marriage of Figaro; The Beggar's Opera; The Three Sisters;* the award-winning *Nicholas Nickleby; On the Razzle*. Film incl: *Heavens Above; For the Love of Ada; Every Good Home Should Have One; Footsteps*. TV incl: *Dixon of Dock Green; The Barber of Stamford Hill; Take a Sapphire; The Wild Geese; Benbow Was His Name; The Three Sisters; Caring; 'Allo 'Allo!; Strangers; The Bill; Press Gang; Murder East, Murder West*. m. J C Davis (dec.); 1 s. John. Address: c/o Richard Stone. Birthsign: Gemini. Hobbies: gardening, needlework, art, yoga. **Most Cherished Possession:** 'My Worshipful Company of Musicians silver medal.' **Favourite Memory:** 'Being pregnant and being able to sing in opera up to five months!'

HILLERMAN, John

Actor, b. 20 December, Denison, Texas. Trained at American Theater Wing, New York, and Theater Club, Washington. Films incl: *The Last Picture Show; Paper Moon; The Naked Ape; The Thief Who Came To Dinner; High Plains Drifter; Blazing Saddles; Chinatown; Sunburn*. TV incl: *Ellery Queen; One Day At a Time; Tales of the Brass Monkey; Magnum; Assault and Matrimony* (TVM); and many guest appearances. Address: c/o McCartt-Oreck Barrett. Birthsign: Capricorn. Hobbies: caviar, electronic toys. **Most Cherished Possession:** 'My accent. It gets me sophisticated, suave parts.' **Favourite Memory:** 'My years on *Magnum*. It's tough living in a luxury home in Hawaii, only yards from the Pacific surf.'

HINDLE, Madge

Actress, b. 19 May 1938, Blackburn, Lancashire. Spent her early days in amateur theatre. Recent theatre incl: *Elsie and Norm's Macbeth*. TV incl: Lily in *Nearest & Dearest;* Renee Roberts in *Coronation Street* (1976–80); *Play For Today; The Two Ronnies; Cannon and Ball; Mr and Mrs Edgehill; Lost Empires*. m. solicitor Michael Hindle (for 25 years); 2 d. Charlotte, Frances. Address: c/o Sandra Griffin. Birthsign: Taurus. Hobbies: gardening, reading, entertaining friends. **Most Cherished Possession:** 'My dishwasher.' **Favourite Memory:** 'The 1961 Edinburgh Festival, which changed my career. I went from teacher to actress.'

HINES, Frazer

Actor, b. 22 September 1944, Horsforth, Yorkshire. A student of the Corona Academy, he started in the 'business' at the age of eight. By the time he was 15 he had appeared in six films. Stage incl: *A King in New York; Happy Birthday; Hedda Gabler; On the Razzle*. Films incl: *Zeppelin; The Last Valley*. TV incl: *Emmerdale* (since its start in 1972); *Doctor Who; Duty Free; Doctor In the House*. m. actress Gemma Craven (dis.). Address: c/o Peter Charlesworth, London. Birthsign: Virgo. Hobbies: amateur jockey, horse breeding, cricket for the Lord's Taverners. **Most Cherished Possession:** 'My horse, Excavator Lady, who has given me so much pleasure as a jockey.' **Favourite Memory:** 'Working with Charlie Chaplin – no it wasn't a silent movie!'

HINGE (Dr Evadne) and BRACKET (Dame Hilda)

Female impersonators since 1972. Many guest appearances on TV and own series *Dear Ladies*. Address: c/o Peter Charlesworth. **Patrick Fyffe (Dame Hilda)** b. 23 January, Stafford. Began as hairdresser. Birthsign: Aquarius. Hobbies: gardening, cooking, antiques, music, old houses. **Most Cherished Possession:** 'My cameo brooch.' **Favourite Memory:** 'Seeing Evadne fall in Aphrodite's well.' **George Logan (Dr Evadne)** b. 7 July, Glasgow. Formerly a computer programmer. Birthsign: Cancer. Hobbies: electronic music, computers, reading. **Most Cherished Possession:** 'My banjo.' **Favourite Memory:** 'Performing with Dame Hilda at Covent Garden.'

HIRD, Thora, OBE

Actress/comedienne, b. 28 May 1913, Morecambe, Lancashire. She had theatrical parents and was an overnight success in her first London appearance in *Flowers For the Living* in 1944. Stage ranges from *Romeo and Juliet* to *No, No, Nanette*. Films incl: *The Entertainer; Term of Trial; Some Will, Some Won't*. Recent TV incl: *In Loving Memory* (five series); *Flesh and Blood; Praise Be; Hallelujah; Last of the Summer Wine; The Tailor of Gloucester*. m. James Scott; 1 d. actress Janette Scott. Birthsign: Gemini. Address: c/o Felix de Wolfe. Hobbies: travel (when time!), reading, gardening. **Most Cherished Possession:** 'Without a doubt, my husband, daughter and grandchildren, Daisy and James.' **Favourite Memory:** 'When my baby daughter was handed to me with the words "Here's your baby!".'

HODGE, Patricia

Actress, b. 29 September 1946, Cleethorpes, Lincolnshire. Trained at LAMDA. Stage incl: *Rookery Nook* (West End debut); *Popkiss; Two Gentleman of Verona; Pippin; The Mitford Girls* (for which she was nominated Best Actress in a Musical, SWET Awards, 1981); *Benefactors; Noel and Gertie*. Films incl: *The Elephant Man; Betrayal; Sunset; Just Ask For Diamonds; The Secret Life of Ian Fleming*. TV incl: *Rumpole of the Bailey; Holding the Fort; Jemima Shore Investigates; Hotel Du Lac* (nominated for Best Television Actress, BAFTA 1986); *The Life and Loves of a She Devil; Exclusive Yarns; The Shell Seekers; The Heat of the Day*. m. musician Peter Owen. Address: c/o ICM. Hobbies: decorating, sewing, painting, music. **Most Cherished Possession:** 'My car – it's a cocoon.' **Favourite Memory:** 'Finishing the last exam I ever had to take.'

HODGSON, Sharyn

Actress, b. 25 August 1968, Sydney, Australia. Trained at the Phillip Street Drama School, Sydney, then worked with the Australian Film and Television School, appearing in films for students. After completing her HSC at school, she worked in a shop, before successfully auditioning for the role of Carly Morris in *Home and Away*. Address: c/o Australian Creative Management, 169 Phillip Street, Sydney, NSW 2000, Australia.

HODSON, Charles

ITN correspondent, b. 20 July 1955, Bourton-on-the-Hill, Gloucestershire. BBC trainee, 1978–9; BBC radio news Brussels journalist, 1979–82; *Channel 4 News* scriptwriter, then reporter, 1982–6; ITN reporter, 1986–7; Channel Four's *Business Programme*, 1988–9; Europe correspondent, *Channel Four Daily*, since 1989. m. Ann Walton (dis.); 2 s. William, Thomas. Address: c/o ITN, 22 Avenue d'Eylau, 75116 Paris. Hobbies: classical music, travel, books, the countryside.

HOLDERNESS, Sue

Actress, b. 28 May 1949, Hampstead, London. In 1967 went to Central School of Speech and Drama. Stage incl: *Hay Fever; Edge of Darkness; When the Lights Go On Again; Duet For One; Why Not Stay For Breakfast?;* and *Our Kid* (one-woman show). Films: *That'll Be the Day; It Could Happen To You.* TV incl: *Canned Laughter; The Sandbaggers; It Takes a Worried Man; The Brief; Only Fools and Horses; End of Part One; Dear John; The New Avengers; Minder.* m. director Mark Piper; 1 d. Harriet, 1 s. Frederick. Address: c/o Peter Browne Management. Birthsign: Gemini. Hobbies: dancing, riding, theatre. **Most Cherished Possession:** 'My credit card.' **Favourite Memory:** 'The safe arrival of my two children into this world.'

HOLMES, Michelle

Actress, b. 1 January 1967, Rochdale, Lancashire. Trained at Oldham Theatre Workshop. Theatre: *Road; Midnight Hour; The Emperor's New Clothes; Homeland; Translations; Me Mam Sez; The Beauty Game.* Film: Sue in *Rita, Sue and Bob Too.* TV: Jenny in *Damon & Debbie;* Susan in *The Practice;* Tina Fowler in *Coronation Street.* Address: c/o Granada TV. Birthsign: Capricorn. Hobbies: going to the gym, collecting musical instruments, singing in the funk band Dunky Dobbers, with actress Sue Devaney. Pets: 'A boyfriend called Billy!' **Most Cherished Possession:** 'My rings on my fingers – they were my Nana's.' **Favourite Memory:** 'Thinking that the Pyramids in Egypt were a building site!'

HOLNESS, Bob

Radio/TV presenter, b. 12 November, Vryheid, Natal. Stage and radio acting before leaving for Britain. On radio he presented *Late Night Extra* for eight years. TV incl: *World In Action; Junior Criss Cross Quiz; What the Papers Say; Today; Blockbusters.* TVTimes award (twice); Variety Club Award for Joint Independent Radio Personality of the Year, 1979 and 1984. m. Mary Rose; 2 d. Carol, Ros, 1 s. Jon. Address: c/o Spotlight. Birthsign: Scorpio. Hobbies: gardening, walking, music of all sorts. Pets: an ailing goldfish. **Most Cherished Possession:** 'A Victorian Polyphon, to remind me of the quality of recorded music, at the turn of the century.' **Favourite Memory:** 'Arriving back in Britain at Southampton Docks. After 10 years away it was marvellous to be home.'

HOPE, Jason

Actor, b. 5 March 1970, Liverpool. Spent his early years in youth theatre. Stage incl: *Pied Piper of Hamelin; Romeo and Juliet; Soaplights.* TV incl: *20/20 Vision* (documentary); *Brookside* (as Rod Corkhill). Address: c/o Brookside Productions. Birthsign: Pisces. Hobbies: tennis, boxing, running, painting, listening to music. **Most Cherished Possession:** 'My tennis racket, because you can't play tennis without it.' **Favourite Memory:** 'When I went to Disneyland as a child, because it is what every kid dreams of.'

HOPKINS, Anthony

Actor, b. 31 December 1937, Port Talbot, Wales. Trained at RADA then worked in rep before successfully auditioning for Laurence Olivier to join the National Theatre at the Old Vic. 1974 appeared in *Equus* on Broadway and spent next 10 years working in US. Recent stage incl: *The Lonely Road* (Old Vic); *Pravda; King Lear; Antony & Cleopatra* (National); *M Butterfly*. Films incl: *The Lion in Winter; Magic; The Elephant Man; The Bounty; 84 Charing Cross Road; The Dawning; A Chorus of Disapproval*. Most recent TV incl: *Othello; A Married Man; Hollywood Wives; Blunt; Across the Lake; Heartland*. m. (1st) Petronella Barker (dis.), (2nd) Jennifer Lynton; 1 d. Abigail (from 1st m.). Address: c/o Peggy Thompson Business Management, Richmond, Surrey. Birthsign: Capricorn. Hobbies: piano, reading history and philosophy, walking.

HOPKINS, Muriel

Actress, b. 2 October 1926, London. Born to professional musical/theatrical parents and worked with them in South Coast revues. Stage incl: *John Gabriel Borkman; Julius Caesar; Twelfth Night; Hamlet; Difference of Opinion; War and Peace; The Chalk Garden; See How They Run*. TV incl: *Young Doctors; Glenview High; Homicide; After Marcuse; Certain Women*. m. (2nd) Maxwell F Wright; 2 step-d. Debbie, Janet, 1 step-s. Steve. Address: c/o Holt Williams Agency, Sydney. Birthsign: Libra. Hobbies: playing piano, tap-dancing, jogging, Trivial Pursuit. **Most Cherished Possession:** 'My piano which has travelled the world and back with me. It was once my mother's.' **Favourite Memory:** 'Accepting a marriage proposal from my second husband, because suddenly it was the most natural thing to do.'

HORDERN, Sir Michael, CBE

Actor, b. 3 October 1911, Berkhamsted, Herts. Started as ASM and understudy. London debut *Othello* in 1937. Stage incl: *King Lear; Richard II; Jumpers; You Never Can Tell*. Films incl: *Alexander the Great; The VIPs; The Spy Who Came In From the Cold; Where Eagles Dare; Alice's Adventures In Wonderland; The Slipper and the Rose; The Missionary; Lady Jane; The Comrades; Danny the Champion of the World*. TV incl: *The Browning Version; Tales of the Unexpected; All's Well That Ends Well; The History Man; Trelawny of the Wells; Paradise Postponed; Scoop; Ending Up*. m. former actress Eve Mortimer; 1 d. Joanna. Address: c/o ICM. Hobbies: fishing, gardening. **Most Cherished Possession:** 'A cottage in Berkshire, because it's home.' **Favourite Memory:** 'It's private.'

HOUSEGO, Fred

Presenter and TV personality, b. 25 October 1944, Dundee. Former London taxi driver. Since winning the title of *Mastermind* in 1980 he has been much in demand for radio: *Start the Week; Just the Ticket*. TV: *History On Your Doorstep; Blankety Blank; The Pyramid Game; This Is Your Life; The Six O'Clock Show*. Book: *Fred Housego's London*. Pye TV Personality of 1981 and is a registered London Tourist Board guide. m. Patricia; 2 d. Kate, Abigail. Address: c/o Peter Charlesworth. Birthsign: Scorpio. Hobbies: photography, books, history, wine. Pets: rabbit and guinea pig ('not mine'). **Most Cherished Possession:** 'A book on troubadours, inscribed by my friends in the TGWU cab section on my winning *Mastermind*.' **Favourite Memory:** '*This Is Your Life*, because I met so many old friends.'

HOW, Jane

Actress, b. 21 December, London. Student of Webber Douglas Academy. Stage incl: *Return of A J Raffles; Crime and Punishment; Cavalcade* and *Oh Kay*. TV incl: *A. D.* and *War and Remembrance* (both mini-series); *General Hospital; Doctor Who; Ten From the Twenties; Shuttlecock; The Foundation; The Spoils of War* (three series); *Cribb; Take Three Women; Kelly Monteith; Seaview; The Citadel; Don't Wait Up* (six series); *EastEnders; Matlock; US Movie of the Week*. m. actor Mark Burns; 1 s. Jack. Address: c/o Barry Burnett. Birthsign: Sagittarius. Hobbies: gardening, interior design, writing, drinking champagne. Pets: cat called Teela. **Most Cherished Possession:** 'My tweezers because they are in constant use.' **Favourite Memory:** 'Being 16 in Paris and thinking I was grown-up.'

HOWARD, Susan

Actress/writer, b. (Jeri Lynn Monney), 28 January, Marshall, Texas. Trained with the Los Angeles Repertory Company. Films incl: *Moonshine County Express; Sidewinder 1.* TV incl: *The Paper Chase; The Flying Nun; Bonanza; I Dream of Jeannie; Petrocelli; Killer On Board; Man With a Gun; House On the Hill;* Donna in *Dallas;* and co-host of the Christian Broadcast Network's *700 Club.* m. (2nd) film executive Calvin Chrane; 1 d. (from 1st m.) Lynne. Address: c/o Herb Tobias and Assocs, 1901 Avenue of the Stars, Suite 840, Los Angles, CA 90067. Birthsign: Aquarius. Hobbies: jogging, health food. Pets: a dog named Moe. **Most Cherished Possession:** 'Our 65-acre ranch in Texas.' **Favourite Memory:** 'When I was named Hollywood Deb Star of the Year, in 1968.'

HOWERD, Frankie, OBE

Comedian, b. 6 March 1922, York. Stage debut at 13. Camp concerts during the war. Revue and stage shows incl: *Out Of This World; Pardon My French; Way Out In Piccadilly; Charley's Aunt; A Midsummer Night's Dream;* Palladium pantomimes, 1968 and 1973. Films incl: *Jumping For Joy; Further Up the Creek; Carry On Doctor; Carry On Up the Jungle; Up Pompeii* (also TV); *Up the Chastity Belt; Up the Front; The House in Nightmare Park.* TV incl: *Fine Goings On; The Frankie Howerd Show; Frankie Howerd Strikes Again; HMS Pinafore; Trial By Jury.* Many Royal Variety performances. Books: *Trumps; On the Way I Lost It* (autobiography). Address: c/o Tessa Le Bars. Hobbies: tennis, swimming, music, reading, walking. **Favourite Memory:** 'It hasn't happened yet.'

HUDD, Roy

Comedian, b. 16 May 1936, Croydon, Surrey. Began in 1957 in boys' clubs followed by holiday camp and summer shows. Stage incl: *Oliver!; Underneath the Arches; Run For Your Wife;* and his touring show, *Roy Hudd's Very Own Music Hall.* Radio incl: *The News Huddlines; Huddwinks.* TV incl: *Not So Much a Programme, More a Way of Life* (TV debut 1964); *The Illustrated Weekly Hudd; The Good Old Days; I Hazard a Guess; Hometown.* m. (1st) Ann (dis.), (2nd) Deborah; 1 s. Max (from 1st m.). Address: c/o Aza Artistes. Hobbies: walking, talking, watching Crystal Palace FC, music hall (history and songs). Pets: several wild toads. **Most Cherished Possession:** 'Membership of the Grand Order of Water Rats.' **Favourite Memory:** 'Is yet to come – whoopee.'

HUGHES, Nerys

Actress, b. 8 November 1941, Rhyl, Wales. Made a name for herself on TV in *The Liver Birds* followed by *The Merchant of Venice; High Summer; Seasons; Diary of a Young Man; How Green Was My Valley; Doctor Who; Jackanory; Play Away; Third Time Lucky; Alphabet Zoo; District Nurse* (three series). Also presented a *QED* documentary on otters. m. Patrick Turley; 1 d. Mari-Claire, 1 s. Benjamin. Address: c/o Barry Burnett. Birthsign: Scorpio. Hobbies: playing with the children, gardening.

HULL, Rod

Entertainer/writer, b. 13 August 1935, Isle of Sheppey, Kent. Inseparable from Emu, who was hatched in Australia. TV incl: *EBC; Emu's World; Michael Parkinson Show; This Is Your Life; Emu's Wide World; EMU-TV.* Created, wrote and hosted first Children's Royal Variety Performance, 1981. Pantomime: *Emu In Pantoland; Aladdin.* Book: *The Reluctant Pote.* m. (1st) (dis.), (2nd) Cheryl; 3 d. Danielle, Debbie (both from 1st m.), Amelia (from 2nd m.), 1 step-d. Katrina, 2 s. Toby, Oliver (both from 2nd m.). Address: c/o International Artistes. Birthsign: Leo. Hobbies: bee-keeping, golf. **Most Cherished Possession:** 'My Zippo lighter which, as a constant pipe-smoker, I'm never without.' **Favourite Memory:** 'Being present at the birth of my children.'

HUMPHRIES, Barry

Comic, b. 17 February 1934, Melbourne, Australia. Experience gained at Union Theatre, Melbourne, and Phillip Street Theatre. Films incl: *Adventures of Barry McKenzie; Barry McKenzie Holds His Own; The Getting of Wisdom*. One-man shows incl: *A Nice Night's Entertainment; Excuse I; A Load of Olde Stuffe; At Least You Can Say You've Seen It; Last Night of the Poms; An Evening's Intercourse With the Widely Liked Barry Humphries;* and *Back With a Vengeance*. TV chat shows, including his own, *The Dame Edna Experience*. Variety Club Showbusiness Personality of the Year 1987. m. Dianne Millstead; 2 d. Tessa, Emily, 2 s. Oscar, Rupert. Address: c/o William Morris. Birthsign: Aquarius. Hobbies: amateur painting, reading ghost stories.

HUNNIFORD, Gloria

TV and radio presenter, and interviewer, b. 10 April, Portadown, Co Amargh. Had own radio programme in Canada, 1959. Her daily Radio 2 programme began in 1982. TV incl: *Good Evening Ulster; Val Doonican Show; Les Dawson Show; Sunday Sunday; We Love TV; Songs of Praise; Tarby and Friends; Give Us a Clue; The Newly-Weds*. *TVTimes* Top Female Personality, 1984. Record: *True Love*. m. Don Keating (dis.); 1 d. Caron, 2 s. Paul, Michael. Address: c/o Jo Gurnett Management. Birthsign: Aries. Hobbies: antiques, tennis. **Most Cherished Possession:** 'Objects made by hand by my children.' **Favourite Memory:** 'Coming home from school to the smell of home-made bread and cakes.'

HUNT, Gareth

Actor, b. 7 February 1943, London. Trained at the Webber Douglas Academy of Dramatic Art. Worked in rep, RSC and the National Theatre. Stage incl: *Conduct Unbecoming; Alpha Beta; Deathtrap; Run For Your Wife*. Films incl: *Licensed To Love and Kill; The World Is Full of Married Men; The House On Garibaldi Street*. TV incl: *Upstairs, Downstairs; The New Avengers; That Beryl Marston . . .!; A Hazard of Hearts; Shaping Up*. m. (1st) Carol (dis.), (2nd) Anette; 2 s. Gareth (from 1st m.), Oliver-Leigh (from 2nd m.). Address: c/o ICM. Birthsign: Aquarius. Hobbies: golf, keep-fit, squash, cricket. **Most Cherished Possession:** 'My father's ring.' **Favourite Memory:** 'Being present at the birth of Oliver.'

HUNTER, Russell

Actor, b. 18 February 1925, Glasgow. A former shipyard worker, began acting as an amateur. Professional debut with Glasgow Unity Theatre 1947. Appeared all over Scotland in one-man show, *Jock*. Other theatre incl: *Lock Up Your Daughters*. Played Andrew Carnegie in a play written to celebrate 150th anniversary of the famous philanthropist. Probably best known on TV for part of Lonely in series *Callan*. Other TV incl: *The Gaffer; Play For Tomorrow; The Dunroaming Uprising*. Address: c/o Marjorie Abel Ltd, 50 Maddox Street, London W1. Birthsign: Aquarius. Hobbies: reading, viewing icons. **Most Cherished Possession:** 'Life itself.' **Favourite Memory:** 'Many – but not as good as tomorrow's.'

ILES, Jon

Actor, b. 17 May 1954, Ripon, Yorkshire. Trained at Rose Bruford College of Speech and Drama. Rep at Worthing, many tours incl: *Macbeth; Romeo and Juliet; The Winslow Boy*. West End Theatre incl: *Jungle Book; Dial M For Murder*. Film: *Those Glory, Glory Days*. TV incl: Det Con Mike Dashwood in *The Bill; Fresh Fields; Never the Twain; Crown Court; Dick Emery* series; *To the Manor Born; Bognor; Supergran; C.A.T.S. Eyes*. Address: c/o Daly Gagan Assocs. Birthsign: Taurus. Hobbies: gym, writing, swimming, art. Pets: one German shepherd dog, Beef, one Cross-breed dog, Chips. **Most Cherished Possession:** 'An Egyptian gold and silver locket – the first piece of jewellery my father gave my mother.' **Favourite Memory:** 'I hope it hasn't happened yet.'

IMRIE, Celia

Actress, b. 15 July 1952, Guildford, Surrey. Theatre incl: Glasgow Citizens' Theatre; Royal Court Theatre, London; Traverse Theatre, Edinburgh; RSC world tour; *The Last Waltz; Particular Friendships; School For Wives; Philanthropist; Yerma.* Films incl: *The Wicked Lady; Assassin; The House of Whipcord; Highlander; Death On the Nile.* TV incl: *Cloud Howe; Bergerac; To the Manor Born; Upstairs, Downstairs; The Nightmare Man; Shoestring; Victoria Wood As Seen On TV.* Address: c/o CDA. Birthsign: Cancer. Hobbies: Tae Kwondo, going to Italy, gardening. Pets: one cat, Mildew. **Most Cherished Possession:** 'Mildew, because she purrs when I stroke her.' **Favourite Memory:** 'Walking up Shahid Bhagat Singh Road in the middle of the night.'

INGLE, Su

TV presenter, b. 23 April 1955, London. After taking a degree in botany at Durham started career as a photographer in London. TV incl: *The Boat Show; Blankety Blank; Child's Play; BBC Conservation Awards; Tomorrow's World; Wildtrack; Motorfair; The Good Food Show; Ten On Saturday; Secrets of the Coast; Don't Ask Me; Photo Assignment; Craft, Design and Technology;* natural history programme for New Zealand TV, 1988–9. LBC Crown FM radio programme *World Outlook,* 1989. Address: c/o Arlington Enterprises. Birthsign: Taurus. Hobbies: sailing, skiing, photography, travel. **Most Cherished Possession:** 'My garden – when British weather permits.' **Favourite Memory:** 'Taking part in Operation Raleigh – visiting breathtaking South Pacific islands, seeing the incredible wildlife, and meeting friendly and fun people.'

INMAN, John

Actor/entertainer, b. 28 June 1935, Preston, Lancashire. At 21, joined a touring rep company, then moved into pantos and summer seasons. Theatre incl: *Ann Veronica; Salad Days; Mother Goose; Pyjama Top.* TV incl: *Are You Being Served?* (also film); *Take a Letter Mr Jones; Odd Man Out; Good Old Days; Blankety Blank; Seaside Special; Top Secret; This Is Your Life.* BBC TV Personality of the Year, 1976. *TVTimes* Funniest Man On Television, 1976. Address: c/o Bill Robertson, W & J Theatrical Enterprises, 51a Oakwood Road, London NW11 6RJ. Hobby: work. **Most Cherished Possession:** 'My health. Without it, I would not have any others.' **Favourite Memory:** 'My ambition was to top the bill and take my curtain-call by descending a huge flight of stairs, dressed in white tie, top hat and tails. I achieved this in 1977 at the Britannia Pier, Great Yarmouth.'

INNOCENT, Harold

Actor, b. 18 April 1936, Coventry, Warwickshire. Scholarship winner to Birmingham School of Speech Training and Dramatic Art. Recent theatre incl: National Theatre; RSC; *Ruddigore; Alice In Wonderland* (operetta). West End theatre incl: *Donkey's Years; School For Scandal; The Magistrate.* Clarence Derwent Award as Best Supporting Actor for *The Second Mrs Tanqueray,* 1982. TV incl: *A Tale of Two Cities; The Canterville Ghost; Porterhouse Blue; Inspector Morse; Minder; The Professionals; Ben Casey; Sea Hunt; Paradise Postponed; Killing Time; Bookmark; An Englishman Abroad; A Woman's Story; The Night of the Simhat Torah.* Address: c/o Susan Angel Assocs. Hobbies: music, particularly opera, reading, travel, history. **Most Cherished Possession:** 'My big brass bed and my CD player.'

IRVING, Jayne

Presenter, b. 30 August 1956, Sheffield. Trained as reporter on the Doncaster *Evening Post.* Moved to Radio Hallam, then IRN, then Thames News as a reporter. Joined TV-am in 1982 as reporter. Promoted to newsreader, then host of *After Nine,* TV-am's women's magazine programme; co-presenter of the BBC's *Open Air* since 1989. Other TV: *The New Statesman; Give Us a Clue; Telly Addicts; Tell the Truth.* Film: *American Roulette.* Address: c/o Jacque Evans Management. Birthsign: Leo. Hobbies: horse-riding, weight-lifting. **Most Cherished Possession:** 'A scrappy bit of notepaper signed by Paul Newman, because he never gives autographs. I asked him not knowing this after interviewing him – and he signed it!' **Favourite Memory:** 'My first date, because I was such a gawky teenager. I thought it was a miracle!'

JACOBS, Joyce

Actress, b. 15 April 1922, Surrey. Started with Lloyds of London Drama Group. Theatre incl leading roles in: *I Remember Mama; View From the Bridge; The Little Foxes; Tonight At 8.30; The Shifting Heart; Flowers For the Living* (Best Actress Award). TV incl: *The Young Doctors;* and as Esme, the town gossip, in *A Country Practice.* m. Ian Jacobs; 1 d. Valerie, 2 s. Brian, Peter. Address: c/o June Reilly Agency, 24th Floor, 54 Pitt Street, Sydney, NSW 2000. Birthsign: Aries. Hobby: tennis. Pets: cats, goldfish. **Most Cherished Possession:** 'My mother's antique china cabinet, because it reminds me of her and England, not forgetting my family.' **Favourite Memory:** 'My first TV sketch, bandaged from head to foot, with only my eyes visible.'

JAMES, Geraldine

Actress, b. 6 July 1950, Maidenhead, Berkshire. Trained at The Drama Centre, London, then rep for four years. Theatre incl: *Passion For Dracula; When I Was a Girl I Used To Scream and Shout; Cymbeline; The Merchant of Venice* (West End and Broadway, with Dustin Hoffman). Films incl: *Sweet William; Night Cruiser; Gandhi; The Tall Guy; The Wolves of Willoughby Chase; She's Been Away* (won her the Venice Film Festival 1989 Best Actress award). TV incl: *The Sweeney; Dummy* (1978 Critics' Award for Best Actress); *The Jewel In the Crown; Blott On the Landscape; Echoes.* m. Joseph Blatchley; 1 d. Eleanor. Address: c/o Julian Belfrage. Hobbies: piano, gardening. **Most Cherished Possession:** 'A tiny gold suitcase. It's the first thing my husband gave me.'

JAMES, John

Actor, b. 18 April, Minneapolis, Minnesota. Trained at the American Academy of Dramatic Arts. Theatre incl: *Butterflies Are Free; Suds.* TV incl: *Search For Tomorrow; The Love Boat; Fantasy Island.* TV film: *He's Not Your Son;* Jeff Colby in *Dynasty* and *The Colbys.* m. Denise Coward. Address: c/o William Morris Agency, 151 El Camino Drive, Beverly Hills, California 90212. Hobbies: skiing, scuba-diving, singing, playing the guitar. **Most Cherished Possession:** 'My Jeep – a big, black steed with a padded roll bar and chrome bumpers. I can drive over anything that gets in my way.' **Favourite Memory:** 'A ride in an air force jet. After that I overcame my fear of flying and I now have a pilot's licence.'

JAMES, Rachel

Actress, b. 29 September 1956, Cottingham, East Yorkshire. Trained at Arts Educational School, then with the National Youth Theatre. Also Children's Theatre, TIE, season at Library Theatre, Manchester, plus work with the Tricycle and Roundhouse Theatres. TV incl: *Juliet Bravo; Alive and Kicking; Our Dog Mick;* Debra Bates in *The Practice;* Judy Maitland in *Capstick's Law.* Working in the south of Spain for the British Council since 1989. Fluent in Spanish. Agent: Janet Welch Personal Management, 486 Chiswick High Road, London W4. Birthsign: Libra. Hobby: tennis. Pets: one dog, Matti Bean. **Most Cherished Possession:** 'My dog, because she adores me!' **Favourite Memory:** 'Seeing the seal sanctuary in Gweek, Cornwall, finally completed.'

JAMESON, Louise

Actress, b. 20 April 1951, Wanstead, London. Trained at RADA. Theatre incl: with RSC in *King Lear; Love's Labour's Lost; Summerfolk; Richard III; Passion Play; As You Like It; A Midsummer Nights Dream; Sleeping Nightie* at Royal Court Theatre London. TV incl: *Cider With Rosie; Z-Cars; The Omega Factor; Tenko; Boy Dominic; Bergerac; Emmerdale Farm; The Gentle Touch; The Secret Diary of* and *The Growing Pains of Adrian Mole.* Lives with artist Martin Bedford; 2 s. Harry, Thomas. Address: c/o Jeremy Conway. Birthsign: Aries. Hobbies: cooking, guitar, piano, theatre-going. Pets: one dog, Dixie, one cat, Sheesh. **Most Cherished Possession:** 'My contact lenses. I'm hopeless without them.' **Favourite Memory:** 'Giving birth to my two boys. It felt like taking part in a miracle.'

JAMIESON, Charles

Actor, b. 12 March 1952, Rutherglen, Scotland. Trained at Glasgow School of Art Drama Club and Texas Christian University Art and Drama Dept. Theatre incl: *Privates On Parades; Twelfth Night; Sailor Beware.* TV incl: *Blake's Seven; The Omega Factor; Goodnight and Godbless;* and as Ruari Galbraith in *Take the High Road.* Has directed for his own theatre group and exhibited widely as a painter. m. Sally Ann Muir. Address: c/o Joan Gray. Birthsign: Pisces. Hobbies: painting, drawing, gardening, cooking. **Most Cherished Possession:** 'My toy train. It reminds me of my happy childhood.' **Favourite Memory:** 'Walking in the Sonoraw Desert by moonlight.'

JANSON, David

Actor, b. 30 March 1950, London. Joined the Phildene Stage School aged nine. Stage debut in 1962 in *Oliver.* Joined the RSC in 1963 with *A Midsummer Night's Dream.* Theatre incl: 1965 season at Stratford: *Hanky Park; Roll On Four O'Clock; She Was Only An Admiral's Daughter; Out of the Crocodile; My Giddy Aunt; Season's Greetings; Taking Steps; The Rivals; Don't Start Without Me; Run For Your Wife.* Film: *A Hard Day's Night.* TV incl: *The Newcomers; Get Some In; Grundy; Don't Rock the Boat; Brush Strokes.* m. actress Debbie Arnold; 1 d. Ciara. Address c/o Peter Graham Assocs at Crouch Salmon Associates. Birthsign: Aries. Hobbies: wildlife, squash. **Most Cherished Possession:** 'Our daughter.' **Favourite Memory:** 'Watching her being born.'

JARVIS, Martin

Actor, b. 4 August 1941, Cheltenham. Trained at RADA. Theatre incl: *Hamlet; Man And Superman; She Stoops To Conquer; The Importance of Being Earnest; Other Places; Woman In Mind; Henceforward; Exchange.* Films incl: *The Bunker; The Last Escape; Ike; Caught In the Act; Buster.* Radio incl: *War and Peace; Great Expectations; Jarvis's Frayn;* also readings and author of several short stories. TV incl: *The Forsyte Saga; After Liverpool; The Pallisers; Make and Break; Rings On Their Fingers; Doctor Who; David Copperfield; Jackanory; Mr Palfrey of Westminster; Oscar Wilde; The Black Tower; Rumpole of the Bailey; Comic Relief.* m. actress Rosalind Ayres; 2 s. Toby, Oliver. Address: c/o Michael Whitehall. Hobbies: music, Indian food, films, interior design.

JASON, David

Actor, b. 2 February 1940, London. Keen amateur actor before his actor brother, Arthur, helped him to get his first professional part in *South Sea Bubble.* A Dick Emery season at Bournemouth led to his role in *Do Not Adjust Your Set,* which established him on TV. Films incl: *The Odd Job; The B.F.G.* TV incl: *Doctor at Large; Doctor In the House; Doctor at Sea; Lucky Fella; The Top Secret Life of Edgar Briggs; A Sharp Intake of Breath; Open All Hours; Only Fools and Horses; Porterhouse Blue; A Bit of a Do.* Address: c/o Richard Stone. Birthsign: Aquarius. Hobbies: skin-diving, restoring motor-cycles, flying. Pets: one three-legged dog. **Most Cherished Possession:** 'Me mum.' **Favourite Memory:** 'Travelling to New Zealand to film, because it's the only time I ever travelled first-class.'

JEAVONS, Colin

Actor, b. 20 October 1929, Newport, Monmouthshire. Trained at the Old Vic Theatre School and his first stage appearance was with the Old Vic in 1951. Recent theatre incl: *Cat On a Hot Tin Roof.* His first film role was in 1962. Films incl: *Absolute Beginners; The French Lieutenant's Woman.* TV incl: *Paradise Postponed; Sherlock Holmes; Brat Farrar; Billy Liar; Great Expectations; Hitch-Hiker's Guide To the Galaxy; Reilly Ace of Spies; Atlantis; Travelling Man; Hitler's SS; Jackanory; Blackeyes.* m. Rosie; 2 s. Saul, Barney. Address: c/o Duncan Heath Assocs. Hobbies: books, records. **Most Cherished Possession:** 'My armchair, because it is so comfortable to go to sleep in!' **Favourite Memory:** 'Seeing *Thanks For The Memory* – it had the last great music hall stars. Superb.'

JEFFRIES, Lionel

Actor/film director/screenwriter, b. 10 June 1926, London. Trained at RADA. Theatre incl: *Hello Dolly; See How They Run*. Films incl: *The Colditz Story; The Prisoner of Zenda; Danny the Champion of the World*. TV incl: ITV's first play, *Facts of Life; Shillingbury Tales; Cream In My Coffee; Ending Up*. Wrote and directed *The Railway Children* (Hollywood Gold Medal award); *The Amazing Mr Blunden*. Directed *The Water Babies; Baxter; Wombling Free*. Paris Gold Medal Melier Award; The Burma Star. m. Eileen; 2 d. Martha, Elizabeth, 1 s. Timothy. Address: c/o John Redway & Assocs. Hobby: painting. **Most Cherished Possession:** 'My family, including my grandchildren Amy and Thomas.' **Favourite Memory:** 'Seeing my name in lights for the first time in the West End.'

JENKINS, Sue

Actress, b. Liverpool. Trained at the Elliott Clarke College of Dance and Drama. Spent twelve years acting in theatre, incl: Rita in *Educating Rita*; Viola in *Twelfth Night*; Desdemona in *Othello*; Beatrice in *The Changeling*; Nora in *The Plough and the Stars*; Doreen (especially written for her by Alan Bleasdale) in *Having a Ball*. TV incl: *How We Used To Live; The Beiderbecke Affair; Coronation Street*. m. David Fleeshman; 1 d. Emily Victoria, 1 s. Richard Jonathan. Address: c/o Spotlight. Birthsign: Leo. Pets: two cats, Whiskey, Charlie. **Most Cherished Possession:** 'I don't treasure material things – they can be replaced. I treasure my family – they can't be!' **Favourite Memory:** 'The birth of my two beautiful children.'

JEPHCOTT, Dominic

Actor, b. 28 July 1957, Coventry, Warwickshire. Trained at RADA, then rep, and tours through India and South East Asia. Joined the RSC performing with it in London and Stratford. TV and film debut both in 1979 in *Enemy At the Door* and *All Quiet On the Western Front*. Since then TV and films have incl: *The Scarlet Pimpernel; Napoleon and Josephine; The Aerodrome; The Jewel in the Crown; Oliver Twist; The Beiderbecke Affair; Hold the Dream; Paradise Postponed; Claws; Rumpole of the Bailey*. Address: c/o Markham & Froggatt, London. Birthsign: Leo. Hobbies: guitar-playing, tennis, trying to land a flight simulator on the runway. **Most Cherished Possession:** 'What I cherish most is my good health.' **Favourite Memory:** 'Every job I ever got.'

JEWEL, Jimmy

Actor/comedian, b. 4 December 1912, Sheffield. Learned tap dancing and acrobatics from his father, also named Jimmy Jewel. Theatre incl: *The Sunshine Boys; Comedians; Death of a Salesman; You Can't Take It With You*; National Theatre Player. Films incl: *Missing Persons; The Krays*. Radio incl: *Up the Pole*. TV incl: *Spring and Autumn; Nearest and Dearest; Thicker Than Water; Funny Man; Oldest Goose In the Business*; many other TV plays and appearances. Won the Variety Club Special Award 1985. m. Belle (dec.); 1 d. Piper, 1 s. Kerry. Address: c/o 96 Troy Court, Kensington High Street, London W8. Birthsign: Sagittarius. Hobby: golf. Pets: one dog. **Most Cherished Possession:** 'My memories – father, mother, Belle, my children.' **Favourite Memory:** 'The day my son was born.'

JOHN, Bartholomew

Actor/singer, b. 24 August 1952, Christchurch, New Zealand. Formal music training at St Andrew's College, Christchurch. Musicals incl: *A Little Night Music; Man of La Mancha; Oliver; The Sound of Music*. Plays incl: *Chapter Two; Private Lives*. TV incl: *The Young Doctors; Skyways; The Challenge*. m. Inese; 1 d. Alexandria, 1 s. Benjamin. Address: c/o Jane Camerons, 120 Victoria Street, Ports Point 2011, Sydney, Australia. Birthsign: Leo/Virgo. Hobbies: squash, golf, surfing, running. **Most Cherished Possession:** 'My home, for it's the backdrop of all of life's struggles and the focus for happy times.' **Favourite Memory:** 'The last night of my first production of *Side By Side By Sondheim*. At the end, everyone stood for 15 minutes.'

JOHNSON, Don

Actor, b. Flat Creek, Missouri. Won a drama scholarship to the University of Kansas and then went on to the American Conservatory Theatre Group in San Francisco. Films incl: *Sweetheart Dance; Cease Fire; Zacharias; Return To Macon Country; Dead-Bang.* TV incl: *The Rebels; From Here To Eternity; Elvis and Me; The Long Hot Summer; Revenge of the Stepford Wives; Miami Vice.* Won Golden Globe award for Best Actor. Released LP *Heartbeat.* m. 1st actress Melanie Griffith (dis.), 2nd Melanie Griffith (remarried); 1 s. Jesse, 1 d. Dakota. Address: c/o Mike Belson, 50 Beverly Drive, Beverly Hills, CA 90212. Hobbies: songwriting, music, golf, fishing. **Most Cherished Possession:** 'My portable sauna to tote around with me on location.' **Favourite Memory:** 'Singing with my grandfather's backwoods church choir.'

JOHNSTON, Sue

Actress, b. 7 December 1943, Warrington, Lancashire. Trained at the Webber Douglas Academy of Dramatic Art. Worked in rep at Farnham, Salford, Lincoln, Manchester, Coventry. Also the Portable Theatre, Coventry's TIE, Bolton Octagon, and was a founder member of the M6 Theatre Company. Starred in Jim Cartwright's *To,* with *Brookside* actor John McArdle. Much radio work. TV incl: *Brookside; Coronation Street.* Autobiography: *Hold On To the Messy Times.* m. (dis.), 1 s. Joel. Address: c/o Brookside. Birthsign: Sagittarius. Hobbies: walking, reading, listening to and playing music, gardening. Pets: two dogs, two cats, two fish. **Most Cherished Possession:** 'My son Joel.' **Favourite Memory:** 'Travelling on my grandfather's steam engine (he was the driver) as a young girl.'

JONES, Freddie

Actor, b. 12 September 1927, Stoke-on-Trent. Trained at the Rose Bruford College of Speech and Drama, followed by rep and with the RSC. Stage incl: *Marat Sade* (and film); *Mister; A Song In the Night* (one-man show). Films incl: *Far From the Madding Crowd; Otley; Goodbye Gemini; The Elephant Man; Firefox; Krull; Dune; Firestarter; And the Ship Sails On.* TV incl: *Sword of Honour; Treasure Island; Cold Comfort Farm; Uncle Vanya; Sweeney Todd; The Ghosts of Motley Hall; In Loving Memory; District Nurse.* Named World's Best TV actor at Monte Carlo TV Festival in 1969 for *The Caesars.* m. actress Jennifer Heslewood; 3 s. Toby, Rupert, Caspar. Address: c/o James Sharkey. Birthsign: Virgo. Hobbies: cooking, gardening.

JONES, Ken

Actor, b. 20 February 1930, Liverpool. Amateur actor before training at RADA and joining Joan Littlewood's Theatre Workshop in *The Hostage.* Recent theatre incl: *When the Wind Blows.* Films incl: *SWALK; File of the Golden Goose; Sherlock Holmes; No Surrender.* TV incl: *Z-Cars; Hunter's Walk; Go For Gold; Germinal; Her Majesty's Pleasure; First Class Friend; Last of the Baskets; The Wackers; The Squirrels; Dead Ernest; Seconds Out; Valentine Park; Boon.* m. actress/writer Sheila Fay. Address: c/o David White Assocs. Birthsign: Pisces.

JONES, Peter

Actor/author, b. 12 June 1920. Wem, Shropshire. Radio incl: *Just a Minute; In All Directions; Hitch-Hiker's Guide to the Galaxy.* TV incl: *The Rag Trade; Long Live the King; Beggar My Neighbour; Mr Digby Darling; Children of Dynmouth; One-Upmanship; Whoops Apocalypse; The Agatha Christie Hour; I Thought You'd Gone; Singles Weekend; Rumpole of the Bailey.* Also guest appearances on many quiz shows. m. American actress Ieri Sauvinet; 1 d. actress Selena Carey-Jones, 2 s. Bill Dare, Charles. Address: c/o Richard Stone, London. Birthsign: Gemini. Hobby: making plans. **Favourite Memory:** 'Holidays when my children were little.'

JONES, Simon

Actor, b. 27 July 1950, Charlton Park, Wiltshire. Started in rep before appearing in *Bloomsbury* 1974 (West End debut). Theatre incl: *Privates On Parade; Benefactors; The Real Thing; My Fair Lady; Candida.* Films incl: *Brazil; Meaning of Life; Reds.* TV incl: *Newheart; Brideshead Revisited; Hitch-Hiker's Guide to the Galaxy; Black Adder II; Claws; Hart To Hart; Muck and Brass; Rock Follies.* m. Nancy Lewis. Address: c/o Duncan Heath Assocs. Birthsign: Leo. Hobbies: keeping a diary, making lists of things to do. **Most Cherished Possession:** 'The stuffed alligator given at Christmas by a friend who knew I'd like it and that my father would be appalled.' **Favourite Memory:** 'My father discovering the alligator under a bed where my mother had hidden it as a surprise.'

JUDD, Lesley

Broadcaster, b. 20 December 1946, London. Trained at the Arts Educational School of Ballet and Drama. Started on the stage as a dancer in such productions as: *Half a Sixpence; Our Man Crichton; Twang!* TV incl: *Blue Peter; Micro-Live; Horizon* (narrator); *Pets In Particular; Holiday Talk; Dance Crazy; This Is Your Right; Let's Go Maths; Business Matters; Adventure Game; The Great Egg Race; Threads.* m. A Relph; 1 d. Marta Carolina, 1 s. Henry Thomas. Address: c/o Arlington Enterprises, London. Birthsign: Sagittarius. Hobby: trying to find the time to do nothing. Pets: one dog, Benji, one cat, Tara. **Most Cherished Possession:** 'My contact lenses – I can't find my glasses without them!' **Favourite Memory:** 'Every time spring comes – a fresh start every year!'

JUNKIN, John

Actor/writer, b. 29 January 1930, Ealing, London. Schoolteacher-turned-scriptwriter. Has written or co-written more than 1500 TV and radio scripts. Devised and chaired *Jump* and *The Unfair Quiz* on radio, and *Ask No Questions* on TV. As an actor, he has made numerous TV, film, radio and stage appearances. Programme associate/consultant, *Bodymatters; Bob's Full House; Opportunity Knocks; The 64,000 Dollar Question.* m. Jennie; 1 d. Annabel. Address: c/o Richard Grenville, London Management. Hobbies: crosswords, sleeping. Pets: one dog, Sophie. **Most Cherished Possession:** 'A letter from Eric Morecambe. I was accused of getting laughs by one of the world's funniest men.' **Favourite Memory:** 'Watching Annabel as Peter Pan in her first school play.'

KANE, John

Actor/writer, b. 27 October 1945, Dundee. Trained at Glasgow College of Dramatic Art and spent seven years with the RSC. TV as an actor incl: *Softly, Softly; Doctor Who; Doctor On the Go; Cymbeline; Love's Labours Lost; The Seagull; Paradise Postponed.* As writer TV incl: *Scott On; Son of the Bride; Black Beauty; The Vamp; Me and My Girl; Funny Ha-Ha; Terry and June; Happy Ever After; All In Good Faith; Never the Twain; Smuggler.* m. Alison Mary Hope Robine; 2 d. Alice, Susanna, 1 s. Simon. Address: c/o Duncan Heath Associates. Birthsign: Scorpio. Hobbies: music, reading, collecting films. Pets: one dog, three cats, two hamsters, one goldfish. **Most Cherished Possession:** 'Land in South France where we hope to build a holiday home.' **Favourite Memory:** 'Most Christmases.'

KAY, Charles

Actor, b. 31 August 1930, Coventry. Attended Birmingham University, then trained at RADA. Has been a member of the RSC, National Theatre and the Old Vic. Films incl: *Hennessey; Nijinsky; Amadeus.* Many TV appearances incl: *Microbes and Men; Fall of Eagles; I, Claudius; Target; Lady Killers; To Serve Them All My Days; Bergerac; My Cousin Rachel; The Citadel; Edge of Darkness; King John; Fortunes of War.* Address: c/o Marmont Management. Birthsign: Virgo. Hobbies: reading, listening to music, watching TV, bridge. **Most Cherished Possession:** 'My faculties, such as they are.' **Favourite Memory:** '1954, listening to a midnight mass in Vienna and emerging to find the city covered in snow. It was Christmas day, and it seemed too perfect to be true.'

KAYE, Gorden

Actor, b. 7 April 1941, Huddersfield, West Yorkshire. No formal training. Seasons at Bolton, Sheffield, Royal Court and Stratford East Theatres in London. West End Theatre incl: *Hobson's Choice; 'Allo 'Allo!* US and Canada tour with the NT. Films incl: *Escape From the Dark; Porridge; Jabberwocky; Brazil.* Much TV incl: *'Allo 'Allo!; Coronation Street; Born and Bred; Fame Is the Spur; King John; Much Ado About Nothing; In the Secret State; Are You Being Served?; It Ain't Half Hot Mum.* Address: c/o Markham & Froggatt, London. Birthsign: Aries. Hobbies: travel, food, cinema. **Most Cherished Possession:** 'A photo of myself with Bob Hope, my longstanding idol.' **Favourite Memory:** 'Opening night in San Francisco 1974, the start of a love affair with the USA.'

KEAVENEY, Anna

Actress, b. 5 October 1949, Runcorn, Cheshire. Trained with Studio '68. Rep at Oldham, Bolton, Pitlochry, Liverpool, Citizens' Theatre in Glasgow, Bristol Old Vic. Theatre incl: *Once a Catholic* at the Royal Court, later Wyndhams; *Neaptide* at the National Theatre, *Translations* at Hampstead Theatre, later the National Theatre; *Touched; Good Fun.* Much radio work. Film: *Shirley Valentine.* TV incl: *Divided We Stand; Within These Walls; Widows; Enemy at the Door;* C4 film *Security;* Marie Jackson in *Brookside.* Address: c/o Stephen Hatton Management, 3–5 St John Street, Smithfield, London EC1M 4AE, tel 071-608 2713. Hobby: going on holiday. **Most Cherished Possession:** 'My home. It gives me independence.' **Favourite Memory:** 'Every job I've ever got.'

KEEL, Howard

Actor/singer, b. 13 April 1917, Gillespie, Illinois. Was an aircraft sales rep but began acting after winning singing scholarship. Theatre incl: *No Strings; Carousel; Oklahoma!; South Pacific; Camelot; Kismet; Kiss Me Kate.* Also variety and singing tours in Britain and USA. Films incl: *Seven Brides For Seven Brothers; Annie Get Your Gun; Calamity Jane; Showboat.* Clayton Farlow in TV's *Dallas.* m. (3rd) Judy; 2 d. Christina, Kaya, 1 s. Gunnar (from previous m.), 1 s. Leslie (from 3rd m.). Address: c/o Lew Sherrell Agency, 7060 Hollywood Blvd, LA, CA. Birthsign: Aries. Hobbies: golf, charity work. Pets: one dog. **Most Cherished Possession:** 'My golf clubs.' **Favourite Memory:** 'As a child, my friends and I would hop rides on trolley cars and freight trains.'

KEEN, Diane

Actress, b. 29 July 1946, London. Brought up in Kenya. Settled in England aged 19. Trained in rep. Unknown until *The Cuckoo Waltz* on TV. Other TV incl: *Crossroads; Fall of Eagles; Softly, Softly; Public Eye; The Legend of Robin Hood; The Sweeney; The Feathered Serpent; Country Matters; Crown Court; The Sandbaggers; Rings On Their Fingers; The Shillingbury Blowers; The Shillingbury Tales; The Reunion; The Morecambe and Wise Show; Bruce Meets the Girls; Foxy Lady; Oxbridge Blues; Killer Waiting; Sleeps Six; You Must Be the Husband; Jekyll & Hyde. TVTimes* Top 10 Best Actress Award 1979. m. Neil Zeiger; 1 d. Melissa. Address: c/o William Morris. Birthsign: Leo. Hobbies: interior design, DIY, exploration. Pets: two cats. **Most Cherished Possession:** 'My collection of Marilyn Monroe books and photographs.'

KEITH, Penelope

Actress, b. 2 April, Sutton, Surrey. Trained at Webber Douglas Academy of Dramatic Art, then rep and the Royal Shakespeare Company. Theatre incl: *Fallen Angels; The Norman Conquests* (and TV); *Donkey's Years* (and TV); *The Apple Cart; The Millionairess; Moving; Hobson's Choice; Captain Brassbound's Conversion; Hay Fever* (and TV); *The Dragon's Tail.* Films incl: *The Hound of the Baskervilles; The Priest of Love.* TV incl: *Private Lives; To the Manor Born; On Approval; Spider's Web; Waters of the Moon; Executive Stress; No Job For a Lady; The Good Life.* Winner of *TVTimes* Top Ten Award 1976–80; Variety Club Award for BBC TV Personality 1979. m. Rodney Timson. Address: c/o London Management. Hobby: gardening. Pets: two dogs, three cats.

KEITH, Sheila

Actress, b. 9 June 1920, London. Trained at Webber Douglas Academy of Dramatic Art. Theatre incl: *Mame* (with Ginger Rogers); *Anyone For Denis?; Deathtrap.* Films incl: *Ooh, You Are Awful; Frightmare; The Comeback; Clockwise.* TV incl: *Never the Twain; Fresh Fields; David Copperfield; Moody and Peg; Within These Walls; Angels; Jubilee; The Cedar Tree; The Pallisers; Heartland; Rings On Their Fingers; Agony; The Other 'Arf.* Address: c/o David White Assocs. Birthsign: Gemini. Hobbies: nature study, browsing in bookshops, antique furniture. Pets: one dog. **Most Cherished Possession:** 'My nearest and dearest – including my black cocker spaniel.' **Favourite Memory:** 'Getting home after my first morning at kindergarten in Aberdeen, aged three.'

KELLY, Barbara

TV personality, b. 5 October, Vancouver, Canada. Began career in CBC Radio, Canada, then in *The Stage Series.* Arrived in Britain in 1949 and offered BBC Radio series. Many TV appearances incl: *Kelly's Eye; Criss Cross Quiz; Leave Your Name and Number.* Joined *What's My Line?* team 1950 and appeared on and off for 15 years. m. Bernard Braden; 1 s. Christopher, 2 d. Kelly, Kim. Address: c/o Prime Performers, 5 Kidderpore Avenue, London NW3 7SX. Birthsign: Libra. Hobbies: sleeping, TV, tennis. Pets: two dogs. **Most Cherished Possession:** 'Having someone to love.' **Favourite Memory:** 'Being able to sleep on my tummy after my first baby was born.'

KELLY, Chris

Writer/producer/presenter, b. 24 April 1940, Cuddington, Cheshire. Started career with Anglia TV, then producer with Granada before going freelance. TV incl: *Clapperboard; World In Action; The Royal Academy Summer Exhibition; The Royal Film Performance; I've Got a Secret; Wish You Were Here; Never Too Early, Never Too Late; Friday Live; Folio; Cinema Scrapbook; Food and Drink.* As writer: *Zero Option:* (two-hour drama for Central TV); *The Telebook.* m. Vivien; 1 d. Rebecca, 1 s. Nicholas. Address: c/o Barry Burnett, London. Birthsign: Taurus. Hobbies: reading, cooking, collecting. Pets: four cats. **Most Cherished Possession:** 'A painting by Fred Hall, of the Newlyn School. It calms me.' **Favourite Memory:** 'Corfe Castle in the evening. Absolute peace.'

KELLY, David

Actor, b. 11 July 1929, Dublin, Ireland. Trained at the Abbey Theatre School. Has appeared many times on stage in Paris, Amsterdam, Oslo, Stockholm, Zurich, and Berlin. Films incl: *The Red Monarch; The Jigsaw Man; Ann Devlin; Pirates.* Dozens of dramas on TV, from *Armchair Theatre* to BBC's Shakespeare series. Best known for many sit-coms, incl: *Robin's Nest; Oh! Brother; Fawlty Towers; Cowboys; Slinger's Day.* m. actress Laurie Morton; 1 d. Miriam, 1 s. David. Address: c/o Joy Jameson. Birthsign: Cancer. Hobby: painting landscapes. Pets: one dog. **Most Cherished Possession:** 'My home. In this profession, to own one is a small miracle.' **Favourite Memory:** 'The first standing ovation I ever got, because it was also the last standing ovation I ever got.'

KELLY, Henry

Reporter/presenter, b. 17 April 1946, Dublin. Trained in daily journalism on *The Irish Times,* where he worked for eight years, travelling all over the world as a reporter. Joined Radio 4 in 1976 and has since done much radio work incl: *The World Tonight; Profile; Woman's Hour; Midweek.* Co-presented TV's *Game For a Laugh* for the first three years. Presenter on TV-am; and of *Monkey Business; Scene '85, '86, '87, '88; Extra Time; Going For Gold.* Book: *How Stormont Fell.* m. Marjorie; 1 d. Siobhan. Address: 8 Sandy Road, London NW3 7EY. Birthsign: Aries. Hobbies: golf, cricket, racing, reading. **Most Cherished Possession:** 'My driving licence – almost clean!' **Favourite Memory:** 'Watching Dawn Run win the 1986 Cheltenham Gold Cup.'

KELLY, Matthew

Actor, b. 9 May 1950, Manchester. First 10 years spent working in theatre, incl variety, rep and West End. TV incl: *The Bonus; Pickersgill People; Holding the Fort* (three series); *The Critic; Room Service; Madabout* (two series); *Relative Strangers* (two series); *The Sensible Show; Game For a Laugh* (three series); *Adventures of a Lifetime* (two series); *Kelly's Eye.* m. Sarah; 1 d. Ruth, 1 s. Matthew. Address: c/o Stella Richards Management. Birthsign: Taurus. Hobbies: travelling, swimming, dancing, talking, laughing. **Most Cherished Possession:** 'A matchbox toy of a lorry called Tiny, cherished from childhood.' **Favourite Memory:** 'Arrival in Sri Lanka on my first visit to the tropics. Feeling the sun hit my legs as I stepped off the plane, I knew I was in Paradise.'

KELLY, Sam

Actor, b. 19 December 1943, Manchester. Trained at LAMDA, 1964–67, and then rep at St Andrews, Liverpool, Sheffield, Manchester, Coventry, Birmingham, Southampton and the Young Vic, London. West End Theatre incl: *'Allo, 'Allo!; Run For Your Wife.* TV incl: *Emergency–Ward 10; The Liver Birds; Porridge; 'Allo, 'Allo!; Who's Who; Grown Ups; Victoria Wood As Seen On TV; Boys From the Blackstuff; Now and Then; Coronation Street; Christabel; Haggard.* Address: c/o Richard Stone, London. Birthsign: Sagittarius. Hobbies: watching cricket, classical music, barber shop singing. **Most Cherished Possession:** 'My Lancashire CCC membership card. It makes me feel that I could just be playing for them.' **Favourite Memory:** 'Holidaying in Queensland.'

KENDAL, Felicity

Actress, b. 25 September, Birmingham. Taken to India when three months old by her parents, who were travelling actors. Returned to Birmingham to live with her aunt. Break in a TV play with John Gielgud, *The Mayfly and the Frog.* Theatre incl: Regent's Park Open Air Theatre; *Keen; The Norman Conquests; Clouds; Amadeus; On the Razzle; The Second Mrs Tanqueray* and *Othello* (all for the National Theatre); *Made In Bangkok; Haggard; Much Ado About Nothing; Ivanov;* (London Evening Standard Drama Awards Best Actress, 1989). Also in *The Real Thing* and *Jumpers* in the West End. Films: *Shakespeare Wallah; Valentino.* TV incl: *Crime of Passion; Love Story; The Woodlanders; Edward the Seventh; The Good Life; Solo; The Mistress.* m. (1st) Drewe Henley (dis.), (2nd) Michael Rudman; 2 s. Charlie (from 1st m.), Jacob (2nd m.). Address: c/o Chatto & Linnit.

KENDALL, Kenneth

Presenter, b. 7 August 1924, South India, but brought up in Cornwall. Former schoolmaster and wartime Captain in the Coldstream Guards. Joined BBC 1948. Newsreader 1955–61 when he left to go freelance, but returned in 1969. Voted best-dressed newsreader by Style International and No 1 newcaster by Daily Mirror readers 1979. Left BBC 1981 and became co-presenter of C4's *Treasure Hunt.* Address: c/o Lewis Joelle, 108 Frobisher House, Dolphin Square, London SW1. Birthsign: Leo. Hobbies: gardening, walking, cooking. Pets: two dogs. **Most Cherished Possession:** 'My dogs, my constant companions.' **Favourite Memory:** 'As a child, sea voyages with my parents between England and India, where my father worked.'

KENNEDY, Cheryl

Actress, b. 29 April 1947, Enfield, Middlesex. Trained at the Corona Stage School. Theatre incl: *Half a Sixpence; The Boy Friend; 1776; Time and Time Again; Absent Friends; Flowers For Algernon; My Fair Lady* (in US with Rex Harrison); *Time and the Conways* (Old Vic); *What a Way To Run a Revolution* (Young Vic). TV incl: Cliff Richard and Mike Yarwood shows; *That's Life; Omnibus; Play For Today; Play of the Month; The Sweeney; Target; The Professionals; Brookside.* m. (dis.); 2 d. Clarissa, Samantha. Address: c/o Larry Dalzell Assocs. Hobbies: stamp collecting, swimming. Pets: three dogs, one goldfish. **Most Cherished Possession:** 'My stamp collection. I have collected stamps since I was twelve years old.'

KENNEDY, Kevin

Actor, b. 4 September 1961, Manchester. Trained at Manchester Polytechnic School of Theatre. Has appeared on stage in *Ducking Out* at the Greenwich Theatre and West End, London; in *Hamlet* at the Crucible Theatre, Sheffield. Radio incl: *The Old Man Sleeps Alone; Metamorphosied Arkwright.* TV incl: *Dear Ladies; The Last Company Car; Keep On Running;* Curly Watts in *Coronation Street* since 1982. m. Dawn; 1 s. Ryan. Address: c/o Saraband Assocs. Birthsign: Virgo. Hobbies: music, football, reading. Pets: one cat, Pencil. **Most Cherished Possession:** 'Ryan, my son, because he makes me laugh.' **Favourite Memory:** 'Manchester City FC winning the League Cup at Wembley in 1976.'

KENNEDY, Sarah

Broadcaster, b. 8 July 1950, Wallington. Worked in radio in Singapore and Germany before joining BBC Radio in London. Radio incl: *String Sound; Start the Week with Richard Baker; Colour Supplement.* TV incl: *Royal Progress; Animal Roadshow; Chipperfield Safari; Game For a Laugh; 60 Minutes; Daytime; Busman's Holiday.* Address: c/o Bagenal Harvey. Birthsign: Cancer. Hobbies: running, swimming, weeding, tennis. **Most Cherished Possession:** 'Health, and my terracotta pots.' **Favourite Memory:** 'Getting the aforementioned pots on to the roof.'

KENNELLY, Sheila

Actress. Trained at the Independent Theatre, eventually giving up an advertising office job to join the Elizabethan Theatre Trust. Worked in music-halls for four years. TV incl: Norma Whittaker in *Number 96; Kingswood Country; Secret Valley;* Floss MacPhee in *Home and Away.* Address: c/o Lee Leslie Management, 72 Glebe Point Road, Glebe, NSW 2037, Australia.

KERCHEVAL, Ken

Actor, b. 15 July, Wolcottville, Indiana. Appeared in summer theatres in California and regional theatres: on Broadway in *Something About a Soldier* and *Fiddler On the Roof.* TV films incl: *Enemy of the People.* TV guest star in: *Trapper John MD; Matlock; Love Boat; Hotel; Mike Hammer.* Cliff Barnes in *Dallas.* Other TV incl: *Naked City; Secret Storm.* m. (1st) (dis.); 2 s. Aaron, Caleb, 1 d. Liza, (2nd) Ava Fox. Address: c/o Triad Agency, 10100 Santa Monica Blvd, LA, CA 90067. Hobbies: antiques, restoring Packard cars, collecting American regional art. Pets: one dog. **Most Cherished Possession:** 'My 1939 Packard V12.' **Favourite Memory:** 'I spent one summer digging sewer tunnels 50 feet underneath Manhattan!'

KERSHAW, Richard

Presenter/reporter, b. 16 April 1934, London. Cambridge graduate and University of Virginia Graduate School. Spent 10 years as member of BBC TV's *Panorama* reporting team; then presenter of *Newsday, Newsweek* and *Nationwide.* Other TV incl: *This Week; Gallery; Tonight; Platform One; The World About Us; The Business Programme; Tomorrow Tonight.* m. (dis.); two children. Address: c/o Arlington Enterprises. Birthsign: Aries. Hobby: sport, particularly cricket. **Most Cherished Possession:** 'My flat, because I live and work there.' **Favourite Memory:** 'First seeing New York from the sea.'

KEY, Janet

Actress, b. 10 July 1945, Bath. Trained at Bristol Old Vic Theatre School. Theatre incl: Bristol Old Vic, Hornchurch, Watford, RSC, National Theatre. Films incl: *Percy; 1984.* TV incl: *Trial; The Dorati Conspiracy; Regan; The Sweeney; Man At the Top; The Cress; Cousin Bette; The Tenant of Wildfell Hall; Vanishing Army; You Don't Have To Fly; Demons; Heart of the Country; Running Wild.* m. actor/writer Gawn Grainger; 1 d. Eliza, 1 s. Charlie. Address: c/o Peter Browne Management. Birthsign: Cancer. Hobbies: reading, jazz dance, tennis. Pets: two tortoises. **Most Cherished Possession:** 'My mother's poetry collection – because I loved her!' **Favourite Memory:** 'The day I met my husband – because I love him!'

KEYS, Richard

Presenter, b. 23 April 1957, Coventry. Started career in journalism at the Wolverhampton *Express & Star,* before moving to a Fleet Street news agency. Then worked for Independent Local Radio in Liverpool and Manchester. Moved to TV-am as sports reporter, then presenter of *Good Morning Britain.* m. Julia; 1 d. Jemma, 1 s. Joshua. Address: c/o TV-am. Hobbies: squash, golf, football, tennis. Birthsign: Taurus.

KILROY-SILK, Robert

Writer/broadcaster, b. 18 May 1942. Birmingham. Labour MP 1974–86. TV incl: *Day To Day; Kilroy!* m. Jan; 1 d. Natasha, 1 s. Dominic. Address: c/o The Kilroy Television Company, Lime Grove, London W12. Birthsign: Taurus. Hobbies: gardening, golf. Pets: ducks, geese, doves, dog and cats. **Most Cherished Possession:** 'An art deco figure.' **Favourite Memory:** 'Being at the birth of Natasha.'

KING, Chris

Actor/entertainer, b. 2 June 1956, Hobart, Tasmania. Trained at the Theatre Workshop and at Hobart Rep. TV incl: *Lindsay's Boy; Pig In a Poke; Ben Hall; Certain Woman; Number 96; A Country Practice;* eight years as Dennis Jamieson in *The Young Doctors.* Tours with his own cabaret show, *The Chris King Show.* m. Susie; 4 d. Eliza Anne, Christina Louise, Belinda Rose, Stacey Lee. Address: c/o PO Box 59, Forestville, NSW 2087. Birthsign: Gemini. Hobbies: cricket, touch football, swimming, collecting badges, hats and T-shirts. Pets: one cat, Jessie. **Most Cherished Possession:** 'My Bible, because it is a constant source of inspiration and wisdom.' **Favourite Memory:** 'The births of all my four daughters. I don't think anything can match the miracle of life.'

KING, Claire

Actress, b. 10 January 1963, Yorkshire. Attended the Actors' Institute at Harrogate College. Theatre incl: *The Pleasure Principle.* Films: *Heart of Fire; Eat the Rich; The Cold Light of Day.* TV: *Watch With Mother; Hot Metal; Starting Out; The Bill;* presenter of American pop programme *Shout;* Kim Tate in *Emmerdale* since 1989. Address: c/o Heidi Cook Personal Management, 47 Greencoat Place, Westminster, London SW1P 1DS, tel 071-828 8185. Birthsign: Capricorn. Hobbies: horse-riding, swimming, rock music. Pets: several goldfish and a black labrador. **Most Cherished Possession:** 'A 6ft cheese plant called George! I've had him for eight years, from a baby, and he's travelled to various homes with me.'

KING, Jonathan

Presenter, b. 6 December 1948, London. Has worked as a pop entepreneur and artist, producer, journalist, owner of a record company, consultant to a major record label, author. Own BBC TV series *Entertainment USA*. Also devised BBC 2's *No Limits*. Address: c/o Carole Broughton, 1 Wyndham Yard, Wyndham Place, London W1H 1AR. Birthsign: Sagittarius. Hobby: self.

KINGSTON, Mark

Actor, b. 18 April 1934, London. Trained at the London Academy of Music and Drama and made his theatre debut at Boscombe Hippodrome 1953, then rep seasons. First London appearance in *Caesar and Cleopatra* at Old Vic. Toured Russia, Poland, Australia and New Zealand with Old Vic Company. Many London appearances since incl: *The Norman Conquests; The Cocktail Party; A Voyage Round My Father; Clouds; Educating Rita; Woman In Black*. TV incl: *United; Beryl's Lot; Time of My Life; Driving Ambition; Shine On Harvey Moon; No Job For a Lady*. m. Marigold Sharman. Address: c/o CDA. Birthsign: Aries. Hobbies: music, golf. **Most Cherished Possession:** 'My health.' **Favourite Memory:** 'My father.'

KIRKBRIDE, Anne

Actress, b. 21 June 1954, Oldham, Lancashire. Trained at Oldham rep. TV incl: *Another Sunday, Sweet FA;* has played Deirdre in *Coronation Street* since 1972. Address: c/o Granada TV. Birthsign: Gemini. Hobby: photography.

KITCHEN, Michael

Actor, b. 31 October 1948, Leicester. Worked with the National Youth Theatre, then a year as ASM before RADA. Appeared at London's Royal Court Theatre, Young Vic and National Theatre, where plays incl: *On the Razzle; Bedroom Farce* (and TV); *Spring Awakening; Rough Crossing; The Pied Piper; Fools of Fortune; The Russian House*. Other theatre incl: *Othello; Macbeth; Charley's Aunt*. Films incl: *The Bunker; Out of Africa; Dracula Today; Breaking Glass*. TV incl: *Brontes of Haworth; The Reporters; Churchill's People; No Man's Land; Fall of Eagles; Brimstone & Treacle; The Long, The Short and the Tall; As Man and Wife; No Man's Land; The Monkey's Paw; Lawrence & Frieda; Savages; The Early Life of Stephen Hind*. Address: c/o Markham & Froggatt. Hobbies: music, tennis, writing, flying.

KLIBINGAITIS, Maxine

Actress, b. 17 May 1964, Ballarat, Victoria. Went into acting straight from school 1983 in *Home*, an Australian TV drama. Other TV incl: Bobbie Mitchell in *Prisoner: Cell Block H;* Terri Inglis in *Neighbours*. Also played leading role in 1987 Australian film *Bibi*. m. director Andrew Friedman. Agent: Lee Leslie Management, 72 Glebe Point Road, Glebe, NSW, Australia. Birthsign: Taurus. Hobby: watching TV, especially videos of *The Young Ones* and *Filthy Rich and Catflap*. Pets: one dog, Henrietta. **Most Cherished Possession:** 'My home, because it is a happy place and very pretty.' **Favourite Memory:** 'My wedding day in 1987, because it was a fairytale day.'

KNOX, Barbara

Actress, b. 1938, Oldham, Lancashire. Left school at 15 to work as a Post Office telegraphist, then in offices, shops and factories. After some amateur acting, joined Oldham Rep and worked extensively in repertory theatre, radio and TV, before joining *Coronation Street* in 1972 as Rita Littlewood, living as 'Mrs Bates' with Harry Bates. The character later married Len Fairclough and was widowed in 1983. Winner, 1989 *TVTimes* Best Actress award. Other TV incl: *Emergency–Ward 10; Mrs Thursday; Never Mind the Quality, Feel the Width; The Dustbinmen; A Family at War*. Film: *Goodbye Mr Chips*. Record: *On the Street Where I Live* (LP, 1973). m. 1st Denis (dis.), 2nd John Knox; 1 d. Maxine (from 1st m.). Address: c/o Granada TV.

KOVE, Martin

Actor, b. 6 March 1947, Brooklyn, New York. Started career at La Mama Theatre, New York, and in rep. Films incl: *Where's Poppa?; Capone; Death Race 2000; Savages; The Four Deuces; Partners; First Blood II; The Karate Kid; Cry For the Stranger; The Sky Trap*. TV incl: *Code-R; The Edge of Night; The Optimist;* plays Isbecki in *Cagney and Lacey*. Hon chairman for the Love of Life Foundation. m. Vivienne; 1 step-s, Sean Raymond. Address: c/o The Agency, 10351 Santa Monica Blvd, LA, CA 90025. Hobbies: tennis, riding, scuba-diving, skiing. **Most Cherished Possession:** 'I'm a Wild West buff and cherish my Wild West mementoes; also my martial arts equipment.' **Favourite Memory:** 'My annual three-day horseback rides to Wyoming where Butch Cassidy's gang hung out a century ago.'

KRAMER, Stepfanie

Actress/director/singer, b. 6 August, Long Beach, California. Trained at the American Academy of Arts/West. Many guest roles on TV incl: *Knots Landing; Starsky and Hutch; Trapper John; Dynasty; The A-Team; Fantasy Island; Vegas; Operation Runway*. TV series incl: *We Got It Made; Hunter* (directed the first episode). TV film: *Terror At the London Bridge*. Address: c/o William Morris Agency, Beverly Hills. Birthsign: Leo. Hobbies: dancing, writing and performing country and rock 'n' roll music. Pets: one dog, Maggie. **Most Cherished Possession:** 'My father died when I was very young. I kept all the sheet music he wrote. It's very special to me.' **Favourite Memory:** 'My mother is an artist. As a child, I loved watching her paint.'

THE KRANKIES

Husband and wife comedy team that began at Pavilion, Glasgow. Voted Comedy Act of the Year 1978 and made Royal Variety Show debut same year. Starred in first Children's Royal Variety Show 1981 and several Royal Shows since, plus summer seasons, pantos and tours. TV incl: *Crackerjack; The Krankies Klub; Krankies Elektronik Komik; Joke Machine; Krankies Television;* own series for BBC, LWT, Border. **Ian Tough**, b. 26 March 1947, Glasgow. Address: c/o International Artistes. Birthsign: Aries. Hobbies: golf, fishing. **Janet Tough**, b. 16 May 1947, Queenzieburn, Stirlingshire. Birthsign: Taurus. Hobbies: golf, swimming in the sea. **Most Cherished Possession:** 'The boots worn by "wee Jimmy". They were Ian's grandad's and have become our good luck charm.'

KWOUK, Burt

Actor, 18 July 1930, Manchester. Grew up in Shanghai, went to USA and returned to England 1953. First break in a *Charlie Drake Show* and the film *The Inn of the Sixth Happiness*. Well known as Peter Sellers's karate-mad houseboy in *The Pink Panther* films. Films incl: *A Shot In the Dark; Madame Sin; Deep End; The Most Dangerous Man In the World; Goldfinger; You Only Live Twice; The Return of the Pink Panther; The Fiendish Plot of Dr Fu Manchu; The Trail of the Pink Panther; Plenty; The Curse of the Pink Panther*. TV incl: *Tenko; Hart To Hart; Supergran; Switch On to English; The Brief; The Lenny Henry Show*. Address: c/o London Management. Birthsign: Cancer. Hobby: time-wasting.

LA RUE, Danny

Actor/entertainer, b. 26 July 1927, Cork, Ireland. Joined Royal Navy 1944. West End Theatre incl: *Come Spy With Me; Danny La Rue At The Palace; Danny La Rue Show; Aladdin*. Three Royal Variety Shows. 1983 became the first man to star as Dolly Levi in *Hello Dolly* at the Prince of Wales Theatre. Films: *Our Miss Fred*. TV incl: *The Good Old Days; Charley's Aunt; Tonight With Danny La Rue; This Is Your Life*. Autobiography: *From Drags To Riches*. Address: c/o Brian Shaw, 140 High Street, Cheshunt, Hertfordshire. **Most Cherished Possession:** 'A cassette recording of a poem, written to celebrate my 50th birthday by my late manager, Jack Hanson.' **Favourite Memory:** 'Sharing the dance floor at my nightclub with my mother, Liberace and his mother, Pete Murray and his mother.'

LACEY, Ronald

Actor, b. 28 September 1935, Harrow, Middlesex. Trained at LAMDA after National Service. Theatre incl: *St Joan; Chips With Everything; The Fourth of June; Private Dick*. Films incl: *Sky Bandits; The Hit Man; Raiders of the Lost Ark; Zulu Dawn; Red Sonia; Firefox; Betrayal; The Likely Lads; Charleston; Sword of the Valient; Nijinsky; Sahara; Flesh and Blood; Buckeroo Banzai; Making the Grade; Invitation to the Wedding; Valmont; Face To Face; Stalingrad*. TV incl: *Unnatural Causes; Boon; Sign of Four; Hart To Hart; Hard Cases; Staircase; Masquerade; Lady Killers; Rothko; Aubrey Beardsley; Tiny Revolutions; Magnum PI; Scarecrow and Mrs King; The Nightmare Years; The Great Escape – The Sequel*. m. (1st) Mela (dis.), (2nd) Joann; 1 d. Rebecca, 2 s. David (both from 1st m.), Matthew (from 2nd). Address: c/o Joyce Edwards. Hobby: photography. Pets: two cats.

LAINE, Cleo, OBE

Singer/actress, b. 28 October 1927, Southall, Middlesex. A hairdresser's apprentice before being introduced to John Dankworth. Signed up to sing with the Dankworth Orchestra 1953. Theatre incl: *A Time To Laugh; Hedda Gabler; Showboat; The Seven Deadly Sins; Facade; A Little Night Music* (US, 1983); *Into the Woods* (US, 1989). Many awards incl Grammy as Best Jazz Vocalist (Female) 1985. m. (1st) George (dis.), (2nd) John Dankworth; 1 d. Jacqueline (from 1st m.), 2 s. Stuart (from 1st), Alex (from 2nd). Address: c/o International Artistes. Birthsign: Scorpio. Hobbies: painting, cooking. **Most Cherished Possession:** 'The first night programme of my daughter Jackie's first production with the RSC.' **Favourite Memory:** 'My son Alex playing bass for me at the Hollywood Bowl.'

LALLY, Teri

Actress, b. 21 April 1961, Coatbridge, Scotland. Trained at drama school in Edinburgh. Theatre incl: *Don't Tell the Wife; Never a Dull Moment; Cinderella; Babes In the Wood; Dick Whittington; Mother Goose*. Films: *Comfort and Joy; Restless Natives*. TV incl: Carol McKay in *Take the High Road; The Video Show; It's Andy Cameron*. m. Ken. Address: c/o Scottish TV. Birthsign: Taurus. Hobbies: reading, cinema, home decoration. **Most Cherished Possession:** 'It must be my "home laundry" – automatic machine and tumble drier!' **Favourite Memory:** 'A holiday spent in the Lake District.'

LAMAS, Lorenzo

Actor, b. 20 January, Los Angeles. The son of Arlene Dahl and the late Fernando Lamas, he trained with the Film Actors' Workshop. Best known for his role as Lance Cumson in the TV soap *Falcon Crest*. Films incl: *Body Rock; Grease; Tilt; Take Down*. Other TV incl: *California Fever; Secrets of Midland Heights; Detour; Love Boat; Hotel; Switch; Sword of Justice*. m. (1st) Victoria Hilbert (dis.), (2nd) Michele Smith (dis.), (3rd) Kathleen Kinmont; 1 d. Shayne, 1 s. Alvaro Joshua (both from 2nd m.). Address: c/o Herb Nanas, 2128 Pico Blvd, Santa Monica, California 90405. Hobbies: surfing, karate, guitar, skiing, riding motorcycles. Pets: three dogs. **Most Cherished Possession:** 'My three tattoos.' **Favourite Memory:** 'The birth of my children.'

LANDEN, Dinsdale

Actor, b. 4 September 1932, Margate, Kent. Trained at Florence Moore School of Theatre, Hove, before National Service with the RAF. Theatre incl: *The Philanthropist; Alphabetical Order; Plunder; The Merchant of Venice; On the Razzle; Uncle Vanya; Bodies; Thark; The Philanderer.* Films incl: *The Valiant; We Joined the Navy; Mosquito Squadron; Morons From Outer Space; Every Home Should Have One.* TV incl: *Pig In the Middle; Glittering Prizes; Devenish; Events In a Museum; This Office Life; Great Expectations; Arms and the Man.* m. actress Jennifer Daniel. Address: c/o Michael Whitehall. Birthsign: Virgo. Hobbies: golf, walking. Pets: two dogs, one cat. **Most Cherished Possession:** 'A house in East Anglia, a veritable retreat.' **Favourite Memory:** 'My first job as the back legs of a horse in *Cinderella* at Worthing Rep.'

LANDON, Michael

Actor/writer/producer/director, b. 21 October 1937, Forest Hills, New York. Films incl: *God's Little Acre; I Was a Teenage Werewolf.* TV incl: Little Joe in *Bonanza; Highway To Heaven; Little House on the Prairie.* Was also creator and producer of latter two, plus *Father Murphy.* m. (1st and 3rd) Cindy Clerico, (2nd) Lynn Noe (dis.); 9 children, 3 s. (1 adopted) and 1 d. with Cindy, 3 s. 2 d. (1 adopted) with Lynn. Address: c/o Malibu, California. Hobby: travel. Pets: cats, eight dogs, rabbits, one parrot. **Most Cherished Possession:** 'My family and my work.' **Favourite Memory:** 'I saw the movie *Samson and Delilah* and grew my hair long to give me strength. It worked. I was 126 pounds and the best high-school javelin thrower in the USA.'

LANDOR, Rosalyn

Actress, b. October 1958, Hampstead, London. Theatre incl: *Arms and the Man; Hay Fever.* Films incl: *The Devil Rides Out; Jane Eyre; The Amazing Mr Blunden; Divorce His/Divorce Hers.* TV incl: *E. Nesbitt; The Need For Nightmares; Edgar Allen Poe; Z-Cars; Dad; Little Girls Don't; Love In a Cold Climate; Rumpole of the Bailey; Sherlock Holmes; C.A.T.S. Eyes; The Speckled Band.* Address: c/o ICM. Birthsign: Libra. Hobbies: music, reading, shopping, travelling.

LANEUVILLE, Eric G

Actor/director, b. 14 July, New Orleans. Trained with the UCLA Theatre Group. Films incl: *Love At First Bite; A Piece of the Action; A Force of One; Backroads.* TV films: *Sacred Straight;* and as director, *The George McKenna Story* and *No Secrets.* Luther Hawkins in TV's *St Elsewhere.* Other TV incl: *Room 222; Hill Street Blues.* Has also directed five episodes of *St Elsewhere.* m. (dis.); 1 s. Sean. Address: c/o Twentieth Century Artists, 3518 Cahuenga Blvd, Los Angeles, California 90068. Birthsign: Cancer. Hobbies: cars, basketball, all sport. **Most Cherished Possession:** 'My golf clubs.' **Favourite Memory:** 'When the Los Angeles Lakers (A basketball team) won the 1987 championship.'

LANG, Robert

Actor/theatre director, b. 24 September 1934, Bristol. Trained at Bristol Old Vic Theatre School then Bristol Old Vic Company. Theatre incl: *Uncle Vanya; Dial M For Murder; Donkey's Years; The Medusa Touch; Rumpole and the Fascist Beast.* TV incl: *Vanity Fair; The Contract; The Birthday Party; That Was the Week That Was; Emergency–Ward 10; For Maddy With Love; 1990; King Lear; The Brack Report.* m. actress Ann Bell; 1 d. Rebecca, 1 s. John. Address: c/o Julian Belfrage Assocs. Birthsign: Libra. Hobbies: photography, pisciculture, gardening. **Most Cherished Possession:** 'My car radio, for bringing plays and people to all those hours of travelling.' **Favourite Memory:** 'Cheese sandwiches beside the Avon the day I caught my first roach.'

LANGFORD, Bonnie

Dancer/singer/actress, b. 22 July 1964, Hampton Court, Surrey. Trained at Arts Educational and Italia Conti stage schools in London. TV debut aged six on *Opportunity Knocks*. West End debut at seven in the musical version of *Gone With the Wind*. Other West End theatre incl: *Peter Pan – the Musical; Cats; Pirates of Penzance; Gypsy* on Broadway; *Me and My Girl*. Films incl: *Bugsy Malone; Wombling Free*. TV series incl: co-host of *Junior Showtime; Saturday Starship; Just William; Doctor Who; Hot Shoe Show*. Other TV incl: *Lena and Bonnie*. Address: c/o Billy Marsh Assocs. Birthsign: Gemini. **Most Cherished Possession:** 'A little medal which I carry with me, even on stage. It's my lucky charm.' **Favourite Memory:** 'Working in America in *Gypsy* and touring such a vast and beautiful country.'

LANGRISHE, Caroline

Actress, b. 10 January 1958, London. Joined the National Youth Theatre, then worked as a showgirl at the Hilton Hotel, London. Films: *Eagle's Wing; Les Misérables*. TV: *The Glittering Prizes; The Brothers; Anna Karenina; Wuthering Heights; The Flipside of Dominic Hide; Fortunes of War; Pulaski, Twelfth Night; The Return of Shelley; Boon; Chancer*. m. actor Patrick Drury; 2 d. Leonie, Rosalind. Address: c/o Duncan Heath Associates. Birthsign: Capricorn.

LANSBURY, Angela

Actress, b. 16 October 1925, London. Trained at Webber Douglas and Feagin schools. Theatre incl: *A Taste of Honey; Sweeney Todd; Hamlet* (three Tony awards). Films incl: *Gaslight; The Harvey Girls; The Picture of Dorian Gray; Samson and Delilah; Bedknobs and Broomsticks; Death on the Nile; The Lady Vanishes; National Velvet; The Pirates of Penzance*. Three Oscar nominations. TV incl: Jessica Fletcher in *Murder, She Wrote*. m. (1st) Richard Cromwell, (2nd) Peter Shaw; 1 s. Anthony, 1 step-s. David, 1 d. Deidre. Address: c/o William Morris Agency, 151 El Camino Drive, Beverly Hills, CA. Hobbies: gardening, involved in social causes, especially violence in the home. **Favourite Memory:** 'Of all my roles, the happiest has been as wife to Peter Shaw.'

LARGE, Eddie

Impressionist/comedian, b. 25 June 1942, Glasgow. First ambition was to be a footballer before accident ended that career. Met Syd Little and teamed up as a singing duo. Turned to comedy before winning *Opportunity Knocks* 1971. TV incl: *Who Do You Do?; Wednesday At Eight; Disneytime; Little and Large*. Also, London, Palladium, pantomimes and summer seasons. m. Patsy Ann; 2 d. Alison, Samantha, 1 s. Ryan. Address: c/o Peter Prichard. Birthsign: Cancer. Hobbies: golf, keep fit, supporting Manchester City FC. **Most Cherished Possession:** 'A very poignant poem that my father wrote about his life just before he died.' **Favourite Memory:** 'The time I sang *Do You Wanna Dance*, backed by Syd Little and The Shadows! Even Cliff never had that experience!'

LATHAM, Bernard

Actor, b. 21 April 1951, Manchester. Trained at Bristol Old Vic Theatre School. Theatre incl appearances at Manchester, Stoke-on-Trent, Cardiff, Exeter, Clwyd, Sheffield and London. Films incl: *The Lovers; Boy Soldier*. Acted in about 30 plays. TV incl: *The Practice; Carrott Del Sol; Tan Tro Nesa; The Danedyke Mystery; Crown Court; Fox; Coronation Street; Hard Times; Sally Ann; Flying Lady*. m. Jane; 1 d. Emily. Address: c/o Michelle Braidman Assocs. Birthsign: Taurus. Hobby: decorating under duress. **Most Cherished Possession:** 'My house in Cardiff, because it's where my video lives!' **Favourite Memory:** 'My recent trip to Africa. Playing Bottom to Africans proved to me that comedy is universal.'

LATHAM, Philip

Actor, b. 17 January, Leigh-on-Sea, Essex. After National Service, trained at RADA and in rep at Farnham. Most recent theatre incl: tours of *The Letter; The Winslow Boy*. Films incl: *Spy Story; Force Ten From Navarone*. TV incl: *Mogul; Maigret; The Troubleshooters; Whose Life Is It Anyway?; No Exit; Time-Lock; Good At Games; The Pallisers; The Cedar Tree; The Professionals; The Killers; Hammer House of Horror; Name For the Day; Nanny; No 10; The Fourth Arm; Man From the Pru*. He is also in demand for his religious readings. m. Eve, 1 d. Amanda, 1 s. Andrew. Address: c/o Bryan Drew Ltd, London. Birthsign: Capricorn. Hobby: golf. **Most Cherished Possession:** 'Freedom of thought.' **Favourite Memory:** 'Many happy "family" times.'

LAWRENCE, Kelly

Actress, b. 31 August 1966, East London. Joined the children's entertainment group Kids International at the age of 14, appearing in *The Les Dawson Show*, BBC TV specials and Children's Royal Variety Performances. Trained at Boden Studios. Theatre: *The Wizard of Oz; Anne of Green Gables; The Crucible*. Film: National Film School production of *Beelzebub*. TV: *Dramarama; The Practice; Travelling Man;* Louise Todd in *Albion Market;* WPC Claire Brind in *The Bill* (1988–9). Plus training videos and a health education film with Rowan Atkinson. Address: c/o LWA. Birthsign: Virgo.

LAWRENCE, Patricia

Actress, b. 19 November, Andover, Hampshire. Trained at RADA (won the Bancroft Gold Medal). West End theatre incl: *Heat of the Day; Funny Sunday/Sometime Never; Five Finger Exercise; Dead Ringer; Man of Mode; Across Oka; Restoration; Some Americans Abroad* (RSC member, 1987–9). Films incl: *Tom Jones; The Hireling; Room With a View*. TV incl: *Our Mutual Friend; Telford's Change; To Serve Them All My Days; Seven Faces of Woman; Barriers; Tenko; The Gentle Touch; Paradise Postponed; They Never Slept*. m. Greville Poke (chairman of LAMDA and Thorndike Theatre); 2 s. James, Christopher. Address: c/o David White Assocs. Hobbies: drawing, needlepoint. **Most Cherished Possession:** 'My wedding ring, made from a ring belonging to my great-great-grandmother.'

LAWRENCE, Stephanie

Actress, b. 16 December, Hayling Island. Trained at Arts Educational School and made first London stage appearance aged 12 in *The Nutcracker*. West End debut in *Forget Me Not Lane*. Other West End incl: the lead in *Evita; The Royal Variety Show* (also TV); *Time;* lead in *Marilyn The Musical; Starlight Express; Kiss Me Kate*. TV incl: *Rod Argent Showcase; The David Frost End of the Year Show; The Two Ronnies;* one-woman show *6.55*. Records incl: *You Saved My Life* (with *Johnny Mathis*); *Only Me; Starlight Express; The Music of Andrew Lloyd Webber*. Films: *Buster; Phantom of the Opera*. Address: c/o Susan James. Hobbies: gardening, clothes, music, water-skiing, riding. Pets: two dogs, one cat. **Most Cherished Possession:** 'My award for *Marilyn the Musical* – a personally signed book by Ingrid Bergman.'

LAWSON, Leigh

Actor, b. 21 July 1943, Atherstone, Warwickshire. Trained at Mountview Theatre School 1964–67 and RADA 1967–69. Worked extensively in rep. Theatre incl: *Yonadab; The Price of Justice; A Touch of Spring; The Cherry Orchard; The Second Mrs Tanqueray; From the Balcony*. Many films, most recent incl: *The Sword of the Valiant; Tess; Madame Sousatzka*. TV incl: *Black Carrian; Journey Into the Shadows; Travelling Man; Lace; Queenie; Deadline*. m. actress Twiggy Lawson; 2 s. 1 d. Address: c/o Duncan Heath Associates. Birthsign: Cancer.

LAWSON, Twiggy

Actress, b. 19 September 1949, London. Hairdresser's assistant-turned-model, became an actress at 20. First film role in *The Boy Friend*. Stage debut in *Cinderella* 1974. Theatre incl: *Captain Beaky's Musical Christmas; My One and Only* (on Broadway). Films incl: *W; Shadow of Evil; There Goes the Bride; The Blue Brothers; The Doctors and the Devils; Club Paradise; Madame Sousatzka; Istanbul.* TV incl: *Twiggs; Twiggy; The Frontiers of Science; Bring On the Girls; Roller Coaster; The Muppet Show; Pygmalion; Jukebox; Sun Child; The Little Match Girl; The Great Diamond Robbery; Charlie the Kid.* Records incl: *The Boy Friend; Twiggy; Here I Go Again; Please Get My Name Right; A Woman In Love; Tomorrow Is Another Day; My One and Only.* Books: *Twiggy* (autobiography); *Unlimited Twiggy* m. Leigh Lawson; 1 d. Carly. Address: c/o Neville Shulman.

LAYTON, George

Actor/writer/director, b. 2 March 1943, Bradford, Yorkshire. Trained at Royal Academy of Dramatic Art. Many stage roles, incl Fagin in *Oliver* (Albery Theatre). Directed and performed in many pantomimes. TV incl: *The Likely Lads; My Brother's Keeper* and the *Doctor* series (co-writer with Jonathan Lynn); *It Ain't Half Hot Mum; Minder; Pass the Buck; That's Life* (presenter in first series). Creator and writer of *Don't Wait Up* and *Executive Stress*. Wrote best-selling book of short stories, *The Fib and Other Stories.* m. Moya; 3 d. Tris, Claudie (from 1st m.), Hannah, 1 s. Daniel. Address: c/o Green & Underwood. Birthsign: Pisces. Hobbies: tennis, learning piano, reading. Pets: one dog, Strudel, two tortoises, Ethel and Albert.

LE VELL, Michael

Actor, b. 15 December 1964, Manchester. Theatre incl: *Kes; Joby; No More Sitting On the Old School Bench; Dick Whittington; Jack and the Beanstalk.* TV incl: *My Son, My Son; Fame Is the Spur; The Last Song; The Hard Word; A Brother's Tale; One By One;* Kevin Webster in *Coronation Street.* Address: c/o Granda TV. Birthsign: Sagittarius. Hobbies: football, pool, snooker, golf.

LEACH, Rosemary

Actress, b. 18 December 1935, Shropshire. Trained at RADA and then rep. Recent theatre incl: *84 Charing Cross Road; Six For Gold.* Films incl: *Room With a View; Crazy Like a Fox; SOS Titanic; The Bride; Turtle Summer.* TV incl: *The Charmer; Sadie It's Cold Outside; Cider With Rosie; Birthday; No That's Me Over Here; Life Begins At Forty; The Jewel In the Crown; The Enemy Within.* m. Colin Starkey. Address: c/o William Morris Agency. Birthsign: Sagittarius. Hobbies: cooking, keep fit, gardening, reading. Pets: one dog, three cats. **Most Cherished Possession:** 'My home and my garden, because they reassure me.' **Favourite Memory:** 'The cherry trees in bloom along the road from Richmond roundabout to Twickenham Bridge, just as it's getting dark.'

LEADER, Carol

Actress, b. 10 November, Colchester, Essex. Gained a BA Hons at York University. London theatre incl: *Topokana Martyrs Day; Bazaar And Rummage; Whole Music.* TV incl: *Sally Ann; Play School; Play Away; Flambards; Chockablock; Honky Tonk Heroes; Young At Heart; Out of Step; Getting On; Studio; Late Starter; Information World; First and Last.* m. Michael Maynard; 1 s. Jonathan. Address: c/o Lou Coulson. Birthsign: Scorpio. Hobbies: gardening, reading, visiting standing stones and ancient religious sites. **Most Cherished Possession:** 'A large old-fashioned style garden in London where I can convince myself that I live in the country.' **Favourite Memory:** 'Hearing my son start to talk.'

LEBOR, Stanley

Actor, b. 24 September 1934, East Ham, London. Trained at RADA. Theatre incl RSC 1964–66 and rep. Films incl: *Personal Services; Superman IV; Flash Gordon; A Bridge Too Far*. TV incl: *Ever Decreasing Circles; The Naked Civil Servant; Holocaust; Reilly Ace of Spies; Paradise Postponed; Minder; Shoestring; Secret Army; All the World's a Stage; Under the Hammer; Beyond the Pale; Hunting Tower*. m. Jill Rodwell; 3 s. David, Thomas, Michael. Address: c/o Essanay at Green & Underwood. Birthsign: Libra. Hobbies: bringing up children, politics, investing in stocks and shares. Pets: cats. **Most Cherished Possession:** 'Good health.' **Favourite Memory:** 'View of Jerusalem from neighbouring hills when filming in Israel, 1984. Why? Sheer beauty.'

LEHMAN, Valerie

Actress. Theatre incl: *Trafford Tanzi; Farewell Brisbane Ladies; Chicago; In Duty Bound; The Foreigner; Cake; A Streetcar Named Desire; A Lie of the Mind; One Extra Dance Co; A Touch of Silk; Who's Afraid of Virginia Woolf?; Coward*. Films: *Kitty and the Bagman; Army Wives*. TV: Bea Smith in *Prisoner: Cell Block H*, 1979–83 (won three Logie awards, two years running for best lead actress in a series, once for most popular lead actress in a series); *A Fortunate Life; Bellbird Wives; Prime Time; The Flying Doctors; Army; Obsession; Power Without Glory; The Saturday Show*; interviewed on *Parkinson: One To One*. m. 1st (dis.), 2nd Charles Collins; 2 d., 1 s. (from 1st m.). Address: c/o London Management.

LEUCHARS, Anne

Journalist, b. 2 August 1953, Kampala, Uganda. Trained on regional TV news magazine programmes. Is now a reporter and newscaster with ITN. Address: c/o ITN, ITN House, 48 Wells Street, London W1P 4DE. Birthsign: Leo. Hobbies: hillwalking, natural history, theatre. Pets: one cat, Sooty. **Most Cherished Possession:** 'My teddy bear – he has helped me through every crisis!' **Favourite Memory:** 'Any one of 100 walks in the Lake District, Northumberland or the Yorkshire Dales.'

LEWIS, Kim

Actor, b. 5 September 1963, Sydney, Australia. Trained at the National Institute of Dramatic Art 1984–87. Film: *Squizzy Taylor*. TV incl: *The Restless Years; Sons and Daughters*. Address: c/o Barbara Leane and Associates, 261 Miller Street, North Sydney, NSW, Australia. Birthsign: Virgo. Hobbies: sky diving, belly dancing. Pets: one fat-tailed sminthopsis, one peach-faced parrot, Mr Pointybird. **Most Cherished Possession:** 'My bed because it never changes, it's warm and comfortable, and it doesn't talk back to me.' **Favourite Memory:** 'My grandfather, because he was a great guy.'

LEWIS, Martyn

Newscaster/reporter, b. 7 April 1945, Swansea. Educated at Trinity College, Dublin. Joined BBC Belfast as a reporter in 1967; 1968–70 reporter/presenter HTV Cardiff. Worked for ITN: 1970–86, Northern correspondent; newcaster *News at 5.45* and *News at Ten*; 1986 joined BBC to present *One O'Clock News; Nine O'Clock News*. Documentaries: *The Secret Hunters; MacGregor's Verdict*. Producer/writer of *Battle For the Falklands* video. Book: *And Finally*. m. Liz; 2 d. Sylvie, Katie. Address: c/o BBC TV. Birthsign: Aries. Hobbies: tennis, photography, reading. **Most Cherished Possession:** 'Lucky takamaka seed found on a remote beach in the Seychelles – brings back memories I couldn't possibly describe here.' **Favourite Memory:** 'Watching my daughters being born.'

LILLICRAP, Christopher

Actor/writer/musician/presenter, b. 14 February 1949, Plymouth. Extensive Rep incl: Nottingham, Canterbury, Cheltenham and Theatre in Education. A self-taught musician. Presenter of *Making the Most Of; Wondermaths; Playboard; Flicks; Knock Knock.* TV incl: *Love Story; King Robert of Sicily;* two plays on Keats. Writer and performer of one-man children's series *Busker.* Also author, with wife of several children's plays, incl: *Christmas Cat and the Pudding Pirates.* m. actress Jeanette Ranger; 1 s. Dominic. Address: c/o Arlington Enterprises. Birthsign: Aquarius. Hobbies: golf, gardening. Pets: three cats, two tortoises. **Favourite Memory:** 'The birth of my son, the most amazing moment of my life. Words cannot explain.'

LINDEN, Jennie

Actress, b. 8 December 1939, Worthing, Sussex. Trained at Central School. Theatre incl: *Killing Jessica; On Approval; Hedda Gabler;* one-woman shows *Sounds Entertaining* and *Twice Brightly.* Films incl: *Corsican Brothers; Women In Love; A Severed Head.* TV incl: *Lillie; The Practice; Sister Mary; Lytton's Diary; Dick Turpin; Breadwinner; Degree of Uncertainty.* m. Christopher Mann; 1 s. Rupert. Address: c/o John Redway & Assocs. Birthsign: Sagittarius. Hobbies: gardening, music, singing, interior design, travel, spiritual research. Pets: two cats. **Most Cherished Possession:** 'My marriage, it is the only truly constructive achievement in my life.' **Favourite Memory:** 'Being invited to sing and dance at a Punch & Judy show when I was four years old.'

LINDSAY, Shona

Actress, b. 4 December 1969, Edinburgh. Professional debut at the age of 11, starring in the national tour of the musical *Annie;* classically trained singer. Theatre incl: national tour of *King's Rhapsody; The Wicked World of Bel-Ami; Dick Whittington.* TV: Barbara Boyer in *The Secret Diary of Adrian Mole Aged 13¾* and *The Growing Pains of Adrian Mole; Lizzie's Pictures; The Ritz;* Sara Briggs in *Crossroads.* Radio: star of BBC Radio 4's musical anthology *Alice In Wonderland.* Pop single: *Goodbye* (BMG, 1988). m. actor James Barron (from July 1990). Address: c/o Eric Glass. Hobbies: 'Sleeping, taking my cat for walks in the park.' Pets: 'Manic blue cat called Ivor (after Novello).' **Most Cherished Possession:** 'James and our home and pussycat.' **Favourite Memory:** 'Winning the part of Annie, which opened the door to my chosen career.'

LIPMAN, Maureen

Actress, b. 10 May 1946, Hull. Trained at LAMDA. Theatre incl: *Candida; Outside Edge; Messiah; Chapter Two; The Meg and Mog Show; On Your Way Riley; Smash; Night and Day; See How They Run* (won her an Olivier award); *Re: Joyce.* Films: *Gumshoe; Educating Rita; Water.* TV incl: *The Evacuees;* Jane Lucas in *Agony; Smiley's People; Couples; Dangerous Davies; The Knowledge; Rolling Home; Outside Edge; Love's Labours Lost; Absurd Person Singular; Absent Friends; Shift Work;* Sheila Haddon in *All At No 20* (won her the *TVTimes* Best Comedy Actress award); *About Face* (starring in six different plays). Radio incl: *Just a Minute; Event of the Season; When Housewives Had the Choice.* Books: *How Was It For You?; Something To Fall Back On.* m. playwright Jack Rosenthal; 1 d. Amy, 1 s. Adam. Address: c/o Saraband. Hobbies: writing, eating marzipan. Pet: one cat.

LITTLE, Syd

Comedian, b. 19 December 1942, Blackpool. Guitarist and singer before teaming up with Eddie Large as singing duo. Turned to comedy before winning *Opportunity Knocks* 1971. TV incl: *Seaside Special; Wheeltappers and Shunters Social Club; Wednesday At Eight; Little and Large.* m. Sheree; 1 d. Donna, 1 s. Paul. Address: c/o Peter Prichard. Birthsign: Sagittarius. Hobbies: making model boats, keep fit. **Most Cherished Possession:** 'A guitar which Paul McCartney played in our dressing room in 1965.' **Favourite Memory:** 'When I played *My Old Man's a Dustman* in a working man's club aged 16. My dad burst out of the gents wearing his jacket inside out, minus teeth, and his hair all spiked up, then walked around the club as I sang!'

LLOYD, Kevin

Actor, b. 28 March 1949, Derby. Trained at East 15 Acting School, London. Appeared at the Royal Court Theatre, London, and member of RSC. Theatre incl: *Love Girl and the Innocent; Stiff Options; The Foreigner.* Films incl: *Link; Brittania Hospital; Trial By Combat.* TV incl: *Auf Wiedersehen, Pet; Dempsey and Makepeace; All In Good Faith; Andy Capp; Coronation Street; Z-Cars; Minder; Hazell; Bergerac; The Borgias; By the Sword Divided; Dear John; Boon;* Det Sgt 'Tosh' Lines in *The Bill.* m. Lesley; 2 d. Sophie, Poppy, 4. s. Mark, James, Henry, Edward. Address: c/o Saraband Assocs. Hobbies: football, cricket, tennis. Pets: two dogs, five rabbits, one duck. **Most Cherished Possession:** 'My family. They make me realise how lucky I am.' **Favourite Memory:** 'Derby winning the Football League in 1972 and 1975.'

LLOYD PACK, Roger

Actor, b. 8 February 1944, London Trained at RADA. Theatre incl: *Kafka's Dick; Futurists; Yerma; Romersholm; Flea In Her Ear;* directed own play *The End.* Films incl: *Prick Up Your Ears; Hamlet; The Virgin Soldiers; The Go-Betweens; Nineteen Eighty-Four; The Cook, the Thief, His Wife and Her Lover; Wilt.* TV incl: *One For the Road; Inspector Morse; Only Fools and Horses; Making Good; Bouncing Back; Video Stars; The Brief; Made In Spain; The Contractor.* m. Jehane Markham; 1 d. Emily, 2 s. Spencer, Hartley. Address: c/o Kate Feast. Hobbies: chess, tennis, reading. Pets: one rabbit, Hazel. **Most Cherished Possession:** 'A letter to me from Samuel Beckett, because he was one of the greatest writers of our time.'

LOCKE, Philip

Actor, b. 29 March 1928, London. Trained at RADA. Royal Shakespeare stage appearances incl: *Richard III; The Tempest; Julius Caesar; Antony and Cleopatra; Amadeus.* Other theatre incl: *A Midsummer Night's Dream; Troilus and Cressida; King Lear.* Films incl: *Thunderball; Escape To Athena; Porridge; Hitler – The Last Ten Days; Ivanhoe; And the Ship Sailed On; The Inquiry; The Secret Garden; Stealing Heaven.* TV incl: RSC's *Antony and Cleopatra; A Night Out; She Fell Among Thieves; Pennies From Heaven; Butterflies; Don't Count; Mill On the Floss; Dead Man's Kit; Dick Turpin; The Omega Factor; Oliver Twist; The Disappearance of Harry; Doctor Who; Codename Icarus; Boy of Delights; The Young Delinquent; Trelaway of the Wills; Connie; The Comic Strip Presents . . .; Bergerac; Jekyll & Hyde; Saracen; Virtuoso; Poirot.* Address: c/o Jeremy Conway.

LOCKLEAR, Heather

Actress, b. 25 September 1961, Los Angeles, California. Educated at UCLA. Film: *Swamp Thing.* TV movies: *City Killer; Jury Duty.* TV incl: *T J Hooker;* Sammy Jo in *Dynasty.* m. heavy metal musician Tommy Lee. Address: c/o ICM, 8899 Beverly Boulevard, Los Angeles, California 90048. Birthsign: Libra. Hobbies: running, lifting weights. Pets: two dogs. **Most Cherished Possession:** 'My TV career. It ranks as one of the easiest in the history of the medium. It's a mystery to me.' **Favourite Memory:** 'My wedding in Santa Bastasa, especially the parachutist who came with a magnum of Moet Chandon.'

LODGE, David

Actor, b. 19 August, Stroud, Kent. Began career in Gang Shows, variety and concert party. Has appeared in over 115 films from *Cockleshell Heroes* to *Return of the Pink Panther* and *Edge of Sanity.* Many TV series and appearances incl: *Lovely Couple; Q8; Murder At the Wedding.* Autobiography: *Up The Ladder To Obscurity.* Awards: Freeman of the City of London (for charity work); Variety Club of Great Britain Silver Heart; Variety Club International Presidential Citation; King Rat, Grand Order of Water Rats, 1990. m. Lyn. Address: c/o CCA. Hobby: charity work. **Most Cherished Possession:** 'The antique desk in my study, bought by my wife, which caused me to sit and write my book.' **Favourite Memory:** 'The first sight of my wife across a crowded room.'

LOE, Judy

Actress, b. 6 March 1947, Urmston, Manchester. Gained a BA Combined Honours English and Drama at Birmingham University. Theatre incl: *No Sex Please, We're British; Class K; Illuminations; Hair*. TV incl: *Yesterday's Dreams; Heartland; Singles; When the Boat Comes In; Home Front; Ripping Yarns; Robin's Nest; The Upchat Line; Ace of Wands. The Chief; Eurocops*. m. actor Richard Beckinsdale (dec.); 1 d. Kate. Engaged to film director Roy Battersby. Address: c/o Peters Fraser & Dunlop. Hobbies: reading, walking with her dog. Pets: one dog, Cassie, two cats, Rita, Ziz. **Most Cherished Possession:** 'People are more important to me than things, though I keep many, cherished for their memories.' **Favourite Memory:** 'The direct and curious stare of my daughter when we first beheld each other.'

LOGAN, Phyllis

Actress, b. 11 January 1956, Paisley. Trained at the Royal Scottish Academy of Music and Drama. Theatre incl: *Threads; On the Edge; The Hired Man*. Also several radio plays. Films incl: *Another Time, Another Place; The Kitchen Toto; The Chain; Every Picture Tells a Story; The Doctor and the Devils; The Dress*. TV incl: *The White Bird Passes; The Goodtime Girls; Off-Peak; Time and the Conways; Extras; Bust; Hemingway; Lovejoy*. Address: c/o CDA. Birthsign: Capricorn. Hobbies: gardening, driving. Pets: one friendly garden robin. **Most Cherished Possession:** 'A photograph of my parents when they were my age.' **Favourite Memory:** 'Family hogmanays of years gone by.'

LONG, Shelley

Actress, b. 23 August, Fort Wayne, Indiana. Trained with Chicago Second City Improvisational Troupe, summer stock theatre. Films incl: *Hello Again; Outrageous Fortune; Night Shift; Caveman; The Money Pit*. TV films incl: *The Cracker Factory; A Promise of Love*. TV series incl: *Cheers;* writer/associate producer/co-host magazine programme *Sorting It Out*. TV guest roles incl: *M*A*S*H; Family; Love Boat*. m. (2nd) Bruce Tyson; 1 d. Juliana. Address: c/o William Morris Agency, 151 El Camino Drive, Beverly Hills, CA 90212. Birthsign: Virgo. Hobbies: writing, music, walking, cooking Italian food. **Most Cherished Possession:** 'My vocabulary – it's increased tremendously.' **Favourite Memory:** 'Winning a national title in original oratory in high school.'

LONGTHORNE, Joe

Singer/impressionist/entertainer, b. 31 May 1957, Hull. Started in local talent shows before TV debut at 14 on *Junior Showtime*, which he hosted for two years. Headlined his own show, *Salute To the Superstars* at Drury Lane Theatre, Chicago. TV incl: *Search For a Star; 3-2-1; Des O'Connor Tonight; Live From the Palladium; Les Dennis's Laughter Show; Joe Longthorne Entertains; The Joe Longthorne Show* (two series); *The Royal Variety Show 1989;* major US TV appearance. Address: c/o Clifford Elson. Hobbies: water-colour painting, cooking, tennis. Pets: two goats, two dogs, 14 fish, one rabbit, 20 chickens, one pigeon. **Most Cherished Possession:** 'A hand-painted Romany flat cart given to me by my father.' **Favourite Memory:** 'Winning *Search For a Star*, which led to my big break.'

LONNEN, Ray

Actor, b. 18 May 1940, Bournemouth. Trained at the Hampshire School of Drama. Started as ASM in Belfast, then rep at York, Worthing, Farnham, Bomley and Coventry. Also stage tour of New Zealand. Sky Masterson in *Guys and Dolls* in Edinburgh. Musical: *Wonderful Town*. Films incl: *Zeppelin; Lady Caroline Lamb; Murder Elite; Maneaters*. TV debut 1965 in *Emergency–Ward 10*. Other TV incl: *The Power Game; Honey Lane; Lovejoy; General Hospital; Pathfinders; The Brief; The Troubleshooters; Z-Cars; The Gentle Touch; Sandbaggers; Glamour Girls; Harry's Game; Yellowthread Street*. 1 d. Amy, 2 s. Thomas, Rhys. Address: c/o CCA, London. Birthsign: Taurus. Hobbies: travel, cinema, music, tennis. **Favourite Memory:** 'Walking out of the school gates for the last time. I wasn't fond of school.'

LOTT, Barbara

Actress, b. 15 May 1920, Richmond, Surrey. Trained at RADA and made first London appearance in *Love For Love*. Then Arts Theatre seasons and toured in *Major Barbara; Man and Superman; Richard III*. Many TV appearances incl: *Nightingale's Boys; Six Days of Justice; Ballet Shoes; The Survivors; Sexton Blake; Kids; Rings On Their Fingers; Sorry; Honeymoon*. m. Stuart Latham. Address: c/o Marmont Management. Birthsign: Taurus. Hobbies: walking, gardening, tapestry, music. **Favourite Memory:** 'All the actors I've worked with.'

LUCAS, William

Actor, b. 14 April 1925, Manchester. Trained at Bradford Civic Theatre after Royal Navy during the war. Rep at Liverpool. London theatre incl: *Amber For Anna; Ring Of Jackals; Dual Marriageway*. Films incl: *Sons and Lovers; The Professionals; Payroll; Bitter Harvest*. TV incl: *Portrait of Alison; The Paragon; The Infamous John Friend; Rigoletto; A Flea Off Pepe; Champion Road; Flowers of Evil; Mogul; Warship; Black Beauty; The Spoils of War; Doctor Who; The Two Ronnies*. m. (dis.); 2 s. Daniel, Thomas. Address: c/o Michael Ladkin. Birthsign: Aries. Hobbies: sailing, waterskiing. Pets: one dog, Staffordshire Bull Terrier.

LULU

Singer/actress, b. Marie Lawrie, 3 November 1948, Lennoxtown, Glasgow. Discovered by Marian Massey, who changed her name to Lulu. Many hit records, incl: *Shout; I'm a Tiger*. Topped US charts 1966 with *To Sir With Love*. 1969 joint winner of Eurovision Song Contest. Films incl: *To Sir With Love*. West End Theatre incl: *Peter Pan; Guys and Dolls*. TV incl: *It's Lulu; Lulu's Back In Town; The Growing Pains of Adrian Mole; Lulu*. Book: *Lulu – Her Autobiography*. m. (1st) Maurice Gibb (dis.), (2nd) John Frieda; 1 s. Jordan (from 2nd m.). Address: c/o Clifford Elson. Birthsign: Scorpio. Hobbies: buying clothes, water-skiing. **Most Cherished Possession:** 'Life itself.' **Favourite Memory:** 'An ice cream birthday cake when I was six.'

LUMLEY, Joanna

Actress, b. 1 May 1946, Shrinagar, Kashmir. A brief period in a craft and furniture shop followed by modelling course in London. After appearing in *Queen* magazine, her career as a model took off. Theatre incl: *Private Lives; Noel & Gertie; Blithe Spirit; Othello; Hedda Gabler*. Films incl: *Some Girls Do; On Her Majesty's Secret Service; Trail of the Pink Panther; Curse of the Pink Panther; Shirley Valentine; A Ghost In Monte Carlo*. TV incl: *The Mark II Wife; Coronation Street; The New Avengers; General Hospital; Sapphire and Steel; Oxbridge Blues; Steptoe and Son; The Weather In the Streets; Mistral's Daughter*. m. (1st) Jeremy Lloyd (dis.); 1 s. James; (2nd) Stephen Barlow. Address: c/o MLR. Birthsign: Taurus. Hobbies: reading, painting, gardening. **Most Cherished Possession:** 'The John Ward painting of my son.'

LUSARDI, Linda

Presenter/actress, b. 18 September 1960, London. Theatre incl: *Pygmalion; Cinderella; Snow White*. TV incl: *Miss Northern Ireland* (co-host); *Royal Variety Show; Tom O'Connor Show; Wogan; Blankety Blank; In at the Deep End; The Jim Davidson Show; The Six O'Clock Show; Good Evening Ulster; The Paul Coia Show; The Chris Stuart Chat Show; 40 Minutes; Open Space*; TV-am; co-host, *A Kind of Magic; Davro's Sketch Pad*. Launched series of six videos, starting with *Making the Most of Yourself*. Has own management and model company, Linda Lusardi Management, launched 1990. Address: c/o Yellow Balloon Productions, Micadam, 21 Fairmile Avenue, Cobham, Surrey KT11 2JA. Hobbies: water-skiing, swimming, making clothes. Pets: one dog, Trina. **Most Cherished Possession:** 'My house. It was built, brick by brick, by my boyfriend Terry, and designed by me. I love it.'

LYE, Jackie

Actress, b. 25 July 1959, Newcastle. Trained at the Central School of Speech and Drama. Best known as Sandra in TV comedy series *Brush Strokes*. Other TV incl: *Casualty; Mog; Hell's Bells; Fresh Fields*. Played Dot in the C4 film *Tides of Laughter*. Address: c/o Carole James Management. Birthsign: Leo. Hobbies: knitting, gardening, reading. **Most Cherished Possession:** 'William, my old blue Mini.' **Favourite Memory:** 'Walking in the snow in Wales, because of the very special person I was with.'

LYNAM, Desmond

Journalist/broadcaster, b. 17 September 1942, Ennis, Co. Clare, Eire. Wide experience of local and network radio and TV. Radio incl: presenting *Sport On 2; Sports Report; Today;* quiz programmes – *Forces Chance; Treble Chance; Midweek;* and music programmes. Commentator for tennis and boxing. TV incl: presenting *Grandstand; Sports Review of the Year; Sunday Grandstand*. Olympics and World Cup commentator, boxing and football. m. (dis.); 1 s. Patrick. Address: c/o BBC TV, London. Birthsign: Virgo. Hobbies: all sports, theatre, poetry. **Most Cherished Possession:** 'My health.' **Favourite Memory:** 'Receipt of a new bicycle, aged 10.'

LYNDHURST, Nicholas

Actor, b. 20 April 1961, Emsworth, Hampshire. Trained at the Corona Academy. Recently starred at the Albery Theatre in *The Foreigner*. TV series incl: *Anne of Avonlea; Heidi; The Prince and the Pauper; Going Straight; The Two of Us; Butterflies; Only Fools and Horses; Spearhead; To Serve Them All My Days; Slimming Down* (play). Address: c/o Chatto & Linnit. Birthsign: Aries. Hobbies: surfing, flying. Pets: one cat. **Most Cherished Possession:** 'My house.' **Favourite Memory:** 'My first solo flight. I'd been waiting for twenty years to do it.'

LYNN, Jonathan

Writer/director/actor, b. 3 April 1943, Bath. Started with Cambridge Footlights Revue, appearing on Broadway. Directed many West End plays and RSC and National Theatre productions plus short film *Mick's People* and feature films *Clive* and *Nuns On the Run*. As an actor, TV incl: *Doctor In the House; The Liver Birds; My Brother's Keeper* (also co-writer); *Barmitzvah Boy; The Knowledge; Outside Edge; Diana; Suspicion*. Wrote TV comedies *Yes, Prime Minister* (winner of the three BAFTA awards) and *Yes Minister* (winner of 1987 BAFTA Writer's Award). Books: *A Proper Man; The Complete Yes Minister; Yes, Prime Minister Vols I and II*. 1 s. Edward. Address: c/o Peters Fraser & Dunlop. Hobbies: 'Changing weight.'

MACARTHUR, Edith

Actress, b. 8 March 1926, Ardrossan, Ayrshire. Began career with Wilson Barrett Company at Royal Lyceum Theatre, Edinburgh. Also Bristol Old Vic, Royal Shakespeare Company, London's West End. Frequent appearances Edinburgh Festival, notably in many prose and poetry recitals, solo performance play *Marie of Scotland*, and *The Thrie Estaites* with the Scottish Theatre Company. Recent theatre incl: *Hay Fever; Death of a Salesman; The Cherry Orchard; Daphne Laureola*. TV incl: *The Borderers; Sunset Song; Weir of Hermiston; Dr Finlay's Casebook; Five Women; Love Story; Heartland; The Sandbaggers; Sutherland's Law;* Elizabeth Cunningham in *Take the High Road* (1980–87); *Menace Unseen; French Fields*. Address: c/o Larry Dalzell. Hobbies: music, reading.

MacCORKINDALE, Simon

Actor/director/writer, b. 12 February 1952, Ely, Cambs. Trained with rep and with Studio 68 in London. As director, theatre incl: *The Merchant of Venice; The Importance of Being Oscar* (his own one-man show). Films incl: *Jaws 3-D; Death On the Nile; Riddle of the Sands.* TV incl: *The Pathfinders; Just William; The Skin Game; I, Claudius; Romeo and Juliet; Wilfred Owen; The Mannions of America; Jesus of Nazareth; Three Weeks; Falcon Crest;* own series *Manimal.* Films produced: *Stealing Heaven; That Summer of White Roses.* m. (1st) actress Fiona Fullerton (dis.), (2nd) actress Susan George. Hobbies: photography, tennis, interior decorating, writing, producing feature and TV films. Address: c/o The Agency, 6380 Wilshire Blvd, Los Angeles, California 90048. Birthsign: Aquarius.

MACDONALD, Aimi

Actress, b. 27 February, Glasgow. Stage incl: *On the Town; The Mating Game; The Sleeping Prince; The Prime of Miss Jean Brodie; Hi-Infidelity; Present Laughter; A Bedful of Foreigners; Whodunnit?.* Films incl: *Vampira; Take a Girl Like You; Vendetta; No 1 of the Secret Service.* Radio incl: *Just a Minute; Jump; Do You Come Here Often?; Definition; Rentaghost;* and many guest appearances. Royal Variety Performance, 1968 and 1983. Various pantomime roles. m. (dis.); 1 d. dancer Lisa Muladore. Address: c/o Peter Charlesworth. Birthsign: Pisces. Hobbies: skating, writing.

MACDONALD, James

Actor/singer/entertainer, b. 9 February 1931, Glasgow. Films incl: *Sense of Freedom.* TV incl: *House On the Hill; The Eric Sykes Show; End of the Line; Aliens; Death On the Mountain; Grey Granite; Take the High Road.* m. Ruby; 1 s. Hugh, 1 d. Joanne. Address: c/o Young's Casting Agency, Glasgow. Birthsign: Aquarius. Hobbies: singing and entertaining. **Most Cherished Possession:** 'A BA from the Open University – great sense of achievement.' **Favourite Memory:** 'My first radio broadcast, my first step on the entertainment ladder.'

MacLEOD, Tracey

Producer/presenter, b. 30 October 1960, Ipswich, Suffolk. Worked as a journalist before entering television. Researcher on *Wogan, Food and Drink* and *The Six O'Clock Show;* reporter, *Network 7* series one; producer, *Network 7* series two; producer/presenter, *The Late Show;* presenter of BBC music specials, including Paul McCartney, Elvis Costello and Eurythmics; presenter, *Edinburgh Nights* (1989 Edinburgh Festival magazine programme); voice-over, *Rapido.* Address: c/o The Late Show, BBC Television, Lime Grove, London W12. Birthsign: Scorpio. Hobbies: 'Recording TV programmes I never get to watch.' **Most Cherished Possession:** 'My contract.' **Favourite Memory:** 'Meeting three of my musical heroes – Randy Newman, Van Morrison and Elvis Costello.'

McARDLE, John

Actor, b. 16 August 1950, Liverpool. Trained at East 15 Acting School, London, followed by rep at Liverpool, Oldham, Sheffield, Manchester, Cardiff. Theatre incl: Jim Cartwright's *To,* with Brookside actress Sue Johnston. TV incl: *Coronation Street; Charlie; Frankie and Johnny; How We Used To Live;* Billy Corkhill in *Brookside.* m. actress Kathy Jamieson; 1 d. Katie, 1 s. Justin. Address: c/o Brookside Productions. Birthsign: Leo. Hobbies: windsurfing, tennis, pub crawling. **Most Cherished Possession:** 'My daughter and son.' **Favourite Memory:** 'Getting into East 15 Acting School, I never knew such places existed.'

McBURNEY, Judy

Actress/comedienne, b. 19 May 1948, Sydney, Australia. Studied acting, voice production, theatre and dancing in Sydney. Theatre incl: *Don't Just Lie There, Say Something; The Clown Who Lost His Circus*. Films incl: *Michael; First Time Round*. TV incl: *Prisoner: Cell Block H; The Young Doctors; A Country Practice; Seven Little Australians; Bellbird; Catwalk; Homicide; Division 4; The Spoiler; Ton-up Trucking; The Box; No 96; Bluey; It Stands To Reason* (Australian version of *Till Death Do Us Part*). Address: c/o RMK Management, 197 Walkeps Street, North Sydney, Australia. Birthsign: Taurus. Hobbies: cooking. **Favourite Memory:** 'Sitting on top of a mountain which was covered in spring wildflowers in Liechtenstein and listening to the sound of cowbells.'

McCALLUM, David

Actor, b. 19 September 1933, Glasgow. First acted with BBC Repertory Company, then went to RADA. Stage incl: *After the Prize; Alfie; Camelot; The Mousetrap; Donkey's Years; Night Must Fall; Run For Your Wife; Sleuth*. Films incl: *A Night to Remember; Billy Budd; Dogs; Freud; The Great Escape; Mosquito Squadron; Three Bites of the Apple; The Secret Place; Watcher In the Woods*. TV incl: Ilya Kuryakin in *The Man From UNCLE; The Colditz Story; The File On Devlin; The Invisible Man; Kidnapped; Sapphire and Steel; Mother Love*. Directed *Charles Montague Doughty (The Explorers)* for the BBC in 1974. m. (1st) actress Jill Ireland (dis.), (2nd) interior designer Katherine Carpenter; 1 d. Sophie, 4 s. Paul, Jason (dec.), Valentine, Peter. Address: c/o 10 East 44th Street, New York 10017.

McCALLUM, Eileen

Actress, b. 2 December 1936, Glasgow. Gained an MA at Glasgow University. Trained at the Royal Scottish College of Music and Drama. Appeared in repertory theatre at the Royal Lyceum, Edinburgh. TV incl: *Just Your Luck; Garnock Way;* Isabel Blair in *Take the High Road* since it began, in 1980. m. Tom Fidelio; 3 s., 1 d. Address: c/o Scottish TV.

McCARDIE, Brian

Actor, b. 22 January 1965, Bellshill, Glasgow. BA (Hons) in theatre arts from Rose Bruford College of Speech and Drama. Theatre: *Street Angels; Red Wind*. TV: PC Ronnie Barker in *Waterfront Beat;* Bunny McKinnon in *The Snow Queen*. Address: c/o Culbertson Reeves, The Studio, 7a North Cross Road, London SE22, tel 081-693 9318. Birthsign: Aquarius. Hobbies: sport, cinema, theatre, Prince, books. **Most Cherished Possession:** 'My Zippo lighter (a gift) and my Walkman, because close friends and music are vital to me.' **Favourite Memory:** 'The first time I heard the name Gorbachev, because he gives me hope.'

McCASKILL, Ian

Weatherman, b. 28 July 1938, Glasgow. After the Royal Air Force attended the Meteorological Office College. Joined the BBC as a weather forecaster in 1978. Weatherman for Central TV, 1982–83. He has made many guest appearances on TV. m. Lesley; 2 d. Victoria, Kirsty. Address: c/o BBC TV Weather Unit. Birthsign: Leo. Hobbies: comic postcards, junk, swimming. **Most Cherished Possession:** 'My wife, who doesn't mind getting wet with me.' **Favourite Memory:** 'Bringing mum and babies home from hospital.'

McCLANAHAN, Rue

Actress, b. 21 February 1935, Oklahoma. Studied drama at University of Tulsa, then with Uta Hagem and Harold Clurman in New York. Theatre incl: *Jimmy Shine; Sticks and Bones; California Suite; Who's Happy Now* (for which she received OBIE Award); *Crystal and Fox; Dylan; Dark Side of the Moon; Picnic.* Films incl: *The Pursuit of Happiness; Players; The People Next Door.* TV incl: *Maude; Mama's Family; The Love Boat; Lou Grant; Golden Girls.* m. 5 times (dis.); 1 s. Mark (from 1st m.). Address: c/o ICM, California. Birthsign: Pisces. Hobbies: gardening, cooking. Pets: three dogs, Sandy, Misty and Harrod, two cats, Fosdick and Celestine. **Favourite Memory:** 'When I was three years old, singing and dancing on the sidewalk of my mother's beauty shop, waving at passing cars.'

McCOWEN, Alec, CBE

Actor, b. 26 May 1925, Tunbridge Wells. Trained for the stage at Royal Academy of Dramatic Art. Stage incl: his one-man show; *St Mark's Gospel; Kipling; The Browning Version; Equus.* Extensive TV appearances incl: *All For Love; Private Lives; Family Dance; Twelfth Night; Mr Palfrey of Westminster.* Address: c/o Jeremy Conway, London. Birthsign: Gemini. Hobby: gardening. **Most Cherished Possession:** 'The family photograph album. The only record of the past.'

McCOY, Sylvester

Actor, b. 20 August 1943, Dunoon, Argyll, Scotland. No professional training. Theatre incl: *The Pied Piper; Twelfth Night* with National Theatre; *Antony and Cleopatra; The Caucasian Chalk Circle; Androcles and the Lion; The Tempest; Buster's Last Stand; Can't Pay, Won't Pay; Abracadabra; Pirates of Penzance; The Ken Campbell Road Show.* Films incl: *Fireworks; The Secret Policeman's Ball.* TV incl: *Doctor Who; Last Place On Earth; Eureka; Starstrider; Dramarama; Tiswas; Jigsaw; Big Jim and the Figaro Club.* m. Agnes; 2 s. Sam, Joe. Address: c/o James Sharkey. Birthsign: Leo. Pets: cat. **Favourite Memory:** 'Informing the local sweet shop that rationing had finished.'

McDONALD, Pat

Actress, b. 1 August, Victoria, Australia. Started her career in live radio and the theatre. Has been awarded three Critics' Awards and four Logies, including the Gold Award which is for top personalities. One of her most recent performances was in *Sons and Daughters.* Is national spokeswoman for the Mascular Dystrophy Association, and does 'talking books' for the Royal Blind Society. m. (dis.); 1 s. Ian. Address: c/o June Gann Management, PO Box 1577 North Sydney, Australia. Birthsign: Leo. Hobbies: music, reading, cooking, travel. Pet: dog. **Most Cherished Possession:** 'My life.'

McDONALD, Trevor

Journalist/newscaster, b. 16 August 1939, Trinidad, West Indies. Worked for local radio in Trinidad before joining the TV station, in 1962, as interviewer for the current affairs programmes *Panorama* and *Dialogue.* In 1969, went to the BBC in London, first as a producer of current affairs programmes for the Caribbean Service, then as a producer for the World Service. Joined ITN in 1973. Diplomatic correspondent, 1980–82; *Channel 4 News* diplomatic correspondent (and presenter), 1982–7; *Channel 4 News* diplomatic editor, 1987–9; a presenter of *News at 5.40,* 1989; a presenter of *News at Ten* since January 1990. Books: biographies of cricketers Viv Richards and Clive Lloyd. m. 1st Josephine (dis.), 2nd Sabrina; 2 s. Tim, Jamie, 1 d. Joanne. Address: c/o ITN. Hobbies: cricket, tennis, golf.

McEWAN, Geraldine

Actress, b. Old Windsor, Berkshire. Began career at the Theatre Royal, Windsor. Has played the lead in many London plays incl: *Who Goes There?; Summertime; The Member of the Wedding; The Entertainer; The School For Scandal; Dear Love; On Approval; Chez Nous;* also member of Royal Shakespeare Company and National Theatre. Many TV roles incl: *The Prime of Miss Jean Brodie; L'Elegance; The Barchester Chronicles; Mapp and Lucia; Oranges Are Not the Only Fruit.* m. Hugh Cruttwell; 1 s. Greg, 1 d. Claudia. Address: c/o Marmont Management. Birthsign: Taurus.

McGANN, Joe

Actor, b. 24 July 1958, Liverpool. No formal training but performed with the Liverpool Everyman Youth Theatre. Theatre incl: *Yakety Yak; Blood Brothers; Canterbury Tales; Arturo Ui; Guys and Dolls; The Long and the Short and the Tall.* Films incl: *No Surrender; Kiss Cross.* TV incl: *Johnny Jarvis; Brothers McGregor; The Gentle Touch; Rockliffe's Babies; Boon; Casualty; Norbert Smith – A Life; The Chronicles of Narnia.* m. (dis.). Address: c/o Marina Martin Management. Birthsign: Leo. Hobbies: music, walking, reading. **Most Cherished Possession:** 'A pastel landscape by friend and artist Ken Draper, because of the spirit in which it was given.' **Favourite Memory:** 'Working in *Yakety Yak* at the Astoria Theatre with my three brothers – happy times.'

McGANN, Mark

Actor. Theatre: *Lennon; Old King Cole; Brown Bitter, Wet Nellies and Scouse; Blood Red Roses; Nineteen Eighty-Four; Yakety Yak; True Romance; Blood Brothers; Up On the Roof; Comedians; Guys and Dolls.* Films: *No Surrender; Business As Usual; Abducted.* TV: *Moving On the Edge; Studio; Scully; Zastrozzi; Les Girls; John and Yoko – A Love Story;* Halliwell in *The Manageress; Yellowthread Street.* Address: c/o Marina Martin Management.

McGANN, Paul

Actor, b. Ireland. Theatre incl: *John Paul George Ringo . . . & Bert; Much Ado; Cain; Oi For England; Yakety Yak; The Genius; Loot; The Seagull; A Lie of the Mind.* Films: *Withnail & I; Tree of Hands; Streets of Yesterday; The Rainbow; Dealers; Paper Mask.* TV incl: *Whistling Wally; Russian Night; Gaskin; Two Weeks In Winter; Give Us a Break;* Percy Toplis in *The Monocled Mutineer; The Importance of Being Earnest; Cariani and the Courtesan; Open Space;* Colin in *Screen 2* film *Drowning In the Shallow End.* Lives with Annie Milner; 1 s. Joe. Address: c/o Marina Martin Management.

McGANN, Stephen

Actor. Theatre incl: *Yakety Yak; The Holiday; Sgt Musgrave's Dance; Class K; Shamrocks and Crocodiles; Not About Heroes; Loot; Up On the Roof; Blood Brothers* (London West End). Film: *Business As Usual.* TV incl: *Missing From Home; Juliet Bravo; Bergerac; Brookside; Help!; Boon; Home Front; Stars In a Dark Night; Streetwise.* Address: c/o Marina Martin Management.

McGEE, Henry

Actor, b. 14 May, London. Trained at Italia Conti School and then spent several years in rep in England and Australia. Stage incl: *Uproar In the House; The Man Most Likely To Be In London; Noises Off; The Cat and Canary; Run For Your Wife.* TV incl: appeared in the award-winning series of Feydeau farces, *Paris 1900; The Worker* (with Charlie Drake); *Let There Be Love;* and his successful association with Benny Hill continues. Address: c/o CDA. Birthsign: Taurus. **Most Cherished Possession:** 'Walking stick fashioned out of a propellor from a World War I Royal Flying Corps aeroplane.' **Favourite Memory:** 'Stradbroke – a small island off the coast of Queensland. A Sea Eagle caught a mullet and then dropped it at my feet.'

McGINTY, Lawrence

Reporter, b. 2 July 1948, Manchester. Studied for a biology degree then went into journalism. Reported for *Channel 4 News* on science, technology and medicine; ITN's science editor since January 1990. m. Joan. Address: c/o ITN, London. Birthsign: Cancer. Hobbies: books, walking, eating, drinking. **Most Cherished Possession:** 'Freedom of thought and expression.'

McKAY, Glenda

Actress, b. 2 February 1971, Leeds. Left school in June 1989 with 10 O-levels and four A-levels. Starred in the musical *Annie* at the Grand Theatre, Leeds, aged 12. Film: Gudrun in director Ken Russell's film adaptation of the D H Lawrence novel *The Rainbow.* Rachel Hughes in *Emmerdale Farm* (now *Emmerdale*) since 1988. Address: c/o Peter Graham Associates, at Crouch Salmon Associates, 59 Frith Street, London W1V 5TA, tel: 071-734 2167. Hobbies: frequent working-out at the gym, swimming, dancing, badminton, skiing, and eating out with family and friends. **Most Cherished Possession:** 'My life, because to have had the opportunity to achieve what I have at such a young age is something I cannot begin to appreciate.' **Favourite Memory:** 'Meeting my present boyfriend – it was absolute love at first sight!'

McKENZIE, Julia

Actress, b. 17 February 1942, Enfield, Middlesex. Trained at the Guildhall School of Music and Drama. Stage incl: *Guys and Dolls; Woman In Mind; Follies.* Film: *Shirley Valentine.* Extensive TV work incl: guest with David Frost, Russell Harty, Mike Douglas (coast to coast in America), Terry Wogan. Music specials of Jerome Kern, Gershwin, Sondheim, Sheldon Harnick and her own *Julia and Company.* Own TV series *Maggie and Her; That Beryl Marston . . .!; Fresh Fields; Fame is the Spur; Blott on the Landscape; Absent Friends; Hotel Du Lac; French Fields.* Won *TV Times* Best Actress on TV award in 1986 and Favourite Comedy Performance on TV 1985, 1986 and 1988. m. actor-director Jerry Harte. Address: c/o April Young. Birthsign: Aquarius. Hobby: cooking.

McKERN, Leo, AO

Actor/writer, b. 16 March 1920, Sydney, Australia. Came to England in 1946; spent three years with the Old Vic and two years with the Royal Shakespeare Company. Stage incl: *Rollo; Othello; A Man For All Seasons; Crime and Punishment; Uncle Vanya; Valpone.* TV incl: *The Prisoner; The Sun Is Good; On the Eve of Publication; The Tea Party; Rumpole of the Bailey.* m. actress Jane Holland; 2 d. Abigail, Harriet. Address: c/o ICM. Birthsign: Pisces. Hobbies: sailing, swimming, ecology, environment preservation. **Most Cherished Possession:** 'My family.' **Favourite Memory:** 'Begetting my family.'

McLAUGHLIN, Lise-Ann

Actress, b. 24 June 1958, Dublin. Started career with the Abbey Theatre, Dublin. Many stage appearances incl: *City Sugar; A Life; Nightshade;* and Royal Court production of *Ourselves Alone.* Film: *Angel.* TV incl: many plays such as *Shadows Of Our Skin; Katie – The Year of a Child; Nobody's Property; 2016; Ties of Blood; Teresa's Wedding; Friends and Lovers;* also the series *We'll Meet Again; The Irish R.M.* (three series); *Dead Entry; Square Deal.* In 1983 was awarded the *TVTimes* Award for the Most Promising Newcomer to Television. Address: c/o Annette Stone. Birthsign: Cancer. Hobbies: music, food, reading. **Favourite Memory:** 'Time spent in Ireland.'

McLEOD, Shelagh

Actress, b. 7 May, Vancouver, Canada. Trained at the Corona Academy in London, has made many TV appearances both here and in the US. Has worked on stage at the Royal Court, London, and at Stratford, Canada. Plays incl: *The Dresser; Love's Labours Lost; Much Ado About Nothing.* Films incl: *Success; Lady Oscar; Indian Summer.* TV incl: *Cream In My Coffee; Keats; Camille; Street Think; Pygmalion* (with Peter O'Toole); *The Winning Streak.* m. James C Jordan. Address: c/o James Sharkey. Birthsign: Taurus. Hobbies: swimming, reading, music, travelling. **Most Cherished Possession:** 'A small wooden Japanese monkey that's about 200 years old. I hold on to him when I'm flying, for luck!' **Favourite Memory:** 'Flying in to New York for the first time.'

McNEILL, Gillian

Actress, b. 25 September 1965, Dundee. Trained at the Royal Scottish Academy of Music and Drama. Theatre incl: *Snow White and the Seven Dwarfs* 1989–90 Christmas pantomime. TV: Lynne McNeil in *Take the High Road* since 1987. Address: c/o Ruth Tarko. Birthsign: Libra. Hobbies: horse riding, socialising, travelling. **Most Cherished Possession:** '"Scarfie", my security blanket, because he's been with me since the beginning.' **Favourite Memory:** 'Getting my Equity card and being phoned to be told that I had my first job.'

McROBERTS, Briony

Actress, b. 10 February 1957, Welwyn Garden City, Hertfordshire. Played at various theatres incl: National, Chichester, Citizens' Theatre, Glasgow, Liverpool Everyman. Stage performances incl: *Hay Fever; Browning Version; Charley's Aunt; Peter Pan.* Films incl: *Captain Nemo and the Underwater City; The Pink Panther Strikes Again.* TV incl: *Bachelor Father; Lucky Jim; Peter Pan; Malice Aforethought; Strangers; Diamonds; The Professionals; Kelly Monteith; Mr Palfrey of Westminster; Butterflies; Don't Wait Up; Fellow Traveller.* m. David Robb. Address: c/o Green & Underwood. Hobbies: watching rugby, cooking and dancing. **Most Cherished Possession:** 'A photograph of my mother.' **Favourite Memory:** 'My wedding day – surrounded by one's best-loved people.'

MACNEE, Patrick

Actor, b. 6 February 1922, London. Won a scholarship to Webber Douglas Academy of Dramatic Art in 1939. Theatre incl: *Little Women; Made In Heaven; The Grass Is Greener; House Guest; Killing Jessica.* Films incl: *The Elusive Pimpernel; Battle of the River Plate; Les Girls; The Sea Wolves.* TV incl: *The Avengers; The New Avengers; Vintage Quiz; Empire; Lime Street; Where There's a Will.* m. (1st) actress Barbara Douglas (dis.), (2nd) actress Catherine Woodville (dis.); 1 d. Jennie, 1 s. Rupert (both from 1st m.). Address: c/o London Management. Birthsign: Aquarius. Hobbies: walking, reading, tennis. **Most Cherished Possession:** 'A few treasured books, particularly Cecil Beaton's Diaries which travel the world on location with me.'

MADELEY, Richard

Presenter, b. 13 May 1956, Romford, Essex. Newspaper journalist, 1972–6; BBC local radio producer 1976–8; Border TV reporter 1978–80; Yorkshire TV reporter 1980–82; Granada TV reporter and presenter since 1982. Also host of quiz show *Runway* and co-presenter of *This Morning* since 1988. m. 1st (dis.), 2nd co-presenter Judy Finnigan; 3 s. twins Tom and Dan (from Judy's 1st m.), Jack, 1 d. Chloe. Address: c/o Granada TV or Arlington Enterprises. Birthsign: Taurus. Hobbies: playing the guitar, reading, sleeping.

MADOC, Philip

Actor, b. 5 July 1934, Merthyr Tydfil. First-rate linguist (seven languages), his studies took him to the University of Vienna where he was the first foreigner to win the Diploma of the Institute of Interpreters. After two years as an interpreter, he went to RADA. TV incl: *Last of the Mochicans; Another Bouquet; The Life and Times of David Lloyd George; Zina; Court Case.* 1 d. Lowri, 1 s. Rhys. Address: c/o Peter Browne Management. Birthsign: Cancer. Hobbies: languages, windsurfing, squash, Pets. cat. **Most Cherished Possession:** 'One particular Father's Day card from my children.' **Favourite Memory:** '21st birthday – a beautiful evening in the Vienna woods listening to the zither music of Anton Karas.'

MADOC, Ruth

Actress/comedienne, b. 16 April 1943, Norwich. Best known on TV as the love-sick Gladys Pugh in BBC's *Hi-de-Hi.* Started career with Nottingham Rep. ASM before training at RADA. Debut in *Under Milk Wood* at Lyric, Hammersmith (also film). Theatre incl: *Fiddler on the Roof* (also film). Other TV incl: *Hunter's Walk; Leave It To Charlie; The Life and Times of David Lloyd George.* m. (1st) actor Philip Madoc, (2nd) manager John Jackson; 1 d. Lowri, 1 s. Rhys (both from 1st m.). Address: c/o Saraband Assocs., London. Birthsign: Aries. Hobbies: gardening, home. Pets: cats. **Most Cherished Possession:** 'Two-way music stand bought with my first salary from *Hunter's Walk.'* **Favourite Memory:** 'Watching the massed bands of the Light Division 1980. My husband was leading them.'

MAGILL, Ronald

Actor, b. 21 April 1920, Hull. Started his career during the Second World War when he toured with *Stars In Battledress.* A year after demob joined a travelling company, Arena, and has since played most theatres outside London. Actor and director at Nottingham Playhouse for nine years. Film: *Julius Caesar.* TV: most well-known as Amos Brearly in *Emmerdale.* Address: c/o Ken McReddie. Birthsign: Taurus. Hobbies: swimming, reading. **Most Cherished Possession:** 'My home, I've never owned one before.' **Favourite Memory:** 'Saying the first words on the stage of the brand new Nottingham Playhouse Theatre.'

MAGNUSSON, Magnus, Hon KBE

Writer/broadcaster, b. 12 October, Reykjavik, Iceland. Has lived in Scotland since he was nine months old. Started as a reporter on the *Scottish Daily Express,* moved to *The Scotsman* as chief feature writer. TV incl: co-presenter of *Tonight* (1964–65); *Chronicle; Checkpoint; Mainly Magnus; Mastermind; Living Legends; Vikings!; BC: The Archaeology of the Bible Lands.* Books incl: *Landlord or Tenant? – A View of Irish History; Magnus on the Move; Lindisfarne, The Cradle Island; Iceland Saga.* m. journalist Mamie Baird; 3 d. Sally, Margaret, Anna, 1 s. Jon. Address: c/o Rogers, Coleridge & White, London. Hobbies: translating Icelandic Sagas and modern novels. Pets: dog, cat, two Icelandic ponies. **Most Cherished Possession:** 'Right now, my Macintosh Apple word processor, which has revolutionised my life!'

MALAHIDE, Patrick

Actor, b. 24 March 1945, Berkshire. Started as a stage manager in St Andrews and worked in rep at Edinburgh, Birmingham, Manchester and Bristol. Appeared at the Royal Court in *Operation Bad Apple*. Films incl: *The Killing Fields; Comfort and Joy; A Month In the Country; December Bride*. TV incl: *Minder; Miss Julie; The One Game; Our Geoff; The Singing Detective; Inspector Morse; Boon; Living With Dinosaurs*. m. Rosie; 1 s. Liam, 1 d. Mairi. Address: c/o Kate Feast. Hobbies: tennis, sailing, walking. Pet: Welsh springer spaniel, Toby. **Most Cherished Possession:** 'A flint axe-head, 50,000 years old, which I found when out walking as a boy.' **Favourite Memory:** 'Riding horseback along a beach in Donegal with my wife.'

MANDEL, Howie

Actor, b. 29 November, Toronto, Canada. Started his career as a stand-up comic at Los Angeles' The Comedy Store. Films: *A Fine Mess; Walk Like a Man*. TV cinemax special: *Howie Mandel: Live From Carnegie Hall*. TV incl: *The Tonight Show; Merv Griffin; Mike Douglas*; HOBO Special: *Bizarre*. Dr Wayne Fiscus in *St Elsewhere*. m. Terry; 1 d. Jackelyn. Address: c/o William Morris Agency, 151 El Camino Drive, Beverly Hills, CA 90212. Birthsign: Sagittarius. Hobbies: collecting pants from mail-order catalogues. **Most Cherished Possession:** 'My blow-up rubber surgical glove – I wouldn't do a show without it.' **Favourite Memory:** 'Peddling carpets a few years ago – it's a real rugs-to-riches success story.'

MANETTI, Larry

Actor, b. 23 July, Pendleton, Oregon. Studied drama at Northwestern University and trained with Sal Dano. Film: *Two Minute Warning*. TV incl: *Emergency; Chase; Switch; Black Sheep Squadron; Battlestar Galactica; The Duke; Ten Speed and Brown Shoe; Fantasy Island; Quincy; Barnaby Jones; Magnum PI; The Mob*. m. actress Nancy; 1 s. Lorenzo. Address: c/o The Artists Group Ltd, 1930 Century Park West, LA, CA 90067. Birthsign: Cancer. Hobbies; tennis, bicycle riding, basketball. **Most Cherished Possession:** 'My 1984 black Ferrari.' **Favourite Memory:** 'The day I got to practise with the LA Fire Department. Since I was a boy I always wanted to be a fireman.'

MANN, Vernon

TV journalist, b. 5 May 1945, Berkeley, Gloucestershire. Began career on Gloucester Citizen moved on to: ABC; ATN Channel 7; UPI, HTV, IRN, ITN Foreign Editor; Washington News Editor (1984); was awarded RTS Home News award 1987. Has covered numerous countries incl Beirut, Iran Revolution, Romania. m. Avril; 1 s. Anthony. Address: c/o ITN. Birthsign: Taurus. Hobbies: walking, sleeping, mountain-biking. Pets: bearded collie, cats. **Most Cherished Possession:** 'Stuffed bantam, amazed that anyone should have taken the trouble to stuff it.' **Favourite Memory:** 'Birth of my son.'

MARINARO, Ed

Actor, b. 31 March, New York, grew up in New Milford, New Jersey. Played professional football with the Minnesota Vikings and the New York Jets. Studied acting with coaches Milton Katselas and Warren Robertson. Stage debut in *It Had To Be You*. Film: *Fingers*. TV incl: *Policewoman Centrefold; Three Eyes; Born Beautiful*; Joe Coffey in *Hill Street Blues; Tonight's The Night; What If I'm Gay; Eischeid; Laverne and Shirley; Dynasty*. Has formed own production company. Address: c/o William Morris Agency, Beverly Hills. Hobbies: all sports, exercising, golf, tennis, travel, racquetball, cooking. **Most Cherished Possession:** 'My home.' **Favourite Memory:** 'Playing professional football for The Vikings and New York Jets.'

MARKS, Alfred, OBE

Actor/comedian, b. 28 January 1921, London. Stage debut at the age of nine in a Boys' Brigade concert; first professional performance at the Kilburn Empire in 1946 in variety. Stage incl: *Where the Rainbow Ends; A Day in the Life of . . .; Spring and Port Wine; The Entertainer; The Sunshine Boys; Fiddler on the Roof.* Films incl: *Desert Mice; There Was a Crooked Man; Frightened City; Scream and Scream Again.* TV incl: *Alfred Marks Time; The Good Old Days; Looks Familiar; Does the Team Think?; Maybury; Parkinson; Sunday Night at The London Palladium* (compere). m. actress Paddie O'Neil; 1 d. Danielle, 1 s. Gareth. Address: c/o Barry Burnett. Birthsign: Aquarius. Hobbies: target shooting, riding. Pets: 2 dogs.

MARSDEN, Roy

Performer, b. 25 June 1941, London. Among his many TV appearances are: *The Sandbaggers; Airline; Goodbye, Mr Chips; Vanity Fair; Inside Story*; and the P D James crime book series playing Det Chief Sup Adam Dalgliesh. m. Polly Hemingway; 1 s. Joe. Address: c/o CAA. Hobbies: sailing, opera. Birthsign: Cancer.

MARSH, Reginald

Actor, b. 17 September 1926, London. Has worked in rep, Royal Shakespeare Company and the National Theatre. Stage incl: *Thark; Relatively Speaking; Henry IV Part I; My Brother's Keeper; The Boundary; Bedroom Farce; The Last Gamble.* Author of a number of plays incl: *The Death Is Announced; The Man Who Came To Die.* Films incl: *The Sicilians; Shadow of Fear; Jigsaw; Young Winston; Sky Pirates.* TV incl: *The Planemakers; Bless This House; The Good Life; Terry and June; Nye; Who Pays the Piper; George and Mildred.* Book: *Much More Than Murder.* m. Rosemary; 3 d. Kate, twins Rebecca, Alison, 3 s. John, Adam, Alexander. Address: c/o Plunket Greene, London. Birthsign: Virgo. Hobbies: writing, gardening. **Favourite Memory:** 'Conducting the BBC Northern Orchestra on television.'

MARTIN, Derek

Actor, b. 11 April 1933, Bow, London. Started acting at 9 years old. Stuntman for 5 years. Acting debut in Paul Temple series followed later with leading roles in *Law and Order; Chinese Detective.* Also appeared in *Sweeney; Professionals; Minder; Hart To Hart; King and Castle.* 2 s. twins David, Jonathan. Address: c/o Jimmy Garrod Management, St Martins, Sandhills Meadow, Shepperton, Middlesex TW17 9HY. Hobbies: golf, horseracing, my sons. **Most Cherished Possession:** 'My twins, they make everything worthwhile.' **Favourite Memory:** 'Working on the film *Ragtime* and acting with my childhood idol James Cagney.'

MARTIN, Jessica

Actress/comedienne, b. 25 August 1962, Fulham. London. Studied English/drama course at London University. Began singing and performing impressions on London cabaret circuit. TV incl: *Spitting Image; Copycats; Bobby Davro's TV Weekly; Summertime Special; Tarby and Friends; Saturday Live; Wogan; We Love TV; Catchphrase; 3-2-1; Des O'Connor Tonight; New Faces; The Television Show; Doctor Who; Telly Addicts; The Royal Variety Show; Family Fortunes.* Address: c/o Saraband Assocs. Hobbies: collecting film memorabilia, drawing, songwriting, dancing. **Most Cherished Possession:** 'Book *A Pictorial History of the Talkies,* a Christmas present at 8 years old.' **Favourite Memory:** 'Meeting Barbra Streisand. How was I to know my impression of her would bring me good fortune?'

MATTHEWS, Francis

Actor, b. 2 September 1931, York. Started career at Leeds Rep at 17 and later at Oxford and Bromley. Recent stage incl: *The Business of Murder; Middle Age Spread; Aren't We All?* Films incl: *No Escape; Bhowani Junction; Roman Holiday.* Radio incl: *Not In Front of the Children; Local Time; Stop the World; Double Trouble.* TV incl: *Paul Temple; A Little Big Business; My Man Joe; Morecambe and Wise Christmas Show,* 1971 and 1978; *Crowther Collection; Tears Before Bedtime; The McGuffin; Brat Farrar; May We Borrow Your Husband?* m. actress Angela Browne; 3 s. Paul, Dominic, Damien. Address: c/o Barry Burnett. Birthsign: Virgo. Hobbies: writing, tennis, cricket. **Favourite Memory:** 'Meeting my wife on *The Dark Island* in 1962.'

MATTHEWS, Sally Ann

Actress, b. 19 September 1970, Oldham, Lancashire. Trained at Oldham Theatre Workshop. Jenny Bradley in *Coronation Street.* Address: c/o Laine Management, Hampson Street Trading Estate, Hampson Street, Manchester 5. Birthsign: Virgo. Hobbies: horse riding, dancing, singing. Pets: a dog called Alex. **Most Cherished Possession:** 'Video of the film *Those Glory, Glory Days,* because it's my favourite film.' **Favourite Memory:** 'Watching Mike Cecere of Oldham Athletic Football Club score a hat trick.'

MAXWELL, Lisa

Singer/dancer/actress/presenter, b. 24 November, London. Trained at the Italia Conti stage school. Professional debut, aged 11, in *The Many Wives of Patrick* on TV. Theatre incl: *Annie* (London West End); national tours of *A Hotel Paradise* and *Babes In Arms;* plus many pantomimes. Films: *The Dark Crystal; Remembrance.* Other TV incl: *Ballet Shoes, A Place Like Home; Danger – Marmalade at Work; The Benny Hill Show; Tripods; The Hello Goodbye Man; Les Dennis's Laughter Show; The Joe Longthorne Show; Noel Edmonds; Saturday Roadshow; The Satellite Show; Relative Strangers.* Presenter of: *No Limits; Splash; The Bizz.* Address: c/o Mike Hughes Entertainments. Birthsign: Sagittarius. Pets: Tibetan spaniel called Fizzgig.

MAYO, Simon

Disc jockey/presenter, b. 21 September 1958, Southgate, London. Before joining Radio 1 he worked for hospital, university and local radio and was lunchtime presenter at Radio Nottingham for two and a half years. As well as fronting Radio 1's weekend early morning shows, he is a frequent presenter of breakfast, lunchtime and teatime shows and is currently one of BBC TV's *Top of the Pops* presenters. Was presenter of *Pilgrimage to the Holy Land* and the instigator of Radio 1's series on pop and politics, *Rebel Yell.* Also working on satellite and cable TV presenting *Multi-track* for the BBC World Service. Address: c/o James Grant, London. Birthsign: Virgo.

MEAGHER, Ray

Actor. Extensive theatre and films. TV: *Mother and Son; Kingswood Country; Pig In a Poke; Secret Valley; A Country Practice; Rafferty's Rules; The Great Bookie Robbery; Vietnam; A Fortunate Life; The Shiralee; True Believer; Spit MacPhee;* Alf Stewart in *Home and Away.* m. agent Lee Leslie. Address: c/o Lee Leslie Management, 72 Glebe Point Road, Glebe, NSW 2037, Australia.

MELLINGER, Leonie

Actress, b. 24 June, Berlin, West Germany. Trained at Central School of Speech and Drama. Theatre incl: Royal Shakespeare Company's production of *The Winter's Tale*; *Titus Andronicus*; *The Cenci*; *Beached*; *Lady Macbeth*. Films incl: *Memoirs of a Survivor*; *Ghost Dance*; *Memed My Hawk*; *Zina*; *The Young Toscanini*. TV incl: *Sons and Lovers*; *Paradise Postponed*; *Mr Palfrey of Westminster*; *Summer Lightning*; *Bergerac*; *Small World*; *Hannay*; *The New Statesman*; *Frederick Forsyth Presents*. Address: c/o ICM. Hobbies: singing, water skiing, swimming, dancing, cricket. **Most Cherished Possession:** 'My body! I can't think of anything else I couldn't live without.' **Favourite Memory:** 'Sailing into Gozo harbour at sunset, one of the happiest moments of my life.'

MERCIER, Sheila

Actress, b. 1 January 1919, Hull. Trained at Stratford-upon-Avon College of Drama. Started career with Sir Donald Wolfit's company as did her brother, Brian Rix. After the war she joined Brian's Whitehall Theatre company in 1955 and was with him for 11 years. Has played Annie Sugden in *Emmerdale* since its start in 1972. m. Peter Mercier; 1 s. Nigel David. Address: c/o Peter Mercier, 36 Coastal Road, Angmering-on-Sea, East Preston, West Sussex BN16 1SJ. Birthsign: Capricorn. Hobby: reading. **Most Cherished Possession:** 'I haven't got one.' **Favourite Memory:** 'Holding my new born son in my arms because he was a very much wanted baby.'

MICHELMORE, Cliff, CBE

Commentator/presenter, b. 11 December 1919, Cowes, Isle of Wight. Started with the British Forces Network in Germany, 1947–49. Joined BBC to produce, direct and write for children's TV. Sports commentaries from 1951 and a nightly interview programme, 1955–57. TV incl: *Tonight*; *24 Hours*; *Our World*; *Holiday*; *Space Programmes*; *General Elections*; *Talkback*; *Wheelbase*; *Chance To Meet*; *Day By Day*; *Home on Sundays*; *Songs of Praise*; *Lifeline*. Still remembered as the presenter of *Family Favourites*. m. broadcaster Jean Metcalfe; 1 s. Guy, 1 d. Jenny. Address: Whitehouse, Upper West Street, Reigate, Surrey. Birthsign: Sagittarius. Hobbies: golf, sailing, walking. **Most Cherished Possession:** 'A water colour of the farm I lived on as a boy painted by my wife.'

MILLIGAN, Spike

Author/actor/comedian, b. 16 April 1918, Ahmaddnagar, India. Stage incl: *The Bed-Sitting Room* (and film). Films incl: *The Last Remake of Beau Geste*; *The Life of Brian*; *The Hound of the Baskervilles*; *History of the World, Part I*. Radio incl: *Crazy People* (which became *The Goon Show*); *The Last Goon Show of All*. TV incl: *Milligan's Wake*; *Q5 to Q10*; *The Other Spike*; *The Best of British*; *Just Like That!*. Records incl: *The Ying Tong Song*; *The Goons*; *The Snow Goose*. Books incl: *Puckoon*; *Adolf Hitler, My Part In His Downfall*; *The Spike Milligan Cartoons*; *Mussolini: His Part In My Downfall*; *Milligan's War*. Serious poetry books: *Small Dreams of a Scorpion*; *Open Heart University*; *The Mirror Running*. m. (3rd) Shelagh Sinclair; 3 d. Laura, Sile (from 1st m.), Jane (from 2nd m.), 1 s. Sean (from 1st m.). Address: c/o 9 Orme Court, London W2. Hobbies: reading, antiques.

MILLS, Adrian

Actor/ TV presenter, b. 16 July 1956, Oakham, Rutland. Trained at the Rose Bruford College of Speech and Drama. From 1973–77 was with the National Youth Theatre Company. Other theatre incl: York Theatre Company, Scarborough Theatre in the Round and the Shaw Theatre Company, London. TV incl: *Doctor Who*; *Minder*; *Play For Today*; *Brookside*; *That's My Boy*; *Breakfast Time*; *That's Life*; *Facing Up To Aids*. Address: c/o Gary Trolan Management, 30 Burraro Road, London NW6. Hobbies: cricket, tennis, football, walking. **Most Cherished Possession:** 'I never seem to throw anything away so everything becomes a cherished possession.' **Favourite Memory:** 'Telling my parents that I'd beaten 4,000 others to present *That's Life!*'

MILLS, Hayley

Actress, b. 18 April 1946, London. Trained at the Elmhurst Ballet School and made her first film, *Tiger Bay*, when she was 12. Made her stage debut in the title role of *Peter Pan* in 1970. Other stage incl: *The Three Sisters; The Wild Duck; Rebecca; A Touch of Spring; The Summer Party; My Fat Friend; Trelawney of the Wells; Importance of Being Ernest; Dial M For Murder; Tallys Folly*. Films incl: *Whistle Down the Wind; The Chalk Garden; The Family Way; Pretty Polly; Truth About Spring*. TV incl: *Only a Scream Away; Deadly Strangers; The Flame Trees of Thika; Parent Trap; Back Home*. Book: *My God* (1988). m. (dis.); 2 s. Crispian, Jason. Address: c/o Chatto & Linnit. Birthsign: Aries. Hobbies: travel, reading, studying philosophy.

MILMOE, Caroline

Actress, b. 11 January 1963, Manchester. No formal training but attended the Contact Youth Theatre, Manchester. Theatre: Mary McGregor in *The Prime of Miss Jean Brodie;* RSC national tours of *The Winter's Tale* and *The Crucible;* Jo in *A Taste of Honey;* Hermia in *A Midsummer Night's Dream*. Films: *The Magic Toyshop; Without a Clue; The Fruit Machine*. TV: Julie Jefferson in *Bread* (first two series); Sandra Lord in *The Practice;* Maureen Delaney in *Brick Is Beautiful; Valentine Park;* Cindy in *Hot Metal;* Laura in *The Bill;* Mary Durrant in *Agatha Christie's Poirot*. Address: c/o Nigel Martin-Smith. Hobbies: reading, travelling, cinema. **Favourite Memory:** 'The first night of *The Prime of Miss Jean Brodie* at the Royal Exchange, Manchester – I'd worked there as an usherette.'

MINOGUE, Kylie

Actress/singer, b. 28 May 1968, Melbourne, Australia. Auditioned successfully for the Australian soap *The Sullivans* at the age of 11 and became a regular in the cast. Later appeared in *Skyways* and *The Henderson Kids*. Left school in 1985 and landed the role of Charlene in *Neighbours*. Left the serial in 1988 to concentrate on her pop recording career. First chart single, *Locomotion*, was followed by a hit LP, a duet with Jason Donovan – *Especially For You* – and a second album, *Enjoy Yourself*. Film: *The Delinquents*. Birthsign: Gemini.

MITCHELL, Warren

Actor, b. 14 January 1926, London. Trained at RADA and went on to become a household name for his role as Alf Garnett in BBC TV's *Till Death Us Do Part*. Theatre incl: *Death of a Salesman; The Caretaker* (both at the National Theatre). Films incl: *Knights and Emeralds; The Chain*. Other TV incl: *The Merchant of Venice; The Caretaker; Moss; In Sickness and In Health*. m. actress Constance Wake; 2 d. Rebecca, Anna, 1 s. Daniel. Address: c/o ICM, London. Birthsign: Capricorn. Hobbies: tennis, sailing, clarinet, supporting Spurs FC. Pets: Bernese Mountain Dog and a Giant Schnauzer. **Most Cherished Possession:** 'My 1968 Jaguar 420. Having to feed my pets means I can't afford a new Jaguar.' **Favourite Memory:** 'Max Miller at the Holborn Empire. Why? "Look at the eyes lady – Mrs Miller's oldest son".'

MOLL, Brian

Actor, b. 19 May 1925, Wanstead, London. Made stage debut in *Androcles and the Lion* at the Arts Theatre, Great Newport Street, in 1941. Emigrated to Australia after the war and worked in PR. TV debut in 1958 in *Captain Carvallo*. Other TV incl: *The Young Doctors; A Country Practice; Great Expectations – The Untold Story; The Petrov Affair; Shut Your Eyes and Think of England*. Address: Richard Kent Management, 6 Goodhope Street, Paddington, New South Wales, Australia 2021. Birthsign: Taurus. Hobbies: reading, watching TV. Pets: Siamese cat called Mitzika. **Most Cherished Possession:** 'Siamese cat because we have a love/hate relationship.' **Favourite Memory:** 'Opening night of my first effort as a producer/director – *No No Nanette*.'

MONKHOUSE, Bob

Entertainer, b. 1 June 1928, Beckenham, Kent. Trained as cartoon film animator. Later became the BBC's first contract comedian. Formed script-writing team with Denis Goodwin and together they wrote thousands of scripts for radio and TV. Stage incl: *Bob Monkhouse Startime; Come Blow Your Horn; Boys From Syracuse*. Films incl: *Dentist in the Chair; Weekend with Lulu; She'll Have a Go*. TV incl: *Candid Camera; Sunday Night at the London Palladium; The Golden Shot; Celebrity Squares; I'm Bob – He's Dickie; Family Fortunes* (1980–83); *The Bob Monkhouse Show; Bob's Full House; The 64,000 Dollar Question*. m. (1st) Elizabeth (dis.), (2nd) Jacqueline; 1 d. Abigail, 2 s. Gary, Simon. Hobbies: collecting vintage films and artwork by great cartoonists. Address: c/o Peter Prichard, London. Birthsign: Gemini.

MONTAGUE, Bruce

Actor/writer, b. 24 March 1939, Deal, Kent. Trained at RADA. Began career at Birmingham Rep, followed by the Old Vic. Recent theatre incl: *Last of the Red Hot Lovers; The Division Belle*. As writer: *Love Bites; 1793; A Touch of Menace*. TV incl: *Crane; Dimensions of Fear; The Saint; The Alpha Plan; Linkmen; Public Eye; Secret Army; Sharon and Elsie;* Leonard in *Butterflies;* Shah in *Whoops Apocalypse; Fresh Fields; The Vision; Agatha Christie's Poirot*. m. Barbara; 1 s. Sam, 1 d. Kate. Address: c/o Peter Graham Assocs at Crouch Salmon Assocs. Hobbies: writing, gardening. Pets: three cats. **Most Cherished Possession:** 'My pen.' **Favourite Memory:** 'Quoin Island, Great Barrier Reef. Pacific paradise visited on Old Vic tour 1961.'

MONTEATH, Alec

Actor, b. 22 May, Doune, Perthshire. Trained at the Royal Scottish Academy of Music and Drama. Has worked in theatre seasons at Glasgow's Citizens', Edinburgh Gateway, Pitlochry Festival, Perth, Edinburgh Lyceum and with the Scottish Theatre Company. Stage incl: *Brief Glory; Journey's End; Swanson; The Birthday Party; Battle Royal; Aladdin*. TV incl: *Omega Factor; Doom Castle; Hess; Take the High Road; Highway*. m. Linna Skelton; 2 s. actor David, Alasdair. Address: c/o Scottish TV. Birthsign: Gemini. Hobbies: cycling, swimming, fishing, Scottish heraldry and history. Pets: golden retriever and matching cat. **Favourite Memory:** 'Walking with my wife over the bridges of the River Degli Schiavoni to Piazza San Marco in Venice.'

MOORE, Roger

Actor, b. 14 October 1927, London. Trained at RADA and soon became a film and TV star. Films incl: *The Man Who Haunted Himself; Gold; Shout At The Devil; The Wild Geese; Escape From Athena*. Has played James Bond, first in 1970 in *Live And Let Die* and subsequently in: *The Man with the Golden Gun; The Spy Who Loved Me; Moonraker; Octopussy; For Your Eyes Only; A View To a Kill;* plus films *Bed and Breakfast; Bullseye*. TV incl: *Ivanhoe; The Alaskans; Maverick; The Saint; The Persuaders*. m. (1st) Doorn van Steyn (dis.), (2nd) Dorothy Squires (dis.), (3rd) Luisa Mattioli; 2 s. Geoffrey, Christian, 1 d. Deborah. Address: c/o ICM. Birthsign: Libra. Hobbies: skiing, tennis, backgammon.'

MOORE, William

Actor, b. 19 April, Birmingham. Trained at Birmingham Rep. Taught at Bristol Old Vic Theatre School. Theatre: *When We Are Married* in London's West End. TV incl: *Coronation Street; Dombey and Son; Sorry; My Husband and I*. m. actress Mollie Sugden; 2 s. twins Robert and Simon. Address: c/o Joan Reddin. Birthsign: Aries. Hobbies: writing poetry, walking.

MORGAN, Garfield

Actor, b. 19 April 1931, Birmingham. After attending Birmingham Drama School went to the Arena Theatre, Birmingham. Was Director of Productions at Marlowe Theatre, Canterbury, 1957–58, and at Manchester's Library Theatre, 1959–60. Associate Director, Northcott Theatre, 1976–78, and Nottingham Playhouse, 1978–80. Stage and Films incl: *The Pumpkin Eater; The Story of Private Pooley; Perfect Friday.* TV incl: *Softly, Softly; Randall and Hopkirk (Deceased); Dear Mother . . . Love Albert; The Sweeney; Shelley; One By One; The Nineteenth Hole; No Job For a Lady.* Address: c/o Michelle Braidman Assocs, London. Birthsign: Aries. Hobbies: golf, photography, showjumping and eventing.

MORGAN, Richard

Actor, b. 12 August 1958, Hobart, Tasmania, Australia. Trained at Herbert Berghoff Studio in New York. Theatre incl: *Zombie Barbeque; The Heiress From Punchbowl,* all with Not Another Theatre Company. Films incl: *The Devil's Playground; Christmas Day; Break of Day; Phar Lap; Voyeur; Silver City.* TV incl: *Homicide; Solo One; The Sullivans; Boy In The Bush; City West; Sons and Daughters; The Last Warhorse; Great Expectations; Four Corners; Prince of the Court of Yarralumla.* Address: c/o Robyn Gardiner Management, 126A Hampden Road, Artarmon, NSW, Australia 1064. Birthsign: Leo. Hobbies: reading, watching sport. **Most Cherished Possession:** 'My leather jacket – keeps me warm.' **Favourite Memory:** 'Getting my first professional job because that meant I could quit school.'

MORIARTY, Paul

Actor, b. 19 May 1946, London. Studied at Manchester University. Has worked at a variety of theatres countrywide, incl: Coventry, Bolton, Liverpool, Bristol, Royal Shakespeare, National Theatre, Royal Court, London. Stage incl: *The Contractor* in the West End. Also founder member of the Enemy Within Theatre group. Films: *Quest For Love; The Chain.* TV incl: *Holly; Pelham; Coronation Street; Z-Cars; Minder; The Sweeney; Jackanory; Love Story; Troilus and Cressida; The Gentle Touch; Casualty; Saracen; The Paradise Club; Troublemakers.* m. Teresa; 1 d. Jessica, 1 s. Matthew. Address: c/o Ken McReddie. Hobbies: walking, reading. **Most Cherished Possession:** 'Whitwell miners badge: reminder that there are good and brave people around.' **Favourite Memory:** 'Being at birth of children.'

MORRIS, Beth

Actress, b. 19 July 1949, Gorseinon, South Wales. Trained at the Cardiff College of Music and Drama, followed by rep at Northampton, Bristol and Birmingham before appearing in London's West End and with the Royal Shakespeare Company. Stage incl: *Man and Superman; Banana Ridge; Travesties; Passion of Dracula; Mrs Grabofskies Academy.* TV incl: *Play of the Week; Play of the Month; Jude the Obscure; Minder; Z-Cars; Softly, Softly; I, Claudius; David Copperfield; Ballroom; District Nurse* (two series)*; Better Days; We Are Seven.* Address: c/o Ken McReddie. Birthsign: Cander. Hobbies: reading, fishing. **Most Cherished Possession:** 'My health.' **Favourite Memory:** 'Walking into Sardis, New York, and everyone applauding after first night of *Travesties.'*

MORRIS, Jonathon

Actor, b. 20 July 1960, Urmston, Manchester. Studied at Bristol Old Vic Theatre School. Theatre incl: *La Cage Aux Folles; As You Like It; The Cherry Orchard; Candida; Wuthering Heights; Tess of the Durbervilles; Rain From Heaven; Diary of a Somebody; Semi Monde.* TV incl: *Beau Geste; Bread; The Consultant; The Prisoner of Zenda; That Beryl Marston; Ties of Blood; Jackanory; The Agatha Christie Hour; The Practice; Bingo, Hells Bells.* Address: ICM. Birthsign: Cancer. Hobbies: All sports; dance, singing, reading. **Most Cherished Possession:** 'My family.' **Favourite Memory:** 'Yesterday.'

MORRIS, Mike

Television presenter, b. 26 June 1947, Harrow, Middlesex. Gained a BA before entering journalism with the *Surrey Comet* in 1969. Joined Sydney-based news agency AAP Reuters as bulletins editor. Moved to United Newspapers in 1974, first as sports reporter, then sports editor. Joined Thames TV as a sub-editor and reporter in 1979. Four years later, became TV-am's main sports presenter and host of *The Saturday Morning Show*. Presenter of *Good Morning Britain* since 1987. m. Alison; 2 d. Sarah, Helen. Address: c/o TV-am. Birthsign: Cancer. Pets: two cats, three guinea pigs, one hamster, one goldfish.

MORRISSEY, Neil

Actor, b. 4 July 1962, Stafford. Studied at the Guildhall School of Music and Drama. Theatre incl: *Daughter In Law*. Film: *Playing Away*. TV incl: *The Bounty; Juliet Bravo; Boon* (four series); *Travellers By Night; Pulaski; William Tell*. Address: Louis Hammond. Birthsign: Cancer. Hobbies: motor bikes. Pets: a fluffy mongrel. **Most Cherished Possession:** 'My necklace.' **Favourite Memory:** 'Getting a job on *The Bounty*. I was only three months out of drama school.'

MORSE, David

Actor, b. 11 October, Beverly, Massachusetts. Worked with the Boston Repertory Company and the Circle Repertory Company in New York. Drama Logie Award for his performance in the Los Angeles production of *Mice and Men*. Films incl: *Inside Moves; Invasion From Mars*. TV incl: *Family Business; Prototype; Shattered Vows;* Dr Jack Morrison in *St. Elsewhere; Personal Foul; Six Against the Rock; The Best Kept Secret; Dawn Payment of Murder*. m. actress Susan Wheeler Duff. Address: c/o Yvette Bikoff Agency, 9120 Sunset Blvd, LA, Calif 90069. Birthsign: Libra. Hobbies: oil painting, drawing, running, charity work. Pets: golden retriever called Lucy. **Favourite Memory:** 'Proposing to my wife.'

MOSES, Billy

Actor, b. 11 November 1959, Los Angeles, California. Went to the University of Southern California and Wesleyan University before starting successful acting career. Film: *Choices*. Cole Gioberti in the TV soap opera *Falcon Crest*. Other TV incl: *Love Boat; Glitter; Finder of the Lost Loves; Battle of the Network Stars*. Address: c/o Leading Artists, 445 North Bedford Drive, Beverly Hills, Calif 90210. Hobbies: basketball, swimming, running; fixing up his house. **Most Cherished Possession:** 'My red Alfa Romeo.' **Favourite Memory:** 'I appeared opposite John Wayne and Rock Hudson.'

MOSLEY, Bryan

Actor, b. 25 August 1931, Leeds. Trained at the Esme Church Northern Theatre School after serving with the RAF in Air Traffic Control. Rep at St Andrews, Perth, Derby, Harrogate, and York. Films incl: *Get Carter; Charlie Bubbles; Far From The Madding Crowd; A Kind of Loving; This Sporting Life*. TV incl: *The Saint; Z-Cars; The Avengers; No Hiding Place; Crossroads;* Alf Roberts in *Coronation Street; Play of the Week; The Villains; Doctor Who; Queenie's Castle*. Expert swordsman, arranges fights for stage, film and TV. m. Norma, 3 d. Jacqueline, Simone, Helen, 3 s. Jonathan, Bernard, Leonard. Address: c/o Granada TV. Hobbies: archery, travel, painting, drawing. **Most Cherished Possession:** 'My Pentax camera because it gives me so many pictures of happy times and marvellous people, particularly my family.'

MOSLEY, Roger E

Actor, b. Los Angeles. Best known for his role as TC, an ex-Vietnam war helicopter pilot, who assists Tom Selleck in the title role of TV's *Magnum PI*. He was a champion wrestler while at college and a founder member of the Watts Reportory Company. Films incl: *Semi-Tough; Leadbelly; The Greatest; Stay Hungry; K-God*. Other TV incl: *Attica; I Know Why the Caged Bird Sings; The Jericho Mile; Love Boat*. m. (1st) (dis.); 5 children. Address: c/o Aimee Entertainment, 13743 Victory Blvd, Van Nuys, Calif 91401. Hobbies: collecting cowboy boots, tennis, basketball (coaches a basketball team). Pets: two dogs. **Most Cherished Possession:** 'My collection of cowboy boots and cars.' **Favourite Memory:** 'Beating Tom Selleck on the basketball court.'

MUIR, Frank, CBE

Scriptwriter/performer, b. 5 February 1920, Broadstairs, Kent. Started writing seriously in 1946. In 1947 teamed up with Denis Norden in *Navy Mixture*. Together for 17 years during which they wrote *Take It From Here; Bedtime With Braden;* and TV series: *And So To Bentley; Whack-O!; The Seven Faces of Jim; Brothers-In-Law*. Radio incl: *My Word!; My Music*. TV incl: *Sound of Laughter; Call My Bluff; How To Be An Alien; We Have Ways of Making Your Laugh*. BBC's Head of Comedy, 1963; LWT's Head of Light Entertainment 1966–69. Books: *You Can't Have Your Kyak and Heat It* (with Denis Norden); *The Frank Muir Book; The Oxford Book of Humorous Prose*. m. Polly; 1 d. Sarah, 1 s. James. Address: c/o April Young, London. Birthsign: Aquarius. Hobbies: collecting books.

MULLIGAN, Richard

Actor, b. 13 November 1932, New York. Started career as a playwright, was mistaken for an actor at a Miami theatre and landed the role of Andy Mayo in *Beyond the Horizon*. Broadway theatre incl: *All the Way Home; Never Too Late; Nobody Loves an Albatross; Thieves*. Films: *The Mixed Up Files of Mrs Basil E Frankweiler; Irish Whiskey; Rebellion; One Potato, Two Potato; The Group; The Big Bus; Little Big Man; Scavenger Hunt; S.O.B.; Trail of the Pink Panther; Meatballs Part II; Teachers; Micki and Maude; Doin' Time; The Heavenly Kid; A Fine Mess; Quicksilver*. TV: *Having Babies; Poker Alice; The Hero; The Diana Rigg Show;* Burt in *Soap* (1980 best comedy actor Emmy); *Harvey; The Public Incident;* title role in *Reggie;* Harry in *Empty Nest* (1989 best comedy actor Emmy). m. 1st Patricia Jones (dis.), 2nd Joan Hackett (dis.), 3rd Leonore Stevens.

MURDEN, Karen

Actress, b. 24 April 1970, Nottingham. Joined the Central Junior Television Workshop at the age of 13, appearing in stage plays *On the Beach, The Gallopers, A Collier's Tuesday Tea, Roses of Eyam, The Boy Friend, Cabaret* and *Bugsy Malone*. TV: BAFTA award-winning *Your Mother Wouldn't Like It* (two series); *Hardwicke House;* Beverley Grice in *Crossroads;* Sheila in *Tales of Sherwood Forest;* Sarah Robbins in new BSB soap *Jupiter Moon*. Lives with dancer Nick Davion. Address: c/o Spotlight. Birthsign: Taurus. Hobbies: socialising. Pets: a cat called Sylvester. **Most Cherished Possession:** 'Sylvester.' **Favourite Memory:** 'Playing Blousy Brown in *Bugsy Malone*.'

MURPHY, Brian

Actor, b. 25 September 1933, Ventnor, Isle of Wight. After National Service with the RAF trained at RADA. Became a stalwart of Joan Littlewood's Theatre Workshop. Stage incl: *On Your Way Riley;* a season with the Royal Shakespeare Company in 1984. TV incl: *Man About the House; George and Mildred; The Incredible Mr Tanner; L For Lester; Lame Ducks*. m. Carol; 2 s. Trevor, Kevin. Address: c/o Saraband Associates. Birthsign: Libra. Hobbies: collecting films. **Most Cherished Possession:** 'Vintage comedies of Will Hay and Laurel and Hardy showing comedy acting at its height.' **Favourite Memory:** 'First glimpse of Venice. History come alive.'

MURRAY, Bryan

Actor, b. 13 July 1949, Dublin, Ireland. Trained at the Abbey Theatre School in Dublin. Went on to become a member of the Abbey Theatre Company where he has played many leading parts, directed and co-wrote two musicals performed by the Company. Joined the National Theatre Company in 1977. Also a member of the RSC. TV incl: *Oscar; I'm a Dreamer Montreal; Strumpet City; Bread Or Blood; Rifleman; The Irish RM; Final Run; Encore; Perfect Scoundrels.* m. actress Angela Harding (sep.); 1 d. Laura. Address: c/o Peters Fraser & Dunlop. Hobbies: music and movies. **Most Cherished Possession:** 'My records.' **Favourite Memory:** 'Being introduced by my young daughter as "Bryan" to her school friend.'

NETTLES, John

Actor, b. 1948, St Austell, Cornwall. Took part in dramatic society productions while at university. Joined the Royal Court Theatre, London; member of the Royal Shakespeare Company, 1976–9. TV incl: Ian Mackenzie in *A Family At War; Black Beauty; Play For Today: Findings On a Late Night; The Merchant of Venice; The Liver Birds* (four series); Jim Bergerac, star of *Bergerac* since 1982. m. Joyce (dis.); 1 d. Emma. Address: c/o Saraband Associates.

NETTLETON, John

Actor, b. 5 February 1929, London. Trained at RADA and spent many years with the Royal Shakespeare Company, National Theatre and Old Vic. Recent theatre incl: *Anyone For Denis?; When the Wind Blows.* Films incl: *A Man For All Seasons; And Soon the Darkness; Black Beauty.* TV incl: *The Citadel; The Flame Trees of Thaika; Brideshead Revisited; Yes Minister; East of Ipswich; A Perfect Spy.* m. Deirdre Doone; 3 d. Sarah, Joanna, Jessica. Address: c/o Marmont Management. Birthsign: Aquarius. Hobbies: gardening, listening to music. Pets: cat. **Most Cherished Possession:** 'A short-haired British cream cat called Jenkins, who is overfed, spoiled and thick, but incredibly beautiful.'

NEWMAN, Nanette

Actress/author, b. Northampton. Trained at RADA and went straight into films incl: *The L-Shaped Room; The Whisperers; The Wrong Box; The Love Ban; Man At the top; The Stepford Wives; The Raging Moon; International Velvet.* TV incl: *Prometheus; Fun Food Factory* (own series); *London Scene; Stay With Me 'Til Morning; Let There Be Love; Jessie* (title role); *Late Expectations; The Endless Game.* As an author, sales over one million. Books incl: *God Bless Love; My Granny Was a Frightful Bore; The Christmas Cookbook; Small Beginnings; Summer Cookpot; Archie; The Best of Love; Small Beginnings; Bad Baby; Entertaining; Sharing.* m. film director/author Bryan Forbes; 2 d. Sarah, Emma. Address: c/o Chatto & Linnit. Birthsign: Gemini.

NICHOLAS, Paul

Actor, b. 3 December 1945, Peterborough. Former rock 'n' roll piano player, started acting 1969 in original production of *Hair.* Followed by *Jesus Christ Superstar* and *Grease.* Theatre incl: *Cats; Blondel; The Pirates of Penzance; Charlie Girl.* Films incl: *Tommy; Stardust; Lisztomania; Sergeant Pepper's Lonely Hearts Club Band; The World Is Full of Married Men; Yesterday's Hero; Alice; The Jazz Singer; Nutcracker.* TV incl: *Three Up Two Down; Chips; The Lady Killers, The Boys From Ipenema; A Little Rocco; Just Good Friends; Doubting Thomas; Bust; Paul Nicholas and Friends; Close to Home.* m. Linzi; 2 d. Natasha, Carmen, 2 s. Oscar, Alexander. Address: c/o Billy Marsh Assocs. Birthsign: Sagittarius. Hobbies: walking with children, snooker, swimming.

NICHOLLS, Sue

Actress, b. 23 November 1943, Wallsall, West Midlands. Trained at RADA then rep and cabaret in England and abroad. Appeared in *London Assurance* on Broadway. Film: *Expresso Slasho!* TV incl: *Crossroads; The Fall and Rise of Reginald Perrin; Solo; The Professionals; Pipkins; Rentaghost; Tycoon; Not On Your Nellie; Heartlands; Coronation Street; Up the Elephant and Round the Castle.* Hit record with *Where Will You Be.* Address: c/o Barry Brown Management. Birthsign: Sagittarius. Hobbies: music, singing, dancing, sauna, films, eating out. **Most Cherished Possession:** 'My radio. It has everything to fit whatever mood, you are never alone.' **Favourite Memory:** 'That one day when I'd lost enough weight and my trousers didn't feel tight!'

NICHOLSON, Michael

Correspondent, b. 9 January 1937, Romford, Essex. University of Leicester BA. Nominated for Emmy Award 1968 for his reports from Biafra. In 1974 received Special Award by British Broadcasting Press Guild for his war coverage in Cyprus; his Battle For Newport Bridge, the last battle in South Vietnam, won him Silver Nymph at Cannes Film Festival 1976; twice Royal Television Society Journalist of the Year. His reporting of Falklands War won him many awards, incl: BAFTA Richard Dimbleby Award 1982. Books: *The Partridge Kite; Red Joker; December Ultimatum; Across the Limpopo; Pilgrim's Rest.* m. Diana; 2 s. Tom, Will. Address: c/o ITN, London. Birthsign: Capricorn. Hobbies: writing, tennis, swimming, skiing. Pets: three dogs, three cats, two donkeys, 30 doves. **Most Cherished Possession:** 'My house and garden.'

NIMMO, Derek

Actor/writer, b. 19 September 1933, Liverpool. Many West End appearances incl: *The Amorous Prawn; Duel of Angels; Charlie Girl; A Friend Indeed; See How They Run* (also TV). Also tours in Australia and the Far East. Film incl: *One of Our Dinosaurs Is Missing.* TV incl: *All Gas and Gaiters; Oh Brother!; Oh Father!; My Hon Mrs; Sorry I'm Single; Life Begins At Forty; Third Time Lucky; Hell's Bells; Neighbours.* m. Patricia; 1 d. Amanda, 2 s. Timothy, Piers. Address: c/o Barry Burnett. Hobbies: sailing, collecting English 17th and 18th century furniture. **Most Cherished Possession:** 'Obtaining Don Bradman's autograph.' **Favourite Memory:** 'Having failed for 30 years to obtain the above, managing to extract it from the Don in Adelaide.'

NORDEN, Denis, CBE

Writer/broadcaster, b. 6 February 1922, Hackney, London. Originally a theatre manager, 1939–42. Wrote for troops shows in RAF, then scriptwriter for variety. Teamed up with Frank Muir, 1947–64, wrote for radio: *Take It It From Here* and *Bedtime With Braden.* For TV: *And So To Bentley; Whack-O!; The Seven Faces of Jim; The Glums; Brothers-In-Law.* Solo writer 1964 and film scripts incl: *Bueno Sera, Mrs Campbell; Every Home Should Have One; The Water Babies.* Radio incl: *My Word!; My Music.* TV incl: *The Name's The Same; How To Be An Alien; Looks Familiar; It'll Be Alright On the Night; With Hilarious Consequences; Ten Years of Alright On the Night; 21 Years of Laughter; In On the Act; Pick of the Pilots.* m. Avril; 1 d. TV producer Maggie, 1 s. Nick. Hobbies: reading, loitering. Address: c/o April Young.

NORMAN, Barry

Writer/presenter, b. 21 August 1933, London. A journalist, mostly with *Daily Mail* until made redundant. *Film* series 1972–81 and *The Hollywood Greats.* 1982 presented *Omnibus* for BBC1 before returning to *Film* series. TV incl: *The British Greats; Barry Norman In Chicago; Barry Norman's Hong Kong; Barry Norman On Broadway; Barry Norman's London Season; Barry Norman In Celebrity City; The Rank Charm School.* Won BAFTA Richard Dimbleby Award 1980. Books incl: *The Movie Greats; Have a Nice Day; Sticky Wicket; The Film Greats.* m. Diana; 2 d. Samantha, Emma. Address: c/o BBC TV. Birthsign: Leo. Hobbies: cricket.

NUNN, Judy

Actress, mother a teacher-turned-actress who also directed drama for ABC radio in Australia. Professional debut, aged 12, at the Perth Playhouse. Moved to Britain, aged 22, and worked in repertory, fringe and London West End theatre, as well as TV and radio, alongside stars such as John Gregson, Wilfred Pickles, Jessie Matthews and Julia Lockwood. Returned to Australia. Theatre incl: *Don's Party*. TV: Vikki Stafford in *The Box*; Irene Fisher in *Sons and Daughters*; Ailsa Hogan in *Home and Away*. Address: c/o June Cann Management, PO Box 1577, North Sydney, NSW 2060, Australia.

OAKLEY, Roger

Actor, 21 August 1943, Auckland, New Zealand. Became interested in acting while studying languages at university. Moved to Britain in 1968, took a part-time theatre course and performed in repertory theatre for five years. He returned to New Zealand in 1973, appearing on radio and TV, and moved to Australia in 1978. Films: *Ground Zero; Travelling North; Sleeping Dogs*. TV incl: Major Barrington in *The Sullivans; Against the Wind; Eureka Stockade; Sara Dane; Women of the Sun; Carson's Law;* Tom Fletcher in *Home and Away*. Melbourne Theatre Company productions incl: *Glen Garry Glen Rose; The Alchemist; Benefactors; The Norman Conquests*. Address: c/o Barbara Leane and Assocs, 261 Miller Street, North Sydney, NSW 2060, Australia.

OBERMAN, Claire

Actress, b. 1956, Holland, brought up in New Zealand. At 16, won a scholarship to the National Drama School, in Wellington, then worked on stage and in radio drama. Wrote her own one-woman stage show, *Lovers and Vagabonds*. New Zealand theatre incl: *The Taming of the Shrew; Twelfth Night; Kennedy's Children; Pygmalion; Time and Time Again; Just Between Ourselves; The Merchant of Venice*. She returned to Holland, then moved to Britain. Theatre incl: *Boeing Boeing; Rose; Move Over Mrs Markham*. Films: *Goodbye Pork Pie* (New Zealand); *The Beautiful End of the World* (Germany). TV incl: *Hunter's Gold; Moynihan; Joe and Koro; Mortimer's Patch* (all New Zealand); Kate Norris in *Tenko; Hi-de-Hi!; Bottle Boys; The Two Ronnies; Paradise Postponed; Ladies Night; Fortunes of War;* Sandy Savage in *Gentlemen and Players; Matlock*. Address: c/o Barry Burnett.

O'BRIEN, Peter

Actor, 25 March 1960, Murray Bridge, Australia. After leaving South Australian College of Advanced Education joined St Martin Youth Theatre and South Australian Theatre Company. Theatre incl: *Romeo and Juliet; The Bear; Runaways*. Films incl: *The Mortal Coil*. TV incl: *Starting Out; Carson's Law; Prisoner: Cell Block H; The Henderson Kids;* Shane in *Neighbours;* Dr Sam Patterson in *The Flying Doctors*. Address: c/o Gary Stewart, M.A.M., Melbourne, Australia. Hobbies: reading, carpentry, water sports, music. **Most Cherished Possession:** 'Great-great-grandparents' bedroom and lounge suites which I restored and now use; plus my book collection.' **Favourite Memory:** 'Childhood days on family farm and hitch-hiking around Australia by myself.'

O'BRIEN, Richard

Actor, b. 25 March 1942, Cheltenham, Gloucestershire. Brought up in New Zealand, but had no formal training as an actor. Theatre incl: *Gulliver's Travels; Hair; Jesus Christ Superstar; The Unseen Hand; The Hostage; The Tooth of Crime; They Used To Star In Movies; Eastwood Ho!; The News;* also as writer for the following: *The Rocky Horror Show; T Zee; Disaster; Top People*. Films incl: *Carry On Cowboy; Fighting Prince of Donegal; The Old Job Man; Flash Gordon; Shock Treatment; Revolution*. TV incl: *A Hymn For Jim; Robin of Sherwood; The Crystal Maze*. m. Jane Elizabeth Moss-O'Brien; 2 s. Linus, Joshua, 1 d. Amelia. Agent: Chatto & Linnit. Birthsign: Aries. Hobbies: reading, drawing, talking. **Most Cherished Possession:** 'An old pair of lizard skin cowboy boots! I've had them for 15 years.'

O'BRIEN, Simon

Actor, b. 19 June 1965, Garston, Liverpool. Landed the role of Damon Grant in *Brookside* (1982–7) when his best friend went to audition for it. Simon accompanied him and was offered the role himself. Starred in the three-part spin-off serial *Damon & Debbie*, in which the character was murdered. TV since then: *Night Network* presenter; *I Can Do That* presenter; *Move It* presenter; *Fraggle Rock* presenter; *Young, Gifted and Broke* (two series). Film: Willy Russell's *Dancin' Thru the Dark*. Theatre: *Stags and Hens; Prisoners.* Address: c/o Annette Stone Associates. Birthsign: Gemini.

O'CONNOR, Des

Entertainer, b. 12 January, Stepney, London. Joined RAF at 18. A former Butlin's Red Coat made his professional debut at the Palace Theatre, Newcastle, 1953. TV incl: *Sunday Night at The London Palladium;* and many *Des O'Connor Shows; Des O'Connor Tonight.* Hit records incl: *Careless Hands; I Pretend; One Two Three O'Leary.* Gold discs for albums: *Just For You; Des O'Connor Now.* TVTimes Favourite Male TV Personality 1969 to 1973. m. (1st) Phylis; (2nd) Gillian; (3rd) Jay; 4 d. Karen (from 1st), Tracey and Samantha (from 2nd), Kristina Eva (from 3rd). Address: c/o IMG. Birthsign: Capricorn. Hobbies: showbusiness, golf. **Favourite Memory:** 'Seeing my mother and father dancing together on their 50th wedding anniversary.'

O'CONNOR, Tom

Comedian, b. 31 October 1939, Bootle, Merseyside. Originally maths and music teacher at St Joan of Arc School, Bootle; *Opportunity Knocks* led to his own TV series – *Wednesday At Eight; London Night Out; Tom O'Connor Show; Tom O'Connor At The Casino.* Host of TV game shows *Zodiac; Name That Tune; Gambit; Password; I've Got a Secret; A Question of Entertainment; Cross Wits.* Recent TV series incl: *Tom O'Connor* and *Tom O'Connor's Roadshow.* m. former teacher Pat; 3 d. Ann, Frances, Helen; 1 s. Stephen. Address: c/o Clifford Elson. Birthsign: Scorpio. Hobbies: golf, snooker, football. **Most Cherished Possession:** 'Pocket watch presented by the boys on leaving St Joan of Arc School.' **Favourite Memory:** 'Seeing my mother's radiant face in the audience when I appeared in my very first Royal Variety Show in 1977, at the London Palladium.'

ODDIE, Bill

Writer/performer, b. 7 July 1941, Rochdale, Lancashire. Was member of Footlights at Cambridge University 1960–63. As writer/performer TV incl: *That Was the Week That Was; Twice a Fortnight; Broaden Your Mind; The Goodies; From the Top;* various ornithological programmes for TV incl: *Oddie In Paradise.* Has written and sung on various Goodie hit records and is the author of several bird books. m. Laura Beaumont (co-writer of recent books and TV); 3 d. Kate and Bonnie (from previous m.) and Rosie. Address: c/o London Management. Birthsign: Cancer. Hobbies: ornithology, music (jazz, rock etc.), painting birds, and a bit of tennis. **Most Cherished Possession:** 'My binoculars.' **Favourite Memory:** 'Hopefully still to come. Never live in the past!'

OGILVY, Ian

Actor, b. 30 September 1943, Woking, Surrey. Started backstage at London's Royal Court Theatre before RADA. Rep at Colchester, Canterbury and Northampton. Films incl: *Stranger In the House; The Sorcerers; Witchfinder General; The Invincible Six; Waterloo; Wuthering Heights; Fengriffin; No Sex Please, We're British; Design For Living; Horses; Anna Karenina.* TV incl: *The Liars; Upstairs, Downstairs; Catherine* (Affairs Of the Heart); *A Walk With Destiny; The Return of the Saint; Tom, Dick and Harriet.* TVTimes Award Most Compulsive Character 1978–79. m. former model Diane; 1 step-d. Emma, 1 s. Titus. Address: c/o Michael Whitehall. Birthsign: Libra. **Most Cherished Possession:** 'My word processor.' **Favourite Memory:** 'The day I bought my word processor.'

ORCHARD, Chris

Actor, b. 6 August 1951, Manchester, England. Began at National Institute of Dramatic Art, Sydney, Australia. Theatre incl: *Sgt. Peppers Lonely Hearts Club Band; On the Road; Othello; The Tempest; The Lower Depths; A Man For All Seasons; The Good Person of Sezchuan; The London Cuckolds; Isadora; Macbeth; Travelling Revue.* Films incl: *Image of Death; Greed; Journey to Hainan.* TV incl: *The Young Doctors; Carson's Law; Prime Time.* m. Diane Jill; 1 s. Adam, 1 d. Emily. Address: c/o M.A.M., 643 St Kilda Road, Melbourne, Vic. 3004, Australia. Birthsign: Leo. Hobbies: playing guitar, chess, squash, tennis. Pets: dog, cat. **Most Cherished Possession:** 'Martin guitar purchased after fifteen years of promising myself one.' **Favourite Memory:** 'Broadway in the rain having just seen *42nd Street* with my wife.'

O'SHEA, Kevin

Actor, b. 7 March 1952, Enfield, Middlesex. Trained with the National Youth Theatre and at Bristol Old Vic Theatre School. Theatre incl: at Glasgow Citizens' Theatre; *Much Ado About Nothing; The Lion In Winter; The Caretaker;* with the Royal Shakespeare Company; *Romeo and Juliet;* directed *As You Like It* in US. Films incl: *SOS Titanic; Black Joy; Woman On a Roof; Inseminoid; Dirty Dozen III.* TV incl: *Thank You Comrades; We Think the World of You; Secret Army; Spearhead; The Professionals; The Gentle Touch; The Scarlet Pimpernel; Kelly Monteith; Grange Hill.* m. (d.). Address: c/o Creative Artists, 11–15 Betterton Street, London WC2. Hobbies: film-making, computer, gliding, cinema, football. **Favourite Memory:** 'Snorkel diving in Israel on New Year's Eve in a coral reserve, it was beautiful.'

O'SULLIVAN, Richard

Actor, b. 7 May 1944, Chiswick, London. Child actor in many films incl: *Stranger's Hand; Dangerous Exile; Cleopatra.* In many Cliff Richard musicals. Theatre incl: *The Government Inspector; Boeing-Boeing;* panto at London Palladium. TV incl: *Doctor At Large; Doctor In Charge; Father, Dear Father* (and film); *Alcock and Gander; Man About the House; Robin's Nest; Dick Turpin; Me and My Girl.* Address: c/o Al Mitchell Assocs, 7 Garrick Street, London WC2 9AR. Birthsign: Taurus. Hobby: soccer (plays in charity matches). **Most Cherished Possession:** 'A medal for playing soccer against the England World Cup team at White City.' **Favourite Memory:** 'Nutmegging the England captain, Bobby Moore, at White City.'

OWEN, Bill, MBE

Actor/author, b. 14 March 1914, Acton Green, London. No academic training. First professional theatre job 1939 Royalty Theatre. Theatre incl: *Who's Afraid of Virginia Woolf?; As You Like It* (New York); *Luther; The Contractor; In Celebration; March On Russia.* More than 60 films, incl: *Laughterhouse; Oh Lucky Man; Singleton's Pluck.* As writer incl: *Lysette; Breakout; Matchgirls; Fruits of Philosophy;* many lyrics for popular songs. TV incl: *Brideshead Revisited* and as Compo in *Last of the Summer Wine.* m. Kathie, former actress; 1 s. Tom, 1 step-d. Kathleen Louise. Address: c/o Richard Stone. Hobby: working in boys' clubs. **Favourite Memory:** 'Holmfirth, West Yorkshire – the home of *Summer Wine.*'

OWEN, Nicholas

Presenter and correspondent, b. 10 February 1947, London. Worked as a journalist since 1964. With BBC TV, before joining ITN in 1984. m. Brenda; 1 d. Rebecca, 1 step-d. Justine, 1 s. Anthony, 1 step-s. Daniel. Address: c/o ITN. Birthsign: Aquarius. Hobbies: reading, walking, sleeping. **Most Cherished Possession:** 'Wife (present one).' **Favourite Memory:** 'Marrying the above.'

OWEN, Nick

TV presenter, b. 1 November 1947, Berkhamsted, Hertfordshire. BA (Hons) Classics. Newspaper journalist and local radio experience before joining ATV/Central 1978 to present news and sport programmes. TV incl: presenting *Good Morning Britain*, TV-am 1983–6; *Midweek Sport Special; Sporting Triangles;* ITV athletics, ice skating, royal premieres; *Hitman.* m. Jill; 3 s. Andrew, Timothy, Christopher, 1 d. Jenny. Address: c/o Severn Management, 36 Chadbrook Crest, Richmond Hill Road, Edgbaston, Birmingham. Hobbies: golf, jogging, watching football and cricket, squash, walking the dog and children! Pets: dog, Suzi. **Most Cherished Possession:** 'Car parking space at Thames TV. Men have killed for less.' **Favourite Memory:** 'Attending the birth of all four children. A most exciting, exhilarating and emotional experience.'

OXENBERG, Catherine

Actress, b. 22 September 1962, New York. Is the daughter of Princess Elizabeth of Yugoslavia. Pursued a successful career as a model on both sides of the Atlantic before studying acting with Stanley Zaraff in New York. Started her career on TV as Lady Diana Spencer in *The Royal Romance of Charles and Diana.* Other TV incl: *The Love Boat; Cover Up; Crazy Like a Fox;* Amanda Bedford in *Dynasty; Saturday Night Live; Roman Holiday; Swimsuit.* Address: c/o ICM, 8999 Beverly Blvd., Los Angeles, Calif 90048. Pets: dog. **Favourite Memory:** 'Being coached in Shakespeare at the age of 13 sitting on the knee of Richard Burton.'

PACE, Norman

Comedian, b. 17 February 1953, Dudley, Worcestershire. Previously a teacher. Formed a double act with Gareth Hale. TV: *Pushing Up Daisies; Coming Next; The Young Ones; Live From The Palladium;* host of *Saturday Live; Just For Laughs; The Saturday Gang; The Management; Hale & Pace* (1989 Golden Rose of Montreux winner). Books (with Gareth Hale): *Falsies; The Hale & Pace Book of Writes and Rons.* LP: *Hale & Pace Live In Concert.* m. Beverley; 2 s. Liam and Charlie, 1 d. Holly. Address: c/o International Artistes. Birthsign: Aquarius. Hobbies: sport, reading, whisky. **Most Cherished Possession:** 'My Walkman, so I can go to sleep listening to the World Service without disturbing my wife.' **Favourite Memory:** 'The birth of my daughter, Holly – no need to say why.'

PAGETT, Nicola

Actress, b. 15 June 1945, Cairo, Egypt. Brought up in Hong Kong and Japan because of her father's work, then returned to Britain in her early teens. Trained at RADA, before going into rep at Worthing. Made her London West End debut in *Widows' Houses,* at the Royal Court Theatre. Films: *The Viking Queen; Anne of the Thousand Days; There's a Girl In My Soup; Operation Daybreak; Frankenstein; Oliver's Story; Privates On Parade; All of You.* TV: *Barlow at Large; The Persuaders; Upstairs, Downstairs; The Rivals of Sherlock Holmes; Napoleon; The Sweeney; French Without Tears; Anna Karenina; War and Peace; Aren't We All; Love Story; Scoop; A Bit of a Do.* m. writer Graham Swannell, 1 d. Eve. Address: c/o James Sharkey. Hobbies: cooking, gardening. **Favourite Memory:** 'My garden, 'cos it's getting older but more beautiful.'

PALMER, Geoffrey

Actor, b. 4 June 1927, London. No formal training but worked as unpaid trainee assistant stage manager at the Q Theatre, London. Most recent theatre incl: *A Friend Indeed; Tishoo; St Joan; The Mask of Moriarty; Kafka's Dick.* Films incl: *O Lucky Man; The Outsider; The Honorary Consul; A Zed and Two Noughts; Clockwise; A Fish Called Wanda.* Many plays on radio. TV incl: *The Fall and Rise of Reginald Perrin; Butterflies; A Midsummer Night's Drama; The Last Song; Absurd Person Singular; Radio Pictures; Fairly Secret Army; Hot Metal; The Insurance Man; Season's Greetings; Inspector Morse.* m. Sally; 1 s. Charles, 1 d. Harriet. Address: c/o Spotlight. Birthsign: Gemini. Hobbies: 'Getting fewer.' **Most Cherished Possession:** 'My wife.' **Favourite Memory:** 'Can't remember.'

PALMER, Toni

Actress, b. 17 September 1932, London. Trained as a dancer, no formal training in drama, learnt everything she knows from Danny La Rue and Joan Littlewood. Theatre incl: *Saturday Night Sunday Morning; Fings Ain't Wot They Used To Be; Steaming; Sweeney Todd; Phantom of the Opera*. Films incl: *The French Lieutenant's Woman; Personal Services; Ellis Island; The Doctor and the Devils; Smashing Time*. TV incl: *The Rag Trade; Within These Walls; Take My Wife; The Confederacy of Wives; Russ Abbot's Madhouse; King and Castle; West End Tales; The Kelly Monteith Show; The Cuckoo Sister; Only Fools and Horses; Mog!' Hi-de-Hi; The Bill*. Address: c/o Barry Brown. Birthsign: Virgo. Hobby: travel. **Most Cherished Possession:** 'Health.'

PAPPS, Alex

Actor. Comes from a showbusiness family – his parents are both theatre directors and his father also occasionally acts on TV. Took a drama and media production course. TV: Vinnie in *The Henderson Kids; Prisoner: Cell Block H; Neighbours;* co-presenter of ABC's Saturday-morning show *The Factory* in Australia; Frank Morgan in *Home and Away*, until 1989. Address: c/o The Actors Agency, 26 Victoria Street, North Sydney, NSW 2060, Australia.

PARKINSON, Michael

Journalist/broadcaster, b. 28 March 1935, Cudworth, Yorkshire. Entered journalism via local paper. TV producer Granada TV. Executive producer LWT. Founder member/director TV-am. TV incl: *Work In Action; What the Papers Say; 24 Hours; Cinema; Tea Break* with wife Mary; *World of Sport; Sports Arena; Give Us a Clue; Parkinson; Parkinson One To One; Where In the World; Movie Quiz; Good Morning Britain*. Radio incl: *Start the Week; Desert Island Discs*. Author of many books incl: *Cricket Mad; Parkinson's Lore*. m. TV presenter Mary Parkinson; 3 s. Andrew, Nicholas, Michael. Address: c/o IMG. Birthsign: Aries. Hobbies: golf, watching cricket. Pets: one old cat. **Most Cherished Possession:** 'One old cat.' **Favourite Memory:** 'One young kitten.'

PARRY, Ken

Actor, b. 20 June 1930, Wigan, Lancashire. Started in rep in the North and later West End and National Theatre. Films incl: *Come Play With Me; What's Up Nurse; Lifeforce; Dardinelle; Taming of the Shrew; Start the Revolution Without Me; Spring and Port Wine; Tom Jones; Lisztomania*. TV incl: *Crossroads; Kings Royal; Filthy Rich and Catflap; The Young Ones; Kelly Monteith; Blott On the Landscape; Horne a Plenty; The Merchant of Venice; Hazell; The Sweeney; A Midsummer Night's Dream*. Address: c/o June Epstein Assocs. Birthsign: Gemini. Hobbies: vintage films, boxing, clairvoyance and spiritual medium. **Most Cherished Possession:** 'My Life.' **Favourite Memory:** 'Being in Rome in 1966 with Zeffirelli, Burton, Taylor, filming *Taming of the Shrew* as the tailor.'

PARSONS, Nicholas

Actor/compere/presenter, b. 10 October 1928, Grantham, Lincolnshire. Engineering apprenticeship at Clydebank, then Glasgow University. Began as an impressionist, then repertory theatre in Bromley, Kent, followed by cabaret and revues in London. Comedian at The Windmill for six months. London West End theatre incl: *Boeing Boeing; Say Who You Are; Uproar In the House;* tour of *Why Not Stay For Breakfast?* Film comedies in the Sixties. TV: straight man to Arthur Haynes for 10 years; *The Benny Hill Show; Sale of the Century* presenter, 1971–85; *Night Network*'s *Alphabet Quiz; Laughlines* on BSB. m. actress Denise Bryer (dis.); 1 d. Suzy, 1 s. Justin. Address: c/o Billy Marsh Assocs. Hobbies: photography, gardening sport. **Most Cherished Possession:** 'A grandfather clock put together from bits and pieces when I was 16 – and still working.'

PASCO, Richard, CBE

Actor, b. 18 July 1926, Barnes, London. Began as student stage manager at the Q Theatre, London, 1943. After the war, trained at the Central School of Speech and Drama. Old Vic Company, 1950–52; Birmingham Rep, 1952–5; English Stage Company, Royal Court, 1956–8; many London West End stage appearances; Bristol Old Vic, 1964–7; Royal Shakespeare Company, 1969–74 and 1979–82; joined National Theatre, 1987, to play the father in *Six Characters In Search of an Author* and Pavel in *Fathers and Sons;* National Theatre, 1990, in *Racing Demon.* An honorary associate artist of the RSC. Film incl: *Room at the Top; Yesterday's Enemy; Arch of Triumph; Wagner.* TV incl: *Let's Run Away To Africa; Pythons On the Mountain; Sorrell and Son; Drummonds.* m. Greta Watson (dis.), 2nd actress Barbara Leigh-Hunt; 1 s. William (from 1st m.). Address: c/o Michael Whitehall.

PAXMAN, Jeremy

Presenter/reporter/writer, b. 11 May 1950, Leeds. Attended Cambridge University, reporter, Northern Ireland (1974–7). Reporter for *Tonight* and *Panorama* (1979–85). Presenter of *London Plus; Six O'Clock News; Breakfast Time; Newsnight.* TV incl: *The Bear Next Door.* Film: *Called To Account – How Roberto Calvi Died.* Won Royal TV Society Award for International Current Affairs 1984. Books: *A Higher Form of Killing; Through the Volcanoes.* Address: c/o BBC TV, London. Birthsign: Taurus. Hobbies: flyfishing, skiing, sleeping in the garden. **Most Cherished Possession:** 'A sense of the absurd.'

PENHALIGON, Susan

Actress, b. 3 July 1949, Manila. Brought up in England and trained at the Webber Douglas Academy of Dramatic Art. Wide rep experience. Films incl: *No Sex Please, We're British; The Land That Time Forgot; Nasty Habits; Under Milk Wood; Leopard In the Snow; Private Road; Patrick.* TV incl: *Public Eye; Country Matters; Bouquet of Barbed Wire; Fearless Frank; Call My Bluff; Give Us a Clue; The Taming of the Shrew; A Fine Romance; A Kind of Loving; Heather Ann; Remington Steele; A Kind of Living* (presenter); *Heart of the Country; Bergerac.* m. David Munro (dis.); 1 s. Truan. Lives with actor Duncan Preston. Address: c/o Jeremy Conway. Hobby: acting. Pets: 1 dog – Bronwyn. **Favourite Memory:** 'Seeing Truan for the first time, indescribable feeling of a new love.'

PENROSE, Tricia

Actress/singer, b. 9 April 1970, Liverpool. Trained at Elliott Clarke Theatre School. Theatre; starred in *Bye, Bye, Birdie.* Films: *Vroom; Cresta Run; Tydi Bywyd yn Boen! (Isn't Life a Pain!)* for the Welsh Fourth Channel; Willy Russell's *Dancin' Thru the Dark; Shooting Stars.* TV: Ruth in *Brookside,* aged 15; *Help!; Albion Market; Boon;* WPC Emma Reid in *Brookside;* Julie in *How To Be Cool; Split Ends.* Plus many TV commercials. Address: c/o ART Casting. Hobbies: singing, listening to music, going out and socialising in pubs and clubs. Pet: a cat called Harry. **Most Cherished Possession:** 'My diaries. I have kept a diary since I was 13. When I feel down, I look back to schooldays.' **Favourite Memory:** 'My first audition for a TV job. I will never forget the weird feeling in my stomach. I loved it.'

PENTELOW, Arthur

Actor, b. 14 February 1924, Rochdale. A cadet clerk in the police, but amateur dramatics in spare time. After Royal Navy during the war became a student teacher. Joined Bradford Civic Theatre School to train as an actor, then rep at Bristol Old Vic. In Orson Welles' *Othello* in London. Best known on TV as Henry Wilkes in *Emmerdale,* which he has played since the series began in 1972. Films incl: *Privilege; Charlie Bubbles; United!* Other TV incl: *Z-Cars; Armchair Theatre; The Troubleshooters Coronation Street; Play For Today.* m. pottery teacher Jacqueline; 2 s. Nicholas, Simon. Address: c/o Green & Underwood. Birthsign: Aquarius. Hobbies: the countryside, gardening, tennis, music.

PERLMAN, Rhea

Actress, b. 31 March, Brooklyn, New York. Took a degree in drama and trained in off-Broadway productions. Carla in TV's *Cheers*, for which she has won three Emmy awards; also appeared in *Taxi* and has made many TV films. m. actor Danny De Vito; 2 d. Lucie, Gracie, Jake. Address: c/o John Kimble, Triad Artists, 10100 Santa Monica Blvd., LA, CA 90067. Birthsign: Aries. Hobbies: roller-skating, watching films and TV, babies, vegetarian cooking. **Most Cherished Possession:** 'I wouldn't part with my 364 Dodge Dart convertible when I moved to Los Angeles.' **Favourite Memory:** 'My appearance in an off-off Broadway play – an all-nude version of *Dracula*. I think we got to wear G-strings.'

PERLMAN, Ron

Actor, b. 13 April 1950, Manhattan, New York, the son of a jazz drummer who performed in Artie Shaw's band. Began performing while at high school, first as a comedian, then as an actor. Joined the Classic Stage Company in New York. Theatre incl: *La Tragedie De Carmen; Teibele and Her Demon; American Heroes* (all on Broadway); *The Architect and the Emperor of Assyria; Woyzeck; Tartusse; Measure For Measure; The Resistible Rise of Arturo Ui.* Films: *Quest For Fire; Ice Pirates; The Name of the Rose; A Stoning.* TV: *Ryan's Hope; The Doctors; Bedrooms; The Fall Guy; Family Honor; Paper Chase; Macgruder and Loud; R.E.L.A.X.;* Vincent in *Beauty and the Beast.* m. fashion designer Opal Stone; 1 d. Blake. Hobbies: keep-fit, all sports, watching LA Dodgers baseball team, travelling, especially in Europe.

PERRIE, Lynne

Actress/singer, b. 7 April 1931, Rotherham, South Yorkshire, sister of comic Duggie Brown. Once a dance-band singer, but worked in a stocking factory until her first cabaret engagement in 1954. Performed as singer-comedienne in clubs in Britain, France, Germany, America and South Africa. Did 12 concerts with The Beatles and four shows with Sacha Distel. Films: *Kes; Yanks.* TV: *Slatterly's Mounted Foot; Leeds United; Follyfoot; Mrs Petty; Queenie's Castle; The Intruders; It Was a Good Story, Don't Knock It;* Ivy Brennan in *Coronation Street* since 1971. m. Derrick Barksby; 1 s. Stephen. Address: c/o Granada TV. Hobbies: horse and greyhound racing.

PERTWEE, Bill

Actor/comedian, b. 21 July 1926, Amersham. First ambition was to be a cricketer, but entered show business in concert party and variety tours, stooging for comics Jon Pertwee, Beryl Reid, Charlie Chester, Ted Ray and Jimmy James. Numerous stage farces incl: *There Goes the Bride; See How They Run; Run For Your Wife.* Radio: *Beyond Our Ken; Round the Horn.* TV incl: *Dad's Army* (played Air Raid Warden Hodges); *Chance In a Million; 3-2-1; Pebble Mill; Spy Trap; Blankety Blank; You Rang, M'Lord?* Best-selling books: *Promenades and Pierrots; By Royal Command; Dad's Army – The Making of a Television Legend.* m. Marion; 1 s. Jonathan. Address: c/o Richard Stone, London. Birthsign: Cancer. Hobbies: cricket, swimming, DIY. Pets: dog – Biffa.

PERTWEE, Jon

Actor/comedian, b. 7 July 1919, London. Trained at RADA. War service in Royal Navy, then radio. Theatre incl: *There's a Girl In My Soup; Irene.* Films incl: *A Funny Thing Happened On the Way To the Forum; The Ugly Duckling; One of Our Dinosaurs Is Missing.* TV incl: *Three of a Kind; Doctor Who; Whodunnit; Worzel Gummidge; Worzel Gummidge Down Under.* Noted for his range of accents and voices. m. (1st) actress Jean Marsh (dis.), (2nd) Ingeborg Rhosea; 1 d. Dariel, 1 s. Sean (both from 2nd m.). Address: c/o Spotlight, London. Birthsign: Cancer. Hobby: skin-diving. **Most Cherished Possession:** 'A small soft likeness to a mole, given to me by my second wife 30 years ago – it's been around the world with me.' **Favourite Memory:** 'Being at the helm of my 20ft jet propelled speedboat going flat out off the island of Ibiza.'

PETTIFER, Julian

Presenter/reporter, b. 21 July 1935, Malmesbury, Wilts. Started with Southern TV 1958; joined *24 Hours* 1965 and moved to *Panorama* 1969. As BBC reporter been to Vietnam, Aden, Hong Kong, the Suez Canal zone and Northern Ireland. BAFTA Reporter of the Year 1968–69. Documentary TV programmes incl: *90 South; War Without End; Millionaire; Vietnam – The Other World; The Regiment; The World About Us; Diamonds In the Sky; Nature Watch; The Living Isles; World Safari; Only One Earth; Automania; Busman's Holiday; Africawatch; Missionaries.* Address: c/o Curtis Brown. Birthsign: Cancer. Hobby: travel.

PHELPS, Peter

Actor, b. 20 September 1960, Sydney, Australia. Attended MacQuarif University, Sydney. Theatre incl: *Nicholas Nickleby* (Sydney Theatre Company); *The Club.* Films incl: *Undercover; Playing Beattie Bow; The Light Horsemen; Starlight Hotel; Uncle Sam's at the Door.* TV incl: *Sons and Daughters; Cowra Breakout; A Country Practice; The Challenge; Dirtwater; Dynasty.* Address: c/o Barbara Leane, 261 Miller Street, North Sydney, NSW, Austria. Birthsign: Virgo. Hobbies: surfing, fishing, French/Italian eating, horseriding. Pets: African hunting dog, two snakes, one mad cat. **Most Cherished Possession:** 'My health. Why? It's an actor's best tool.' **Favourite Memory:** 'Winning under 15s rugby grand final by scoring the winning try. I was famous for a day.'

PHILBIN, Maggie

Broadcaster, b. 23 June 1955, Manchester. After taking a degree in English and Drama, has appeared on TV incl: *Swap Shop; Ticket To Ride; The Show Me Show; Tomorrow's World; The Saturday Picture Show; The Quest; Hospital Watch; Radio 1 Weekend Show; Bodymatters Roadshow.* m. TV presenter Keith Chegwin; 1 d. Rose Elizabeth. Address: c/o Dave Winslett Entertainments. Birthsign: Cancer. Hobbies: riding, writing, reading. Pets: two dogs, four cats, three horses. **Most Cherished Possession:** 'My cat, Pooh – she's the most bad-tempered creature I know!' **Favourite Memory:** 'Passing my driving test – I never thought I'd make it!'

PHILLIPS, Siân

Actress, b. 14 May, Carmarthenshire. Joined BBC Repertory Company, then trained at RADA. Theatre incl: *Pal Joey; Dear Liar; Peg; Love Affair; Gigi; Vanilla.* Films incl: *Goodbye Mr Chips; Murphy's War; Clash of the Titans; Dune; Valmont.* TV incl: *How Green Was My Valley; I, Claudius; Tinker, Tailor, Soldier, Spy; Crime and Punishment; Winston Churchill – The Wilderness Years; Smiley's People; Barriers; Language and Landscape; Vanity Fair; Heartbreak House; Lady Windermere's Fan; Shadow of the Noose; Snow Spider.* Book: *Sian Phillips Needlepoint.* Hon Doc Litt University of Wales. m. (1st) actor Peter O'Toole (dis.), (2nd) Robin Sachs; 2 d. Kate, Pat (both from 1st m.). Address: c/o Saraband. Hobbies: gardening, needlepoint. Pets: three Burmese cats. **Most Cherished Possession:** 'Our garden.'

PICKERING, Ron, OBE

Commentator/compere, b. 4 May 1930, London. Attended Carnegie College of Physical Education and Leicester University. TV journalist for 20 years. Five Olympic Games for BBC; *The Superstars; We Are the Champions.* Documentaries for TV incl: *South African Sport and Apartheid; The Birmingham Bid.* m. former Olympic and European long jump champion Jean Desforges; 1 d. Kim, 1 s. Shaun. Address: c/o Bagenal Harvey. Birthsign: Taurus. Hobbies; golf, photography. **Most Cherished Possession:** 'Good health, without which I couldn't work a 70 hour week.' **Favourite Memory:** 'Lynn Davies winning his Olympic gold medal in Tokyo 1964 because I was there.'

PICKLES, Christina

Actress, b. 17 February, Yorkshire, niece of actor Wilfred Pickles. Trained at RADA and pursued her career in the US, appearing on Broadway and at the Joe Papps Shakespeare Festival. Nurse Helen Rosenthal in TV's *St Elsewhere*. Other TV incl: *Lou Grant; The Andros Targets; The White Shadow; The Guiding Light; Another World*. Theatre incl: *Undiscovered Country; Death of a Buick*. Film: *Masters of the Universe*. 1 s. 1 d. Address: c/o Paul Kohner Agency, 9169 Sunset Blvd., LA, CA 90069. Birthsign: Aquarius. Hobbies: running, tennis, gardening, reading, cooking pasta.

PIGOTT-SMITH, Tim

Actor, b. 13 May 1946, Rugby. Trained at Bristol Old Vic Theatre School. Member of the RSC London 1972–75. Theatre incl: *Bengal Lancer; Antony and Cleopatra; Benefactors; Entertaining Strangers*. Films incl: *Clash of the Titans; Escape To Victory; Richard's Things*. TV incl: *Eustace and Hilda; Lost Boys; Meausure For Measure; Henry IV (I); No, Mama, No; Hannah; Winston Churchill – The Wilderness Years; Fame Is the Spur; I Remember Nelson; The Jewel In the Crown* (1984 BAFTA, Broadcasting Press Guild and *TVTimes* best actor awards); *Struggle; Man In a Fog; Dead Man's Folly; Life Story; The Chief*. Artistic director, Compass Theatre. m. Pamela Miles; 1 s. Tom. Address: c/o Michael Whitehall. Hobbies: reading, music, yoga.

PINDER, Steven

Actor, b. 30 March 1960, Whalley, Lancashire. Trained at MYT and Drama Centre, London. Theatre incl: *Macbeth*, Shaw Theatre; *Valere, Miser*, Birmingham rep. TV incl: *Foxy Lady; C.A.T.S. Eyes; Now and Then;* Roy Lambert in *Crossroads; Crown Court; Scotch and Wry*. Address: c/o Peter Browne. Birthsign: Aries. Hobbies: all sports, football and cricket in particular. **Most Cherished Possession:** 'My grandfather clock, it's been in the family years.' **Favourite Memory:** 'I played in a celebrity football match before the FA Cup Final '87 between Spurs and Coventry at Wembley.'

PINNER, Steven

Actor, b. 28 December 1961, Maidstone, Kent. Trained at the Guildhall School of Music and Drama then The Theatre, Chipping Norton. Toured the Middle and Far East With Derek Nimmo and his Intercontinental Hotels Entertainment Company. Joined the Royal Shakespeare Company 1985 season at Stratford-upon-Avon; Liverpool Playhouse. Film: *Link* with Terence Stamp. TV incl: *The Life and Times of John Wycliffe; The Eye of the Yemanger;* Jonathan Gordon-Davies in *Brookside*. Address: c/o Shane Collins Assoc, 24 Wardour Street, London W1. **Most Cherished Possession:** 'My contact lenses – without them I'd be lost!' **Favourite Memory:** 'Taking time out from my lunch while filming *Brookside* in Vancouver to play a black baby grand piano and look out over the water, across Stanley Park to the north shoreline and the mountains.'

PLANER, Nigel

Actor/writer/comedian, b. 22 February 1953, London. Trained at LAMDA, and has appeared on stage at Traverse Theatre, Leeds Playhouse, Young Vic, Lyric Theatre, Hammersmith. Co-founder of London's Comic Strip and original Comedy Store comedian. As actor films incl: *Yellowbeard; Brazil; Supergrass*. TV incl: *Shine On Harvey Moon; The Young Ones; The Comic Strip Presents . . .; Roll Over Beethoven; King and Castle*. As writer creator of 'Neil' character in *The Young Ones* on TV, and numerous live appearances as Neil incl Hammersmith Odeon in London. Hit single: *Hole In My Shoe*. Co-author: *Neil's Book of the Dead*. Co-author: *The Comic Strip* film. Address: c/o Peters Fraser & Dunlop. Birthsign: Pisces. Hobbies: scuba and ornithology.

PLATER, Alan

Writer, b. 15 April 1935, Jarrow-on-Tyne. Trained as an architect; full-time writer since 1961. Films: *The Virgin and the Gypsy; Juggernaut; It Shouldn't Happen to a Vet; Priest of Love*. Original TV series incl: *Oh No It's Selwyn Froggitt; Middlemen; Get Lost; The Beiderbecke Affair; The Beiderbecke Tapes; The Beiderbecke Connection*. TV dramatisations incl: *Flambards; Barchester Chronicles; Fortunes of War; A Day In Summer; A Very British Coup*. TV contributions incl: *Z-Cars; Softly, Softly; Miss Marple; Tales of Sherwood Forest; Campion*. Many stage plays. m. (2nd) Shirley Rubinstein; 2 s. Stephen, David, 1 d. Janet (all from 1st m.); 3 stepsons, Peter, John, Paul. Address: c/o Margaret Ramsay. Hobbies: books, theatre, listening to jazz, being with friends, following fortunes/misfortunes of Hull City FC. Pet: Red setter The Duke (after Ellington).

PLUMB, Gwendoline, MBE

Actress/announcer, b. Sydney, Australia. Professional stage debut 1948 in *See How They Run*. Numerous theatre appearances incl: *Entertaining Mr Sloane; Blithe Spirit; Steaming*. Own radio programme for 26 years covering major events and interviewing celebrities. Starred in *Blue Hills*, Australia's longest running radio serial, and in TV's *The Young Doctors*. Also own show and many guest appearances. Address: c/o ICS, 147A King Street, Sydney, Australia. Birthsign: Leo. Hobbies: swimming, travel, reading, entertaining. **Most Cherished Possession:** 'My beach house filled with memorabilia of stage and travel.'

POLLARD, Su

Entertainer, b. 7 November 1949, Nottingham. Numerous cabaret appearances and concerts. In an all-girl singing group Midnight News. Theatre incl: *The Desert Song; Rose Marie; Godspell; Big Sin City; Oh Mr Porter; Grease*. Also many pantomimes incl: *Aladdin* at Manchester. TV debut *Opportunity Knocks*. TV since incl: *Summer Royal; The Comedians; Golden Gala; Get Set For Summer; Clock On; The Saturday Show; Two Up Two Down*; as Peggy in *Hi-de-Hi!* (also on stage); *You Rang, M'Lord?*. m. teacher Peter Keogh. Address: c/o Noel Gay. Birthsign: Scorpio. Hobbies: reading Mills & Boon books, talking, dancing. Pets: cat called Dulcie. **Most Cherished Possession:** 'My husband – 'cos I luv him.' **Favourite Memory:** 'Getting part of Peggy in *Hi-de-Hi!*'

PORTEOUS, Shane

Actor, b. 17 August 1942, Coleraine, Victoria, Australia. Studied Art at Queensland University and worked as book designer, illustrator and animator. Joined Old Tote Theatre, Sydney in 1968 in *Rosencrantz & Guildenstern Are Dead*. Other theatre incl: *Hamlet; Major Barbara; Death of a Salesman; King Oedipus; Love's Labours Lost*. Films incl: *Scobie Malone, Puzzle; Round the Bend; Burning Man*. TV incl: *Taming of the Shrew; Chopper Squad; Sullivans; A Country Practice*. m. Jennifer; 2 d. Fiona, Polly, 1 s. Benjamin. Address: c/o June Cann Management, Sydney, Australia. Birthsign: Leo. Hobbies: tennis, cricket, painting, bush-walking, reading. Pets: cat. **Favourite Memory:** 'Playing in same cricket XI as Frank Tyson, and getting a wicket.'

POTTER, Dennis

Playwright, b. 17 May 1935. Joined the BBC as a current affairs journalist in 1959, then wrote for national newspapers, before success as a playwright. TV plays and series: *Vote Vote Vote For Nigel Barton* (SFTA award); *Stand Up Nigel Barton; Where the Buffalo Roam; A Beast With Two Backs; Son of Man; Traitor; Paper Roses; Casanova; Follow the Yellow Brick Road; Only Make Believe; Joe's Ark; Schmoedipus; Late Call; Brimstone and Treacle; Double Dare Where Adam Stood; Pennies From Heaven* (BAFTA award); *Blue Remembered Hills* (BAFTA award); *Blade On the Feather; Rain On the Roof; Cream In My Coffee* (Prix Italia); *Tender Is the Night; The Singing Detective; Visitors; Blackeyes; Secret Friend*. Film screenplays: *Pennies From Heaven; Brimstone and Treacle; Gorky Park; Dreamchild; Track 29*. Plus books and novels.

POWELL, Jennifer

Presenter, b. 8 April 1968, Ilford, Essex. Trained at the Italia Conti Academy. Presenter of three series of rock show *No Limits;* regular *Top of the Pops* presenter; *Children's BBC* presenter of *Two By Two* and *UP24;* radio presenter for Metro FM. Address: c/o Arlington Enterprises. Birthsign: Aries; Hobbies: cooking, dancing. Pets: Border Collie called Shep and a Cairn Terrier called Hamish. **Most Cherished Possession:** 'My ring, it's the only piece of jewellery that I haven't managed to lose, yet.' **Favourite Memory:** 'My first love . . . but that's all I'm saying.'

POWELL, Robert

Actor, b. 1 June 1944, Salford, Lancashire. Theatre incl: *Travesties; Terra Nova; Private Dick.* Films incl: *Mahler; Tommy; The Thirty-Nine Steps; Harlequin; Jane Austen In Manhattan; Imperative; The Jigsaw Man.* Since appearing in *Doomwatch* in 1970, TV incl: *Shelley; Jude the Obscure; Mr Rolls and Mr Royce; Looking For Clancy; Jesus of Nazareth; Mrs Warren's Profession; You Never Can Tell; Frankenstein; Pygmalion; Hannay.* m. Barbara; 1 s. Barnaby, 1 d. Katherine. Address: c/o ICM. Birthsign: Gemini. Hobbies: cricket, tennis, golf. **Most Cherished Possession:** 'A very old cricket bat.' **Favourite Memory:** 'Hitting ball out of ground with most cherished possession.'

POWLEY, Mark

Actor, b. 4 October 1963, Chelmsford, Essex, brought up in Swindon, Wiltshire. Graduated from the London Academy of Music and Dramatic Art (LAMDA) in 1985, then played Angelo in *Piaf* on stage and appeared in pantomime in Colchester. TV: *Victoria Wood; Rockliffe's Babies; Bergerac;* PC Melvin in *The Bill.* Film: *Time Warp Terror.* m. ex-dancer Janis Jaffa. Address: c/o CCA. Birthsign: Libra. Hobbies: scuba diving, riding, snooker, golf, listening to jazz.

PRAED, Michael

Actor, b. 1 April 1960, Gloucestershire. Trained at the Guildhall School of Music and Drama, London. Theatre incl a season at Southampton and at Civic Theatre, Chesterfield. Played leading role in West End production *The Pirates of Penzance* for a year, and in *Abbacadabara* at Lyric Theatre, Hammersmith. Also in *The Three Musketeers* on Broadway. TV incl: *The Gentle Touch; The Professionals; Rothko; Video Entertainers; Dynasty.* Played Robin in *Robin of Sherwood.* Address: c/o Duncan Heath Assocs. Birthsign: Aries.

PRESLEY, Priscilla

Actress, b. 24 May, Brooklyn, New York. Attended school in Germany, where she lived until moving to US to marry Elvis Presley. Studied acting with Milton Katselas and co-hosted TV series *Those Amazing Animals.* Film: *Naked Gun.* Jenna Wade in TV's *Dallas.* Other TV incl: *Comeback.* Book: *Elvis and Me.* m. Elvis Presley (dis. 1973); 1 d. Lisa Marie, 1 s. Navarone (by Marco Garibaldi). Address: c/o Norman Brokow, William Morris Agency, 151 El Camino Drive, Beverly Hills, California 90212. Hobbies: karate (brown belt), modern jazz, exercising. **Favourite Memory:** 'The birth of my children.'

PRINCIPAL, Victoria

Actress/authoress, b. 3 January 1950, Fukuoka, Japan. Brought up in Ruislip, Middlesex, where her father was stationed with US Air Force. Studied ballet at Royal Academy before going to Hollywood, where she studied law. A former Miss Miami, films incl: *Earthquake; Vigilante Force.* TV incl: *Fantasy Island,* which led to her role as Pam Ewing in *Dallas; Mistress.* Books: *The Body Principal; The Beauty Principal; The Diet Principal.* m. Christopher Skinner (dis.), (2nd) Dr Harry Glassman. Address: c/o ICM, Los Angeles. Birthsign: Capricorn. Hobbies: business, real estate, swimming, exercise. Pets: two Dobermans. **Most Cherished Possession:** 'My husband.' **Favourite Memory:** 'Studying ballet at The Royal Academy. I was the only American accepted at the time, it was quite an honour.'

PRINGLE, Bryan

Actor, b. 19 January 1935, Glascote, Staffordshire. Trained at RADA and was with the Old Vic 1955–57, rep at Birmingham, Nottingham. West End theatre incl: *Long and the Short and the Tall; Fings Ain't What They Used To Be; One More River; Big Soft Nellie; Lower Depths; The Birthday Party; End Game; Billy; The Passion; Crime Strike; Corocle.* Films incl: *Saturday Night, Sunday Morning; HMS Defiant; The Boy Friend; Bullshot; Brazil.* TV incl: *Portsmouth Defence; Dustbinmen; On Giant's Shoulders; Love Story; Still Waters; Diary of a Nobody; Paradise Postponed; Auf Wiedersehen Pet;* Mr Crusty in *The Management.* m. actress Anne Jameson; 1 d. Kate, 1 s. Craster. Address: c/o Markham & Froggatt, London. Birthsign: Capricorn.

PROSKY, Robert

Actor, b. 13 December, Philadelphia. Trained at the American Theater Wing School and Arena Stage, Washington DC. Films incl: *Thief; Christine; The Keep; The Lords of Discipline; The Natural; Outrageous Fortune; Things Change.* TV films incl: *Carney Case; The Ballad of Mary Phagan; Into Thin Air.* TV mini series: *World War II; Adams Chronicles.* Sgt Stan Jablonski in TV's *Hill Street Blues.* m. Ida; 3 s. Address: c/o Smith Freedman & Assoc, 123 N San Vicente Blvd, Beverly Hills, California 90211. Birthsign: Sagittarius. Hobby: restoring old houses and furniture. Pets: one cat. **Most Cherished Possession:** 'Our vacation home in the historic Cape May, New Jersey.' **Favourite Memory:** 'Performing at the Moscow Art Theatre in Russia.'

PYNE, Frederick

Actor, b. 30 December 1936, London. Started as a farmer in Cheshire and Cambridgeshire. He signed on with the RAF and became interested in the theatre. Trained at RADA, then rep and four years with the National Theatre at the Old Vic 1966–70. TV incl: *Crossroads; Dixon of Dock Green; Justice; Emmerdale Farm.* Address: c/o Peter Graham Assocs at Crouch Salmon Assocs. Birthsign: Capricorn. Hobbies: music, gardening, foreign travel. Pets: three cats, one dog. **Most Cherished Possession:** 'Some pieces of Nankins china from the Gelder Mal Sen because of the history behind it and that it lay on the seabed from 1752.' **Favourite Memory:** 'A visit, two years ago, to New Zealand to see members of my family.'

QUAYLE, Anna

Actress, b. 6 October 1937, Birmingham. Trained at RADA after touring in Douglas Quayle's Company (her actor/producer father) for whom she made stage debut aged four. Theatre incl: *Full Circle* (which she wrote); *Out of Bounds; Pal Joey; Kings and Clowns;* Old Vic season 1964; *The Boy Friend.* Films incl: *Chitty Chitty Bang Bang; SOS Titanic; The Seven Per Cent Solution; Towers of Babel.* m. Don Baker; 1 d. Katy Nova. Address: c/o CDA. Birthsign: Libra. Hobbies: reading and travel. Pets: four cats, one Pekinese. **Most Cherished Possession:** 'My father's yellow pullover because it reminds me of him.' **Favourite Memory:** 'The birth of my daughter Katy.'

QUAYLE, John

Actor, b. 21 December 1938, Lincoln. Trained at RADA and has worked extensively in rep. London Theatre incl: *Habeas Corpus; When We Are Married; Watch On the Rhine; Noises Off; Life Begins At Forty*. Films incl: *Charles and Diana; Privates On Parade*. TV incl: many comedy series; *Upstairs, Downstairs; Jumbo Spencer; The King's Dragon; Nanny; Pig In the Middle; Jane; This Office Life; Majorie and Men;* two series of *Farrington of the FO;* three series of *Terry and June; Tricky Business; The Nineteenth Hole*. m. Petronell. Address: c/o Barry Burnett. Hobbies: horses, donkeys, post and railing paddocks. **Most Cherished Possession:** 'My contact lenses, they enable me to see who's in the audience!' **Favourite Memory:** 'My father putting his hat on with great panache.'

QUICK, Diana

Actress/writer, b. 23 November 1946, Kent. Member of the National Youth Theatre aged 16. Has appeared at London's Royal Court Theatre; Bristol Old Vic; Open Space; Royal Exchange; Soho Poly; Lyric; Hammersmith; Greenwich; West End. Also National Theatre and Royal Shakespeare Company; London Old Vic. Films incl: *Nicholas and Alexandra; The Duellists; The Big Sleep; The Odd Job; Ordeal By Innocence; 1919; May Mon Amour; Vroom*. TV incl: *Christ Recrucified; Complete and Utter History of Britain; At Last It's Friday; Brideshead Revisited; The Woman White; Chekhov in Yalta; Cariana and the Courtesans; Flesh and Blood; The Justice Game*. Address: c/o Duncan Heath Assocs. Birthsign: Scorpio. Hobbies: reading, writing, gardening, cooking, skiing, restoring furniture.

QUILLEY, Denis

Actor, b. 26 December 1927, London. Trained with the Birmingham rep, where he made his debut in 1945. Numerous theatre appearances incl: *Death Trap; Sweeney Todd; Antony and Cleopatra; La Cage aux Folles*. Films incl: *Life At the Top; Anne of the Thousand Days; Evil Under the Sun; King David; Privates On Parade*. TV incl: *Murder In the Cathedral; the Crucible; Honky-Tonk Heroes; Gladstone In No. 10; The Bretts; After the War; The Interrogation of John;* hosted the Olivier Awards. m. Stella Chapman; 2 d. Sarah, Joanna, 1 s. David. Address: c/o Bernard Hunter Assocs, London. Hobby: playing music. Pets: two dogs and two cats. **Favourite Memory:** 'A play called *The Lady's Not For Burning*. I met my wife, Richard Burton and John Gielgud all in the same play.'

QUINTEN, Christopher

Actor, b. 12 July 1959, Middlesbrough. Trained at Billingham Theatre School. Film: *International Velvet*. Brian Tilsley in *Coronation Street*, 1978–89. Other TV incl: *Warship; Target; The Pink Medicine Show; The Little Big Show; Quatermass*. m. TV chat show host Leeza Gibbons (sep); 1 d. Jordan. Address: c/o Peter Charlesworth. Birthsign: Cancer. Hobbies: golf, tennis, football. **Most Cherished Possession:** 'My Action Man – it was my first toy.'

QUIRKE, Pauline

Actress, b. 8 July 1959, London. Drama training at Anna Scher theatre and while still at school appeared on TV in *Dixon of Dock Green, Kids About Town, Days of Hope* and *You Must Be Joking*. Turning point in career as the autistic child in *Jenny Can't Work Any Faster*. Other TV incl: *Pauline's Quirkes; Pauline's People; Baby Talk; A Name For the Day; The Story of the Treasure Seekers; Shine On Harvey Moon; Angels; Birds of a Feather*. Address: c/o Anna Scher Theatre Management. Birthsign: Cancer. Hobbies: reading autobiographies, watching plays, decorating, eating out.

RACHINS, Alan

Actor/writer/director, b. 3 October 1942, Boston, Mass. Trained with William Ball, Harvey Lembeck, Kim Stanley, American Film Institute. Received a degree in film production from Empire State College. Theatre incl: *After the Rain; Hadrian the Seventh; Oh, Calcutta.* Film: *Always.* TV incl: *Paris;* Douglas Brackman in *L.A. Law; Mistress.* Written for TV: *Hart To Hart; The Fall Guy; Hill Street Blues.* m. actress Joanna Frank (who portrays his screen wife Sheila Brackman in *L.A. Law*); 1 s. Robby. Address: c/o Jimmy Koda, Artists Agency, 10000 Santa Monica Blvd, LA, Calif. 90067. Birthsign: Libra. Hobbies: avid reader, tennis, family life. Pets: two cats. **Most Cherished Possession:** 'My family photo albums, I'm a real family man.' **Favourite Memory:** 'My life.'

RANTZEN, Esther

TV journalist, b. 22 June 1940. Berkhamstead, Hertfordshire. Went to Oxford University and started career in radio studio management, TV research and production. First appeared on TV as a reporter on *Braden's Week* and went on to produce and present *That's Life!* (since 1973) and *That's Family Life!* Also producer/reporter for *The Big Time.* Launched *Childline* Freefone service offering help to abused children. m. independent TV producer/writer Desmond Wilcox; 2 d. Emily, Rebecca, 1 s. Joshua. Address: c/o Noel Gay. Birthsign: Cancer.

RASHAD (was Ayers-Allen), Phylicia

Actress, b. 19 June, Houston. Trained at the Negro Ensemble Company. Stage incl: *The Wiz; Dream Girls; Ain't Supposed to Die a Natural Death; Duplex.* TV incl: *One Life To Live; The Cosby Show.* Awards: People's Choice Award for Favourite Female Performer 1985; Image Award from NAACP; Delco Award for her performance in the title role of *Zora.* m. sportscaster Ahmad Rashad; 1 d. Condola Phylea, plus 1 s. William from previous m. Address: c/o Jimmy Cota, Artists Agency, 10000 Santa Monica Blvd., LA, California 90067. Birthsign: Gemini. **Favourite Memory:** 'When my husband proposed to me on nationwide TV on Thanksgiving Day 1985.'

RASHLEIGH, Andy

Actor/writer, b. 23 January 1949, East London. Trained at Bretton Hall College of Education; taught drama. Many stage roles. Films: *The Ploughman's Lunch; Acceptable Levels; Ends and Means.* TV incl: *Life For Christine; Brideshead Revisited; Juliet Bravo; Mitch; Dear Ladies; Strangers; Coronation Street; Crown Court; The Adventures of Sherlock Holmes; The Practice; Albion Market; The Bill;* Chef in *Crossroads;* Ted Sharp in *Emmerdale Farm; Making Out; Hale & Pace; EastEnders;* Eliot Creasy in new BSB soap *Jupiter Moon.* Numerous radio plays. Writing incl: stage productions *Robeson; Never Trust a City Slicker; Hell Fire Club;* radio serial *The Archers;* TV soap *Crossroads.* Lives with Maggie Wilkinson. Address: c/o Michelle Braidman. Hobbies: gardening, cricket, reading. Pet: Russian blue cat Gnasher.

RATCLIFF, Sandy

Actress, b. 2 October 1950, London. Trained as a designer/pattern cutter and photographic fashion model before acting. Theatre incl: *Lucky Strike; Chorus Girls; The Workshop.* Films incl: *Family Life; Yesterday's Hero.* TV incl: known as Sue Osman in *EastEnders; Cork and Bottle; Shoestring; Cast Off; Danger U.X.B.; Hazell; Couples; The Sweeney; Minder.* 1 s. William. Address: c/o Markham & Froggatt. Birthsign: Libra. Hobbies: writing, playing guitar, swimming, knitting. **Most Cherished Possession:** '1930's opaque reclining lady lamp – love the period. Bought with my first week's wages from first major film role *Family Life.*' **Favourite Memory:** 'Birth of William. Immediate communion with universal consciousness and love.'

RATZENBERGER, John

Actor/writer, b. 6 April 1947, Bridgeport, Connecticut. Studied at the Sacred Heart University and joined drama club. Films incl: *The Ritz; Valentino; Hanover Street; Yanks; A Bridge Too Far; Superman; Superman II; Ragtime; The Empire Strikes Back; Ghandi; The Bitch*. TV incl: *House II; Time Stalkers;* Cliff Calvin in *Cheers* (nominated for Emmy for best supporting actor); *Small World*. m. Georgia; 1 s. James. Address: c/o Russ Lyster, The Agency, 10351 Santa Monica Blvd, LA, Calif 90025. Hobbies: carpentry, sailing, world history. Pets: two dogs, Pete and Sally. **Most Cherished Possession:** 'My Swiss army knife – you have to be prepared for anything.' **Favourite Memory:** 'Putting a new roof on my home in the middle of the night during a blizzard.'

RAVENS, Jan

Actress/broadcaster, b. 14 May 1958, Bebington, Merseyside. Trained as a drama teacher at Cambridge and was a member of Cambridge footlights (first woman president). Broadcaster for Capital Radio's Sunday Brunch. TV incl: *Just Amazing; Getting Into Shape; Carrott's Lib; The Lenny Henry Show; The Kenny Everett Show; Friday People; Farrington of the F.O.; All In Good Faith; Saturday Live; C.A.T.S. Eyes;* voices for *Spitting Image; No Frills; Alexei Sayle's Stuff*. m. composer/performer Steve Brown; 1 s. Alfie. Address: c/o Barry Burnett. Birthsign: Taurus. Hobbies: music, dance, reading. **Most Cherished Possession:** 'My son (even though he's not strictly a "possession").' **Favourite Memory:** 'Falling in love with my husband.'

RAWLE, Jeff

Actor/writer, b. 20 July 1951, Birmingham. Worked at Sheffield Playhouse until he went to the London Academy of Dramatic Art. Musical and West End theatre incl: *Equus; Once a Catholic; Bent; Butley*. Much radio work. TV incl: star of *Billy Liar; Beryl's Lot; The Cost of Loving; Van Der Valk; Send In the Girls; Wilde Alliance; Leave It To Charlie; Singles; Juliet Bravo; Whose Child; Angels; Bergerac; Doctor Who; Singles Weekend; Country and Irish; Boon II; Call Me Mister; Fortunes of War; Run For the Lifeboat; South of the Border; The Bill; Beyond the Pale; Vote For Them; The Gift*. Address: c/o Louis Hammond. Hobbies: Genealogy. **Most Cherished Possession:** 'A Mexican bus.' **Favourite Memory:** 'Getting the Mexican bus home from Mexico.'

RAY, Robin

Writer/presenter, b. London. Trained at RADA. Extensive experience on stage and in TV and radio. Associate director, Meadowbrook Theater, USA. First classical music programme on British commercial radio, *The Robin Ray Collection* for Capital Radio, London. Also the station's record reviewer for seven years. Other radio: *Revolutions In Sound* and *The Tingle Factor* for BBC Radio 4; *Robin Ray's Waxworks* and *Robin Ray On Record* for BBC Radio 2. Author *Cafe Puccini* (Wyndham's Theatre) and drama critic for *Punch* magazine, 1986–7. Artistic director, Classic FM. m. TV presenter Susan Stranks; 1 s. Rupert. Address: c/o David Wilkinson Associates. Hobbies: cinema, music.

RAYNER, Claire

Journalist/agony aunt/author, b. 22 January 1931, London. Trained as an SRN and midwife. Radio incl: *Woman's Hour; Schools; Today; Contact;* a regular spot on the *Michael Aspel Show*, Capital Radio. TV incl: Family Advice slot on *Pebble Mill;* co-presenter *Kitchen Garden; Claire Rayner's Casebook;* TV-am. Author of 70 books incl: medical subjects, childcare and fiction. Medical Correspondent for *Woman's Own* and Agony Aunt for *Sunday Mirror*. m. Desmond Rayner; 1 d. Amanda, 2 s. Adam, Jason. Address: c/o TV-am. Birthsign: Aquarius. Hobbies: cooking, party giving, reading, talking, swimming. **Favourite Memory:** 'Being pulled out of the rubble in which I'd been buried for 28 hours after an air raid in 1940.'

REDDIN, Jacqueline

Actress/presenter, b. 1956, Dublin, moved to Britain at the age of two. Trained at the Bristol Old Vic Theatre. Theatre: *City Sugar; The Boy Friend; Knots and Bumps; Relatively Speaking; This Happy Breed; Grease; Dick Whittington; Cinderella; Table Manners.* TV: *Play For Today: Brencham People; The Duchess of Duke Street; The Professionals; Return of The Saint; Emmerdale Farm; Minder; Florence Nightingale; Tickle On the Tum; Hold Tight; Hale & Pace.* Lives with singer Maynard Williams; 1 d. Jemma, 1 s. Luke. Address: c/o Hamper-Neafsey Associates.

REDING, Nick

Actor, b. 31 August 1962, London. Began career as a stage hand. Theatre: *Easter/Strindberg; A Christmas Carol.* Also acted in and co-directed four productions for the Elephant Walk Children's Theatre Company. TV: *Last Summer's Child; Stalky & Co; Henry IV Part III; Richard III; Play For Today: The Remainder Man; Love and Marriage: Dearly Beloved; Oscar Wilde; Paradise Postponed; Chance In a Million; The Monocled Mutineer; District Nurse; My Family and Other Animals; EastEnders;* PC Ramsey in *The Bill;* Channel Four film *The Final Frame.* Films: *Real Life; Captive; Heroine.* Address: c/o William Morris. Birthsign: Virgo. Hobbies: travel, sports. **Favourite Memory:** 'Many travel memories.'

REES, Ken

TV correspondent, b. 26 January 1944, Cardiff, Wales. Worked as a newscaster for HTV Wales, then as a reporter with HTV Bristol. He joined ITN in 1978 and became their Northern correspondent 1979–1982; has been a Washington correspondent since 1985, which was also the year he became the Royal Television Society Journalist of the year. m. Lynne; 1 d. Samantha, 1 s. Christian. Address: c/o ITN, Wells Street, London. Birthsign: Aquarius. Hobbies: work, old films, reading on planes.

REES, Roger

Actor, b. 5 May 1944, Aberystwyth, Wales. Trained as a fine artist at Slade School of Fine Art in London, before taking up acting. Royal Shakespeare Company debut 1966 in *The Taming of the Shrew.* Played title role of Nicholas Nickleby in RSC production London and New York (where he won a Tony Award), also on TV. Recent theatre incl: *Hamlet; Love's Labours Lost; Archangels Don't Play Pinball; The Real Thing; Hapgood.* Films incl: *A Christmas Carol.* Directing incl: *Turkey Time; Julius Caesar; John Bull* (as Associate Director Bristol Old Vic). TV incl: *Under Western Eyes; Bouquet of Barbed Wire; The Ebony Tower; Singles; Cheers.* Address: c/o ICM, Los Angeles. **Most Cherished Possession:** 'My dog.' **Favourite Memory:** 'The White Rose Bar in New York – a very pleasant memory.'

REGALBUTO, Joe

Actor, b. 14 August 1949, Brooklyn, New York. Trained at the Academy of Dramatic Arts, in regional theatre and in the New York Shakespeare Festival. Norman Tuttle in TV's *Street Hawk.* Films incl: *Missing; Lassiter; Star Chamber; Six Weeks; The Sicilian; Raw Deal.* TV incl: *The Associates; Barney Miller; Mork and Mindy; Betray of Trust; Knots Landing; Our House; J J Starbuck; Ace Crawford, Private Eye; Divorce Wars; You the Jury.* m. Rosemary; 2 s. Nicholas, Michael, 1 d. Gina. Address: c/o Triad Artists, 10100 Santa Monica Blvd, LA, Calif. 90067. Hobbies: photography, cooking Italian food. Pets: one homeless rabbit. **Most Cherished Possession:** 'My family.' **Favourite Memory:** 'Working on the film *Missing,* and the birth of my three children.'

REGAN, Brian

Actor, b. 2 October 1957, Liverpool. Went to Yewtree Comprehensive School. Trained at the Liverpool Playhouse. Appeared in many productions at the Liverpool Playhouse and on TV in *Murphy's Mob* and as Terry Sullivan in Channel Four's soap opera *Brookside* since 1983. Address: c/o Brookside Productions. Birthsign: Libra. Hobbies: playing and watching football, reading music. Pets: a Rottweiler dog. **Most Cherished Possession:** 'My dog because he's a great friend and companion and doesn't answer back.' **Favourite Memory:** 'When Liverpool won the League and FA Cup double. Because I can't remember much about it!'

REID, Beryl

Actress, b. 17 June 1920, Hereford. First appearance in a concert party in Bridlington 1936. Well known as Monica in radio's *Educating Archie*. Worked in TV, radio, clubs variety and revues before first serious stage play, *The Killing of Sister George* (1965) then *Entertaining Mr Sloane*. Recent Theatre incl: *School For Scandal; Gigi*. Films incl: *The Belles of St Trinian's; Yellowhead; Doctor and the Devils*. TV incl: *The Rivals; Father, Dear Father; Smike; The Apple Cart; When We Are Married; Tinker, Tailor, Soldier, Spy; Minder; Late Starter; Beiderbecke Tapes*. Autobiography – *So Much Love*. m. (1st) Bill Worsley (dis.), (2nd) musician Derek Franklin (dis.). Address: c/o Robert Luff, 294 Earls Court Road, London SW5 9BB. Hobbies: gardening, cooking, driving.

REITEL, Enn

Actor, b. 21 June 1950, Forfar. Trained at Central School of Speech and Drama. Made his stage debut in the West End production of *Me and My Girl* at the Adelphi Theatre 1986/87. Radio and TV voice overs. TV incl: *Misfits; Further Adventures of Lucky Jim; The Optimist; Mog; Spitting Image*. Address: c/o Roger Carey. Birthsign: Gemini. Hobbies: horse racing, cartoonist for *Racing Post*, author of *Turf Luck*, a cartoon book. Pets: two cats, six horses. **Most Cherished Possession:** 'Choice of Critics, an 11 year old racehorse on whom I've learnt to ride race style.' **Favourite Memory:** 'Falling off Choice of Critics.'

RICE, Anneka

TV presenter, b. 4 October 1958, Cowbridge, Wales. From 1979–82 worked in Hong Kong in radio, on TV as newscaster and producer and edited a children's book on Hong Kong. In the UK, TV incl: *CBTV; Treasure Hunt; Sporting Chance; Show Business; Family Trees; Wish You Were Here . . .?; Name and Games; Driving Force; World Circus Championships; Aspel & Company; Give Us a Clue*; presenter of *TVTimes 1987 Top 10 Awards; Good Morning Britain; Challenge Anneka; The Other Side of Christmas*. Address: c/o Thames TV. Hobbies: tennis. **Most Cherished Possession:** 'Old diaries. From the ages of nine to 15 I kept a page-a-day diaries which are almost too nostalgic to read!' **Favourite Memory:** 'Packing up the family car for annual seaside holidays in the Isle of Wight.'

RICHARD, Cliff, OBE

Singer, b. 14 October 1940, Lucknow, India. Came to England aged seven. On leaving school worked as a clerk. First TV *Oh Boy!* series in 1958 with The Shadows. Films incl: *Serious Charge; Expresso Bongo; The Young Ones; Summer Holiday; Wonderful Life; Finders Keepers; Two a Penny; Take Me High*. Has had over 100 hit records. First record *Move It* (1958). No 1 hit: *We Don't Talk Anymore*. Thirteen Gold discs, 32 Silver discs. Theatre incl: lead role in the rock musical *Time* 1986/87. Address: c/o Gormley Management, PO Box 46C, Esher, Surrey. Birthsign: Libra. Hobby: tennis. Pets: a dog. **Most Cherished Possession:** 'A framed photograph reminding me of my first encounter with 3rd World problems in Bangladesh.'

RICHARD, Eric

Actor, b. 27 June 1940, Margate, Kent. Acted with many rep companies incl: Nottingham, Liverpool, Sheffield, Birmingham and Manchester. Two years touring with Paines Plough. In London has performed at the Royal Court Theatre, E15 and The Bush. TV incl: *Shoestring; The Onedin Line; Mitch; Angels; Juliet Bravo;* Mike Leigh's *Home Sweet Home; Made In Britain; Games Without Frontiers; Shogun;* Sgt Bob Cryer in *The Bill.* m. Christine; 1 s. Richard, 1 d. Frances. Address: c/o Louis Hammond Management. Birthsign: Cancer. Hobbies: motorcycling, music, sport. **Most Cherished Possession:** 'Life.'

RICHARD, Wendy

Actress, b. 20 July, Teeside. Trained at the Italia Conti Stage School. Theatre incl: *No Sex Please, We're British; Blithe Spirit.* Films incl: *On the Buses; Bless This House; Doctor In Clover.* TV drama incl: *The Newcomers; Harpers West One; No Hiding Place; Joe Nobody; Making of Jericho; Z-Cars;* Pauline Fowler in *EastEnders.* Comedy incl: *Please Sir!; Fenn Street Gang; Not On Your Nellie; Hugh and I; Dad's Army; Are You Being Served?* (also stage and film). Address: John Mahoney Management, London. Birthsign: Cancer. Hobbies: collecting frogs, clowns, condiment sets, tapestry work, plants. **Most Cherished Possession:** 'I have never had a garden, now I have a small patio, with lots of plants. My pride and joy!' **Favourite Memory:** 'Getting the keys for the first time to my very own home.'

RICHARDS, Tom

Actor/cartoonist, b. Brisbane, Australia. Trained in theatre in Queensland. Films incl: *Dawn; The Spook; Raw Deal.* TV incl: *Matlock Police; The Box; Chopper Squad; The Sullivans; Sons and Daughters.* Address: Lee Leslie, Australia. Birthsign: Aries. Hobbies: outdoors – rowing, waterskiing. **Most Cherished Possession:** 'Wave ski – many enjoyable hours surving the white surf off the Australian coast line.' **Favourite Memory:** 'My first performance as a professional actor in television.'

RIDLEY, Joanne

Actress, b. 23 March 1970, London. Trained at the Arts Educational School and Guildhall School of Music and Drama. Appeared in the film *The World Is Full of Married Men* aged six. Has appeared on TV in *A Question of Guilt* and *Mackenzie.* Played Samantha in LWT's *Me and My Girl.* Address: c/o Garricks, 7 Garrick Street, London WC2E 9AR, tel 071-240 0660. Birthsign: Aries. Hobbies: skiing, tennis, water-skiing, walking. **Most Cherished Possession:** 'My futon Japanese mattress – the best buy ever! couldn't live without it!' **Favourite Memory:** 'Sorry, haven't had it yet – I'll let you know.'

RINGHAN, John

Actor, b. 10 February, Cheltenham, Gloucestershire. Started as ASM. 12 years of rep., West End Theatre. Over 250 appearances on TV incl: *Age of Kings; Just Good Friends.* Has also worked in France, Italy, Germany, Switzerland. m. Hedwig Felizitas; 2 d. Jessica, Hannah, 2 s. Max, Ben. Address: c/o Joseph & Wagg, 78 New Bond Street, London W1Y 9DA. Birthsign: Aquarius. Hobbies: playing the piano, allotmenting, writing, school parent/teacher association. Pets: two cats. **Most Cherished Possession:** 'My Grotrian-Steinweg piano whose companionship is sometimes as good as a fellow human's.' **Favourite Memory:** 'Touring India with Bristol Old Vic. Magic from beginning to end.'

RIPPON, Angela

Television presenter, b. 12 October, Plymouth. Began her career at BBC Plymouth and has since had numerous appearances on TV incl: *Nine O'Clock News; News Extra* for BBC; TV-am; Arts and Entertainments Editor for Channel 7, Boston; *Masterteam 1985; Day Out With Angela Rippon; Morecambe and Wise Christmas Show; Angela Rippon Meets . . .; The Antiques Roadshow; People In Power; In the Country; Top Gear; The Rippon Reports; Come Dancing; What's My Line?;* Eurovision Song Contest; BBC General Election coverage; Royal Wedding 1981 BBC coverage; Nobel Prize Ceremony for USA and various other award shows. m. Christopher Dare. Address: c/o IMG. Birthsign: Libra. Hobbies: riding, golf.

ROACH, Pat

Actor, b. 13 May, Birmingham. Films incl: *Adventures of the Spaceman and King Arthur; Clash of the Titans; Red Sonia; Clockwork Orange; Barry Lyndon; Conan the Destroyer; Rising Damp; Raiders of the Lost Ark; Indiana Jones and the Temple of Doom; Never Say Never Again; Willow; Indiana Jones and the Last Crusade; Return of the Musketeers.* TV incl: *Auf Wiedersehen, Pet; The Last Place On Earth; Minder; Bullseye; Three Wishes For Jamie; Hazell; Gangsters; Juliet Bravo; Tiswas; Lenny and Jerry Show; We Love TV; Saturday Show; Jim Davidson Show; Harry's Kingdom.* Address: Peter Charlesworth. Birthsign: Taurus. Hobbies: running a health club in Birmingham. **Favourite Memory:** 'Whenever I return to Britain after a long stay away.'

ROACHE, William

Actor, 25 April 1932, Ilkeston, Derbyshire. After five years in the army, in which he reached the rank of captain in the Royal Welsh Fusiliers, went into rep at Nottingham and Oldham. Films incl: *Behind the Mask; His and Hers; Queen's Guards.* Has played Ken Barlow in *Coronation Street* since it began in 1960. Runs a production company with his wife, presenting plays and chat shows. m. Sara; 1 d. Verity Elizabeth, 1 s. William James. Address: c/o Granada TV, Manchester. Birthsign: Taurus. Hobby: golf. Pets: six dogs, five cats. **Most Cherished Possession:** 'A good family and good health.' **Favourite Memory:** 'Playing golf with Gary Player in the pro-celebrity golf.'

ROBB, David

Actor, b. 23 August 1947, London, brought up in Edinburgh. Trained at Central School of Speech and Drama, London. West End theatre incl: *Abelard and Heloise; Cowardy Custard; Betzi.* Films: *Conduct Unbecoming; The Four Feathers; The Deceivers.* TV incl: *The Glittering Prizes; I, Claudius; The Legend of King Arthur; The Flame Trees of Thika; Fanny By Gaslight; Ivanhoe; The Last Days of Pompeii; Off Peak; Wallenberg; First Among Equals; Dreams Lost, Dreams Found; Wally of Tyranny; The Man Who Lived at The Ritz; Taggart; Parnell.* m. actress Briony McRoberts. Address: c/o William Morris. Hobbies: watching rugby, running marathons, reading. **Most Cherished Possession:** 'A Scottish Jacobite drinking glass.' **Favourite Memory:** 'My wedding day, for obvious reasons.'

ROBBIE, Sue

Presenter, b. 5 July 1949, London. Before working in television taught English in a comprehensive school for four years; worked with the Richmond Fellowship rehabilitating ex-psychiatric patients and drug addicts, and was also an air stewardess with British Airways for four years. TV presenter for programmes incl: *First Post; Hold Tight; Sneak Preview; Cartoon Crackers; Connections; Ark Royal – The Rock Show; Video Active; The Dodo Club;* BBC *Breakfast Time; Showreel; Streetwise; This Morning: Emergency; Consumer File.* Address: c/o Arlington Enterprises. Hobbies: riding, walking, swimming, yoga, cinema, theatre. **Most Cherished Possession:** 'My mother's bible, it was given to me when I was a little girl.' **Favourite Memory:** 'Watching the sunset, sitting on a verandah in the middle of the Kenyan Bush.'

ROBERTS, Ivor

Actor, b. 19 July 1925, Nottingham. After war service in the Royal Navy, returned to the theatre. Theatre incl: *Objections To Sex and Violence; The Unvarnished Truth; The Government Inspector; Pravda; The Attractions.* Films incl: *The Sailor's Return; Hopscotch; Sweet William; Another Country; Portrait of Evil; Personal Services; We Think the World of You.* TV incl: *Secret Army; Bergerac; Sam; Born and Bred; Dombey and Son; Yes Minister; Minder; Sorry; The New Statesman; Coronation Street; The Bretts; Shadow of the Noose; Snow; Better Days; We Are Seven; The Nineteenth Hole.* m. Iris; 1 d. Melanie. Address: c/o Howes & Prior. Hobbies: swimming, crosswords. **Favourite Memory:** 'As a child proudly watching my father perform a trapeze act. I had no idea he could do anything like that.'

ROBINSON, Anne

Journalist, b. 26 September, Crosby, Liverpool. Has written a column for *Daily Mirror* for several years. Radio incl: Anne Robinson show for BBC. TV incl: *Points of View; Blankety Blank.* m. John Penrose; 1 d. Emma. Address: c/o IMG. Birthsign: Libra. Hobbies: reading, spending money, theatre. Pets: Old English Sheep Dog. **Most Cherished Possession:** 'My daughter, Emma.' **Favourite Memory:** 'Two cheques from the BBC on one day.'

ROBINSON, Jancis

Writer/presenter, b. 22 April 1950, Cumbria. Began by editing monthly wine and spirit trade journal then in 1980 joined the *Sunday Times* as a wine correspondent. 1987 joined *The Evening Standard.* Was awarded Master of Wine. Several books incl: *Jancis Robinson's Food and Wine Adventures.* Has written and presented three series of *The Wine Programme* for C4; other TV incl: presenting BBC's Design Awards; *The Dump; Jancis Robinson Meets.* m. Nick Lander; 1 d. Julia, 1 s. William. Address: c/o Curtis Brown. Birthsign: Taurus. Hobbies: family, food, wine. **Most Cherished Possession:** 'Screwpull lever corkscrew and my memory, tho' they're not compatible.'

ROBINSON, Robert

Commentator, b. 17 December 1927, Liverpool. Entered journalism after Oxford University. First broadcast 1955. Radio incl: *Today 1971–74; Stop the Week; Brain of Britain.* TV incl: *Points of View; Ask the Family; Call My Bluff; The Fifties; Robinson's Travels; The Book Programme; Word For Word; The Book Game; Robinson Country; Behind the Headlines.* Books incl: *Conspiracy; Landscape With Dead Dons; Inside Robert Robinson; The Dog Chairman; Everyman Book of Light Verse; Bad Dreams.* m. Josephine; 2 d. Lucy, Suzy, 1 s. Nicholas. Address: c/o BBC TV, London. Birthsign: Sagittarius. Pets: a dog called Fred and Charles the cat. **Most Cherished Possession:** 'My hairstyle.' **Favourite Memory:** 'The first time I was actually paid for writing something.'

RODGERS, Anton

Actor/director, b. 10 January 1933, Wisbech, Cambridgeshire. Trained at Italia Conti Stage School and was a child actor before rep and going to the London Academy of Dramatic Art. Has appeared in and directed many stage plays. Most recent appearances incl: *St Joan; Two Into One; Windy City; Passion Play.* Films incl: *Rotten To the Core; The Man Who Haunted Himself; Scrooge; The Fourth Protocol.* TV incl: *The Organisation; Zodiac; Rumpole of the Bailey; Lillie; Flaxborough Chronicles; Fresh Fields; Comeback; Talking Takes Two; May To December; After the War; French Fields; Goodbye and I Hope We Meet Again.* m. (2nd) Elizabeth Garvie; 1 d. Talia, 1 s. Adam (both from 1st m.), 3 s. Barnaby, Dominic, Luke (from 2nd m.). Address: c/o Michael Whitehall. Hobbies: fly fishing, antique collecting.

ROËVES, Maurice

Actor/director/writer, b. 19 March 1937, Sunderland. Trained at the Royal College of Drama, Glasgow. Theatre incl: *Macbeth; Othello; Tunes of Glory; Carnegie; There Was a Man.* Films incl: *Young Winston; A Day at the Beach; The Eagle Has Landed; Transfusion; When Eight Bells Toll; SOS Titanic; Escape To Victory; Hidden Amendment; The Big Man.* TV incl: *Danger UXB; Inside the Third Reich; Heather Ann; Magnum PI; Remington Steele; The Quest; Lytton's Diary; North and South Book II; Bergerac; Tutti Frutti; Bookie; Unreported Incident; Jake and the Fatman; Hunter.* Writer of two situation comedies: *Father, Son 'n' Holy Terror; Middle For Diddle.* m. Annie (sep.); 1 d. Sarah. Address: c/o Richard Stone. Hobbies: five-mile runs, seven-card stud poker. Pets: two cats, Alex and Samantha.

ROGERS, Jean

Actress, b. 2 February 1942, Perivale, Middlesex. Trained at Guildhall School of Music and Drama. Member of National Theatre and Chichester Festival Company. Has made more than 1500 radio broadcasts and been a presenter and writer for *Listen With Mother.* TV incl: *George and Mildred; Callan; Comedy Playhouse; General Hospital; The Harry Worth Show; Charge;* Nurse Rogers in *Emergency–Ward 10;* Julie Shepherd in *Crossroads;* presenter of BBC schools programme *Watch;* Dolly Skilbeck in *Emmerdale* since 1980. m. 1st Terry Moakes (dis.), 2nd Philip Hartley; 1 d. Justine, 1 s. Jeremy (from 1st m.), four stepchildren. Address: c/o Daly Gagan. Hobbies: cooking, wine-making, gardening, badminton, yoga. Pets: two cats. **Most Cherished Possession:** 'My mother's wedding ring. She died of leukaemia just weeks before I joined *Emmerdale.*'

ROGERS, Katharine

Actress, b. 21 December 1960, London. Joined Anna Scher's Children's Theatre, aged 15, then trained at RADA. Theatre: *This Green and Pleasant Land; Women at War; Linda's; Camberwell Beauty; And All Things Nice; Twelfth Night; The Oedipus Plays; Fugue; The Seagull; Yerma; Our Town; Action Replay; The Piggy Bank.* Royal Shakespeare Company appearances: *A Midsummer Night's Dream; Romeo and Juliet; Camille; The Party; Today; Golden Girls; Red Noses; The Castle; Crimes In Hot Countries.* Joint founder director of Not The RSC, which has organised festivals in Newcastle and London, and performed *The Barker Poems* and Howard Barker's *The Possibilities.* Film: *Quadrophenia.* TV: *Bloody Kids; The Magnificent One; Johnny Jarvis; Only Yesterday;* Firewoman Josie Ingham in *London's Burning.* Address: c/o Hope & Lyne.

ROGERS, Ted

Comedian, b. 20 July 1935, London. Started in bookshops and reached star status the hard way, via touring guest appearances, cabaret and winning a talent contest. After National Service in the RAF became a Butlin's Redcoat. On stage has played both the London Palladium and Savoy Hotel 11 times and has appeared in Las Vegas, New York, Miami, Toronto, Hong Kong and Sydney. Started in TV 1963 in *Billy Cotton's Band Show* and had own show, *And So To Ted.* Other TV incl: *Sunday Night At The Palladium; 3-2-1.* His first radio series was in 1979. m. (1st) Margie (dis.), (2nd) Marion; 3 d. Dena, Fenella (from 1st m.), Canna, 1 s. Danny. Hobby: playing polo at Cowdray Park, Sussex. Address: c/o Yorkshire Television. Birthsign: Cancer.

ROSE, Clifford

Actor, b. 24 October 1929, Hamnish, Herefordshire. Began career with Elizabethan Theatre Company, then rep and 10 years with the Royal Shakespeare Company. Films incl: *The Marat/Sade; Work is a Four-Letter Word; The Wall; The Cold Room; The Good Family.* TV incl: *Roads To Freedom; The Pallisers; Secret Army; Buccaneer; Kessler* (title role); *Reilly Ace of Spies; Oxbridge Blues; Love's Labours Lost; One By One; The Mozart Inquest; Oedipus the King; War and Remembrance; Fortunes of War; Gentlemen and Players; Inspector Morse; Poirot.* m. actress Celia Ryder; 1 d. Alison, 1 s. Jonathan. Address: c/o ICM. Hobbies: music, travel, languages, gardening. **Most Cherished Possession:** 'My garden – a heaven of rest and relaxation, and good for learning lines.'

ROSENTHAL, Jim

TV presenter/reporter, b. 6 November, Oxford. Began at the *Oxford Mail* and *The Times* before moving to BBC radio Sport Unit progressing to ITV Sport. His TV incl: *Sport On Two; Sports Report; 1978 World Cup; Wimbledon 78; Grand National.* Joined LWT 1980. With England team in 1982 & 86 World Cups. Presenter *Big Match Live* 1983–86 ITV athletics presenter; boxing commentaries on European and world title fights; *World of Sport* presenter. m. Chrissy. Address: c/o John Hockey Associates, London. Birthsign: Scorpio. Hobbies: trying to keep in shape and playing Sunday football with an ageing commentators XI. **Favourite Memory:** 'Presenting the *Big Match Live* from Wembley when my team Oxford United, who I watched in short trousers playing in the Southern League, won the Milk Cup in 1986.'

ROSS, Jonathan

Presenter, b. 17 November 1960, London. After grammar school worked as a TV researcher for many game shows. 1st TV, *Last Resort* (three series); other TV incl: *Have Words; George Michael; The Jonathan Ross Show; The Incredibly Strange Film Show; One Hour With Jonathan Ross.* Radio: *Drug Alert.* Address: c/o Gary Farrow, Suite 3, 15 Clanricarde Gardens, London W2 4JJ. Birthsign: Scorpio. Hobbies: chess, films, music. **Most Cherished Possession:** 'My credit cards – I'd be lost without them.' **Favourite Memory:** 'Singing with Tom Jones.'

ROSS, Nick

Broadcaster/journalist/presenter, b. 7 August 1947, London. Began broadcasting while at university in Belfast, reporting for and presenting BBC TV Northern Ireland's news and current affairs programmes, moving to network radio and to national TV. Radio incl: *The World At One; The World This Weekend; The World Tonight; Newsdesk; You the Jury; Any Questions; Call Nick Ross.* TV incl: *Man Alive; Out of Court; Fair Comment; Did You See?; Sixty Minutes; Horizon; Breakfast Time; Crimewatch UK; Watchdog; A Week In Politics.* TV producer for programmes incl: *The Fix; The Cure; The Biggest Epidemic of Our Times.* m. Sarah; 3 s. Adam, Sam, Jack. Address: c/o Jon Roseman Assocs, London WC2H 0DT. Hobbies: skiing, scuba-diving. **Most Cherished Possession:** 'Children – because they won't be children long.'

ROSSINGTON, Norman

Actor, b. 24 December 1928, Liverpool. Originally an office boy at Liverpool Docks, but started acting as an amateur and trained at Bristol Old Vic Theatre School. An original cast member of *Salad Days.* Has acted with the Royal Shakespeare Company, London Old Vic. Recent theatre incl: *Guys and Dolls.* Films incl: *Saturday Night and Sunday Morning; The Longest Day; A Hard Day's Night; Tobruk; Double Trouble; The Charge of the Light Brigade; Digby the Biggest Dog In the World; Man In the Wilderness; Young Winston.* TV incl: *Hunter's Walk; Crime of Passion; Comedy Playhouse; Armchair Theatre; Village Hall; Budgie; Follow That Dog; Spooner's Patch; Big Jim and the Figaro Club.* Address: c/o Peter Charlesworth. Birthsign: Capricorn. Hobbies: woodwork, skiing, golf.

ROTHWELL, Alan

Actor/director/writer, b. 9 February 1937, Oldham. Trained at RADA. Many years' work in the theatre. Films: *Linda; Nothing But the Best; Zeppelin.* TV incl: David Barlow in *Coronation Street* (1960–68); presenter, writer and producer of *Picture Box; The Lie; Z-Cars; Crown Court;* Nicholas Black in *Brookside; Top Secret; Angel Voices; All Creatures Great and Small.* m. Maureen; 2 s. Tobe, Ben. Address: c/o Elspeth Cochrane Agency, 11–13 Orlando Road, London SW4 0LE. Birthsign: Aquarius. Hobbies: music, walking, reading. **Most Cherished Possession:** 'A computer.' **Favourite Memory:** 'Conversations with a truly wise man.'

ROWLANDS, Patsy

Actress, b. 19 January 1940, London. Trained at the Guildhall School of Music and Drama. First professional appearance was in the chorus as a singer. Her big break came in Falmouth. Films incl: *Tess; Joseph Andrews; Little Lord Fauntleroy;* several *Carry On* films. TV incl: *Bless This House; The Squirrels; Ladies; The History of Mr Polly; Hallelujah; George and Mildred; Robin's Nest; In Loving Memory; Little Princess; Imaginary Friends; Charlie the Kid; Crimestrike.* m. Malcolm Sircom (dis.); 1 s. Alan. Address: c/o Saraband Associates. Birthsign: Capricorn/Aquarius. Hobbies: painting, collecting anything Victorian. Pets: one dog, Polly. **Favourite Memory:** 'Thursdays meant picnics after school with my mum, my dad, and my gran. A lovely childhood.'

ROYLE, Carol

Actress, b. 10 February 1954, Blackpool. Father actor Derek Royle, mother film make-up artist Jane Royle, sister actress Amanda Royle. Trained at Central School of Speech and Drama, London, before joining Harrogate Repertory Company. RSC stage appearances. Films: *Tuxedo Warrior; When the Walls Come Tumbling Down; Deadline.* TV incl: *The Cedar Tree; Blake's Seven; Waxwork; Heartland; The Professionals; Girl Talk; The Racing Game; The Outsider; Bergerac; Oxbridge Blues; Ladies In Charge; Hedgehog Wedding; Life Without George; The London Embassy; Blackeyes.* m. Julian Spear; 1 s. Taran. Address: c/o Hutton Management. Hobbies: reading, drawing, tapestry, writing. Pets: Irish setter and a mongrel. **Favourite Memory:** 'The thin metal strands that run in squares in the windows of some lift doors. Some friends of mine lived in flats with such a lift.'

RUSHTON, William

Actor/writer/comedian, b. 18 August 1937, London. After National Service, a solicitor's articled clerk then a freelance cartoonist, helping to found and edit *Private Eye.* Theatre incl: *The Private Eye Revue; Pass the Butler.* Films incl: *Those Magnificent Men In Their Flying Machine; The Bliss of Mrs Blossom; Adventures of a Private Eye.* TV incl: *That Was the Week That Was; Not So Much a Programme, More a Way of Life.* Many guest appearances on TV panel shows. Recent TV incl: *The Cobblers of Umbridge; The Kenny Everett Show.* Many books incl: *Great Moments In History; French Letters; W G Grace's Last Case.* m. actress Arlene Dorgan; 1 s. Tobias, 2 step-s. Matthew, Sam. Address: c/o Roger Hancock. Birthsign: Leo. Hobbies: ping pong, cricket.

RUTTER, Barrie

Actor, b. 12 December 1946, Hull, Yorkshire. National Youth Theatre 1964, leading player 1968, when he was voted Most Promising Actor by London Critics for *Apprentices.* Theatre incl: seasons at Nottingham Playhouse with the Royal Shakespeare Company and at the National Theatre. TV incl: *Apprentices; Queenie's Castle; Our Kid; Bavarian Nights; Astronauts; The Oresteia; The Big H; Way Up Stream; Great Writers – South Bank Show; Countdown To War; The Saint.* m. Dr Carol Rutter (author/university lecturer); 2 d. Bryony Rose, Rowan Jess. Address: c/o ICM. Hobbies: rugby league, making wine. Pets: a dog, Welsh border collie/labrador cross. **Most Cherished Possession:** 'Brandy glass in celebration of good food and drink.' **Favourite Memory:** 'The birth of our children.'

RYAN, Helen

Actress, b. 16 June 1938, Liverpool. After RADA and various rep companies, *Madras House* and *The Cherry Orchard* with the National Theatre; *Terra Nova* at Chichester; *Making Noise Quietly* at the Bush Theatre, London; *Lettice & Lovage* at the Globe Theatre, London. Films incl: *The Elephant Man.* Radio incl: *A Room With a View.* TV incl: *Edward the Seventh; Hannah; My Father's House; C.A.T.S. Eyes.* m. Guy Slater (dis.) 1 s. Daniel, 1 d. Rebecca. Address: c/o Joyce Edwards. Birthsign: Gemini. Hobbies: photography, music, tennis, reading, swimming. Pets: a dog called Nuts. **Most Cherished Possession:** 'The collection of good luck drawings and cards made by Daniel and Rebecca as children.' **Favourite Memory:** 'My children's births.'

SACHS, Andrew

Actor/writer, b. 7 April 1930, Berlin, Germany. Came to England just before the war. Stage incl: *A Voyage Round My Father; Habeas Corpus; No Sex Please, We're British; Jumpers*. TV incl: *Fawlty Towers* (Variety Club Award for Most Promising Artist, 1977); *The Tempest; History of Polly; Rising Damp; Galactic Garden, When In Spain* and *Berliners* (all three also as writer); *Bergerac;* wildlife-programme and other TV commentaries. Has written frequently for radio and stage, incl: *Made In Heaven* for the Chichester Festival. m. actress Melody Lang; 1 d. Kate, 2 s. John, William. Address: c/o Richard Stone. Hobbies: photography, wildlife concerns, art. Pets: two Cavalier King Charles Spaniels. **Most Cherished Possession:** 'Health and a sense of humour.' **Favourite Memory:** 'As a child, walking in the mountains of the Austrian Tyrol.'

SADLER, Brent

News correspondent, b. 29 November 1950, Manchester. Trained at the National Council for the Training of Journalists. Before entering TV, worked for the *Harrow Observer* and the *Reading Evening Post.* Reporter/news producer for Southern TV; reporter/presenter for Westward TV; presenter/reporter for HTV's *Report West* and *Report Extra.* Joined ITN as a reporter in 1981. He is their Middle East correspondent. m. Debby; 1 d. Brooke. Address: c/o ITN. Birthsign: Sagittarius. Hobbies: snow-skiing, sailing, water-skiing, riding, travel.

SALEM, Pamela

Actress, b. 22 January, Bombay, India. Trained at the Central School of Speech and Drama. Stage incl: rep; English tours of *Secretary Bird; Linden Tree;* and *Nightcap;* and foreign tours of *The Constant Wife; Phoenix Too Frequent; Romantic Comedy; Betrayal.* Films incl: *The Bitch; Never Say Never Again; After Darkness; Salome.* TV incl: *The Professionals; Lytton's Diary; Ever Decreasing Circles; Magnum; Boon; EastEnders.* m. actor Michael O'Hagan. Address: c/o Marina Martin Management. Birthsign: Aquarius. Hobbies: shell collecting, watching wild animals. Pets: Husband, dog and tropical fish. **Most Cherished Possession:** 'My dog, Joseph, for lots of reasons.' **Favourite Memory:** 'A chorus of nightingales at the start of summer.'

SALIH, Nejdet

Actor, b. 23 December 1958, London. Trained at Mountview Theatre School for three years. Stage appearances incl: *Old Tyme Music Hall;* puppeteering for TIE. TV incl: *The Brief; Auf Wiedersehen, Pet; West;* and the BBC soap opera, *EastEnders.* m. Sue; 1 d. Sophia. Address: c/o Bill McLean, 23b Deodar Road, London SW15 2NP. Birthsign: Capricorn. Hobbies: music, football, doing up old cars. **Most Cherished Possession:** 'My record collection – records bring back many memories – and a Volvo P1800.' **Favourite Memory:** 'The Alps in Switzerland. They are absolutely breathtaking, especially the Blue Glacier. Also the birth of my daughter, Sophia.'

SALLIS, Peter

Actor, b. 1 February 1921, Twickenham, Middlesex. Studied at RADA. Recent stage incl: *Sisterly Feelings; Run For Your Wife; Pride and Prejudice; Three Sisters; Ivanore; Much Ado About Nothing.* Films incl: *Sarah; Julie; The VIPs; Full Circle; The Divine Sarah; Witness For the Prosecution.* Radio incl: *End of Term* (play he wrote himself). TV incl: *Into the Dark; How To Murder Your Wife; The Pallisers; Softly, Softly; Yanks Go Home; You're Not Watching Me, Mummy; She Loves Me; Strangers and Brothers; The Bretts; Mountain Men;* and perhaps his best known role as Cleggy in *Last of the Summer Wine.* Played Cleggy's 'father' in subsequent *First of the Summer Wine.* m. actress Elaine Usher; 1 s. Crispian. Address: c/o Duncan Heath Associates. Hobbies: painting, gardening. Pets: three cats.

SALTHOUSE, John

Actor/writer, b. June 1951, London. Trained at LAMDA after retiring from professional football. Stage incl: seasons at Lancaster, Liverpool's Everyman, Leicester, Stratford East, Sheffield's Crucible; *Man Is Man*; *Abigail's Party*; *Ten Times Table*; *Red Saturday*. Also four years with the National Theatre. Appearances there incl: *The Long Voyage Home*; *The Iceman Cometh*; *Dispatches*; *The Shoemaker's Holiday*. Films incl: *A Bridge Too Far*; *An American Werewolf In London*; *Give My Regards To Broad Street*; *Pick Up Your Ears*. TV incl: *Man Above Men*; *Not Quite Cricket*; *The Bill*; *Abigail's Party*; *Glamour Night*; *Making Out*. m. actress Heather Tobias; 1 s. William. Address: c/o Roxanne Vacca, PTA, Bugle House, 21a Noel Street, London W1V 3PD. Hobbies: cricket, music, most sports. **Favourite Memory:** 'The birth of my son.'

SANDERSON, Joan

Actress, b. 24 November 1912, Bristol. Trained at RADA then rep. Stage incl: *See How They Run*; *The Bad Seed*; *Let's Get a Divorce*; *A Lady Mislaid*; *Anyone For Denis?*; *Semi-Detached*; *Doctor At Sea*; *The Mousetrap*. Radio incl: *After Henry*. TV incl: *Please Sir!*; *Mixed Blessings*; *Me and My Girl*; *Fawlty Towers*; *Rising Damp*; *Ripping Yarns*; *Upstairs, Downstairs*; *After Henry*. m. Gregory Scott. Address: c/o Bryan Drew. Birthsign: Sagittarius. Hobbies: gardening, reading, prowling around antique shops. **Most Cherished Possession:** 'A ring of my mother's. It's the only piece of her jewellery I have left – everything else has been lost or stolen.' **Favourite Memory:** 'First sight of coast of North Africa at dawn when arriving by sea. Such wonderful colours.'

SANDS, Leslie

Actor/ writer/playwright. b. 19 May 1921, Bradford, Yorkshire. Professional stage debut Lyceum, Sheffield, in 1941; London debut in *Antony and Cleopatra* in 1946. Stage incl: *Hobson's Choice*; *Measure For Measure*; *Ducking Out*. Films incl: *The Deadly Affair*; *One More Time*; *The Ragman's Daughter*. TV incl: *My Brother's Keeper*; *The Winning Streak*; *Man About the House*; *Fresh Fields*; *Two Ronnies*; *Wilderness Road*; *A Sort of Innocence*. m. actress Pauline Williams; 1 d. Joanna. Address: c/o Peters Fraser & Dunlop. Birthsign: Taurus. Hobbies: photography, sound recording. Pets: Matey, the biggest Yorkshire Terrier in the world! **Most Cherished Possession:** 'My typewriter, because I make half my living by it.' **Favourite Memory:** 'My last part – whatever it was!'

SAUNDERS, Jennifer

Comedienne/actress, b. 12 July 1958, Sleaford, Lincolnshire. Trained at the Central School of Speech and Drama, London, where she met Dawn French. They teamed up and toured in cabaret, starting at the Comedy Store, London. French and Saunders have appeared in many *Comic Strip Presents . . .* films, mostly made for TV incl: *Five Go Mad In Dorset*; *Five Go Mad On Mescalin*; *Consuela*; *Mr Jolly Lives Next Door*, *Strike* (winner 1981 Golden Globe); *Spaghetti Hoops*; *Le Kiss*; *Supergrass* (feature film). Other TV incl: *Girls On Top*; *Happy Families*; *French and Saunders* (three series); *Sapsorrow*. Theatre incl: *An Evening With French and Saunders*; co-directed, with John Cleese, *The Secret Policeman's Biggest Ball*. m. comedian and actor Adrian Edmondson; 2 d. Address: c/o Peters Fraser & Dunlop.

SAVALAS, Telly

Actor, b. 21 January 1925, Garden City, New York. Has appeared in numerous films and TV programmes. Films incl: *The Birdman of Alcatraz*; *The Slender Thread*; *Beau Geste*; *The Dirty Dozen*; *The Dirty Dozen III*; *On Her Majesty's Secret Service*; *The Border*. Title role as TV's *Kojak*. Nominated twice for Best Actor and twice for Best Director for *Kojak*. TV also incl: *The Equalizer*; *J J Starbuck*; the mini-series *Alice In Wonderland*. m. (4th) Julie; 3 d. Christina, Candace, Ariana, 2 s. Nicholas, Christian. Address: c/o ICM, 8899 Beverly Blvd, Los Angeles, CA 90048. Hobbies: reading, sports, racehorses. Pets: two dogs. **Most Cherished Possession:** 'My lollipop – it's worth millions.' **Favourite Memory:** 'Watching my children grow up.'

SAYLE, Alexei

Actor/writer/comedian, b. 7 August 1952, Liverpool. Went to Southport and Chelsea Schools of Art and had odd jobs, drifting into cabaret and then stand-up comedy. Films incl: *The Secret Policeman's Other Ball; Gorky Park; The Bride; Supergrass.* TV incl: *OTT; The Young Ones; Whoops Apocalypse; Didn't You Kill My Brother?* Records: *'Ullo John, Gotta New Motor?; Didn't You Kill My Brother?; Alexei Sayle's Stuff; Stuff.* Books: *Train To Hell; Geoffrey the Tube Train; The Fat Comedian.* m. Linda. Address: c/o Mayer Management. Birthsign: Leo. Hobbies: cycling, drinking, re-using envelopes. **Most Cherished Possession:** 'Possessions tie you down, man.' **Favourite Memory:** 'I'm not telling you!;

SCALES, Prunella

Actress, b. 22 June, Sutton Abinger, Surrey. Trained at the Old Vic Theatre School and with Uta Hagen in New York. Stage incl: *When We Are Married; Single Spies; An Evening With Queen Victoria.* Films incl: *Hound of the Baskervilles; Boys From Brazil; Wagner; The Wicked Lady; Hobson's Choice; The Lonely Passion of Judith Hearne; A Chorus of Disapproval.* TV incl: *Fawlty Towers; Target; Bergerac; Jackanory; An Evening With Queen Victoria; Never the Twain; Slimming Down; Mapp & Lucia; Beyond the Pale; After Henry.* m. actor Timothy West; 2 s. Samuel, Joseph. Address: c/o Jeremy Conway. Birthsign: Cancer. Hobbies: gardening, languages, listening to music. Pets: two cats called Lily and Baylis.

SCANNELL, Tony

Actor, b. 14 August 1945, Kinsale, Co Cork, Eire. Trained at the E15 Acting School and Theatre Workshop after leaving RAF, followed by rep, then National Theatre. Also directed two plays: *The Plough and the Stars; A Streetcar Named Desire.* Films incl: *Flash Gordon; Blue Money;* lead role in *Cheap Perfume,* which won the silver plaque at Chicago Film Festival. TV incl: *Cribb; All the Fun of the Fair; Little Lord Fauntleroy; Up the Elephant;* Det Sgt Ted Roach in *The Bill; Flying Lady.* m. (dis.); 1 s. Sean. Address: c/o Annette Stone. Birthsign: Leo. Hobbies: golf, music, cycling. **Most Cherished Possession:** 'None. I have an unfortunate habit of giving things away.' **Favourite Memory:** 'I live in the present and don't dwell on the past.'

SCHOFIELD, Philip

Actor, b. 1 April 1962, Oldham, Lancashire. His first broadcasting job was for Television New Zealand, fronting their new pop show, *Shazam.* He went on to make regular TV and radio shows, plus specials ranging from live concerts to pop interviews and music award ceremonies. On returning to Britain he landed the job of fronting Children's BBC. Other TV incl: *Take Two; Saturday Superstore; Newsround;* Breakfast TV; *Royal Variety Performance;* and, with Sarah Greene, joint presenter of *Going Live.* Also a Radio 1 disc jockey. Address: c/o James Grant. Birthsign: Aries.

SCOTT, Brough

Sports presenter/journalist, b. 12 December 1942, London. Was professional National Hunt jockey, 1962–71. Joined ITV commentary team in 1977. *Sunday Times* sports journalist; editorial director, *Racing Post;* trustee, Injured Jockeys Fund and Racing Welfare. Radio incl: *The Throughbred.* Racing Journalist of the Year 1977; Sports Journalist of the Year, 1983; Sports Feature Writer of the Year, 1986. Books: *The World of Flat Racing; On and Off the Rails.* m. former British skier Susier McInnes; 2 d. Sophie, Tessa, 2 s. Charlie, Jamie. Address: c/o *Racing Post,* 120 Coombe Lane, Raynes Park, London SW20 0BA. Hobby: making bonfires. **Most Cherished Possession:** 'My earpiece – I can't survive without it on TV.' **Favourite Memory:** 'My first TV interview, with star jockey Yves St Martin – he answered only in French!'

SCOTT, Mike

TV presenter/interviewer, b. 8 December 1932, London. Entered showbusiness in 1954, after National Service. Began as a stagehand with the Festival Ballet, before joining the Rank Organisation as a production trainee, then Granada TV as a floor manager when the ITV company opened in 1956. Directed many programmes – including early episodes of *Coronation Street* – and, in 1963, became a producer and presenter of factual programmes. Hosted *Cinema* and was an interviewer for *World In Action*. In 1979, he became Granada TV's programme controller. Left in 1987 to become presenter of *The Time . . The Place . . .* m. Sylvia; 1 d. Julia. Address: c/o Thames TV.

SCOTT, Terry

Comedian, b. 4 May 1927, Watford. Began in rep, then worked in clubs, pubs, summer shows and pantomimes before teaming up with Bill Maynard for *Great Scott, It's Maynard*. Stage incl: *The Mating Game; A Bedful of Foreigners*. Films incl: several of the *Carry On* films. TV incl: *Hugh and I; The Gnomes of Dulwich; Happy Ever After; Terry and June*. m. (2nd) former ballet dancer Margaret Pollen; 4 d. Sarah, Nicola, Lindsay, Alexandra. Address: c/o Richard Stone. Birthsign: Taurus. Hobbies: gardening, chickens. **Most Cherished Possession:** 'My garden in the lovely countryside.' **Favourite Memory:** 'In a lift in South Africa and a stranger tapped me on the shoulder and said "Hello Terry". It was Sir Stanley Matthews.'

SECOMBE, Sir Harry, CBE

Entertainer, b. 8 September 1921, Swansea, South Wales. Forces shows during the war, and Windmill Theatre on demob. First break on radio in *Variety Bandbox*, then *Welsh Rarebit* and *Educating Archie* before *The Goon Show*. Made his musical comedy debut in 1963 as Pickwick. Films incl: *Oliver!; Song of Norway*. TV incl: *Highway*. Books incl: *Goon For Lunch; Welsh Fargo; Twice Brightly; Arias and Raspberries*. Knighted in 1981. m. Myra; 2 d. Jennifer, Katherine, 2 s. Andrew, David. Address: c/o 46 St James's Place, London SW1. Birthsign: Virgo. Hobbies: golf, photography, sketching. Pets: a cat called Moriarty. **Most Cherished Possession:** 'My family.' **Favourite Memory:** 'Meeting Myra at a Mumbles Pier dance.'

SEED, Graham

Actor, b. 12 July 1950, London. Trained at RADA. Worked in rep at Manchester's Library Theatre and two seasons at the Chichester Festival. London West End theatre incl: Mole in *Toad of Toad Hall;* Gerald in *Me and My Girl;* tour of *Tons of Money*. TV incl: *I, Claudius;* Mike Leigh's *Who's Who; Brideshead Revisited; Bergerac; Edward VII; CAB; Good and Bad at Games; Crossroads*. Radio incl: P G Wodehouse's *Summer Lightning;* Nigel Pargetter in *The Archers*. m. Clare Colvin; 1 d. Nicola, 1 s. Toby. Address: c/o Saraband Assocs. Birthsign: Cancer. Hobbies: cricket, food. **Most Cherished Possession:** 'My body and taking care of it.' **Favourite Memory:** 'Approaching Venice at dawn by motor launch from the airport. Magic!'

SELBY, David

Actor, b. 5 February, Morgantown, West Virginia. Films incl: *Rich and Famous; Up the Sandbox; Super Cops; Rich Kids; Raise the Titanic*. Richard Channing in *Falcon Crest*. Other TV incl: *Dark Shadows; The Waltons; Kojak; Family; Washington; Behind Closed Doors; Flamingo Road; Knightrider*. m. Chip; 1 s. Todd, 2 d. Brooke, Amanda. Address: c/o William Morris Agency, 151 El Camino Drive, Beverly Hills, CA 90212. Hobby: all outdoor sports. **Most Cherished Possession:** 'My wife and my children.' **Favourite Memory:** 'Hopping a train with 25 dollars for New York City to become an actor. I had never been out of West Virginia before that.'

SELBY, Tony

Actor, b. 26 February 1938, Lambeth, London. Trained at the Italia Conti Stage School and made stage debut in 1950 in *Peter Pan*. Other stage incl: *Alfie; Saved; Man and Superman; Fiddler On the Roof*. TV incl: *Up the Junction; Another Day, Another Dollar; Shine a Light; Ace of Wands; Moody and Peg; Get Some In; Hideaway;* Glitz in *Doctor Who*. m. (1st) (dis.), (2nd) Gina Sellers; 1 d. Samantha, 1 s. Matthew (both from 1st m.). Address: c/o AIM, 5 Denmark Street, London WC2H 8LP. Hobbies: football (he's played for the Showbix XI since 1964), swimming, tennis. **Most Cherished Possession:** 'I don't really have one, but my loved ones and friends have always been most important.' **Favourite Memory:** 'Watching my daughter being born. It seemed like a miracle.'

SELLECCA, Connie

Actress, b. Concetta Sellecchia, 25 May, Bronx, New York. Began as a fashion and commercial model; took acting classes in New York. TV incl: *The Greatest American Hero; Flying High; She's Dressed To Kill; Somebody's Killing The World's Greatest Models; The Bermuda Depths; Captain America II;* Christine Francis in *Hotel; Downpayment On Murder; The Last Fling.* m. (sep.) actor Gil Gerard; 1 s. Gilbert Vincent. Address: c/o William Morris Agency, 151 El Camino Drive, Beverly Hills, CA 90212. Hobby: working out. **Favourite Memory:** 'As a model in New York I shared an apartment with four girls, one bedroom, one bathroom and one toilet!'

SELLECK, Tom

Actor, b. 29 January 1945, Detroit, Michigan. Studied drama at Valley College and started his career in TV commercials. Films incl: *Myra Breckenridge; High Road To China; Lassiter; Three Men and a Baby; An Innocent Man; Quigley Down Under.* TV incl: *The Young and the Restless; The Rockford Files; Magnum PI.* TV movies: *Returning Home; Divorce Wars.* Emmy Award: Best Actor for *Magnum*. m. (1st) Jacki Ray (dis.), (2nd) actress Jilly Mack; 1 s. Kevin (step-s. from 1st m.), 1 d. Hannah. Address: c/o McCartt-Oreck Barrett. Hobbies: swimming, volley ball, basketball, softball, making furniture, restoring antiques. **Most Cherished Possession:** 'The gold Rolex watch my father gave me when I turned 21.' **Favourite Memory:** 'I had a bit part in the movie *Coma*. I played a dead body!'

SERLE, Chris

Journalist, b. 13 July 1943, Bristol. Former actor (with the Bristol Old Vic), radio producer (*Petticoat Line; Brain of Britain; Late Night Extra*), and TV director. A former presenter of BBC TV's *That's Life!* Other TV incl: *Medical Express; The Computer Programme; Greek Language and People; 60 Minutes; In at the Deep End; Runway; Windmill; People; Friday Now.* m. Anna; 2 s. Harry, Jack. Address: c/o Curtis Brown. Birthsign: Cancer. Hobbies: sailing, gliding, jazz drumming. Pets: three cats and and expanding family of guinea pigs. **Most Cherished Possession:** 'I cannot choose between my appointments diary, without which my life would collapse, and my son's latest painting.'

SHAKESBY, Patricia

Actress, b. 6 November 1942, Cottingham, Yorkshire. Started in rep at the age of 16. West End plays incl: *The Real Inspector Hound; Night of the Iguana; Suddenly at Home;* and the RSC's *Romeo and Juliet; Hamlet; Troilus and Cressida; Love Girl and the Innocent; La Ronde.* TV incl: *Howards' Way; Late Starter; Sapphire and Steel; Yes Minister; The Pity of It All; Flowering Cherry; Coronation Street; Z-Cars; Saturday While Sunday; War and Peace; Crime and Punishment.* m. (dis.). Address: c/o Roger Carey. Birthsign: Scorpio. Hobbies: painting, music. **Most Cherished Possession:** 'A brooch with my late mother's name on, given to her by a much loved friend of mine.' **Favourite Memory:** 'My late mother, because I miss her.'

SHANNON, Johnny

Actor, b. 29 July 1932, London. Made his acting debut in the Warner Brothers' film, *Performance*. Other films incl: *That'll Be the Day; The Great Rock and Roll Swindle; Flame; Runners; Absolute Beginners; Queenie; Scandal*. TV incl: *Gold Robbers; Beryl's Lot; Man; Watch All Night; Give Us a Break; Big Deal; The Dick Emery Show; Never Mind the Quality, Feel the Width; Minder; The Sweeney; The Professionals; The Morecambe and Wise Show; Supergran; The Kenny Everett Show; Keep It In the Family; Coast To Coast; Bust; High Street Blues*. m. Rose; 1 s. Gary, 1 d. Terry. Address: c/o Chatto & Linnit, London. Birthsign: Leo. Hobbies: watching boxing, horse racing.

SHARP, Andrew

Actor, b. 26 May 1953, Sydney. Australian theatre experience incl: The Artful Dodger in *Oliver!;* Brad Majors in *The Rocky Horror Show; Hamlet; As You Like It*. West End stage incl: *Beyond the Rainbow; Stage Struck; Deathtrap; Men*. Films incl: *Summer of Secrets; Buddies; Undercover*. TV incl: *Shannon's Mob; Homicide; Bobby Dazzler; Tenko; Taurus Rising; Glass Babies; Sword of Honour* (US mini-series); Andrew Baxter in *The Young Doctors*. Address: c/o International Casting Service, 147a King Street, Sydney, NSW 2000, Australia. Birthsign: Gemini. Hobby: writing. **Most Cherished Possession:** 'My radio, to listen to *Desert Island Discs*.' **Favourite Memory:** 'Working in London's West End, feeling right at home.'

SHARROCK, Ian

Actor, b. 20 December 1959, Harrogate, Yorkshire. Trained at the Corona Academy of Music and Dramatic Art. Has appeared in more than 20 films, incl: *Walt Disney's Candleshoe*. Has acted in over 30 radio plays, incl: the award-winning *Equus* with Peter Barkworth. TV incl: *Smike; Peter Pan; Games; Emmerdale Farm*, 1980–89. m. Pamela; 1 d. Natalie. Address: c/o Susan Angel. Birthsign: Sagittarius. Hobbies: golf, spending as much time as possible with Natalie. Pets: Barney – almost a labrador! **Most Cherished Possession:** 'Our lovely home, a converted barn, in our Yorkshire village.' **Favourite Memory:** 'The birth of our daughter Natalie. She proved that I had never really been happy before.'

SHATNER, William

Actor/director, b. 22 March 1931. Montreal, Canada. Studied Law at University. After rep, appeared in the Stratford Shakespeare Festival, Ontario. Films incl: *Star Trek I, II, III, IV* and star and director of *Star Trek V; The Brothers Karamazov; The Intruder; The Outrage; Big Bad Mama; Judgement At Nuremberg; Airplane II*. TV incl: *Go Ask Alice; The Horror At 37,000 Feet; Beachwood and Rawhide* (TV movie); *Saturday Night Live;* the series *Barbary Coast;* title role in *T J Hooker;* Capt Kirk in *Star Trek*. m. (1st) Gloria Ranel, (2nd) Marcy Lafferty; 3 d. Leslie, Lisabeth, Melanie (all from 1st m.). Birthsign: Aries. Hobbies: horse riding, raising champion Dobermans, jogging. **Most Cherished Possession:** 'My beloved horses and new horse ranch in Kentucky.' **Favourite Memory:** 'Horseback riding as a child.'

SHAW, Martin

Actor, b. 21 January 1945, Birmingham. Trained at LAMDA, followed by rep. Stage incl: *They're Playing Our Song;* and as Elvis Presley in *Are You Lonesome Tonight?* Films incl: *Macbeth; Operation Daybreak*. TV incl: *Electra; The Professionals; Cream In My Coffee; The Last Place On Earth; Run the Gauntlet; The Most Dangerous Man In the World*. m. Maggie; 2 s. Luke, Joe, 2 d. Sophie, Kate. Address: c/o Hutton Management. Birthsign: Aquarius. Hobbies; gliding, walking, music. Pets: Siamese cat called Korky. **Most Cherished Possession:** 'My cottage in Galloway, for peace, relaxation and solitude.' **Favourite Memory:** 'Landing a glider after my first solo flight, directly opposite a camera crew filming the event, and dad saying: "What a pro!"'

SHELLEY, Cindy

Actress, b. 23 March 1960, Barnet. Trained at New School of Speech and Drama. Stage incl: *A Taste of Honey; Magic;* Foco Novo. TV incl: *Going To Work; Cockles; Long Live the Babe* (play); *Tenko; Tenko Reunion; Howards' Way.* m. Philip; 1 d. Hannah. Address: Brunskill Management. Birthsign: Aries; Hobbies: dancing, piano, gardening. Pets: two cats. **Most Cherished Possession:** 'A bracelet made up of five medals won by my grandfather for running, 1930–34, and inherited from my grandmother.' **Favourite Memory:** 'Hannah's first giggle.'

SHEPHERD, Cybill

Actress, b. 18 February 1950, Memphis, Tennessee. Was a top fashion model who in 1968 was voted CBS Fashion Model of the Year. Stage incl: *A Shot In the Dark; Picnic; Vanities; The Seven Year Itch; Lunch Hour.* Films incl: *The Last Picture Show; At Long Last Love; The Heartbreak Kid; Daisy Miller; Taxi Driver; The Lady Vanishes; Chances Are.* TV incl: *The Yellow Rose; Hot Summer* (mini-series); *Secrets of a Married Man; Guide For the Married Woman; Seduced* (all TV movies); Maddie Hayes in *Moonlighting.* m. (1st) David Ford, (2nd) Bruce Oppenheim; 2 d. Clementine (from 1st m.) and Ariel, and twin brother Zach. Address: c/o Rogers and Cowan, 10000 Santa Monica Blvd, Los Angeles, CA 90067. Birthsign: Aquarius. Hobbies: horse riding, swimming.

SHEPHERD, Jack

Actor/director/writer, b. 29 October 1940, Leeds. Trained at London Drama Centre. Stage incl: *Glengarry Glen Ross* (Actor of the Year, 1983). Films incl: *The Virgin Soldiers; The Bedsitting Room.* TV incl: *Bill Brand; A Room For the Winter; Escape From Sobibor; Scoop; The Party; The Hospice; Cracking Up; Balltrap On Cote D'Azur; Nobody Here But Us Chickens.* m. (1st) Judy Harland (dis.), (2nd) Ann Scott; 1 d. Jan, 1 s. Jake (both from 1st m.), 2 twin d. Victoria, Catherine, 1 s. Ben (all from 2nd m.). Hobbies: sport, jazz, writing, art. Pets: elderly guinea pig. Address: c/o Markham & Froggatt. **Most Cherished Possession:** 'A battered baritone saxophone given to me by parents on my 21st birthday.' **Favourite Memory:** 'Waking up on the first day of summer holiday and thinking . . . no school for six whole weeks.'

SHERIDAN, Dinah

Actress, b. 17 September 1920, Hampstead Garden Suburb, London. Trained at Italia Conti Stage School. Stage debut in *Where the Rainbow Ends.* After many films, retired from acting in 1953 to bring up two children, but returned in 1967. The first actress to appear on TV from Alexandra Palace, in October 1936, in *Picture Page,* and in the first three-act play from Alexandra Palace, *Gallows Glorious,* in 1938. Films incl: *Where No Vultures Fly; Genevieve; The Railway Children; The Mirror Cracked.* Other TV incl: *Winning Streak; Don't Wait Up* (six series). m. 1st Jimmy Hanley (dis.), 2nd John Davis (dis.), 3rd John Merivale (dec.); 1 d. actress/presenter Jenny Hanley. Address: c/o ICM. Hobbies: gardening, cooking, tapestry. Pets: Shih-tzu dog called Coley. **Favourite Memory:** 'A surprise family dinner for my 60th birthday and being totally caught for *This Is Your Life.*'

SIKKING, James

Actor, b. 5 March, Los Angeles, California. BA in Theatre Arts from UCLA. Stage incl: *The Big Knife* in London. Films incl: *The Terminal Man; Outland; Von Ryan's Express; Scorpio; The Magnificent Seven; The Electric Horseman; Ordinary People; Star Chamber; Star Trek III; Soul Man.* TV incl: guest appearances in *Charlie's Angels; The Incredible Hulk; Starsky and Hutch; M*A*S*H.* Other TV incl: *Turnabout; General Hospital;* Lt Howard Hunter in *Hill Street Blues; Dress Grey;* and the TV films, *Jesse Owen's Story; First Steps; Bay Coven.* m. Florine; 1 s. Andrew, 1 d. Emily. Address: c/o McCartt-Oreck Barrett. Hobbies: golf, skiing, racquetball, collecting wine, cooking. Pets: four dogs. **Favourite Memory:** 'Skiing with my family.'

SILVERA, Carmen

Actress, b. Toronto, Canada. Trained in classical ballet, then studied drama at LAMDA. Stage incl: *Serious Charge; Let's Get a Divorce; El Baille; People Are Living There; On the Rocks; Torrents of Spring; Waters of the Moon; Hobson's Choice; A Coat of Varnish; The Unexpected Guest; The Cherry Orchard; 'Allo, 'Allo!;* and many guest appearances in provincial theatres. TV incl: *Compact; Dad's Army; Beggar My Neighbour; New Scotland Yard; Within These Walls; Maggie and Her; The Gentle Touch; Two Women; Lillie; Tales of the Unexpected; 'Allo, 'Allo!* Address: c/o Barry Burnett. Birthsign: Gemini. Hobbies: antiques, interior decor, reading, bridge, scrabble and golf.

SIMS, Joan

Actress, b. 9 May 1930, Laindon, Essex. Trained at RADA. After rep work, her first major West End role was in *Intimacy At 8.30.* Other stage incl: *The Lord Chamberlain Regrets; Instant Marriage; Uproar In the House; The Country Wife; Good Time Johnny; In Order of Appearance.* She has appeared in more than 50 films, including many of the *Carry On* series and has appeared in over 100 TV productions, incl: *The Dick Emery Show* (co-starred for nine months); *Carry On Laughing; Till Death Us Do Part; Howerd's Confessions; Lord Tramp; East Lynne; Your Move; Born and Bred; Worzel Gummidge; In Loving Memory; Lady Killers; Farrington of the F O; Simon and the Witch.* She has broadcast regularly since 1954. Address: c/o John Mahoney. Birthsign: Taurus.

SINDEN, Donald, CBE

Actor, b. 9 October 1923, Plymouth. Fellow of the Royal Society of Arts. Trained at the Webber Douglas School of Dramatic Art and first appeared on TV in *Bullet In the Ballet* in 1948. Films incl: *The Cruel Sea; Mogambo; Doctor In the House; Doctor At Large; Eyewitness; Decline and Fall; The Day of the Jackal; The Island At the Top of the World; The Children.* TV incl: *The Organisation; Our Man From St Mark's; Two's Company; Never the Twain; Discovering English Churches.* Books: *A Touch of the Memoirs; Laughter In the Second Act* (autobiographies); *The English Country Church.* m. Diana Mahoney; 2 s. Jeremy, Marc. Address: c/o Michael Whitehall. Birthsign: Libra. Hobbies: theatrical history, ecclesiology, serendipity.

SINDEN, Jeremy

Actor, b. 14 June 1950, London. Trained at LAMDA. Spent 1969 season at Pitlochry; 1970–72 with the RSC, 1975 at Chichester. Stage incl: *The Winslow Boy* (as director); *The Philanthropist; An Ideal Husband.* Films incl: *Star Wars; Ascendancy; Chariots of Fire; Madame Sousatzka.* TV incl: *Crossroads; Danger UXB; Brideshead Revisited* (Emmy award nomination); *Holding the Fort; Never the Twain; Squadron; The Far Pavilions; Fairly Secret Army; Lytton's Diary; Three Up, Two Down; Robin of Sherwood; Harem; Bergerac; Fortunes of War; After the War; Square Deal* (two series); *Virtuoso.* m. Delia Lindsay; 2 d. Kezia, Harriet. Address: c/o ICM. Hobbies: walking, photography, tree climbing, travel, croquet. Pets: dog. **Most Cherished Possession:** 'My virginity.' **Favourite Memory:** 'Losing my virginity.'

SINDEN, Leon

Actor, b. 20 July 1927, Ditchling, Sussex. Started in MESA, a Brighton-based ENSA, in 1941, then with Wilson Barret Company, including six seasons at Pitlochry as actor and director, one year with the RSC. Stage incl: *Ross* (two years at Haymarket Theatre); *Semi-Detached; London Assurance* (both on Broadway). On Council of Equity. TV incl: *Assassination Run; Rebecca; Scoop;* Mr Carradine in *Take the High Road.* Radio incl: *The Eliza Stories* for *Morning Story.* Address: c/o Spotlight. Birthsign: Cancer. Hobbies: antiques, classical music. Pets: cat. **Most Cherished Possession:** 'A plaster relief of my mother at age five.' **Favourite Memory:** 'A walk on the banks of Loch Lomond which changed my life.'

SINDEN, Marc

Actor, b. 9 May 1954, London. Trained at Bristol Old Vic Theatre School, then spent five years as a jeweller! Numerous stage appearances, incl West End. Films incl: *Clash of Loyalties; The Wicked Lady; White Nights; Manges D'Hommes.* TV incl: *Dick Turpin; If You Go Down To the Woods Today; Home Front; Bergerac; Strange But True; Crossroads; Magnum PI; All At No 20; Rumpole of the Bailey; Never the Twain; Fiddlers Green; Wolf To the Slaughter; Oratory; The Country Boy.* m. Joanne; 1 s. Henry. Address: c/o CCA. Hobbies: ethology, zoology, motor racing, history of stunt-work, theatrical history, cricket. **Most Cherished Possession:** 'My correspondence with David Niven.' **Favourite Memory:** 'My 30th birthday spent in Geneva.'

SINER, Guy

Actor, b. 16 October 1947, New York City. Trained at the Webber Douglas Academy and in 1971 won the Rodney Millingon Award. Has worked with various repertory companies. London stage incl: *Cowardy Custard* (debut); *Biograph Girl; Nickleby and Me; Off the Peg; Toad of Toad Hall;* and tours of *Barefoot In the Park; Sunshine Boys.* TV incl: *'Allo, 'Allo!; I, Claudius; Life At Stake; Doctor Who; Secret Army; Softly, Softly; Z-Cars.* He also appeared in cabaret at the Ritz. Address: c/o Barry Burnett. Birthsign: Libra. Hobbies: dining out, travel, photography. **Most Cherished Possession:** 'None, because possessions aren't that important to me.' **Favourite Memory:** 'Falling in love, of course.'

SINGLETON, Valerie

TV journalist, b. 9 April 1937, Hitchin, Hertfordshire. Won scholarship to RADA, worked for five years as an actress on TV advertising magazines and did TV commercial voice-overs, before joining the BBC as an announcer. Joined *Blue Peter* in 1962. Other TV incl: *Blue Peter Special Assignments; Blue Peter Royal Safari; Val Meets the VIPs; Nationwide; Tonight; The Money Programme.* Radio incl: *PM* Radio 4, Mondays and Tuesdays. Address: Arlington Enterprises. Birthsign: Aries. Hobbies: exploring London, museums, photography, sailing, riding, water and snow skiing, reading. Pets: two sister cats called Pansy and Daisy. **Most Cherished Possession:** 'My battered box of plugs for anywhere in the world. They have been everywhere with me and I'd be lost without them.' **Favourite Memory:** 'Too many to list.'

SISSONS, Peter

Television journalist, b. 17 July 1942, Liverpool. Joined ITN from Oxford University as a general trainee in 1964. Subsequently a general reporter, foreign correspondent, news editor, industrial editor, presenter of *News at One,* presenter and associate editor of *Channel 4 News.* Winner of Royal Television Society's 1989 Judges' Award. Joined the BBC in 1989 as presenter of the *Six O'Clock News* and chairman of *Question Time.* m. Sylvia; 1 d. Kate, 2 s. Jonathan and Michael. Address: c/o BBC TV. Birthsign: Cancer. Hobbies: relaxing. Pets: thirty fish, two cats, one guinea pig.

SLOANE, Doreen

Actress, b. 24 February 1934, Birkenhead, Wirral. Trained at the Elliott Clarke Theatre School, Liverpool. Various repertory seasons. Films incl: *Yanks; Chariots of Fire.* TV incl: *Coronation Street* (four different parts); *Emmerdale Farm* (two parts); *Victorian Scandals; Nearest and Dearest; Last of the Summer Wine; All For Love;* Annabelle Collins in *Brookside.* Also radio plays and serials. m. (1st) (dis.), (2nd) Len; 2 s. Angus, Bruce, 2 d. Sarah, Jane. Address: c/o Brookside Productions. Hobbies: horse riding, *Telegraph* crossword, reading, brass band music. Pets: cat called Emma. **Most Cherished Possession:** 'Silver locket my father gave me on my 21st birthday.' **Favourite Memory:** 'Touring Cornwall with a theatre company when I was 18.'

SMETHURST, Jack

Actor/producer, b. 9 April 1932, Collyhurst, Manchester. Stage incl: West End and tours of Australia and Far and Middle East; also tours, with *Run For Your Wife; Educating Rita; Season's Greetings.* Many TV appearances, incl: *The Casualties; No Hiding Place; Plane Makers; Z-Cars; Coronation Street; Parables; Love Thy Neighbour,* and *For the Love of Ada* both made into films; *Hilary.* m. Julie; 3 d. Perdita, Merry, Jane-Louse, 1 s. Adam. Address: c/o Richard Stone. Birthsign: Aries. Hobbies: reading, talking, travelling. **Most Cherished Possession:** 'My family – when we are together the house is filled with laughter.' **Favourite Memory:** 'My own *This Is Your Life.* Everybody seemed so happy!'

SMITH, Elaine

Actress, b. 23 April 1962, Scotland, brought up in Perth, Australia. Studied at the Western Australian Institute of Technology for her BA (English) and Double Major in Theatre Arts and Literature. She played a number of roles for Western Australian Playwrights' Workshop. Theatre also incl: *Once a Catholic; What the Butler Saw; Erphingham Camp; Mr Ugg and the Bionic Budgie.* Film: *Possessed.* TV incl: *Carson's Law; Sons and Daughters;* mini-series *Flair.* Leads pop quartet *Suitably Rough.* Address: c/o Frog Promotions, 2a Armstrong Street, Middle Park, Victoria, Australia 3206. **Most Cherished Possession:** 'My teddy bear. It arrived at hospital on the day I was born and has been with me ever since.'

SMITH, Giles

TV journalist, b. 23 May 1944, Beaconsfield, Buckinghamshire. Started in journalism on the *Harrow Observer.* Specialising in industrial matters, he became industrial correspondent for the *Western Mail,* Cardiff, and later joined *The Times* as industrial reporter and then the BBC in the same capacity before moving to ITN in 1974, later becoming its Industrial Editor. Sports correspondent since 1987. Address: c/o ITN. Birthsign: Gemini. Hobbies: cricket, squash, Bob Dylan. **Most Cherished Possession:** 'My cricket bat because it is so exciting wondering if it will ever score any runs.' **Favourite Memory:** 'Bob Dylan's concert at Wembley Stadium in 1984.'

SMITH, Jay

Actor, b. 24 May 1951, Larne, Northern Ireland. Trained at the Royal Scottish Academy of Music and Drama. Began his career at Perth rep and then the Royal Lyceum, Edinburgh. Tours: *Joseph and His Amazing Technicolor Dreamcoat; Rock Nativity.* Films incl: *How He Lied to Her Husband; Heavenly Pursuits.* TV incl: *Sutherland's Law; Strangers; The Camerons; Take the High Road.* m. Margaret; 2 d. Siobhan, Catriona, 2 s. Jamie, Brendan. Address: c/o Ruth Tarko. Birthsign: Gemini. Hobbies: bridge, gardening, politics. Pets: rabbit called Flopsy. **Most Cherished Possession:** 'My Rover 2.6S car – when it is working properly.' **Favourite Memory:** 'Being elected as a district councillor for the town I live in.'

SMITH, Mike

Broadcaster, b. 23 April 1955, Hornchurch, Essex. Started in hospital radio, then moved to Capital Radio, London, and Radio 1. Won 1987 Variety Club Radio Personality of the Year award and, in 1986 and 1987, the Sony Awards DJ of the Year. Founder member of BBC TV's *Breakfast Time* presenting team (1983–6). Other TV: *Speak Out; First AIDS; The Late, Late Breakfast Show; The Royal Tournament; The Royal Wedding; Trick Or Treat; That's Showbusiness;* Boat Shows; Motor Shows; own chat show on BSB from 1990. m. TV presenter Sarah Greene. Address: c/o Duncan Heath Assocs. Hobbies: motor racing, flying, sitting still. Pets: Kevin the carp. **Most Cherished Possession:** 'My Hard Rock (Cafe) Gold Card.' **Favourite Memory:** '21 June 1989 (wedding day).'

SMITH, Ray

Actor, b. 1 May 1936, Trealaw, Rhondda, Wales. Appeared in weekly rep, then *Hamlet; Woyzeck; What the Butler Saw; Pygmalion; The Dresser*. Films incl: *The Painted Smile; Under Milk Wood; Operation Daybreak; Rogue Male; Masada*. TV incl: *Country Matters; Sam; Like I've Never Been Gone; We'll Meet Again; Mill On the Floss; Little Lord Fauntleroy; Colditz; Dempsey and Makepeace; District Nurse*. Radio incl: numerous plays, poetry readings and stories for World Service; he was winner of the 1986 Sony Award for Best Actor. m. (dis.); 2 s. Branwen, Justin. Address: c/o Felix de Wolfe. Birthsign: Taurus. Hobbies: writing, gardening, DIY. **Most Cherished Possession:** 'Portrait of my father who died when I was a child.'

SMITS, Jimmy

Actor, b. July 1955, Manhattan, raised in Brooklyn, New York. His acting career took shape at Brooklyn College, Cornell University, where he received a Master's Degree in Theater, and at the New York Shakespeare Festival. Stage incl: *Hamlet; Ballad of Soapy Smith*. Films incl: *Running Scared; The Believers; Old Gringo*. TV incl: *Miami Vice; Rockabye* (TV movie); Victor Sifuentes in *L.A. Law*. m. with two children, Taina and Joaquin. Address: c/o STE Agency, 211 South Beverly Drive, Beverly Hills, CA 90212. Birthsign: Cancer. Hobbies: horseback riding, playing softball and basketball.

SPALL, Timothy

Actor, b. 27 February 1957, London. Trained at RADA where he was awarded the Bancroft Gold Medal. Stage incl: *Merry Wives of Windsor; Nicholas Nickleby; Knight of the Burning Pestle; Baal* (all with the RSC); *St Joan; Dauphin; Aunt Mary; Man Equals Man; To Kill a Priest*. Films incl: *The Missionary; The Bride; The Sinking of the Titanic; Predator; Gothic; Sheltering Skies*. TV incl: *Auf Wiedersehen, Pet; Brylcream Boys; Cotswold Death; Home Sweet Home; Three Sisters; Vanishing Army; Body Contact*. m. Shane; 2 d. Pascale, Mercedes, 1 s. Rafe. Address: c/o Markham & Froggatt, London. Birthsign: Pisces. Hobbies: strolling around London, bumping into old friends. Pets: two goldfish. **Most Cherished Possession:** 'My credit cards. I couldn't leave home without them.' **Favourite Memory:** 'Getting my first acting job.'

SPEAR, Bernard

Actor, Freeman of the City of London, b. 11 September 1919, London. Started showbusiness career in music halls and in cabaret. Film: *Yentl* (with Barbra Streisand). TV incl: *The Kelly Monteith Show; Never Mind the Quality, Feel the Width; The Lenny Henry Show; Target; Barmitzvah Boy; The Schoolmistress; Albion Market; 3-2-1*. m. Mary Logan; 1 s. Julian. Address: c/o London Management. Birthsign: Virgo. Hobbies: golf, cooking. **Most Cherished Possession:** 'Good health.' **Favourite Memory:** 'Meeting my wife in Great Newport Street rehearsal rooms. It changed everything – for the better.'

SPENDLOVE, Rob

Actor, b. 1 May 1953, London. Studied drama at Middlesex Polytechnic and was a teacher before setting up his own theatre company, touring London schools, then working in fringe and repertory theatre. Film: *Tai-Pan*. TV: *Strangers;* Roger Huntington in *Brookside; Lizzie's Pictures; Winds of War; Queenie;* starred as Rick Sneaden in *Closing Ranks; That's Love; Hard Cases;* Det Chris Tierney in *Tecx*. m. actress Sandy Hendrickse. Address: c/o Julian Belfrage Associates. Birthsign: Taurus.

SPINETTI, Victor

Actor, b. 2 September 1933, Cwm, South Wales. Trained at the Cardiff College of Music and Drama. Stage incl: *Expresso Bongo; Every Man In His Humour; The Hostage; Fings Ain't Wot They Used T'Be; Oh! What a Lovely War; Jesus Christ Superstar; Windy City.* As stage director, incl: *Deja Revue; Let's Get Laid; Yes, We Have No Pyjamas; In His Own Write* (co-author); *King Rat.* Films incl: all The Beatles' films; *The Taming of the Shrew; The Pink Panther; The Voyage of the Damned; The Attic; The Krays.* TV incl: *Two In Clover; Take My Wife; The Sea; SuperTed; The Paradise Club; Van Gogh.* Address: c/o Howes & Prior. Birthsign: Virgo. Hobbies: writing, talking. **Most Cherished Possession:** 'My health.' **Favourite Memory:** 'Opening night of the stage show *Oh! What a Lovely War* – so exciting!'

ST CLEMENT, Pam

Actress, b. 12 May 1942, Harrow-on-the-Hill, Middlesex. Trained at Rose Bruford College of Speech and Drama, and Rolle College, Devon. Stage incl: *Once a Catholic; I Am a Camera; Macbeth;* and RSC. Films incl: *Biggles; Scrubbers; The Bunker; Dangerous Davies; Hedda.* TV incl: *The Tripods; Partners In Crime; A Horseman Riding By; Ladykillers; Matilda's England; Enemy At the Door; Within These Walls; Bottle Boys; Shoestring; Shall I See You Now?;* Connie in *Play For Today: Not For the Likes of Us;* Pat Butcher in *EastEnders.* m. (dis.). Address: c/o Saraband Associates. Birthsign: Taurus. Hobbies: music, country life, watching films, sharing food, drink and conversation with friends, travelling at home and abroad. Pets: two dogs.

STABLEFORD, Howard

TV/radio presenter, b. 12 April 1959, Poynton, Cheshire. After graduating from Durham University he went into local radio in Lancashire and Northampton. TV incl: *Tomorrow's World;* various children's programmes. Address: c/o Dave Winslett Entertainments. Birthsign: Aries. Hobbies: rugby, scuba-diving, motorcyling, music. **Most Cherished Possession:** 'My decisive nature. No, my briefcase. No, no, I mean my mother . . .' **Favourite Memory:** 'Racing Formula 1 round the streets of Milton Keynes!'

STACY, Neil

Actor, b. 15 May 1941, Stowupland, Suffolk. Trained in Youth Theatre and Oxford University Dramatic Society. Recent stage incl: *The Second Mrs Tanqueray* (National); *A Patriot For Me;* (Chichester); *Holiday Snap* (Theatre of Comedy); *Canaries Sometimes Sing* (Albery); *Blithe Spirit* (The Lyric, Hammersmith). Recent TV incl: *To Serve Them All My Days; Shackleton; Fourth Arm; Strangers and Brothers; Nanny; Rumpole of the Bailey; Duty Free; Three Up, Two Down; Haggard.* Address: c/o Michael Whitehall. Birthsign: Taurus. Hobby: medieval history. **Favourite Memory:** 'The lines of whatever part I'm playing.'

STAFF, Kathy

Actress, b. 12 July 1928, Dukinfield, Cheshire. Started her career with a touring company in Scotland and then rep. Stage incl: two West End shows for Theatre of Comedy; *Two Into One* and *When We Are Married;* national tour of *The Rivals;* and various pantomimes. Films incl: *A Kind of Loving; The Dresser; The Family Way; Camille; Little Dorrit.* TV incl: *Coronation Street; Separate Tables; The Benny Hill Show; Crossroads; Open All Hours;* and as Nora Batty in *Last of the Summer Wine.* m. John; 2 d. Katherine, Susan. Address: c/o London Management. Birthsign: Cancer. Hobbies: choral singing, church work. **Most Cherished Possession:** 'My wedding ring because it binds me to my family.' **Favourite Memory:** 'Being the subject of *This Is Your Life.*'

STARDUST, Alvin

Singer/entertainer, b. 27 September, London, Bernard Jewry. Stage debut, aged five, in pantomime *Babes In the Wood*. At 17, joined a pop group and changed his name to Shane Fenton. With his group The Fentones, he toured Britain and Europe, and had hit singles. Changed his name to Alvin Stardust in the early Seventies. Hit singles incl: *My Coo-Ca-Choo; Jealous Mind; Good Love Can Never Die; I Feel Like Buddy Holly*. TV incl: *Let's Rock; Starlight Ballroom; The Rock Gospel Show; Countdown Apollo; It's Stardust*. Subject of *This Is Your Life*. Starred in national tour of *Godspell* and in Andrew Lloyd Webber–Tim Rice concept musical *Cricket*. m. (1st) Iris (dis.), (2nd) actress Liza Goddard (dis.), 2 s. Shaun, Adam (from 1st m.), 1 d. Sophie (from 2nd m.). Address: c/o Susan James Management. Hobbies: writing – has written several books – horse-riding.

STALLARD, Margaret

Actress, b. 30 April 1929, Birmingham. Trained at LAMDA and is also a capable dancer, including acrobatics. TV incl: *Emmerdale Farm; Juliet Bravo; Grange Hill; Last of the Summer Wine; Lovejoy; Divided We Stand;* Mrs Babbit in *Crossroads*. m. musician John Davis; 3 d. Caroline, Deborah and twins Miranda and 1 s. Benjamin. Address: c/o Actors Alliance, Bon Marché Building, 444 Brixton Road, London SW9 8EJ. Hobbies: dancing, swimming, sketching, music (mostly listening). Pet: ginger cat called Orlando. **Most Cherished Possession:** 'My family chamber music group – an incredible home-grown luxury.' **Favourite Memory:** 'The first time they played a Mozart flute quartet and I realised it had been worth putting up with all that practice.'

STANDING, John

Actor, b. 16 August 1934, London. Real name Sir John Leon, the fourth baronet. Acting in his family for seven generations (his mother was the actress Kay Hammond). After deciding he wasn't good enough to be an artist, he joined the RSC. London stage incl: *The Biko Inquest; Rough Crossing*. Films incl: *The Eagle Has Landed; The Elephant Man; The Sea Wolves*. TV incl: *Rogue Male; Tinker, Tailor, Soldier, Spy; The Other 'Arf; All the World's a Stage; The Young Visiters; L.A. Law; Chameleons; The Endless Game*. m. (1st) actress Jill Melford (dis.), (2nd) Sarah Forbes; 2 s. Alexander (from 1st m.), Archie, 2 d. India, Octavia (from 2nd m.). Address: c/o William Morris. Birthsign: Leo. Hobbies: painting, fishing. **Most Cherished Possession:** 'My family.' **Favourite Memory:** 'Watching Len Hutton bat.'

STEELE, Tommy, OBE

Actor, b. 17 December 1936, London. Was discovered while playing in The Two I's Coffee Bar in London. Within 10 weeks was a teenage idol. Stage incl: variety shows; pantomime; *She Stoops To Conquer; Half a Sixpence; The Servant of Two Masters; Meet Me In London; Hans Andersen; An Evening With Tommy Steele; Singin' In the Rain*. Films incl: *Half a Sixpence*. TV incl: *The Tommy Steele Show; Twelfth Night; In Search of Charlie Chaplin; A Special Tommy Steele; Tommy Steele and a Show; Quincy's Quest*. Book: *Quincy*. m. former dancer Ann Donoghue; 1 d. Emma. Address: c/o Isobel Davie. Hobbies: squash, painting. Birthsign: Sagittarius.

STENNETT, Stan, MBE

Comedian/actor, b. 30 July 1927, Pencoed, Mid-Glamorgan. First big break as resident comic on radio's *Welsh Rarebit*, then *Show Band* and *The Black and White Minstrels*. Film: *Possessions*. TV incl: *Stan At Ease; Road Show; The Good Old Days; Those Wonderful TV Times; The Golden Shot; Celebrity Squares; Top Town; Leeds United; What a Performance; Cries From a Watchtower;* a trilogy of plays written by his son, Roger, *1,2,3;* and the role of Sid Hooper in *Crossroads*. m. Elizabeth; 2 s. Roger, Ceri. Address: c/o George Bartram Associates. Birthsign: Leo. Hobbies: golf, flying, football. **Most Cherished Possession:** 'My guitar, trumpet, and clown outfit.' **Favourite Memory:** 'Playing the London Palladium for the first time.'

STEPHENSON, Pamela

Comedienne, b. 4 December, Auckland, New Zealand. Trained at the Australian National Institute of Dramatic Art. Came to England in 1976. Stage incl: *Not In Front of the Audience; The Pirates of Penzance;* plus her own one-woman shows, *Small But Perfectly Formed, Naughty Night Nurses Without Panties Down Under No 2* and *Shocking Behaviour.* Films incl: *History of the World, Part 1; The Secret Policeman's Other Ball; Superman III; Finders Keepers.* TV incl: *Not the Nine O'Clock News* (which won an Emmy and BAFTA Award, 1981); *Move Over Darling. Lost Empires;* and, in America, NBC's *Saturday Night Live; The Johnny Carson Show.* Lives with comedian Billy Connolly; 3 d. Daisy, Amy, Scarlett Layla Stephenson-Connolly. Hobbies: practical joker! Address: c/o John Reid Enterprises.

STEVENS, Ronnie

Actor/director, b. 2 September 1930, London. Trained at RADA and PARADA. Began in revue, his earliest success being *Intimacy At 8.30; For Amusement Only; The Lord Chamberlain Regrets.* Other stage incl: *King Lear; Twelfth Night; St Joan; Romeo and Juliet; The Government Inspector; 84 Charing Cross Road; The Gingerbread Man; HMS Pinafore;* and in 1988, *Easy Virtue.* Films incl: several of the Doctor series; *I'm All Right Jack; A Home of Your Own.* TV incl: *Twelfth Night; Cover Her Face; Margery and Men; Hi-de-Hi; Fresh Fields; Terry and June; Yes, Prime Minister.* m. Ann Bristow; 2 s. Paul, Guy. Address: c/o CDA. Birthsign: Virgo. Hobbies: painting, music, yoga. **Most Cherished Possession:** 'My family.'

STEWART, Alastair

ITN newscaster and correspondent, b. 22 June 1952, Emsworth, Hampshire. Began career with Southern ITV, now TVS, as a reporter. Joined ITN as Industrial Correspondent in 1980. Newscaster since 1982. Main presenter of *News At 5.40;* presenter of *News At Ten* since May 1989; ITN's Washington correspondent since January 1990. Reported and commentated on the Pope in Britain; royal weddings; first live TV from House of Lords; co-presented General Election special 1987. m. Sally; 1 s. Alexander, 1 d. Clementine. Address: c/o ITN. Hobbies: food, wine, reading, writing. **Most Cherished Possession:** 'The envelope to a love letter from my grandfather to grandmother, dated 10 November 1922.' **Favourite Memory:** 'Births of my two children, both of which I was present at.'

STEWART, Allan

Entertainer, b. 30 July 1950, Glasgow. He made his first record at the age of 10 and has been working the clubs, theatre and TV since he was 12. On stage he's appeared at the London Palladium and in Royal Shows as well as in summer seasons and pantomime. Has made many appearances for BBC Scotland, and has also had his own radio show. TV incl: five series for STV; *Copy Cats* (four series); *The Allan Stewart Tapes; Hello, Good Evening, Welcome; Go For It; Live From . . .; Chain Letters.* Address: c/o International Artistes. m. Jane; 1 s. David. Birthsign: Leo. Hobbies: watching TV, talking on the telephone, tennis. **Most Cherished Possession:** 'My new wife and baby.' **Favourite Memory:** 'Going round on the revolving stage in the finale on *Sunday Night At The London Palladium* in 1972.'

STILGOE, Richard

Presenter/writer/performer, b. 28 March 1943, Camberley, Surrey. A product of the Cambridge Footlights revue. Has since had wide experience in radio and TV incl: *A Class By Himself; Nationwide; And Now the Good News; That's Life!; Finders Keepers; Stilgoe's Around;* Royal Variety Performance, 1982. Wrote *Starlight Express* with Andrew Lloyd Webber. Plays 14 instruments, sings in opera and tours Britain with his one-man show. m. Annabel; 2 d. Jemima, Holly, 3 s. Rufus, Jack, Joe. Address: c/o Noel Gay Artists, London. Birthsign: Aries. Hobbies: sailing, DIY.

STOPPARD, Miriam, MB, BS, MD, MRCP

Doctor/medical reporter, b. 12 May 1937, Newcastle upon Tyne. Worked in clinical medicine, specialising in dermatology. Joined pharmaceutical industry, became research director. TV incl: *Where There's Life; The Health Show; So You Want To Stop Smoking*. Books incl: *Miriam Stoppard's Book of Babycare;* and *Book of Healthcare; The Face and Body Rock; Marks & Spencer Book of Babycare; Marks & Spencer Book of Childcare*. Also regular contributor to magazines. m. playwright Tom Stoppard; 2 step-s. Oliver, Barnaby, 2 s. William, Edmund. Address: c/o Yorkshire TV, Leeds. Birthsign: Taurus. Hobbies: family, gardening, photography. **Most Cherished Possession:** 'My garden because it's the only reliable source of tranquility.'

STOURTON, Edward

TV news reporter, b. 24 November 1957, Lagos, Nigeria. Joined ITN as graduate trainee in 1979. Has worked on *News At One; News At 5.40; News At Ten;* and has contributed to ITN specials incl: The Royal Wedding; The Papal Visit. Founder member of *Channel 4 News* team and has since been writer, Home News Editor, Chief Sub-Editor, reporter covering foreign and domestic news and specialist coverage of religious affairs. Washington correspondent, *Channel 4 News*, 1986–8; Paris correspondent, BBC TV, 1988–9; Diplomatic Editor, ITN, since January 1990. m. Margaret McEwen; 2 s. Ivo, Thomas, 1 d. Eleanor. Address: c/o ITN. Birthsign: Sagittarius. Hobbies: tennis, 19th-century novels.

STRACHAN, Michaela

Presenter, b. 7 April 1966, Ewell, Surrey. Took a three-year course in dance, drama and singing at the Arts Educational College, London, then went into pantomime. Theatre incl: *Seven Brides For Seven Brothers*, various pantomimes. TV: *Wide Awake Club; Wacaday; Wac Extra; The Hit Man and Her; OWL TV; But Can You Do It On TV?; Boogie Box* (for Music Box cable TV); guest presenter, *Freetime*. Pop singles: *Happy Radio* (London, 1989), *Take Good Care of My Heart* (London, 1990). Address: c/o Michael Ladkin. Birthsign: Aries. Hobbies: theatre, cinema, jogging. **Most Cherished Possession:** 'My convertible Herbie car (VW Beetle)!' **Favourite Memory:** 'The day I got my first TV job, on *Wide Awake Club*.'

STRAULI, Christopher

Actor, b. 13 April 1946, Harpenden, Herts. Trained at RADA before joining the Old Vic in Bristol in 1970. Has worked in rep, and West End appearances incl: *The Licentious Fly; Lover; Season's Greetings*. TV break came with the part of Bunny in *Raffles*. Other TV incl: *Harriet's Back In Town; Owen MD; Family At War; Warship; Angels; For Tea On Sunday; Gentle Folk; Measure For Measure; Romeo and Juliet; Only When I Laugh; Edward the Seventh; Eustace and Hilda; Dempsey and Makepeace; Lytton's Diary; Full House; A Crack In the Ice; Fortunes of War*. m. Lesley; 2 d. Belinda, Hanneli, 2 s. Barnaby, Dominic. Address: c/o Ellison Combe Assocs. Birthsign: Aries. Hobbies: DIY, computers, video, games, music, gardening, golf. **Most Cherished Possession:** 'My home.'

STREET-PORTER, Janet

Presenter/producer, b. 27 December 1946, London. Worked in newspaper journalism before moving to television. TV: presented *The London Weekend Show; Saturday Night People; Twentieth Century Box* (two series); *Around Midnight;* co-presenter of LWT's *The Six O'Clock Show;* producer *Paintbox* and *Bliss;* deviser *Get Fresh*. Winner of 1988 BAFTA originality award for *Network 7*. Head of Youth Programmes, BBC TV, since 1988, incl: *Reportage; A Rough Guide To the World; A–X of Belief; Behind the Beat; Smash Hits; Style Trial*. Books: *The British Teapot; Scandal!* m. (1st) Tim Street-Porter (dis.), (2nd) Tony Elliott (dis.), (3rd) Frank Cvitanovich (dis.). Address: c/o BBC TV. Hobbies: long walks. **Most Cherished Possession:** 'Ready wit.' **Favourite Memory:** 'Completing the coast-to-coast walk – 190 miles.'

STRIDE, John

Actor, b. 11 July 1936, London. Trained at RADA; professional debut at Liverpool Rep in 1957 before joining the army. On demob went to the Old Vic. Five years with the National Theatre before his TV break. Films incl: *Bitter Harvest; Brannigan; Macbeth; Juggernaut; The Omen; A Bridge Too Far.* TV incl: *The Main Chance; Lloyd George In Number 10; Klaus Barbie; Jumping the Queue; Chelworth.* m. actress April Wilding; 3 d. Philippa, Lindsay, Eleanor. Address: c/o Hatton & Baker. Birthsign: Cancer. **Most Cherished Possession:** 'A pair of cufflinks from Yugoslavia – I don't know why!' **Favourite Memory:** 'Stepping off a windsurf board into a warm sandy beach for the first time; because it was much better than falling off into the water as usual!'

STRONG, Gwyneth

Actress, b. 2 December 1959, London. Made stage debut in the Royal Court production of *Live Like Pigs,* at the age of 11. Other stage incl: *Shout Across The River; Heroes; Care; Sugar and Spice; Strangers In the Night; Glad Hand; Woyzeck; Loving Women; It's a Lovely Day Tomorrow; Inside Out, Paradise Postponed; King of the Ghetto; Only Fools and Horses.* Address: c/o Markham & Froggatt, London. Birthsign: Sagittarius. Hobbies: theatre, swimming, going on holiday! **Most Cherished Possession:** 'Any car that works – I love the freedom that driving has given me.' **Favourite Memory:** 'Happy romantic moments that have occurred over the last five years.'

STUART, Susanne

Actress, b. 29 September, New South Wales, Australia. Spent her early days in Sydney Theatre and was also a radio announcer. Stage incl: *Come Blow Your Horn.* TV incl: *The Young Doctors; People In Conflict; Beyond Reasonable Doubt.* m. (dis.); 2 children, Garth, Shahn. Address: c/o Central Casting, 169 Phillip Street, Sydney 2000, NSW, Australia. Birthsign: Libra. Hobbies: physical fitness, meditation. Pets: black cat called Petunia. **Most Cherished Possession:** 'Presents my children made for me.' **Favourite Memory:** 'Lying on the grass, blossoms falling on me, besides Chalice Well, Glastonbury, England – absolute peace!'

STUBBS, Una

Actress/dancer, b. 1 May 1937, London. Trained as a dancer and made her stage debut in *A Midsummer Night's Dream* at Windsor. Other stage incl: *The Knack; Cowardy Custard; Oh, Mr Porter; Baggage; Secret Life of a Cartoon.* Films incl: *Summer Holiday; Wonderful Life.* TV incl: *Cool For Cats; Till Death Us Do Part; Fawlty Towers; Worzel Gummidge; In Sickness and In Health; Happy Families; Worzel Gummidge Down Under; Morris Minor's Marvellous Motors.* m. (1st) actor Peter Gilmore (dis.), (2nd) actor Nicky Henson (dis.); 3 s. Jason, Christian, Joe. Address: c/o Richard Stone. Birthsign: Taurus. Hobbies: embroidery, driving. Pet: a robin, which wanders around the kitchen while she's cooking. **Most Cherished Possession:** 'My health.' **Favourite Memory:** 'A good day with the children.'

STUYCK, Joris

Actor, b. 23 April 1952, Orpington, Kent. Took part in many of the productions that were staged while he was studying at McGill University, Montreal, Canada. Stage incl: *The Normal Heart.* Films incl: *The Shooting Party; The Razor's Edge.* TV incl: *We'll Meet Again; Reilly Ace of Spies; A Woman of Substance; Tender Is the Night.* Address: c/o Kate Feast Management. Birthsign: Taurus. Hobbies: sailing, music, travel. **Most Cherished Possession:** 'My guitar, which is always sympathetic.' **Favourite Memory:** 'Saying goodbye to restaurant work for my first professional acting job.'

SUCHET, David

Actor, b. 2 May 1946, London. Trained at LAMDA. Has appeared on stage in many RSC productions. Films: *A Tale of Two Cities; The Hunchback of Nôtre Dame; The Trenchcoat; Master of the Game; Red Monarch; The Little Drummer Girl; The Falcon and the Snowman; Gulag; Song for Europe; Mussolini; Thirteen to Dinner; Murrow; Iron Eagle; Harry and the Hendersons; The Last Innocent Man; Why the Whales Came; A World Apart; Cripples/More Than a Touch of Sin.* TV incl: *Oppenheimer; The Last Day; Being Normal; The Life of Freud; Blott On the Landscape; The Muse; Playing Shakespeare; Ulysses; Cause Celebre; Once In a Lifetime; Bingo; Nobody Here But Us Chickens; Agatha Christie's Poirot.* m. actress Sheila Ferris; 1 s. Robert, 1 d. Kate. Address: c/o Brunskill Management. Birthsign: Taurus. Hobbies: photography, music, ornithology

SUCHET, John

ITN newscaster, b. 29 March 1944, London. Began career with Reuters, followed by the BBC. ITN's Washington correspondent, 1981–1983. As an ITN reporter he covered major news events, incl: Iran Revolution; Soviet occupation of Afghanistan; Phillipines Revolution. In 1986/87 he received the RTS TV Journalist of the Year award. m. (1st dis.), (2nd) Bonnie; 3 s. (1st m.) Damian, Kieran, Rory. Address: c/o ITN, London. Birthsign: Aries. Hobbies: classical music, photography. **Most Cherished Possession:** 'Two gold rings – one from my wife, one from my mother!' **Favourite Memory:** 'A poodle eating an apple – it changed my life.'

SUGDEN, Mollie

Actress, b. 21 July 1922, Keighley, Yorks. Trained at the Guildhall School of Music and Drama, and was made a Member. Spent eight years in rep. TV incl: *Hugh and I; Please Sir!; the Doctor* series; *For the Love of Ada; The Liver Birds; Coronation Street; Whodunnit?; Come Back Mrs Noah; That's My Boy; My Husband and I;* and perhaps her best-known role in *Are You Being Served?* m. William Moore; twin s. Robin, Simon. Address: c/o Joan Reddin. Birthsign: Cancer. Hobbies: cooking, gardening.

SULLIVAN, Dean

Actor, b. 7 June 1955, Liverpool. After leaving Lancaster University with B.Ed (Hons), taught for six years before becoming an actor. Professional debut at the Pitlochry Festival Theatre, 1984. Theatre incl: *On the Razzle; Cowardy Custard; Wild Oats;* Phil Redmond's *Soaplights; Road; The Northern Mystery Plays; Snow White; Babes In the Wood.* TV incl: presenter, *All I Want For Christmas;* Jimmy Corkhill in *Brookside* since 1986. Radio incl: BBC Radio 4 plays; Sam Jackson in BBC Radio Merseyside soap *The Merseysiders* since 1988. Formed the Liverpool Theatre Company in 1989 and has directed *The Importance of Being Earnest, Talent, Ghost Story* and *Hay Fever.* Address: c/o Brookside. Hobby: laughing. **Most Cherished Possession:** 'My PSION organiser – I'd be lost without it!' **Favourite Memory:** 'Carrying a spear the first time on stage in *Oedipus Rex!*'

SULLIVAN, Susan

Actress, b. 18 November, New York. Trained at American Academy of Dramatic Arts. Maggie Gioberti in *Falcon Crest.* Other TV incl: *Last Summer at Bluefish Cove* (play); *Swat; Julie Farr, MD; It's a Living; Having Babies; Rich Man, Poor Man; Taxi; The Incredible Hulk; Breaking Up Is Hard To Do; The New Maverick; The Ordeal of Dr Mudd.* Address: c/o Richard Grant, 8500 Wilshire Blvd, Suite 520, Beverly Hills, CA 90211. Birthsign: Scorpio. Hobbies: collecting art, literature, music, travel, skiing, charity work. **Most Cherished Possession:** 'My white Mercedes 450SL.' **Favourite Memory:** 'Dating Cary Grant when I was 22.'

SUMMERS, Jill

Actress/comedienne, b. 10 December 1910, Eccles, Lancashire. Was born into the profession. TV incl: *Summers Here; Castle Haven; How We Used To Live; Agatha; Stay With Me Till Morning; This Year, Next Year;* Phyllis Pearce in *Coronation Street; The Royal Variety Performance; This Morning; Wogan.* m. Dr C Simpson-Smith (dec.). Address: c/o Granada TV. Birthsign: Sagittarius. Hobbies: cooking, entertaining, travel. **Most Cherished Possession:** 'Good health – what can you do without it?' **Favourite Memory:** 'Joining the cast of *Coronation Street.*'

SWIFT, Clive

Actor, b. 9 February 1936, Liverpool. Started in rep at Nottingham before joining the Royal Shakespeare Company. Also directed at LAMDA and RADA. Films incl: *Excalibur; A Passage To India; Pack of Lies.* Many TV plays and series incl: *South Riding; Clayhanger; Roll On Four O'Clock; Waugh On Crime; Churchill; The Wilderness Years; Lucky Jim; The Barchester Chronicles; The Gentle Touch; Pickwick Papers; First Among Equals; Inspector Morse; Cause Celebre; A Very Peculiar Practice; Journey's End; Shelley; Othello.* Plus two books on acting. m. writer Margaret Drabble (dis.); 1 d., 2 s. Address: c/o PTA, Bugle House, 21a Noel Street, London W1V 3PD. Birthsign: Aquarius. Hobbies: music, The Actors' Centre. **Most Cherished Possession:** 'My flat near Lords cricket ground.' **Favourite Memory:** 'The birth of my daughter Rebecca, which I saw.'

SYKES, Eric

Comedian/writer, b. 4 May 1923, Oldham, Lancashire. Toured extensively with Jimmy Edwards in *Big Bad Mouse* and with his own show, *A Hatful of Sykes.* Films incl: *The Bargee; One Way Pendulum; Those Magnificent Men In Their Flying Machines; Rotten To the Core; Spy With a Cold Nose; The Plank* (scripted, directed and acted in); *Shalako; Monte Carlo Or Bust; Rhubarb; Theatre of Blood; Ghost in the Noonday Sun.* Radio scripts incl: *Educating Archie; Variety Bandbox;* own shows. TV incl: *Curry and Chips; Charley's Aunt; Mr H Is Late* (wrote, directed, starred); *The Nineteenth Hole.* Books: *Sykes of Sebastopol Terrace; The Great Crime of Grapplewick.* Freeman of the City of London. m. Edith Milbrandt; 3 d. Catherine, Susan, Julie, 1 s. David. Address: c/o 9 Orme Court, London W2. Hobby: golf.

SYMS, Sylvia

Actress, b. 6 January 1936, London. Trained at RADA and first play was *The Apple Cart* 1953. Much theatre experience incl: *The Vortex; Entertaining Mr Sloane; Ghosts.* Film debut in 1956 *My Teenage Daughter.* Other films incl: *Operation Crossbow; The Tamarind Seed; There Goes the Bride; Run Wild, Run Free.* TV credits incl: *My Good Woman* (with Leslie Crowther); *The Life of Nancy Astor; A Murder Is Announced; Time For Murder.* m. Alan Edney; 1 s. Benjamin, 1 d. Beatrice. Address: c/o Barry Brown. Birthsign: Capricorn. Hobbies: gardening, horse riding. **Most Cherished Possession:** 'A ring my husband gave me.' **Favourite Memory:** 'A weekend spent in Paris with my husband and children and their delight over a huge French meal.'

T, Mr

Actor, b. Chicago, Illinois. Born Lawrence Tureaud, he excelled in athletics and as a wrestling champion and football player. After serving as a military policeman, became a bodyguard. Best known for his role as BA (for Bad Attitude) Baracus in TV's *The A-Team.* Films incl: *Penitentiary; D C Cab; Rocky III.* Other TV incl: *Mr T; T and T.* 1 d. Lisa. Address: c/o Larry Soldinger, Blackman & Kallick, 300 Stn. Riverside Plaza, Chicago 60606. Birthsign: Gemini. Hobbies: working out, being with my children. **Most Cherished Possession:** 'My gold – enough to stock a warehouse.' **Favourite Memory:** '*The A-Team* – it made me a multi-millionaire, so it served its purpose.'

TALLIS, Sonja

Actress, b. 24 September 1943, Sydney, Australia. Graduated from Ensemble Studios and has appeared in many TV incl: *Young Doctors; Prisoner; Prime Time; Five Mile Creek; Butterfly Island; Sweet and Sour; A Kindred Spirit; Captives of Care; The Best of Friends.* Address: c/o Barbara Leane & Assocs, 261 Miller Street, North Sydney 2060 NSW, Australia. Birthsign: Libra. Hobby: painting. Pets: a cat and dog. **Most Cherished Possession:** 'The family photograph album – moments captured that cannot be replaced.' **Favourite Memory:** 'Seeing the house where my grandmother was born in Norway which had not changed it all since she lived there.'

TANDY, Donald

Actor, b. 20 December 1918, London. Spent 4 years as PoW and helped organise theatres and various shows. Then various rep in northern England and Wales. Early TV at Lime Grove and Ally Pally from Gillie Potter to Shakespeare. Theatre incl: *The Dish Ran Away; Biggest Thief In Town.* Films incl: *The Captive Heart; World of Suzy Wong; Jekyll and Hyde.* Best known as Tom Clement in *EastEnders; Timewatch.* m. Diana Buckland; 1 s. Timothy John. Address: c/o Hamilton & Sydney, 21 Goodge Street, London W1P 1FD. Birthsign: Sagittarius. Hobbies: walking, reading, music, occasional golf. Pets: a dog. **Most Cherished Possession:** 'Current good health and family.' **Favourite Memory:** 'After several unsuccessful attempts finally escaping in Czechoslovakia a week before VE Day, and joining Patton's army.'

TANDY, Mark

Actor, b. 8 February 1957, Athlone, Ireland. Started with the RSC where work included *Nicholas Nickleby.* Other theatre incl: *Major Barbara* for the National Theatre; *The Lucky Chance* at the Royal Court; *Beauty and the Beast* at the Old Vic, both for the Women's Playhouse Trust; *Siblings; Study In Scarlet.* Films incl: *Defence of the Realm; Captive;* Lord Risley in *Maurice; Wings of Fame.* TV incl: *Aubrey Beardsley; The Jewel In the Crown; Nicholas Nickleby; Gems; Murder Not Proven; Call Me Mister; Hedgehog Wedding; Catherine; Pulaski; Hannay; Inspector Morse; Vote For Hitler; Saracen; Gibraltar Inquest; Tygo Road; Portrait of a Marriage.* Address: c/o Julian Belfrage.

TANDY, Steven

Actor, b. 23 October 1952, Sydney, Australia. Graduate of National Institute of Dramatic Art. Theatre incl: *Juno and the Paycock; The National Health; Love For Love; Love's Labours Lost.* Translations; *Three Sisters; The Winter's Tale.* Films incl: *Jog's Trot; Gone Tomorrow.* TV incl: Tom Sullivan in *The Sullivans; Spyforce; Over There; All Rivers Run; Possession; Sons and Daughters.* Address: c/o ICS, 147A King Street, Sydney, Australia. Birthsign: Libra/Scorpio. Hobbies: music, golf, movies, reading, horse racing, tennis. **Most Cherished Possession:** 'A personal letter from Laurence Olivier received during my first visit to London in 1978.' **Favourite Memory:** 'Meeting Ingrid Bergman backstage at Haymarket Theatre and feeling the warmth of her smile.'

TARBUCK, Jimmy

Comedian/entertainer, b. 6 February, Liverpool. Started career at 18 as a compere with a rock 'n' roll show then as a Butlin's redcoat. Turned professional 1963 working in clubs in Liverpool and Manchester. TV debut 1963 *Comedy Bandbox.* Other TV incl: *Sunday Night At The London Palladium; It's Tarbuck; Tarbuck's Back; Winner Takes All; Live From Her Majesty's; Tarby and Friends; Bring Me Sunshine; This Is Your Life (1983); Live From The Palladium; Live From The Piccadilly; The Frame Game.* Books incl: *Tarbuck On Golf.* m. Pauline; 2 d. Lisa, Cheryl, 1 s. James. Address: c/o Peter Prichard. Birthsign: Aquarius. Hobbies: golf, football, all sports.

TARMEY, William

Actor, b. 4 April 1941, Manchester. Originally worked in the building trade while accepting singing engagements by night. TV: *Strangers; Crown Court; The Glamour Girls*; Jack Duckworth in *Coronation Street* since 1979, after several 'bit' parts in the serial. m. Alma; 1 s. Carl, 1 d. Sara. Address: c/o Granada TV. Birthsign:

TARRANT, Chris

TV/radio presenter/producer, b. 10 October 1946, Reading. Studied for Central Office of Information. ACTT Director Course Degree in English. Numerous TV incl: LWT's *Six O'Clock Show; Through the Keyhole; Blimp Over Britain; Hotline; Tiswas; OTT; Saturday Stayback; Blankety Blank; Punchlines; Give Us a Clue; Child's Play; Harty; PSI; Everybody's Equal; The Disney Christmas Special; Tarrant on TV*. Radio: host of Capital Radio's weekday breakfast show. Books: *Kens's Furry Friends; Fishfriars Hall*. m. (dis.); 3 d. Helen, Jennifer, Samantha. Address: c/o PVA. Hobby: fishing. **Most Cherished Possession:** 'A garage full of fishing tackle.'

TAYLEFORTH, Gillian

Actress, b. 14 August 1955, London. Trained as a secretary before taking up acting at evening classes with Anna Scher Theatre. First professional part in a BBC TV Play For Today. Film: *The Long Good Friday*. TV incl: *Zigger Zagger; The Rag Trade; Phyllis Dixie; Thunder Cloud; Little Girls Don't; Watch This Space; Hi-de-Hi; Big Jim and the Figaro Club; Sink Or Swim; On Safari; The Gentle Touch; EastEnders; Minder; Fast Hand*. Address: c/o Saraband Associates. Birthsign: Leo. Hobbies: dancing, keeping fit, reading, music, swimming, cooking, any sport. Pets: family dog. **Most Cherished Possession:** 'My Frank Sinatra and Fred Astaire records: they are brilliant!' **Favourite Memory:** 'When my nephew Jamie was born.'

TAYLOR, Benedict

Actor, b. 18 April 1960, London. Joined RSC as a child in 1969 worked with them on and off over 5 years. Theatre incl: *Winter's Tale; Man of Mode; Macbeth*, all with the RSC. Other theatre incl: *Peter Pan; In Praise of Rattigan; Semi Mode*. Films incl: *Say Hello To Yesterday; Watcher In the Woods; Far Pavilions; Last Days of Pompeii; First Modern Olympics; Black Arrow; Every Time We Say Goodbye; London Assurance*. TV incl: *The Other Woman; Union Castle; Mitch; Gentle Touch; Beau Geste; Jackanory; My Brother Jonathan; The Corsican Brothers; 13 At Dinner; 92 Grosvenor Street; A Perfect Spy; South Bank Show; Vanity Fair; The Facts of Life; Bergerac; The Dirty Dozen*. Address: c/o Hamper-Neafsey. Birthsign: Aries. Hobbies: fencing, climbing, diving, music, writing, painting.

TAYLOR, Gwen

Actress, b. 19 February 1939, Derby. Eight years as a bank clerk, before attending the E15 Acting School. Theatre incl: *Clouds; Ripen Our Darkness; Top Girls; Trumpets and Raspberries; The Maintenance Man; Light Up the Sky; The Guardsman*. TV incl: *Play For Today: The Land of Green Ginger; Rutland Weekend Television; Ripping Yarns; Sounding Brass; Only When I Laugh; Forever Young; Duty Free; Ties of Blood; Slip Up; Yes, Prime Minister; Colin's Sandwich; Sob Sisters; A Bit of a Do; Sauce For the Goose; Happy Christmas, I Love You*. Films: *Monty Python's Life of Brian; Richard's Things*. Lives with playwright Graham Reid. Address: c/o James Sharkey. **Most Cherished Possession:** 'Two terracotta replicas of standing stones from Ireland – benign influence.' **Favourite Memory:** 'Being a success as part of the cast of *Top Girls* in New York.'

TEALE, Owen

Actor, b. 20 May 1961, Swansea. Trained at the Guildford School of Acting. Theatre: *Cabaret; Charley's Aunt; Run For Your Wife; Waltzing Matilda; The Fifteen Streets; When She Danced; Comedy of Errors.* Films: The Unknown Soldier in *War Requiem.* TV: *The Mimosa Boys; Doctor Who; Knights of God; David Copperfield; One By One; The Bureaucracy of Love; Way Out of Order; Strife;* John O'Brien in *The Fifteen Streets;* Det Sgt Mike McCarthy in *Waterfront Beat;* Bentley Drummle in *Great Expectations.* m. actress Dilys Watling; 1 s. Ion-Rhys. Address: c/o William Morris. Birthsign: Taurus. Hobbies: golf, tennis, water sports. Pets: two Burmese cats. **Most Cherished Possession:** 'My house – it is very beautiful indeed.' **Favourite Memory:** 'Playing John O'Brien in *The Fifteen Streets* – I learned so much about myself.

TENNANT, Victoria

Actress, b. 30 September 1950, London, father theatrical agent Cecil Tennant, mother Russian prime ballerina Irina Baronova. Trained at Elmhurst Ballet School and Central School of Speech and Drama. Films: *The Ragman's Daughter; Nullpunkt; Sphinx; Strangers Kiss; All of Me; The Holcroft Covenant; Flowers In the Attic; Best Seller; Foolsmate; The Handmaid's Tale.* TV incl: *The Speckled Band; The Winds of War; Tales of the Unexpected; Dempsey; Chiefs; Funniest Guy In the World; Under Siege; George Burns Comedy Theatre; The Twilight Zone; Hitchcock; War and Remembrance; Maigret; Voice of the Heart; Tattingers; Act of Will.* m. (1st) Peppo Vanini (dis.), (2nd) comedian Steve Martin. Address: c/o Hatton & Baker. Birthsign: Libra.

TEWSON, Josephine

Actress, b. 26 February, London. Trained at RADA. Theatre incl: *The Real Inspector Hound; Habeas Corpus; Rookery Nook; Noises Off; Woman In Mind.* Film: *The Hound of the Baskervilles; Last of the Red Hot Lovers; The Reluctant Debutante; Spider's Web* (director); *Brighton Beach Memoirs* (director). Film: *Wilt.* On TV has been the fall for comedians incl: Ronnie Barker; Ronnie Corbett; Dick Emery; Jimmy Tarbuck; Bruce Forsyth; Les Dawson; Frankie Howerd; Charlie Drake. Other TV incl: *Lord Rustless Entertains; Son of the Bride; Odd Man Out; Shelley; Clarence.* m. (1st) the late actor Leonard Rossiter (dis.), (2nd) (dec.). Address: c/o International Artistes. Hobbies: watching cricket, music. **Most Cherished Possession:** '1970 Rover car belonged to my husband – it's so comfortable and a joy to drive.'

THAW, John

Actor, b. 3 January 1942, Manchester. Trained at RADA. Stage debut 1960 Liverpool Playhouse in *A Shred of Evidence.* London debut at Royal Court Theatre 1961 in *The Fire Raisers.* Recent theatres incl: *Henry VIII; Pygmalion.* Film debut: *The Loneliness of the Long Distance Runner.* Other films incl: *Sweeney; Sweeney 2; Cry Freedom.* TV incl: *Redcap; The Younger Generation; Thick As Thieves; The Sweeney; Drake's Venture; Killer Waiting; Mitch; Home To Roost; Inspector Morse; Bomber Harris.* m. (1st) Sally Alexander (dis.), (2nd) actress Sheila Hancock; d. Abigail (from 1st m.), Joanna (from 2nd m.). Address: c/o John Redway, London. Birthsign: Capricorn. Hobbies: music, reading.

THOMAS, Betty

Actress, b. 27 July, St Louis, Missouri. Started as a waitress, then joined the Second City Improvisational Theatre in Chicago. Films incl: *Loose Shoes; Used Cars; Tunnelvision; Jackson County Jail.* TV incl: Sgt Lucy Bates in TV's *Hill Street Blues;* for which she received an Emmy. Other TV incl: *Outside Chance; Nashville Grab.* Address: c/o Nancy Geller, ICM, 8899 Beverly Blvd, LA, Calif. 90048. Birthsign: Leo. Pets: two dogs. **Favourite Memory:** 'Performing with Chicago's famed Second City Comedy Troupe.'

THOMAS, Gareth

Actor. Trained at RADA and theatre experience at Yvonne Arnaud Theatre, Guildford; Liverpool Playhouse; Derby Playhouse; with the Royal Shakespeare Company and Welsh Actors Company; Theatre Royal, Windsor, English Shakespeare Company; *King Lear* at Northcott Theatre, Exeter. TV incl: *Stocker's Copper; How Green Was My Valley; Who Pays the Ferryman?; Blake's Seven; Hammer House of Horror; The Bell; The Citadel; Love and Marriage; Sherlock Holmes; Dog Food Dan and the Carmarthen Cowboy; By the Sword Divided; Morgan's Boy; Better Days; Chelworth; London's Burning.* Address: c/o Julian Belfrage Assocs, London.

THOMAS, Philip Michael

Actor, b. 26 May, Columbus, Ohio. Started career in off-Broadway and Broadway plays. Theatre incl: *Reggae; Selling of the President; Hair.* Films incl: *Stigma; Sparkle Book of Numbers; Coonskin.* TV incl: *This Man Stands Alone; Starsky and Hutch; Medical Center; Roots: The Next Generation; Police Woman; Wonder Woman.* Now best known for his role as Detective Ricardo Tubbs in TV's *Miami Vice.* Latest TV movie *Society's Child.* m. (dis.) 8 children (3 from 1st m.). Address: c/o Kate Porter, Exclusive Artists, 2501 West Burbank Blvd, Burbank, Calif 91505. Birthsign: Gemini. **Most Cherished Possession:** 'My home in Florida, it's Shangri-la.' **Favourite Memory:** 'Being cast in the musical *Hair*. I loved the show – especially the nude scene, I did it with relish.'

THOMPSON, Derek

Racing and sports presenter, b. 31 July 1950, Stockton, Co Durham. Presents racing on Channel Four and The Morning Line. Equestrian commentator, Sky TV. Racing correspondent for the Nottingham *Evening Post* and RTE of Ireland. Presenter of Ladbroke's Racing Service, daily into 1800 betting shops, and presenter of the *Daily Mail* Review of the Racing Year. Own hotline: (0898) 400606. m. Janie; 2 s. Alexander, James. Address: c/o Channel 4 Racing, LWT. **Most Cherished Possession:** 'My London Marathon medal – although how I ran 26 miles in 1984 seems unbelievable.' **Favourite Memory:** 'Riding Classified to victory at Plumpton racecourse in 1980 with HRH Prince of Wales in second place – I'll never get the MBE!'

THOMPSON, Jeremy

News correspondent, b. 1947. Joined ITN in 1982 as sports correspondent, after 11 years with the BBC as a radio and television correspondent. Covered major sports events worldwide, 1982–6, including 40 Test cricket matches, two Olympic Games, soccer's World Cup, rugby internationals, Wimbledon tennis, and golf's Ryder Cup and Open tournament. Appointed ITN's first Asia correspondent in October 1986, based in Hong Kong, reporting on a region stretching from Pakistan to Japan and Mongolia to New Zealand. ITN's main reporter covering the Queen's historic tour of China and the student uprising in Tiananmen Square. Based in London as a senior correspondent since January 1990. m. with 2 s. Address: c/o ITN.

THOMSETT, Sally

Actress, b. 3 April 1950, Sussex. Trained at drama school. Many theatrical tours and pantomimes. Film: *Straw Dogs.* TV appearances incl: *Railway Children; Man About the House;* many commercials. m. Claus Hede Nielsen. Address: c/o PVA. Birthsign: Aries. Hobbies: travel, stock market, working out, shopping, swimming. **Most Cherished Possession:** 'Very large stuffed lion, birthday present from Yootha Joyce and Richard O'Sullivan.' **Favourite Memory:** 'When the pilot for *Man About the House* entered the ratings at No. 2.'

THOMSON, Craig

Actor. While studying acting part-time, he worked in many jobs, including as an apprentice green keeper, a dustbinman and a labourer. Involved in amateur boxing for three years. Trained at the Australian Theatre For Young People. TV: Martin Dibble in *Home and Away*. Address: c/o Sydney Talent Company, PO Box 139, Seven Hills, NSW 2147, Australia.

THOMSON, Gordon

Actor, b. 2 March, Ottawa, Canada. Trained at the Shakespearian Festival, Ontario. Theatre incl: *Loot; The Fantasticks; King John; Godspell*. Films incl: *Explosion; Leopard In the Snow; Acts of Love; The Intruder*. Well known on TV for his portrayal of Adam Carrington in *Dynasty*. Other TV incl: *Flappers; Fantasy Island; After Nine* (TV-am); *Ryan's Hope*. m. Maureen (dis.). Address: c/o William Morris Agency, 151 El Camino Drive, Beverly Hills, Calif 90212. Hobbies: cooking, gardening, reading. Pets: two dogs, Jack and Lilly. **Most Cherished Possession:** 'My books. I rarely dated as teenager and wasn't athletic – my books were my best friends.' **Favourite Memory:** 'Spending my last dollars on a bottle of champagne. I did it often when I was a penniless, struggling actor.'

THORNE, Angela

Actress, b. 25 January 1939, Karachi, Pakistan. Trained at the Guildhall School of Music and Drama. Made her London debut in *You Never Can Tell* at the Haymarket Theatre 1966. Other theatre incl: *The Rivals; The Merchant of Venice; Prometheus Bound; The Golden Age; Yahoo; Anyone For Denis?; Happy Family; London Assurance*. TV incl: *Take a Saphire; The Canterville Ghost; That Was the Week; Ballet Shoes; Horizon; To the Manor Born; The Demon Lover; Paying Guests; Farrington of the F O; Three Up Two Down*. m. Peter; 2 s. Rupert, Laurence. Address: c/o Michael Whitehall. Hobbies: reading, sewing. Pets: one dog, one cat. **Most Cherished Possession:** 'A china tray given to me on the 1st night of *You Never Can Tell* by Sir Ralph Richardson – it was a very special turning point.'

THRELFALL, David

Actor, b. 12 October 1953, Manchester. Trained at Manchester Polytechnic School of Theatre. Many theatre credits incl: *Bed of Roses; Not Quite Jerusalem*. With the Royal Shakespeare Company incl: *Julius Caesar; Nicholas Nickleby; The Party*. Films: *When the Whales Come; The Russia House*. TV incl: *Scum; The Kiss of Death; Red Monarch; Rolling Home; The Gathering Seed; Nicholas Nickleby; Dog Ends; King Lear* (Olivier's); *The Daughter-in-Law; Paradise Postponed; The Marksman; Jumping the Queue; Murders Among Us; Casualty of War; Nightingales*. Address: c/o James Sharkey. Birthsign: Libra; Hobby: 'Keeping fit.' **Favourite Memory:** 'My father.'

THROWER, Debbie

Journalist/TV presenter, b. 17 November 1957, Nairobi, Kenya. Studied at Kings College, London University (French BA Hons). Worked as a reporter on *South London Guardian; Lynn News and Advertiser;* Radio Leicester. Moved to Radio Solent, where she worked as a producer, then to BBC TV South as a reporter/presenter on *South Today;* then reporter BBC TV News and newsreader. Now freelance. Programmes: *Hospital Watch; You and Yours; Coast To Coast; Songs of Praise; The Thrower Report*. m. Peter. Address: c/o BBC TV. Birthsign: Scorpio. Hobbies: cooking, swimming and travelling. Pets: two Siamese cats and a labrador. **Most Cherished Possession:** 'A huge collection of photo albums.' **Favourite Memory:** 'Can't remember – that's why I need the photo album.'

TILBURY, Peter

Actor/scriptwriter, b. 20 October 1945, Redruth, Cornwall. Started as assistant stage manager and actor at Chelmsford rep. Later with Welsh Drama Company, Royal Shakespeare Company and National Theatre as actor. Films incl: *Our Day Out; Breaking Glass; Those Glory, Glory Days.* TV incl: *The Expert; Perils of Pendragon; Dixon of Dock Green; My Son Reuben; Diamond Cracked Diamond; Whodunnit?; C.A.T.S. Eyes; Miss Marple; Fortunes of War; First Born; Casualty, This Is David Lander; The Bill.* As writer TV incl: *Sprout* (with Anthony Matheson); *Sorry, I'm a Stranger Here Myself; Shelley; It Takes a Worried Man* (in which he starred). Address: c/o Jill Foster. Birthsign: Libra. Hobbies: music, Art Deco. **Most Cherished Possession:** 'My word processor because it saves the all night type of scripts!'

TODD, Bob

Character actor, b. 15 December 1923, Faversham, Kent. A cattle breeder whose business failed at the age of 42. Turned to acting and made his TV debut 1963 in *Citizen James.* Been foil to top comics incl: Dick Emery; Marty Feldman; Michael Bentine; Des O'Connor; Benny Hill. Film: *The Return of the Three Musketeers.* TV series: *In For a Penny.* Other TV incl: *What's On Next?; Allan Stewart Show; The Generation Game; Steam Video Show; Rhubarb; Give Us a Clue; This Is Your Life.* m. Monica; 1 d. Anne, 2 s. Patrick, John. Address: c/o International Artistes. Birthsign: Sagittarius. Hobbies: keeping horses and preserving the countryside. Pets: two dogs, Jenny and Lucy. **Most Cherished Possession:** 'My wife and family.' **Favourite Memory:** 'Getting married 44 years ago.'

TODD, Richard

Actor, b. 11 June 1919, Dublin. Trained at Italia Conti School and made his debut in 1936. Founder member of Dundee Rep Co. From 1948 to 1965 worked mostly in films including *Robin Hood; The Dam Busters; The Longest Day.* Later films incl: *The Big Sleep; Jenny's War.* Numerous theatre appearances incl: *An Ideal Husband; Dear Octopus; Sleuth; Equus; The Business of Murder.* In 1970 formed Triumph Theatre Productions. TV incl: *Wuthering Heights; The Brighton Mesmerists; Boy Dominic.* Awarded Hollywood Golden Globe, Best Actor Oscar nomination and British national film award for *The Hasty Heart.* m. (1st) Catherine Grant-Bogle, (2nd) Virginia Mailer; 1 s. Peter, 1 d. Fiona (from 1st m.), 2 s. Andrew, Seumas (from 2nd m.). Address: c/o Richard Stone. Hobbies: shooting, farming, gardening. Pets: two labradors.

TRAVANTI, Daniel J

Actor, b. 7 March, Kenosha, Winsconsin. Trained at Yale Drama School and Bucks County Playhouse. Theatre incl: *Who's Afraid of Virginia Woolf?; Othello; Twigs; The Taming of the Shrew.* TV films incl: *A Case of Libel; Adam; Aurora; Murrow; Midnight Crossing; Millenium.* Plays Captain Frank Furillo in TV's *Hill Street Blues,* two Emmys as outstanding lead actor in a drama series. Is also a regular cast member of *General Hospial.* TV guest roles incl: *The Defenders; Route 66; Kojak; The FBI; Hart To Hart; Knots Landing.* Address: c/o William Morris Agency, 151 El Camino Drive, Beverly Hills, CA 90212. Hobbies: cooking, sports. Pets: two dogs and two cats. **Favourite Memory:** 'Winning Fellowship to Yale School of Drama.'

TREACHER, Bill

Actor, b. 4 June, London. Trained at Webber Douglas Academy of Dramatic Art. West End debut in 1963 in *Shout For Your Life.* On TV is best known as Arthur Fowler in *EastEnders.* Other TV incl: *Bless This House; The Professionals; Angels; Maggie and Her; Grange Hill; Fanny By Gaslight; Sweet Sixteen.* m. actress Kate Kessey; 1 s. Jamie, 1 d. Sophie. Address: c/o BBC TV, Elstree. Birthsign: Gemini. Hobbies: sailing, reading. Pets: Toto the dog and Lizzie the cat. **Most Cherished Possession:** 'I don't cherish possessions, but I'm rather fond of my car!' **Favourite Memory:** 'Apart from my wedding, the day I was demobbed – I could get on with my life.'

TREVES, Frederick

Actor, b. 29 March 1925, Cliftonville, Margate. Served in Merchant Service and Royal Navy. National Theatre work incl: *Coriolanus*. Films incl: *The Elephant Man; Defence of the Realm*. TV incl: *The Cherry Orchard; Country; A Flame to the Phoenix; The Last Viceroy; My Brother Jonathan; Silas Marner; Bratt Farrar; Strangers and Brothers; The Jewel In the Crown; Wynne and Penkovsky; The Good Doctor Bodkin Adams; The Man Eaters of Kumaon; Game, Set and Match; Shadow On the Sun; Death of a Son; Rumpole of the Bailey; Gentlemen and Players; Bomber Harris; Summer's Lease; Paper Mask*. m. Margaret Jean; 2 s. Frederick Simon, Patrick Conwyn, 1 d. Jennet Sarah. Address: c/o April Young. Hobbies: walking, reading, gardening.

TROUGHTON, David

Actor, b. 9 June 1950, Hampstead, London. Had no formal training. Theatre incl: *Terra Nova* (Watford); *A Midsummer Night's Dream, The Rover, Macbeth, Everyman In His Humour* (RSC); *Fool For Love, Don Juan* (National Theatre). Films incl: *Dance With a Stranger; The Chain*. TV incl: *David Copperfield; Our Mutal Friend; Chips With Everything; Wings; Man of Destiny; Molière; The Norman Conquests; Tales of Sherwood Forest; A Very Peculiar Practice*. m. Alison Groves; 3 s. Sam, Jim, William. Address: c/o David White. Birthsign: Gemini. Hobbies: real tennis, cricket, swimming. **Most Cherished Possession:** 'The washing-up machine. I can't stand washing up!' **Favourite Memory:** 'Bowling figures of 9-27 on a good batting wicket!'

TROUGHTON, Michael

Actor, b. 2 March 1955, Hampstead, London. Began as acting ASM at the Arts Theatre. Then Watford, Young Vic and Leeds Playhouse. Theatre incl: *Hay Fever*. RSC tour with *Taming of the Shrew* and a musical *Happy End*. TV incl: *Backs To the Land; The Mill On the Floss; A Moment In Time; Nancy Astor; A Fatal Spring; Night Life; Grudge Fight; Sorrell and Son; A Crack In the Ice; Minder; C.A.T.S. Eyes; Boon*. m. Caroline Rake; 1 s. Matthew, 1 d. Sally. Address: c/o Joseph & Wagg, 78 New Bond Street, London W1Y 9DA. Hobbies: collecting old toys, model-making, golf, gardening. **Most Cherished Possession:** 'My wife and children, if possessions is the right word!' **Favourite Memory:** 'Meeting my wife as she was my make-up lady for *Testament of Youth*.'

TUCKER, Michael

Actor, b. Baltimore, Maryland. Studied at Carnegie Tech Drama School and Arena Stage in Washington DC. Theatre incl: *Comedy of Errors; Waiting For Godot; Modigliani; The Rivals; Mother Courage*. Films incl: *A Night Full of Rain; Radio Days; The Purple Rose of Cairo; An Unmarried Woman; Tin Men; The Eyes of Laura Mars; Diner; Checking Out*. TV incl: *Assault and Matrimony; Vampire; The Quinns; Concealed Enemies; Hill Street Blues*. Stuart Markowitz in *L.A. Law*. m. Jill Eikenberry (2nd m.); 1 d. Alison (1st m.), 1 s. Max (2nd m.). Address: c/o Writers and Artists Agency, 11726 San Vicente Blvd, Suite 300, LA, CA 90049. Hobbies: golf, tennis, skiing. **Favourite Memory:** 'As a child I would accompany my father on business trips to New York and see a show or two. My love affair with the stage began.'

TULLY, Susan

Actress, b. 20 October 1967, Highgate, London. Training of Anna Scher Theatre, London. Theatre incl: *A Little Like Drowning*. TV incl: *Our Show; Saturday Banana; Why Can't I Go Home?; Never Never Land; Grange Hill*; plays Michelle in *EastEnders*. Address: c/o Saraband Assocs. Birthsign: Libra. Hobbies: cinema, theatre, tapestry, music. **Most Cherished Possession:** 'My bits and bobs box. Memorabilia personal and professional.' **Favourite Memory:** 'Telephone call from my dad in 1978 telling me my sister Linda, had been born.'

URE, Gudrun

Actress, b. 12 March 1926, Campsie, Scotland. Began in broadcasting while still at school. Joined the Children's Theatre, before moving to Glasgow's Citizens' Theatre. Has worked at the Bristol and London Old Vic, Edinburgh Festival, Royal Court. Theatre incl: *Othello; Comedy of Errors; The Kingfisher; Something Unexpected.* Films incl: *Doctor In the House; Million Pound Note; Thirty-Six Hours.* Much radio experience, incl. *Agatha Christie's Unexpected Guest.* TV incl: *Nanny; Supergran; Doctor Finlay's Casebook; Sutherland's Law; Going Holliday.* m. John. Address: c/o French's. Birthsign: Pisces. Hobbies: art galleries, the theatre. **Favourite Memory:** 'As a child, seeing a vase of orange blossoms in the sitting room.'

USTINOV, Peter

Actor/producer/director/novelist/playwright, b. 16 April 1921, London. Trained at London Theatre School. Theatre appearances incl *Beethoven's Tenth*, which he also wrote and directed. Films incl: *Memed My Hawk* (also directed); *Evil Under the Sun; Ashanti.* TV incl: *The Life of Samuel Johnson* (Emmy award); *Barefoot In Athens* (Emmy award); *The Well Tempered Bach* (Emmy nomination); *Peter Ustinov's Russia; Peter Ustinov In China; Around the World In 80 Days.* Books incl; *Dear Me; My Russia; The Disinformer.* Writer of 23 plays. Records incl: *The Little Prince; Peter and the Wolf.* m. (3rd) Helene Du Lau D'Allemans; 3 d. Tamara (from 1st m.), Pavla, Andrea, 1 s. Igor (all from 2nd m.). Address: c/o J Y Publicity. Hobbies: cars, sailing, records. Pets: one English sheepdog.

VALENTINE, Anthony

Actor, b. 17 August 1939, Blackburn, Lancashire. Trained at the Valery Glynne Stage School. Debut at 10 in the film, *No Way Back*. As child actor, stage incl: two seasons at Sadler's Wells Opera; *Anniversary Waltz; Two Stars For Comfort; Sleuth; Half a Sixpence.* TV incl: *Vice Versa; Children of the New Forest; Rex Milligan; Billy Bunter.* As an adult, films incl: *Damned; To the Devil a Daughter; Murder Is Easy; Escape To Athens; Masada.* TV incl: *An Age of Kings; The Donati Conspiracy; Colditz; Raffles; The Dancing Years; Tales of the Unexpected; Minder; Robin of Sherwood; Dangerous Corner; The Fear.* m. Susan Skipper. Address: c/o London Management. Birthsign: Leo. Hobbies: squash, boardsailing, skiing, photography.

VAUGHAN, Norman

Entertainer, b. 10 April 1927, Liverpool. Stage debut aged 14 with a boys' troupe. At 15 formed his own trio, *The Dancing Aces*, and toured until the war. Army shows with Harry Secombe, Spike Milligan and Ken Platt. Theatre incl: *There Goes the Bride; Strippers; Calamity Jane; Boeing-Boeing; Play It Again, Sam; The Happy Apple; The Tempest; No, No, Nanette; Once More Darling; Wizard of Oz; Love At a Pinch; A Bedful of Foreigners; No Sex Please, We're British;* plus pantos and summer seasons. TV incl: Compere of *Sunday Night At The London Palladium; The Golden Shot;* and many guest appearances and quiz shows. m. ex-dancer Bernice; 1 s. David. Address: c/o Richard Stone, London. Birthsign: Aries. Hobbies: driving, reading, golf.

VAUGHAN, Peter

Actor, b. 4 April 1924, Shropshire. Joined Wolverhampton Rep after school. Theatre incl: *Entertaining Mr Sloane; Portrait of a Queen; Season's Greetings; The Overgrown Path.* Films incl: *Twist of Sand; The Naked Runner; The Bofors Gun; Hammerhead; Alfred the Great; Straw Dogs; The Man Outside; Death In Rome; The Mackintosh Man; Valentine; Zulu Dawn; The French Lieutenant's Woman; The Razor's Edge; Forbidden; Brazil; Mountains of the Moon; King of the Wind.* TV incl: *The Gold Robbers; Oliver Twist; Great Expectations; Citizen Smith; Winston Churchill – The Wilderness Years; Bleak House; Codename Kyril; Porridge; Monte Carlo; Sins; The Bourne Identity; War and Remembrance; Countdown To War.* m. (1st) actress Billie Whitelaw (dis.), (2nd) actress Lillias Walker; 1 s. David (from 2nd m.). Address: c/o ICM.

VERNON, Richard

Actor, b. 7 March 1925, Reading, Berkshire. Trained at the Central School of Speech and Drama. Theatre incl: *Peter Pan; Any Other Business?; Hay Fever; Saturday, Sunday, Monday; The Passion of Dracula; Pack of Lies*. Films incl: *The Human Factor; Gandhi; Evil Under the Sun; Lady Jane; A Month In the Country*. TV incl: *Man In Room 17; Sextet; Sarah; Upstairs, Downstairs; The Duchess of Duke Street; Ripping Yarns; Suez; The Sandbaggers; The Hitch-Hiker's Guide To the Galaxy; Something In Disguise; Nanny; Waters of the Moon; Roll Over Beethoven; Paradise Postponed; The Return of the Antelope; Yes, Prime Minister; A Gentleman's Club*. 1 d. Sarah, 1 s. Tom. Address: c/o Julian Belfrage Assoc, London. Birthsign: Pisces. Hobby: sailing. **Most Cherished Possession:** 'My boat.'

VEZEY, Pamela

Actress, b. 19 September, Bath. Trained at Bristol Old Vic Theatre School and then with the company and at various reps incl: Watford, Guildford, Farnham, Edinburgh, Exeter, Richmond, Coventry, Birmingham, Windsor. Other theatre incl: *The Pyjama Game; The Ha-Ha*. TV incl: *The Common* (Play Of the Month); *Billy Liar; Grange Hill; Sounding Brass; Crossroads*. Address: c/o Howes & Prior. Birthsign: Virgo. Hobbies: reading, walking.

VILLIERS, James

Actor, b. 29 September 1933, London. After two years at RADA he spent a season at Stratford-on-Avon before his West End debut in *Toad of Toad Hall* in 1954. Then spent two years with the Old Vic in England and America and a year with the English Stage Company. Theatre incl: *Write Me a Murder; Henry IV; The White Devil; The Way of the World; Saint Joan; The Burglar; The Doctor's Dilemma*. Films incl: *The Amazing Mr Blunden; For Your Eyes Only; King and Country; Under the Volcano; Nothing But The Best*. TV incl: *Fortunes of War; The First Churchills; The Other 'Arf; Lady Windermere's Fan; Pygmalion*. Address: c/o Duncan Heath. Birthsign: Libra. Hobby: watching sport. Pets: one spaniel. **Most Cherished Possession:** 'Lucinda, because she is beautiful.'

VINE, David

Sports commentator/interviewer/presenter/consultant, b. 3 January 1936, Barnstaple, Devon. Started on local weekly newspaper, then writer and news/sports interviewer for Westward TV 1962, then BBC 1966. Specialises in equestrian sport, winter sports and bowls. TV incl: *The Superstars*; commentaries for the Olympic Games, Commonwealth Games, Horse of the Year Show, World Ski Cup, Wimbledon Tennis Championships. m. Mandy. Address: c/o BBC TV. Birthsign: Capricorn. Hobby: taking time off. Pets: two dogs, 35 Japanese Koy Carp. **Most Cherished Possession:** 'Mandy.' **Favourite Memory:** 'Our last holiday – repeat needed soon!'

VINE, John

Actor, b. 20 February 1951, Banbury, Oxfordshire. Trained at the Bruford College of Speech and Drama and has since worked in rep, fringe and revue theatres, and London's West End. Films incl: *Richard's Things; Gandhi; Eureka; The Keep*. TV incl: *Knights of God; Bust; Moneymen; Seven Dials Mystery; Kings Royal; Kate the Good Neighbour; Death Of An Expert Witness; Shroud For a Nightingale; Cover Her Face; Murder Not Proven; QED; Not a Penny More; The Franchise Affair; Rockliffe's Folly; Boon*. m. Alex; 2 s. Tom, Oliver. Address: c/o Jeremy Conway, London. Birthsign: Pisces. Hobbies: comedy writing, all sports and games, especially snooker. **Most Cherished Possession:** 'Not really a possession, I know, but it's my family!' **Favourite Memory:** 'I'm afraid it's quite unprintable!'

VORDERMAN, Carol

Presenter/writer, b. 24 December 1960, Bedford. Gained an MA (Cantab) Honours degree in engineering from Cambridge University. Worked as an engineer for a couple of years, then as statistician on *Countdown*. Began on TV as the first woman on C4 on 2 November 1982 on *Countdown*. Other TV incl: *Take Nobody's Word For It; Software Show; Through the Keyhole; Wide Awake Club; Book Tower; So We Bought a Computer; Power Base; Search Out Science; Postcards From Down Under; Drive My Car*. Address: c/o Jon Roseman Associates. Birthsign: Capricorn. Hobbies: flying, swimming, dance, computers, puzzles, science.

VOSBURGH, Tilly

Actress, 17 December 1960, London. Theatre incl: *Landmarks; Outskirts; Raspberry; Strange Fruit; Johnny Oil 2; The Hungry Ghosts; Last Summer In Chulimsk; Touch and Go; Up Against It; The Lower Depths; Soul Night/Please and Thank You; My Sister In This House*. Films: *The Pirates of Penzance; The Missionary;* Un in *Erik the Viking*. TV: *Two People; Starting Out; Maria Martin; Minder; The Victoria Wood Show;* Ruby in *Hold the Back Page; Treatment; File On Jill Hatch; Tears Before Bedtime;* director Mike Leigh's *Film On Four Meantime; You'll Never See Me Again; Raspberry; The Function Room;* Hanna in *Strong Poison;* Debbie in the *Screen 2* film *Will You Love Me Tomorrow; The Bill; A Perfect Spy; Radical Chambers; Agatha Christie's Poirot*. Address: c/o Annette Stone Associates.

VROOM, Peter

Actor, b. 5 October 1968, Tamworth, Australia. After leaving school in 1986, he worked as a motor mechanic, then a deckhand on a ferry. Joined the Australian Theatre For Young People and appeared in amateur plays. TV incl: Lance Smart in *Home and Away*. Address: c/o Seven Network, TV Centre, Mobbs Lane, Epping, NSW 2121, Australia.

WADDINGTON, Bill

Comedian/character actor/after-dinner speaker, b. 10 June 1916, Oldham, Lancashire. Started in variety and concert party and has starred in every variety theatre in Britain. First radio broadcast 1940. First TV 1946 with Margaret Lockwood. Plays Percy Sugden in TV's *Coronation Street*. Other TV incl: *Talent; Family at War; Fallen Hero; Second Change*. m. (dec.); 2 d. Barbara Denise. Address: c/o Granada TV, Manchester. Birthsign: Gemini. Hobby: breeding thoroughbred racehorses. **Most Cherished Possession:** 'The small woollen figure – my mascot – made by my late wife when we first me.' **Favourite Memory:** 'Being honoured by selection for the Royal Variety Performance in 1965, and, more recently, *This Is Your Life*.'

WALDHORN, Gary

Actor, b. 3 July 1943, London. Trained at Yale University Drama School. Theatre incl: The National at the Old Vic; *Sleuth* (Australia, New Zealand and the West End); *Waiting For Godot; Two; Good; Joe Egg; Turning Over; Crime and Punishment*. Films incl: *Zeppelin; The Chain; Escape To Victory; Sir Henry At Rawlinson End*. TV incl: *Outside Edge; All For Love; Love and Marriage; After Pilkington; Minder; Mr Palfrey of Westminster; Brush Strokes; Drummonds*. m. (dis.); 1 s. Joshua. Address: c/o London Management. Birthsign: Cancer. Hobbies: snooker, tennis, travelling. **Most Cherished Possession:** 'A kilim rug – artistry, craftsmanship and colour.' **Favourite Memory:** 'The birth of my son – an awe-inspiring and humbling experience.'

WALKER, Roy

Comedian/entertainer, b. 31 July, Belfast. Boy soprano at 14 with the Francis Langford Choir. After National Service, worked as a comedian and straight man in Belfast. In 1969, moved to Britain, entertaining in Northern clubs. Shot to fame in the ITV talent show *New Faces* (1977). Other TV incl: *Licensed For Singing and Dancing; Live From Her Majesty's; Des O'Connor Tonight; Live From The Palladium; Wogan; The Russ Abbot Show; The Laughter Show; The Paul Daniels Show; The Comedians*; hosted *Summertime Special*; host of quiz show *Catchphrase*. Many pantomime appearances. m. Jean (dec.), 1 d. Joanne, 2 s. Mark, Phil. Address: c/o Mike Hughes Entertainments. Hobbies: golf, keeping fit.

WALLER, David

Actor, b. 27 November 1920, Street, Somerset. Trained under Eileen Thorndike at the Embassy School of Acting. Rep before and after the war, then Old Vic 1951–53 and 1957–58. Joined RSC 1964 and is an associate artist. Author of play *Happy Returns*. Films incl: *Work Is a Four Letter Word; Perfect Friday; Lady Jane*. TV incl: *Rumpole of the Bailey; All Passion Spent; Hannay; Edward and Mrs Simpson; Airport Chaplain; Waxwork; Enemy At the Door; The Tempest; Cribb; The Brack Report; PQ17; The Pickwick Papers; Shadowlands; The Woman He Loved*. m. Elisabeth Vernon. Address: c/o Peters Fraser & Dunlop Ltd, London. Birthsign: Sagittarius. Hobbies: gardening, cooking, painting.

WALLER, Kenneth

Actor, b. 5 November 1927, Huddersfield, Yorkshire. After National Service in the RAF, began career at Huddersfield Theatre Royal. West End debut at Savoy Theatre 1957 in *Free As Air*. Other West End theatre incl: *Salad Days; The Importance of Being Earnest*. Films incl: *Room At the Top; Scrooge; Chitty Chitty Bang Bang; Fiddler On the Roof*. TV incl: *Bread; Are You Being Served?; All Creatures Great and Small; Doctor Who; Big Deal; Coronation Street*. Address: c/o Hamilton & Sydney, 21 Goodge Street, London W1P 1FD. Hobbies: music (plays piano and organ), choral singing, playing bridge. **Most Cherished Possession:** 'My gramophone record collection.' **Favourite Memory:** 'Running down from the top of Snowdon in a thunderstorm and diving into the icy-cold Lyn Ogwen.'

WALLING, Mike

Actor/writer, b. 8 July 1950, Salford, Lancashire. Former English teacher. After working in a comedy double act, became an actor in 1977. Films incl: *Pirates of Penzance; The Disappearance of Harry*. TV incl: *Just Liz; Slimming Down; Badger By Owl-Light; Round and Round; Bootle Saddles; Brush Strokes*. He also writes for TV and has contributed to: *Relative Strangers; Me and My Girl; Valentine Park*; and with Tony Millan has written for two series, *A Small Problem* and *Not with a Bang*. Address: c/o Daly Gagan Assocs. Birthsign: Cancer. Hobby: watching Fulham RLFC. **Most Cherished Possession:** 'Dog Food's live double album, because it's signed by every member of the band.'

WALTERS, Julie

Actress, b. 22 February 1950, Birmingham. Stage debut in *The Taming of the Shrew*, Liverpool. Recent theatre incl: *When I Was a Girl; Jumpers; Fool For Love; Frankie and Johnny In the Clair de Lune*. Films: *Personal Services; Educating Rita*, for which she was nominated for an Oscar, and won Golden Globe, BAFTA and Variety Club Best Actress awards; *She'll Be Wearing Pink Pyjamas; Buster; Killing Dad*. TV incl: *Victoria Wood As Seen On TV* (two series and a special); *Wood and Walters; Talent; Something Happened; Living Together; Boys From the Blackstuff; The Secret Diary of Adrian Mole Aged 13¾; Talking Heads; Victoria Wood*. Address: c/o ICM. Hobbies: travel, Patricia Highsmith's novels. Pets: cats. **Most Cherished Possession:** 'My passport.' **Favourite Memory:** 'The birth of my daughter.'

WANAMAKER, Zoe

Actress, b. 13 May 1949, New York. Trained at Central School of Speech and Drama in London. Joined RSC 1976 and theatre incl: *Bay At Nice; Wrecked Eggs; Wild Oats; Once In a Lifetime; Piaf* (also New York); *Twelfth Night; Comedy of Errors; Mother Courage; Othello; The Importance of Being Earnest; Mrs Klein.* Musicals incl: *Guys and Dolls; Cabaret.* Films incl: *The Hunger; The Last 10 Days of Hitler; Inside the 3rd Reich.* TV incl: *The Silver Mask; Village Hall; Beaux Stratagem; The Devil's Crown; Baal; Strike; All the World's a Stage; Richard III; Paradise Postponed; Edge of Darkness; Poor Little Rich Girl; Ball Trap On the Côte Sauvage; The Dog It Was That Died.* Address: c/o Jeremy Conway. Hobbies: travel, painting, reading, music, theatre, cinema.

WARD, Tracy Louise

Actress, b. 22 December 1958, London. Trained at the Drama Studio, Ealing. Solo cabaret around the London circuit. Theatre incl: *Our Day Out* at Nottingham Playhouse; *Intimacy* in the West End. Film: *Dance With a Stranger.* TV incl: *If Tomorrow Comes; Doctor Who; C.A.T.S. Eyes; Mussolini.* m. Harry Worcester. Address: c/o London Management. Birthsign: Sagittarius. Hobbies: riding, walking, reading. **Most Cherished Possession:** 'My husband – he would be my saddest loss.' **Favourite Memory:** 'My life at 17, alone in Paris.'

WARING, George

Actor/director, b. 20 February 1927, Eccles, Lancashire. Joined RAF at 18 and its Rep Company. Then more rep and West End theatre. Films: *Squaring the Circle; God's Outlaw.* TV inc: *Andy Capp; Z-Cars; Mrs Thursday; Doctor Who; Softly, Softly; Coronation Street, Emmerdale Farm; Mixed Blessings; No Place Like Home; After the War; The Bill.* m. (1st (dis.), (2nd) actress Geraldine Gwyther; 1 d. Georgina, 1 s. Geoffrey. Address: c/o Joseph & Wagg, Studio One, 2 Tunstall Road, London SW9 8BN. Hobbies: tennis, reading, good music, cooking Asian-style meals. Pets: two cats. **Most Cherished Possession:** 'My wok – the finest, most versatile cooking utensil devised by man.' **Favourite Memory:** 'Furtwangler conducting Beethoven in a shabby suit in post-war Hamburg.'

WARREN, Marcia

Actress. Trained at Guildhall School of Music and Drama. Regional theatre incl: Bristol Old Vic for four years; and at Liverpool, Birmingham, Greenwich, Oxford, Guildford, Scarborough, Hornchurch, Northampton, Canterbury, Ipswich, Colchester, Croydon, Leatherhead. London theatre incl: *Joking Apart; Season's Greetings; Music Hall In the Skies; Suburban Strains; Stepping Out; Blithe Spirit.* Film incl: *Mr Love.* Radio incl: *The Skin Game; The Critic; Spiggot.* TV incl: *Now and Then; Kids; London Belongs To Me; Rivals of Sherlock Holmes; Public Eye; Rainbow; Tolpuddle Inheritance; Crown Court; No Place Like Home; History of Mr Polly; The World of J B Priestley; Crossroads; We'll Think of Something.* Address: c/o Scott Marshall, 44 Perryn Road, London W3 7NA.

WARREN, Michael

Actor, b. 5 March, South Bend, Indiana. Won an athletics scholarship to UCLA where he studied film. Emmy nomination for his role as Officer Hill in TV's *Hill Street Blues.* Film debut in *Drive, He Said,* first as a basketball adviser, then given an acting role. Other films incl: *Norman, Is That You?; Fast Break; Butterflies Are Free.* Other TV incl: *Adam – 12; Marcus Welby, MD; Mod Squad; Paris; Sierra; The White Shadow.* m. Susie (dis.); 1 d. Koa, 1 s. Cash. Address: c/o Sandy Bressler and Assocs, 15760 Ventura Blvd, Encino, California 91436. Hobbies: reading, music, basketball, tennis. **Most Cherished Possession:** 'My children.'

WARWICK, James

Actor, b. 17 November 1947, Broxbourne, Hertfordshire. Trained at Central School of Speech and Drama. TV debut as an ostrich in *Late Night Line-Up*. Many rep and West End theatre productions. Films: *The Secret Adversary*. TV incl: *The Onedin Line*; *The Terracotta Horse*; *Rock Follies*; *Edward VII*; *Turtle's Progress*; *Tales of the Unexpected*; *Doctor Who*; *The Nightmare Man*; *The Bell*; *Why Didn't They Ask Evans?*; *The Seven Dials Mystery*; *Partners In Crime*; *Scarecrow and the King*; *Dead Head*; *Howards' Way*; *Bergerac*; *Blore MP*; *Don't Wait Up*. Address: c/o Barry Burnett. Birthsign: Scorpio. Hobbies: gardening, swimming, music. **Most Cherished Possession:** 'My health.' **Favourite Memory:** 'A holiday in Kenya.'

WARWICK, Richard

Actor, b. 29 April 1945, Dartford, Kent. Trained at RADA. Theatre incl: Higgins in *My Fair Lady*; *In Praise of Love*; *The Real Thing*. Films incl: *Romeo and Juliet*; *If . . .*; *First Love*; *The Bedsitting Room*; *Nicholas and Alexandra*; *The Breaking of Bumbo*; *Alice In Wonderland*; *Sebastiane*; *The Tempest*. TV incl: *The Vortex*; *Please, Sir*; *Last of the Mohicans*; *School Play*; *A Fine Romance*. Address: c/o ICM. Birthsign: Taurus. Hobbies: sailing, tennis, travel. **Most Cherished Possession:** 'My record collection. It contains every piece of music I've loved since I was 15.' **Favourite Memory:** 'Being flown off to Rome, aged 21, to make *Romeo and Juliet*.'

WASHINGTON, Denzel

Actor, b. 28 December, Mt Vernon, New York State. Trained with the American Conservatory Theater. Theatre incl: *Ceremonies In Dark Old Men*; *The Mighty Gents*; *Coriolanus*; *When Chickens Come Home To Roost*; *Othello*; *Malcom X*; *A Soldier's Play*. Films incl: *Cry Freedom*; *Carbon Copy*; *For Queen and Country*. TV film: *The George McKenna Story*. Dr Phillip Chandler in TV's *St Elsewhere*. Other TV incl: *Wilma*; *Flesh and Blood*. m. Paulette Pearson; 1 s. John David, 1 d. Katia. Address: c/o William Morris Agency, 151 El Camino Drive, Beverly Hills, CA 90212. Birthsign: Capricorn. Hobbies: travel, skiing, chess, reading, stereo buff. **Most Cherished Possession:** 'My family.; **Favourite Memory:** 'The birth of my son, John – it was a miracle.'

WATERMAN, Dennis

Actor/singer, b. 24 February 1948, London. Acting debut aged 11 in *Night Train To Inverness*. Trained at Corona Stage School and by 16 had been in *The Music Man*, a season at Stratford-upon-Avon, starred in the first TV *Just William* and been to Hollywood. Theatre incl: *Windy City*; *Cinderella*; *Same Time Next Year*. Films incl: *Up The Junction*; *Sweeney*; *Sweeney 2*. TV incl: *Sextet*; *The Sweeney*; *Give Us a Kiss*; *Christabel*; *Minder* (five series); *The World Cup – A Captain's Tales*; *The Life and Loves of a She-Devil*; *Mr H Is Late*. Also writes, sings and records. m. (1st) Penny (dis.), (2nd) actress Patricia Maynard (dis.), (3rd) Rula Lenska; 2 d. Hannah, Julia (both from 2nd m.). Address: c/o ICM. Birthsign: Pisces. Hobbies; playing guitar, writing songs.

WATERS, Nick

Actor, b. 4 September 1951, Melbourne, Australia. Studied drama and mime at the Claremont Theatre, Melbourne 1970. Other theatre: The Playbox Theatre; La Mama; St Martin's; The Alexander Theatre. Films incl: *The Great McCarthy*; *Strike-Bound*; *The Humpty-Dumpty Man*; *The Lighthorsemen*; *Snowy River II*. TV incl: *Rush*; *Against the Wind*; *The Last Outlaw*; *The Sullivans*; *The Anzacs*. m. Joanne; 2 s. Sean, Oliver. Address: c/o The Actors Agency, Melbourne, Australia. Birthsign: Virgo. Hobbies: cricket, horse-training, music, fishing and crosswords. Pets: two dogs. **Most Cherished Possession:** 'A very early American Washurn guitar, because they don't make them like that anymore.' **Favourite Memory:** 'The image of my wife when I met her for the first time.'

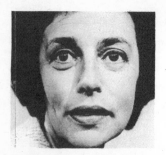

WATFORD, Gwen

Actress, b. 10 September 1927, London. Trained at the Embassy Theatre, London, then rep and Old Vic. Theatre incl: *Singles; Bodies; Present Laughter* (SWET Award 1981); *The Jeweller's Shop; Fall*. Films incl: *Never Take Sweets From a Stranger; The Very Edge; Cleopatra*. Many TV roles incl: *Second Time Around; The Train Now Standing . . .; A Bit of An Adventure; A Provincial Lady; A Suitable Case For Killing; Love Me To Death; Don't Forget To Write; Present Laughter; Sorrell and Son; The Body In the Library*. m. actor Richard Bebb; 2 s. Mark, Owen. Address: c/o Peters Fraser & Dunlop. Birthsign: Virgo. Hobbies: piano, gardening. **Most Cherished Possession:** 'My piano.'

WATSON, Ken

Actor, b. London. Trained at RADA. Rep at Wolverhampton, Colchester, Oxford, Aberdeen and Edinburgh. London theatre incl: *St Joan At the Stake; Ticket of Leave Man*. Films incl: *Great White Hope; Belstone Fox; Doctor Who and the Daleks*. TV incl: *Diamond Run; The Undoing; King and Country; The Barratts of Wimpole Street; The Brothers; Emergency–Ward 10; Crown Court; Darwin; Take the High Road; Roll On Four O'Clock; Losing Her; Too Close To the Edge; Singles; Airline*. As writer/script editor on: *From Inner Space; The Westerners; Fancy That*. m. TV make-up artist Joan Watson; 1 d. Kate, 1 s. Jamie. Address: c/o Joan Gray. Hobbies: DIY, collecting books. Pets: one cat, Charlotte. **Most Cherished Possession:** 'A Minton pot, reputed to have belonged to Sir Henry Irving.'

WATSON, Moray

Actor, b. 25 June, Sunningdale, Berkshire. Trained at the Webber Douglas Academy, then rep before London's West End and his first hit, *The Grass Is Greener* (also film version with Cary Grant). Other theatre incl: *The Incomparable Man* (one-man show); *Married Love; Star Quality; Lettice and Lovage*. Films incl: *Operation Crossbow; The Sea Wolves*. TV incl: *Upstairs, Downstairs; The Pallisers; Rumpole of the Bailey; Pride and Prejudice; Doctor Who; Minder; Rude Health; The Body In the Library; Nobert Smith – A Life*. m. Pam Marmont; 1 d. Emma, 1 s. Robin. Address: Neaves Park Farm, Hartfield, East Sussex. Hobby: gardening. Pets: two dogs. **Most Cherished Possession:** 'My father's watch. It was on his wrist when he was killed a week before Dunkirk and was returned by a Belgian farmer's wife to my mother 25 years later.'

WATT, Tom

Actor, b. 14 February 1956, Wanstead, London. BA Hons Drama at Manchester University. Theatre incl: *Alberto Y Los Trios Paranoias;* in San Francisco with rep and improvisational companies; Europe tour with East West Co; UK and India tour with Graeae Theatre; *The Foreigner* and *The Cherry Orchard* (West End). TV incl: *The Old Firm; A Kind of Loving; My Father's House; Never the Twain; Family Man; EastEnders; Night Network; And a Nightingale Sang*. Birthsign: Aquarius. Hobbies: Walford Boys Club FC, swimming, writing, sweet soul music. **Most Cherished Possession:** 'Several house plants and my blue suede shoes.' **Favourite Memory:** 'The week in May 1971 when I watched Arsenal do the double.'

WAXMAN, Al

Actor/director, b. 2 March 1935, Toronto, Canada. Studied film technique in London and New York. Much theatre experience in rep, off-Broadway and in London's West End. Films incl: *Wild Horse Hank; Double Negative; Atlantic City; Tulips Deathbite; Class of '84*. On TV has acted in *The King of Kensington;* Lt Bert Samuels in *Cagney and Lacey*. Has directed on TV: *The Crowd Inside; The Littlest Hobo; Cagney and Lacey*. m. Sara; 1 d. Tobaron, 1 s. Adam. Birthsign: Pisces. Hobbies: tennis, film- and theatre-going. Pets: one dog. **Most Cherished Possession:** 'My family.' **Favourite Memory:** 'I have wonderful memories of living in London, walking in the rain, collecting walking sticks.'

WEBB, Lizzie

Fitness presenter, b. 12 August 1948, London. Trained as a teacher of English, drama and dance, then taught at a boy's school, and spent a year teaching disturbed adolescents. From 1975, taught at Richmond Ice Rink, Guildford School of Acting and stage schools incl Italia Conti. Also worked as a choreographer. Has been with TV-am since May 1983 as its 'keep-fit lady'. Has made several videos and written *Lizzie Webb's Total Fitness Book*. m. (dis.); 1 s. Ben. Address: c/o TV-am. Hobbies: walking dogs, music and theatre. Pets: two dogs. **Most Cherished Possession:** 'My family.' **Favourite Memory:** 'A holiday in Paris after a mammoth workload!'

WEBSTER, Mark

ITN journalist, b. 21 November 1953, Birmingham. Address: c/o ITN. Birthsign: Scorpio. Hobbies: 'Anything physical.' **Most Cherished Possession:** 'Idi Amin's medical records.' **Favourite Memory:** 'Hearing my dentist say, "They're all perfect."'

WEEKS, Alan

Sports commentator, b. 8 September 1923, Bristol. Public address announcer at Brighton Sports Stadium 1946–65. First BBC TV commentary on ice hockey 1951. Has presented: *Summer Grandstand* 1959–62; Olympic Games 1960–64; World Cup 1962; *Pot Black* 1970–84. Commentated on: soccer 1956–78; Winter Olympics 1964–88; World Cup 1966–78; Olympics 1966–88; Commonwealth Games 1970–86; ice skating; ice hockey; swimming. m. Barbara Jane; 1 d. Beverly; 2 s. Nigel (dec.), Roderick. Address: c/o Bagenal Harvey. Birthsign: Virgo. Hobbies: swimming, football. **Favourite Memory:** 'Brighton Tigers Ice Hockey Club 1946–47 – the best in Britain, and one of the best in Europe.'

WEITZ, Bruce

Actor, b. 27 May 1943, Norwalk, Connecticut. Trained with Long Wharf Rep Theatre; Tyrone Guthrie Theatre. Acted on Broadway in: *Death of a Salesman; Norman, Is That You?; Shakespeare In the Park*. In Los Angeles. TV incl: *Quincy; Kojak; One Day At a Time; The White Shadow; Lou Grant;* Det Mick Belker in *Hill Street Blues* (one Emmy award and two nominations). Other TV incl: *Happy Days; Mork and Mindy; Kaz; The Rockford Files*. m. (dis.). Address: c/o William Morris Agency, 151 El Camino Drive, Beverly Hills, CA 90212. Hobbies: gourmet cooking, racquetball, scuba-diving, travel. **Most Cherished Possession:** 'My swimming pool.' **Favourite Memory:** 'Meeting Nancy Reagan.'

WELLAND, Colin

Actor/writer, b. 4 July 1934, Liverpool. Was an art teacher before joining Manchester's Library Theatre. Briefly compere of BBC's *North at Six* and an appearance in *The Verdict* before becoming PC Graham in *Z-Cars* for three years. Other TV: *Blue Remembered Hills; United Kingdom; Cowboys*. Took to writing and his plays incl: *Leeds United; Kisses at Fifty; The Wild West Show; Your Man From Six Counties; Say Goodnight To Grandma; Roll On Four O'Clock; Bangelstein's Boys*. Acted in many of his own plays. Also presenter *How To Stay Alive*. Films incl: *Kes; Villain; Straw Dogs; Sweeney; Yanks* (wrote film's script); *Chariots of Fire* (won an Oscar for his film script); *Twice In a Lifetime; A Dry White Season*. m. former teacher Pat; 3 d. Genevieve, Catherine, Caroline, 1 s. Christie. Address: c/o Peter Charlesworth. Hobbies: cricket, rugby singing.

WELLING, Albert

Actor, b. 29 February 1952, London. Six seasons with the National Youth Theatre, then BA Hons Drama at Manchester University. Has since acted with the RSC; Royal Court Theatre, London; the Actors' Company; Nottingham Playhouse; Liverpool Playhouse; Young Vic; Royal Exchange, Manchester. TV incl: *Lovejoy; EastEnders; Howards' Way; Tales of the Unexpected; Bulman; Telford's Change; Auf Wiedersehen, Pet; The Gathering Seed; A Voyage Round My Father; Wish Me Luck; Inspector Morse; Boon; Casualty.* m. Judy Riley; 2 s. Benedict, Kaspar. Address: c/o David White Assocs. Hobbies: music, swimming, walking, snooker. Pets: two dogs. **Most Cherished Possession:** 'A scratched, deleted recording of Mozart's C Minor Mass, because it's irreplaceable.'

WELSBY, Elton

Sports presenter, b. 28 May 1951, St Helens, Lancashire. Trained with the Merseyside Group of Weekly Newspapers 1969–74, then worked for Radio City 1974–78 (Sound of Merseyside). TV incl: *Kick Off; Match Time; Results Service; The Big Match Live;* ITV bowls presentation (Liverpool Victoria Insurance Superbowl); *Midweek Sport Special.* m. Joyce; 1 d. Laura, 1 s. Christopher. Address: c/o Bagenal Harvey. Birthsign: Gemini. Hobbies: golf, snooker, bowls (crown green and flat). **Most Cherished Possession:** 'My family and my golf clubs, although not necessarily in that order.' **Favourite Memory:** 'Pioneer days of independent local radio in Liverpool during the end of the 70s when so much was learned from so many mistakes.'

WENDT, George

Actor, b. 17 October, Chicago, Illinois. Trained and acted with Chicago's Second City Comedy Workshop. Norm Peterson in TV's *Cheers.* Other TV incl: *Soap; Taxi; Alice; Hart To Hart; The Twilight Zone; St Elsewhere; Roseanne;* and as TV spokesman for Meister Brau Beer. Films incl: *House; Gung Ho; Airplane II; Dreamscape; No Small Affair; Fletch; The Ratings Game; Glory Days.* m. Bernadette; 1 d. Hilary, 2 step-s. Joshua, Andrew. Address: c/o Writers And Artists Agency, 11726 San Vicente Blvd, LA, CA 90049. Hobbies: basketball, baseball, football, writing. **Most Cherished Possession:** 'A bar stool and a mug of beer.' **Favourite Memory:** 'I spent two-and-a-half years traipsing around Europe and North Africa on a $5-a-day travel itinerary.'

WENZEL, Brian

Actor, b. 24 May 1929, Adelaide, South Australia. Started as a chorus boy at 17. Worked as a semi-professional for many years. Moved from Adelaide to Sydney in 1971 and has rarely been out of work since. Films incl: *The Death Train; Caddie; Allison's Birthday; The Odd Angry Shot.* TV incl: *Certain Women; Punishment; A Country Practice; Division 4; Young Ramsey; Matlock Police; Homicide; Ryan; Boney.* m. Linda. Address: c/o June Cann Management. Birthsign: Gemini. Pets: one dog, one cat, one canary. **Most Cherished Possession:** 'Our house. Why? Because *A Country Practice* allowed me to pay the mortgage off.' **Favourite Memory:** 'My childhood, because it was a lifetime or two. I was an adult at eight years.'

WEST, Timothy, CBE

Actor, b. 20 October 1934, Bradford. Son of theatrical couple, started as assistant stage manager Wimbledon, 1959, in *Caught Napping.* Films incl: *Nicholas and Alexandra; The Day of the Jackal; Agatha; The Thirty-Nine Steps; Rough Cut; Oliver Twist.* TV incl: *Hard Times; Henry VIII; Brass; Tender Is the Night; The Monocled Mutineer; The Good Doctor Bodkin Adams; A Roller Next Year; What the Butler Saw; When We Are Married; A Shadow On the Sun; The Contractor; Strife; Blore MP.* m. actress Prunella Scales; 1 d. Juliet, 2 s. Samuel, Joseph. Address: c/o James Sharkey. Hobbies: listening to music, travel. Pets: two cats, goldfish. **Most Cherished Possession:** 'A canal boat. It's slow, quiet, and has no telephone.' **Favourite Memory:** 'Making *Brass* for Granada – wonderful to be paid for acting badly!'

WHICKER, Alan

Writer, b. 2 August 1925, Cairo, Egypt. After service on Italian warfront as major commanding battle cameramen, became Fleet Street foreign correspondent in Korea. Joined BBC 1957 at start of *Tonight* programme. *Whicker's World* began in 1958. Joined ITV 1968 and returned to BBC 1982 for *Whicker's World – The First Million Miles; South Pacific* series; *A Slow Boat To China; Whicker's New World; Whicker's World Down Under; Whicker's World – Hong Kong*. Winner of many awards incl Richard Dimbleby Award. Wrote bestseller *Within Whicker's World*, also *Whicker's New World* and *Whicker's World Down Under*. Address: c/o Jersey, Channel Islands. **Most Cherished Possession:** 'My 1964 Bentley Continental – for showing that elegance and style can overcome age.' **Favourite Memory:** 'For a fortunate and happy man, it's always yesterday.'

WHITE, Betty

Actress/comedienne, b. 17 January 1922, Oak Park, Illinois. TV incl: *Life With Elizabeth; The Betty White Show; Date With An Angel; Mama's Family; The Mary Tyler Moore Show* (won two Emmys for her role as Sue Ann Nivens); *Golden Girls* (Emmy Award); hosted game show *Just Men!* (won another Emmy). Was member of the board of directors of the LA Zoo. Has written two books about animals. m. (1st) Lane Allen (dis.), (2nd) TV game show host Allen Ludden (dec.); 2 step-d. Martha, Sarah, 1 step-s. David. Address: c/o William Morris Agency, Los Angeles. Hobbies: animals, travel. Pets: two dogs, one cat. **Most Cherished Possession:** 'My animals. At one time, I had 26 dogs!' **Favourite Memory:** 'Twenty years of marriage with Allen Ludden.'

WHITE, Frances

Actress, b. 1 November 1938, Leeds, Yorkshire. Trained at Central School of Speech and Drama. First West End play was *Fit To Print* in 1962. Other theatre incl: *A Severed Head; Appearances*. Films incl: *Pumpkin Eater; Mary, Queen of Scots; Press For Time*. Numerous TV appearances incl: *Raging Calm; I, Claudius; Prince Regent; Looking For Vicky; Crossroads; Nobody's Perfect; Paradise Postponed; A Very Peculiar Practice; A Perfect Spy; Chelworth; May To December*. m. Anthony Hone (dis.); 1 d. Kate. Address: c/o Bryan Drew. Birthsign: Scorpio. Hobbies: gardening, reading, listening to music. **Most Cherished Possession:** 'A portrait of my daughter, painted by my father.' **Favourite Memory:** 'I have quite a few, so I don't want to be tied down to one!'

WHITE, Mela

Actress, b. 28 March, Woodford, Essex. Performed in revues and musicals and later acted in films. Theatre incl: Alan Ayckbourn's *The Westwoods*. TV incl: *Casualty; Bergerac; Angels; Shoestring*. m. actor Ronald Lacey (dis.); 1 d. Rebecca, 1 s. Jonathan. Address: c/o Thomas & Benda Assocs, 361 Edgware Road, London W2 1BS, tel 071-723 0083.

WHITE, Robin

TV reporter, b. 21 July 1955, London. Started his career as a newspaper reporter in 1973. Joined Independent Radio in 1977, then went to ITN as a scriptwriter in 1979. Joined the ITN Crime Unit in 1987. m. Anne. Address: c/o ITN. Birthsign: Cancer. Hobbies: music, golf, writing, wine. **Most Cherished Possession:** 'A collection of books by the author Alan White, who is my father.' **Favourite Memory:** 'Honeymooning in Mauritius.'

WHITEHEAD, Amanda

Actress, b. 12 March 1965, Oldham, Lancashire. Appeared in the Alan Bleasdale play *No More Sitting On the Old School Bench* at Oldham Coliseum, aged 15, then attended Oldham Theatre Workshop and took an A-level in theatre studies. Trained at the Royal Scottish Academy of Music and Drama, gaining a diploma in dramatic art. Theatre: *Alice In Wonderland; Beauty and the Beast; Wuthering Heights; Waving and Drowning; Snow White and the Seven Dwarfs.* TV: 'extra' in *Tutti Frutti* while at college; Emma Aitken in *Take the High Road* since 1989. Address: c/o Scottish TV. Birthsign: Pisces. Hobbies: cinema, theatre, swimming. Pets: a dog, Harry. **Most Cherished Possession:** 'Happiness – if you can possess it.' **Favourite Memory:** 'Too many to mention.'

WHITEHEAD, Geoffrey

Actor, b. 1 October 1939, Sheffield. Trained at RADA, then rep at Canterbury, Coventry and Sheffield and Bristol. TV incl: *Z-Cars; Jane Eyre; Sweeney; Some Mothers Do 'Ave 'Em; Affairs of the Heart; Upstairs Downstairs; Crown Court; Hadleigh; Avengers; Kit Curran; Who Dares Wins; Reilly – Ace of Spies; Robin's Nest; Rivals of Sherlock Holmes; Alas Smith and Jones; Pinkerton's Progress; The Doll; Chelmsford 123; War and Remembrance; Executive Stress; Shelley; Peter the Great.* m. Mary Hanefey; 1 d. Clare, 1 s. Jonty. Address: c/o Bryan Drew. Hobbies: music, all sports, Sheffield Wednesday. Pets: one dog, Walter. **Most Cherished Possession:** 'My Filofax. How did I exist without it?' **Favourite Memory:** 'Coming round after a hernia operation.'

WHITELEY, Richard

Presenter, b. 28 December 1943, Bradford, West Yorkshire. Educated at Giggleswick School, North Yorkshire, and Christ's College, Cambridge. Editor, *Varsity*, 1965. Became an ITN trainee 1965–68. Joined Yorkshire TV 1968. Presenter of *Calendar* and associated programmes, incl: *Calendar Sunday; Calendar Tuesday; Calendar People; Calendar Forum; Good Morning Calendar; Goodnight Calendar; Calendar Commentary;* presenter of *Countdown* on C4 since 1982 – was the first face on C4. Address: c/o Yorkshire TV. Hobby: pottering around the Yorkshire Dales. **Most Cherished Possession:** 'One of the oldest clipboards in ITV – one of the originals in ITN in 1955, given to me when I left.' **Favourite Memory:** 'Thirty seconds of excruciating pain when attacked by a marauding ferret.'

WHITFIELD, June, OBE

Comedy actress, b. 11 November, London. Trained at RADA and appeared on stage in shows such as *Love From Judy.* Came to the fore as Eth in radio series *Take It From Here* (1953). Recent radio: *News Huddlines.* Theatre incl: *An Ideal Husband; Ring Round the Moon; Over My Dead Body.* Films incl: *Carry On Abroad; Bless This House; The Spy With the Cold Nose.* On TV has been the foil to the best funny men in the business. TV incl: *Beggar My Neighbour; The Best Things In Life; Hancock's Half Hour; Scott On . . .* First worked with Terry Scott in 1969 and they have made five series of *Happy Ever After* and ten series of *Terry and June.* Recent TV: *It Doesn't Have To Hurt!* m. surveyor Tim Aitchison; 1 d. actress Suzy. Address: c/o April Young. Hobby: cooking.

WHITTAKER, Sally

Actress, b. 30 May 1963, Middleton, Manchester. Trained at Mountview Theatre School. Theatre incl: Abbadaba Theatre Company; pantomime at Oldham Coliseum; fringe theatre in London. TV incl: *Juliet Bravo; The Practice; Coronation Street;* various commercials. Address: c/o Barry Brown. Birthsign: Gemini. Hobbies: horse riding, walking. keep fit. Pets: one cat. **Most Cherished Possession:** 'My passport. I love to travel.' **Favourite Memory:** 'Being on holiday in Israel and lying in the Dead Sea, floating. It was great fun trying so hard to stand up.'

WIGGINS, Jim

Actor, b. 13 March 1922, Birkenhead. Was a civil servant and a teacher. Spent many years as an amateur with the Merseyside Unity Theatre. Turned professional in 1973. Has performed in BBC radio dramas, and as an actor/director with the Theatre-in-the-Round. TV: Paul Collins in *Brookside*. m. (1st) Rosamond Patterson (dec.), (2nd) journalist Patricia Hart (dec.); 1 s. Peter (from 1st m.), 2 d. Claire, Kerry Ann (both from 2nd m.). Address: c/o Kerry Gardner Management. Birthsign: Pisces. Hobbies: music, travel, ironing. **Most Cherished Possession:** 'My father's retirement wristwatch, given to me by him when he was gravely ill.' **Favourite Memory:** 'Receiving a parcel from home on my 21st birthday in Tunisia during the African Campaign.'

WILCOX, Paula

Actress, b. 13 December 1949, Manchester. Joined National Youth Theatre while at school and started in TV after leaving school. Theatre incl: *Romeo and Juliet; The Cherry Orchard; The Birthday Party; Heartbreak House; Time and the Conways; Pygmalion; Hedda Gabler; Bedroom Farce; Blithe Spirit* (Australia, in the Middle and Far East); *See How They Run; Shirley Valentine*. TV incl: *The Lovers* (also film); *Man About the House* (also film); *Miss Jones and Son; Remember the Lambeth Walk?; The Bright Side; Boon*. m. Derek Seaton (dec.). Address: c/o Barry Burnett. Birthsign: Sagittarius. Hobbies: swimming, walking, cinema, watching football, theatre, concerts. **Favourite Memory:** 'I really don't look back. I enjoy what I'm doing now too much!'

WILLIAMS, Michael

Actor, b. 9 July 1935, Manchester. Trained at RADA, joined Nottingham Playhouse 1959, appeared in *Celebration* at the Duchess Theatre, the revue *Twists* at Arts Theatre, and some TV work. Joined Royal Shakespeare Company 1963, and appeared in plays incl: *Comedy of Errors; The Merchant of Venice; As You Like It; King Lear*. Films incl: *Marat Sade; Eagle In a Cage; Dead Cert; Enigma*. Many TV credits incl: *Elizabeth R; Comedy of Errors; My Son, My Son; Love In a Cold Climate; Amnesty; Shakespeare Master Class; A Fine Romance; Double First; Behaving Badly*. m. actress Dame Judi Dench. Birthsign: Leo. Address: c/o Michael Whitehall. Hobby: 'My family.'

WILLIAMS, Simon

Actor, b. 16 June 1946, Windsor, Berkshire. One of the tallest actors in the business (6ft 4in) he started in pantomime 1965 then rep. West End theatre incl: *A Friend In Need; Hay Fever; The Collector; No Sex Please, We're British; Gigi; See How They Run*. Films incl: *Jabberwocky; The Prisoner of Zenda; The Fiendish Plot of Dr Fu Manchu*. TV incl: Captain Bellamy in *Upstairs, Downstairs; Wodehouse Playhouse; Mr Big; Liza; Agony; Strangers; Kinvig; Sharing Time; Don't Wait Up*. Novel: *Talking Oscars*. m. Lucy Fleming; s. Tamlyn. Address: c/o Michael Whitehall. Birthsign: Gemini. Hobbies: riding, reading, writing. Pets: dogs, cats, horses. **Most Cherished Possession:** 'My make-up box - it's so old and full of possibilities.' **Favourite Memory:** 'Getting my first bicycle, my first car, my first job, my first girlfriend.'

WILLIAMSON, Trish

Broadcast journalist, b. 3 January 1955, Newcastle upon Tyne. Fellow of the Royal Geographical Society. Worked as a magazine and newspaper journalist, before becoming a TV researcher. TV-am reporter, presenter and weather forecaster, 1985–7. ITN reporter and weather presenter since 1988. Freelance work includes Anglia TV's *Sailaway* series (1989 and 1990) and LWT's 1989 *Time For Christmas* campaign. Lives with Russell Wickens. 1 s. Dominic. Address: c/o ITN or Jacque Evans. Birthsign: Capricorn. Hobbies: any sport to do with horses, cross-country, polo, running, aerobics, fitness in general, travel.

WILLIS, Bruce

Actor, b. 19 March 1955, Germany. Raised in New Jersey. Attended Montclair State College, then did commercials and acted in local theatres. Theatre incl: *Fool For Love*. Films incl: *Blind Date; The Verdict; Prince of the City; Die Hard*. TV incl: David Addison in *Moonlighting; Hart To Hart; The Return of Bruno* (album also). m. actress Demi Moore; 1 d. Rumer Glenn. Address: c/o Triad Agency, 10100 Santa Monica Blvd, LA, CA 90067. Hobbies: playing his mouth harp, swimming, stand-up comedy. **Most Cherished Possession:** 'My mint condition black 166 Corvette with a white interior.' **Favourite Memory:** 'Getting myself elected student council president in high school.'

WILLITS, Adam

Actor. Began performing for amateur musical societies at the age of nine. Within three years, he had appeared in the Australian Film and Television School's film *Marbles* and the Ensemble Theatre's play *All My Sons*. Films: *Anna; Damsels Be Damned; Weekend of the Lonesome Rustler; Mad Max: Beyond Thunderdome*. TV movie: *The Perfectionist*. TV: *Maestro's Company;* Steven Matheson in *Home and Away*. Address: c/o Bedford and Pearce Management, 275 Alfred Street North (Suite 206), North Sydney, NSW 2060, Australia.

WILMOT, Gary

Entertainer, b. 8 May 1954, Kennington, London. Started in showbusiness entertaining in a bar in Spain. Formed a double act, Gary Wilmot and Judy, when back in Britain and toured theatres and clubs, then won TV's *New Faces* three times. Went solo 1979 and has appeared on many TV shows incl: *The Six O'Clock Show; Ebony; Royal Variety Show; Royal Night of 100 Stars; Saturday Gang; Cue Gary; This Is Your Life*. Variety Club Award as Most Promising Artiste 1986. m. Carol Clark; 2 d. Katie, Georgia. Address: c/o Dee O'Reilly Management. Birthsign: Taurus. Hobbies: football, running, rugby, DIY.

WILSON, Francis

Broadcaster, b. 27 February 1949, Irvine, Ayrshire. BSc from Imperial College, London University. Associate, Royal College of Science; Fellow, Royal Meteorological Society; member, Institute of Environmental Sciences. Forecaster at Prestwick, Edinburgh. Atmosphere researcher, RAE Farnborough with the Met Research Flight. Started TV career with *Thames News* in London. Joined BBC's *Breakfast Time* in 1983. Books: *Spotter's Guide To Weather* (1978); *Guide To Weather Forecasting* (1980); *Weather Pop-Up Book* (1987). m. Eva; 1 s. Joshua. Address: c/o BBC TV. Birthsign: Pisces. Hobbies: walking the dog. Pets: three cats, one dog. **Most Cherished Possession:** 'A tandem made in 1940.' **Favourite Memory:** 'Coming second in the annual school cross-country race.'

WILSON, Jennifer

Actress, b. 25 April, London. After training at RADA, worked in rep. and on tour to US, Canada, India. Theatre incl: *Spring and Port Wine; Pygmalion; The Grass Is Greener; 84 Charing Cross Road; Fallen Angels; Intimate Exchanges; Widening Gyre; Ladies In Retirement*. More than 300 TV plays. Played Jenny Hammond in *The Brothers* for six years. Other TV incl: *Nicholas Nickleby; The Befrienders*. m. (1st) S Swain (dis.), (2nd) actor/director Brian Peck; 1 d. Melanie. Address: c/o PBR Management, 138 Putney Bridge Road, London SW15 2NQ. Hobbies: collecting pictures, cooking, dividing time between London and new home in France. **Most Cherished Possession:** 'A gold neckchain with my grandmother's wedding ring on it, and a locket with a photo of my husband and daughter.'

WILSON, Richard

Actor/director, b. 9 July 1936, Greenock, Renfrewshire. Gave up career as a research scientist for the stage at 27. Trained at RADA, then in rep. Recent theatre incl: *An Honourable Trade; Some of My Best Friends Are Husbands*. Also directed stage productions, and was an associate director Stables Theatre, Manchester. Recent stage direction: *An Inspector Calls; A Wholly Healthy Glasgow; Prin*. Films incl: *A Passage To India; Pick Up Your Ears; How To Get Ahead In Advertising; A Dry White Season; Fellow Traveller*. Recent TV: *Poppyland; Tutti Frutti; Whoops Apocalypse; Room At the Bottom; High and Dry*. Directed for TV: *A Wholly Healthy Glasgow; Under the Hammer; Changing Step*. Address: c/o Jeremy Conway. Hobbies: squash, eating, photography.

WILSON, Sean

Actor, b. 4 April 1965, Ashton-under-Lyne, Lancashire. Joined Oldham Theatre Workshop before teaming up with a friend to do a cabaret act around pubs and clubs. Rejoined Oldham Theatre Workshop to appear in *The Mother* on stage. Spent a year in community theatre, in the Manchester area and at the Edinburgh Festival, during which he co-wrote a play, *The Bogeymaster*. TV: *Crown Court; Travelling Man*; Mozart in the Channel Four *Film On Four Mozart's Unfinished*; Martin Platt in *Coronation Street* since 1985, after being turned down for the roles of Terry Duckworth and Kevin Webster. Address: c/o Granada TV.

WILTON, Penelope

Actress, b. 3 June 1947, Scarborough. Trained at Drama Centre, London. Theatre incl: *King Lear; Song of Songs; The Norman Conquests; Pearcross Girls; Widowing of Mrs Holroyd; Othello; Country*. Films incl: *Laughterhouse*. TV incl: *The Monocled Mutineer; The Sullen Sisters; Ever Decreasing Circles*. m. actor Daniel Massey (sep.); 1 d. Alice. Address: c/o Julian Belfrage Assocs. Birthsign: Gemini.

WINDING, Victor

Actor, b. 30 January 1929, London. Trained as a draughtsman but acted in amateur dramatics and taught drama at night school. At 29 joined Farnham Rep and three years later the Old Vic, London. West End theatre incl: *Poor Bitos; The Merchant of Venice*. Films incl: *The System; The Medusa Touch; Sailor's Return*. TV incl: *Yes, Prime Minister; Strike It Rich; The Saint; Doctor Who; The Expert; It Takes a Worried Man; Crossroads; Warship; Bognor; Shelley; Little and Large; Jemima Shore Investigates; Angels; Menance Unseen; The Bill; Telly Addicts*. m. Rosalind (dis.); 3 d. Celia, Kay, Jane, 1 s. Julian. Address: c/o Richard Stone. Birthsign: Aquarius. Hobbies: music, travel, gardening. **Most Cherished Possession:** 'My health.' **Favourite Memory:** 'Buying my first cow and calf – a totally new experience.'

WING, Anna

Actress, b. 30 October 1914, Hackney, London. Trained at Croydon School of Acting. Theatre incl: *Heartbreak House; A Place On Earth* (one-woman show). Films incl: *Full Circle; Providence; Runners*. TV incl: *Sink Or Swim; Sorry!; Father's Day*; Lou Beale in *EastEnders*. m. (1st) Peter Davey (dis.), (2nd) Philip O'Connor (dis.); 2 s. actor Mark Wing-Davey and Jon Wing O'Connor. Address: c/o Clifford Elson. Birthsign: Scorpio. Hobbies: painting, music, walking by the sea. **Most Cherished Possession:** 'A pair of gaudy earrings bought for me when my son was seven years old.' **Favourite Memory:** 'When I had given a diabolical performance and had bad revues, and my son said: "It doesn't matter Mum, as long as you keep on trying!"'

WISE, Ernie, OBE

Comedian, b. 27 November 1925, Leeds. Child entertainer with his father in working men's clubs. Formed double act with Eric Morecambe in 1941. Films incl: *The Intelligence Men; That Riviera Touch; The Magnificent Two*. TV incl: *Sunday Night At The London Palladium; The Morecambe and Wise Show*. Many awards incl: five BAFTA awards; Best Light Entertainment 1973; Freeman of the City of London 1976; *TVTimes* Hall of Fame 1980–81. Went solo after death of Eric Morecambe 1984. m. Doreen. Address: c/o Billy Marsh Assocs. Birthsign: Sagittarius. Hobbies: swimming, boating, tennis. Pets: one cat, Tabatha. **Most Cherished Possession:** 'My clogs. If the jokes fail, I never miss with my clog dance.' **Favourite Memory:** 'When I received my OBE at Buckingham Palace.'

WITCHELL, Nicholas

TV news correspondent/presenter, b. 23 September 1953, Cosford, Shropshire. Joined the BBC on News Training Scheme 1976. Has been reporter for BBC Northern Ireland, reporter BBC TV News London, correspondent in Ireland, Beirut and the Falklands. Presenter *Six O'Clock News*, 1984–9; presenter *BBC Breakfast News* since 1989. BBC TV News correspondent with Margaret Thatcher for the 1983 General Election. Book: *The Loch Ness Story*. Address: c/o BBC TV News, BBC TV Centre, London W12. Birthsign: Libra. Hobbies: reading, travel.

WITHINGTON, Shane

Actor, b. 22 August 1958, Toowoomba, Queensland, Australia. Trained at the Twelfth Night Theatre. Theatre incl: *Twelfth Night; How Does Your Garden Grow; Rookery Nook;* 1986 casino show, *Everybody Makes Mistakes*. Films incl: *A Cry For Help; Dawn*. TV incl: *The Young Doctors; Glenview High; Timeless Land; Chopper Squad; A Country Practice* (Logie Award for Best Actor 1984); *Willing & Abel*. Address: c/o Harry M Miller & Company Management, 153 Dowling Street, Kings Cross, Sydney, Australia. Birthsign: Leo. Hobbies: sailing, fishing. Pets: one axolotl, Russell the 'walking fish'. **Most Cherished Possession:** 'My good luck charm – a lead toy-rocking horse.' **Favourite Memory:** 'Floating on a shikahah on Lake Nigan in Kashmir.'

WOGAN, Terry

Broadcaster, b. 3 August 1938, Limerick, Ireland. Many awards incl: Radio Personality of the Year; *TVTimes* Award Most Popular TV Personality for 10 successive years 1978–1987; Variety Club Showbusiness Personality Award 1984. Radio incl: *Terry Wogan Show; Pop Score; Punchlines; Twenty Questions; Quote, Unquote; Year In Question*. Many TV appearances incl: *Lunchtime With Wogan; You Must Be Joking;* weekly and then thrice-weekly chat show *Wogan*. m. former model Helen Joyce; 1 d. Katherine, 2 s. Alan, Mark. Address: c/o Jo Gurnett. Birthsign: Leo. Hobbies: family, reading, golf.

WOOD, Janine

Actress, b. 30 December 1963, Bournemouth, Dorset. Took an A-level drama course, followed by training at The Drama Centre, London. Joined a children's theatre company, touring schools in London and the South East. Theatre: *Romeo and Juliet; A Midsummer Night's Dream; The Kiss; The Hired Man; Black Coffee; Habeas Corpus; Mrs Warren's Profession; Dealing With Clair*. TV: Clare in *After Henry* (five series); *Davro's Sketch Pad; Give Us a Clue*. TV commercials for National Westminster Bank and Alliance and Leicester. Address: c/o Jane Lehrer. Hobbies: theatre, cinema, reading, horoscopes, playing card games, Vietnamese food, daydreaming. **Most Cherished Possession:** 'A bracelet given to my mother on her 18th birthday and passed down to me on mine.' **Favourite Memory:** 'Taking the pot with a royal flush in a game of poker.'

WOOD, Victoria

Comedienne/writer, b. 19 May 1953, Prestwich, Lancashire. Drama degree at Birmingham University. Theatre incl: *Talent; Good Fun; Funny Turns;* one-woman show *Lucky Bag.* TV plays: *Talent; Happy Since I Met You.* Series: *Wood and Walters; Victoria Wood As Seen On TV* (two series, both BAFTA winners); *Victoria Wood Now; An Audience With Victoria Wood* (BAFTA winner); *Victoria Wood.* Other TV incl: *New Faces; Give Us a Clue; Call My Bluff; Jackanory.* m. Geoffrey Durham (The Great Soprendo); 1 d. Address: c/o Richard Stone. Hobby: 'No time.' **Most Cherished Possession:** 'My contact lenses, I can't see without them.' **Favourite Memory:** 'Doing a sketch with Julie Walters at the Bush Theatre and hearing the audience laugh – it was the first sketch I ever wrote (I must use it again!).'

WOODWARD, Edward, OBE

Actor, b. 1 June 1931, Surrey. Trained at RADA, then with the RSC. Theatre incl: *Becket; Young Winston.* Films incl: *Breaker Morant; King David; Champions.* TV incl: *Callan; Rod of Iron; Codename Kyril; Arthur the King;* Robert McCall in the *The Equalizer.* Awards incl: BAFTA award for TV Actor of the Year; *TVTimes* Award as Most Compulsive Male TV Character. Has recorded 14 albums. m. (1st) actress Venetia Barratt (dis.), (2nd) actress Michele Dotrice; 2 d. Sarah (from 1st m.), Emily Beth (2nd), 2 s. Timothy, Peter (both from 1st m.). Address: c/o McCartt-Oreck Barrett, Los Angeles. Hobbies: boating, reading. **Favourite Memory:** 'Winning my first talent competition at the age of five. I recited a poem.'

WOODWARD, Tim

Actor, b. 24 April 1953, London, son of actor Edward Woodward. Trained at RADA but left to tour with the Glasgow Citizens' Theatre. Recent theatre incl: *The Taming of the Shrew.* Films: *Galileo; The Europeans; Pope John Paul; King David; Salome; Personal Services.* TV: *Chips with Everything; Tales of the Unexpected; Wings; East Lynne; The Irish RM; A Killing On the Exchange; Piece of Cake.* Address: c/o Larry Dalzell Associates. Birthsign: Taurus. Hobbies: motorbikes.

WOOLLARD, William

Presenter/producer, b. 20 August 1939, London. Joined RAF after Oxford, then worked for an oil company. Learnt Arabic at Foreign Office school in Beirut. Worked in social science before joining BBC producing, directing and then presenting films for *Tomorrow's World.* Other TV incl: *The Risk Business; The Secret War; Too Hot To Handle; 2001 and All That; Top Gear; Policing the Eighties Connections.* Now runs own production company. 1 d. Jessica, 2 s. Julian, Alexander. Address: c/o Jon Roseman Assocs. Birthsign: Leo. Hobbies: sailing, golf, skiing, windsurfing. **Most Cherished Possession:** 'A small Tang jade horse. It reminds me of my years in the Far East.' **Favourite Memory:** 'Holding my daughter when she was a few minutes old.'

WORTH, Helen

Actress, b. 7 January 1951, Leeds, grew up in Morecambe, Lancashire. First TV role in *Z-Cars*, at the age of 10. On the London West End stage in *The Sound of Music* two years later. Went into repertory theatre at Watford, Hornchurch, Richmond-upon-Thames and Northampton after leaving school. TV: *Doctor Who;* Gail Tilsley in *Coronation Street* since 1974. Lives with actor Michael Angelis. Address: c/o Granada TV. Hobbies: gardening, cooking, eating.

WRAY, Emma

Actress/singer, b. 22 March 1965, Birkenhead, Jill Wray (changed her professional name because there was already an actress namesake). Appeared as a dancer in a charity show at the Drury Lane Theatre, London, aged seven, and a year later on the ITV children's talent show *Junior Showtime*. Trained at the Rose Bruford drama school, in Kent, then sang with a three-part harmony group, The Blooming Tulips. Landed the role of Brenda in *Watching* (four series) and sang the theme song. Other TV: *Minder; Defrosting the Fridge; Stay Lucky* (second series). Address: c/o Louis Hammond Management. Birthsign: Aries.

WYMAN, Jane

Actress, b. 5 January, St Joseph, Missouri. Was hired by Paramount Studio as a chorus dancer and extra. Films incl: *My Man Godfrey; The Yearling; Johnny Belinda; Princess O'Rourke; Stage Fright*. Angela Channing in TV's *Falcon Crest*. Other TV incl: *The Jane Wyman Theater; Love Boat; The Incredible Journey of Dr Meg Laurel*. m. (1st) Myron Frutterman (dis.), (2nd) Ronald Reagan (dis.), (3rd) bandleader Fred Karger (dis. twice); 1 d. Maureen, 1 s. Michael. Address: c/o Michael Mesnick, 500 South Sepulveda Blvd, LA, CA 90049. **Most Cherished Possession:** 'I'm a professional painter and cherish my oil paintings.' **Favourite Memory:** 'Winning the Best Actress Oscar for *Johnny Belinda* (1948). I so little expected to win, I didn't hear them announce my name.'

YARDLEY, Stephen

Actor, b. 24 March 1942, Ferriby, Yorkshire. Trained at RADA. Countless rep. Numerous films. TV incl: *XYY Man; Widows; Z-Cars; Secret Army; War and Peace; Howards' Way; Roads To Freedom; Coronation Street; Harriet's Back In Town; Napoleon and Love; Remington Steele; Blood Money; Tom Gratton's War; Dr Finlay's Casebook; Germinal; Nana; Tale of Two Cities; Fanny By Gaslight*. m. (separated); 1 d. Rebecca, 1 s. Joshua. Address: c/o Hilda Physick, 78 Temple Sheen Road, London SW14. Birthsign: Aries. Hobbies: squash, sailing, painting. **Most Cherished Possession:** 'Paris Marathon medal and the Munich Marathon medal, for a combination of achievement and decided madness.' **Favourite Memory:** 'The birth of my two children.'

YARWOOD, Mike, OBE

Comedian/impressionist, b. 14 June 1941, Bredbury, Cheshire. Started in showbusiness by entering a pub talent contest. Warm-up for *Comedy Bandbox* led to engagements throughout the country, the London Palladium and Royal Variety Performances. Recent tour of *One For the Pot*. TV incl: *Will The Real Mike Yarwood Stand Up; The Best of Mike Yarwood; Mike Yarwood In Person*; documentary, *Mike Yarwood – and This Is Him!* Autobiographies: *And This Is Me; Impressions of My Life*. m. ex-dancer Sandra Burville; 2 d. Charlotte, Clare. Address: c/o Billy Marsh Assocs. Hobbies: football, golf, tennis. **Most Cherished Possession:** 'My late mother's wedding ring.' **Favourite Memory:** 'My first appearance at the Palladium, 1964.'

YATES, Marjorie

Actress, b. 13 April 1941, Birmingham. Trained at Guildhall School of Music and Drama. Theatre incl: Royal Court *Small Change, Touched, Sea Anchor;* National Theatre *As You Like It, Inner Voices;* RSC *Outskirts, Good, Richard III; Thatcher's Woman*. Films incl: *Wetherby; Priest of Love; Stardust; The Optimists*. TV incl: *Kisses At Fifty; Marks; All Day On the Sands; Change In Time; Morgan's Boy; Couples; A Very British Coup; June*. m. University administrator and councillor Michael Freeman; 1 d. Polly, 1 s. Carl. Address: c/o Jeremy Conway. Birthsign: Aries. Hobbies: birdwatching, pond-dipping. **Most Cherished Possession:** 'My mother's engagement ring.' **Favourite Memory:** 'Arriving home after five months on Broadway.'

YATES, Pauline

Actress, b. 16 June, St Helens, Lancashire. Went to Oldham rep straight from school. Also worked in rep at Liverpool, but career mainly in TV, incl: *Hancock; The Second Interview; Rooms; The Fall and Rise of Reginald Perrin; England's Green and Pleasant Land; Keep It In the Family*. Films: *She'll Be Wearing Pink Pyjamas; Hold the Dream; The Four Feathers*. Theatre incl: *Pride and Prejudice; O'Malley's Talk of the Devil*. m. actor/writer Donald Churchill; 2 d. Jemma, Polly. Address: c/o Kate Feast. Birthsign: Gemini. Hobbies: reading, swimming, tapestry. **Most Cherished Possession:** 'A photo album of my family. It's such fun to look back on our laughter, high times and low times.' **Favourite Memory:** 'Coming back home from holiday – any holiday.'

YIP, David

Actor, b. 4 June 1951, Liverpool. A shipping clerk for British Rail, before becoming assistant stage manager at Liverpool's Neptune and Everyman theatres. Trained at the E15 Acting School, London. Theatre incl: *Antony and Cleopatra; Romeo and Juliet; Rosencrantz and Guildenstern Are Dead* (all at the Young Vic); *Hair* (London West End). Films: *Indiana Jones and the Temple of Doom; Empire of the Sun; A View To a Kill; Ping Pong*. TV movie: *Murder On the Moon*. TV incl: *Savages; Quatermass; Whodunnit?; Spies; The Chelsea Murders; Doctor Who; Mystery of the Disappearing Schoolgirls; Going To Work; It Ain't Half Hot Mum; 3-2-1; The Cuckoo Waltz;* starred as Det Sgt John Ho in *The Chinese Detective; The Caucasian Chalk Circle; King and Castle; Making Out;* Michael Choi in *Brookside*. m. 1st Liz Bagley (dis.). Address: c/o Brookside Productions.

YOUNG, John

Actor, b. 18 June 1916, Edinburgh. Trained in rep at Edinburgh Lyceum, Theatre Royal Glasgow and Wolverhampton Grand Theatre. More recently appeared at Glasgow Citizens' Theatre Company. Films incl: *Ring of Bright Water; The Life of Brian; Chariots of Fire; Time Bandits; The Dollar Bottom*. TV incl: *McKenzie; Hamlet; Square Mile of Murder; The Walls of Jericho; Her Mother's House;* Rev McPherson in *Take the High Road; Brigadista*. m. Winifred (Freddie); 1 s. actor Paul. Address: c/o Young Casting. Birthsign: Gemini. Hobbies: making home movies. **Most Cherished Possession:** 'Collection of family movies.' **Favourite Memory:** 'My first visit to a pantomime at the age of four, as it seemed to be sheer magic.;

YOUNG, Paul

Actor, b. 3 July 1944, Edinburgh. Trained at Royal Scottish Academy of Music and Drama. Theatre incl: *Willie Rough; The Bevellers; The Passion* (European tour); *The Three Estates*. Films incl: *Geordie; Submarine X-1; SOS Titanic; Another Time – Another Place; Chato's Land*. TV incl: *Sunset Song; Homework; Take the High Road; Holy City; Something's Got To Give; Doom Castle; Taggart; Brond; House On the Hill; Brigadista; Extras; No Job for a Lady; Leaving; The Justice Game*. m. journalist Sheila Duffy; 2 d. Kate, Hannah. Address: c/o Hutton Management. Birthsign: Cancer. Hobbies: fishing, birdwatching, wine collecting. **Most Cherished Possession:** 'A fishing creel that belonged to Scottish comedian, Will Fyffe.' **Favourite Memory:** 'Being present at the birth of both our children – a most moving experience.'

ZMED, Adrian

Actor, b. 14 March, Chicago, Illinois. Trained at the Goodman School of Drama. Theatre: *Beginner's Luck*. Films incl: *Bump In the Night; Grease II; Bachelor Party*. TV incl: *Love On the Run; Victim For Victims; Flatbush;* host of *Dance Fever*. Plays Vince Romano in *T J Hooker*. Guest appearances incl: *Starsky and Hutch; Good Time Girls; Bosom Buddies*. m. Barbara; 1 s. Zachary. Address: c/o The Gersh Agency, 222 North Canon Drive, Beverly Hills, Calif 90210. Hobbies: singing rock, dancing. Pets: one English Setter. **Most Cherished Possession:** 'A $15,000 short-haired wig that I wore to church to hide my shoulder-length hair. My father was a Romanian Orthodox priest!' **Favourite Memory:** 'Playing football in High School. I wanted to turn pro, but broke my leg and then turned to acting.'

UNFORGETTABLES

ANDREWS, Éamonn, CBE

Commentator/interviewer/compere, b. 19 December 1922, Dublin, d. 5 November 1987. One of the most celebrated television personalities of our time, his easy manner and polished professionalism endeared him to millions. As a schoolboy, he was the All-Ireland Amateur Junior Boxing Champion (Middleweight) and made his first broadcast at the age of 16, on Radio Eirann, as a boxing commentator. From 1941 to 1950, he was a regular sports commentator and interviewer on Radio Eirann, and in 1949 was a columnist on the *Irish Independent*. In 1950, he presented the BBC's famous radio quiz *Ignorance Is Bliss*, and the following year chaired BBC television's *What's My Line?* It made him a household name, consolidated four years later by *This Is your Life*. In 1964, he switched to ITV as the first presenter of *World of Sport* and, later, as host of *The Éamonn Andrews Show*, which ran for four years. In 1978, he brought back *This Is Your Life*, and in 1984 revived *What's My Line?* Among other activities, he presented children's programmes *Crackerjack!* and *Playbox*, wrote two autobiographical books, *This Is My Life* and *Surprise of Your Life*, and had extensive business interests. A devoutly religious man, he received a papal knighthood in 1964 for his charitable works, and in 1970 he was made a CBE. Éamonn was married for 36 years, to Grainne, and had three adopted children – a son and two daughters.

Lady BARNETT, Isobel

TV personality/panellist, b. 30 June 1918, Aberdeen, d. 20 October 1980. One of television's best-known faces throughout the Fifties. Educated in York, she studied medicine at Glasgow University and qualified as a doctor in 1940. The following year, she married Sir Geoffrey Barnett, solicitor and company director. In 1948, she gave up practising medicine and for the next 20 years was a Justice of the Peace. In 1953, she became one of the original panellists of BBC TV's quiz *What's My Line?* and appeared regularly in it until 1963. Her charm, knowledge and intuition won her a huge following among television audiences and she was much in demand as an after-dinner speaker. She also appeared in *Any Questions?, Twenty Questions, Many a Slip* and *Petticoat Lane*. She published her biography, *My Life Line*, in 1965, and was involved in charitable work. Lady Barnett's husband died 10 years before her and she left a son.

BLAKELY, Colin

Actor, b. 23 September 1930, Bangor, Northern Ireland, d. 7 May 1987. An actor of great power and presence, chiefly working in the theatre but also in television and films. He started work at 18 in a sports goods stores, then as a timber-loader in railways. He finally joined the family business in Belfast. In 1957, after a spell of amateur dramatics with the Bangor Operatic Society, he turned professional with the Group Theatre, Belfast. From 1957 to 1959, he was at the Royal Court Theatre, appearing in *Cock-A-Doodle Dandy, Sergeant Musgrave's Dance* and – to critical approval – *The Taming of Murderers Rock*. In 1961, he joined the Royal Shakespeare Company at Stratford-upon-Avon and from, 1963 to 1968, was with the National Theatre at the Old Vic. Among his many plays were *The Recruiting Officer, Saint Joan, Royal Hunt of the Sun, Volpone* and *Oedipus*. He returned to the Royal Shakespare in 1972 in Harold Pinter's *Old Times* and was subsequently in many West End plays. In 1969, his controversial study of Jesus Christ in Dennis Potter's *Son of Man* gained him wide recognition. Other TV roles included *Peer Gynt, The Birthday Party* and John Mortimer's saga *Paradise Postponed*. His films included *This Sporting Life, Equus, The Dogs of War* and *Charlie Bubbles*. Colin was married to actress Margaret Whiting for 26 years and had three sons.

BRYANT, Margot

Actress, b. 1898, Hull, d. New Year's Day 1989. Celebrated as Minnie Caldwell, the character she created in *Coronation Street*. The daughter of a doctor, she moved with her family to London while still a child. Attracted to a career in the theatre while a teenager, she started in pantomime as a chorus girl, progressing to musical comedy – 'though I'd never trained to do either'. She subsequently appeared in the Fred Astaire stage musical *Stop Flirting* in London's West End. Her first TV appearance was in a play, *My Mother Said*. In 1960, she joined Episode 3 of *Coronation Street* and stayed with the serial for the next 16 years, until forced to leave through ill health. She spent most of the last years of her life in a Manchester nursing home.
Although she played the loveable, put-upon character Minnie, forever drinking milk stout in the Rovers with the garrulous Ena Sharples, she was very different in real life. William Roache, who was also in the original cast, says: 'Margot wasn't a bit like Minnie. She liked to shock people and always had a twinkle in her eye.'

CARSON, Violet, OBE, MA

Actress, b. 1 September 1905, Manchester, d. 26 December 1983. As the irascible Ena Sharples, she created a character loved by millions and became the first of *Coronation Street*'s superstars. She began to play the piano at the age of three and, by 15, was relief pianist at a Manchester cinema, accompanying silent films. She married at 26, but was widowed two years later and never remarried. To support herself, she continued to play the piano at clubs, socials and cinemas. In 1935, she made her first broadcast, when she joined the BBC as a pianist and singer of anything from comic songs to operatic arias. In 1946, she became known as Auntie Vi on radio's *Children's Hour*, and travelled the country entertaining servicemen. In the same year, she teamed up with Wilfred Pickles in the celebrated radio show *Have A Go*, and stayed with it for six years. She then spent four years with *Woman's Hour* as an interviewer and panellist, from which she graduated to radio drama and features and, finally, BBC television. In 1960, she joined ITV's *Coronation Street*, playing the aggressive, hairnetted Ena Sharples, and appeared in 2000 episodes, until her departure in 1980. Violet was made an OBE in 1965 and an Honorary MA at Manchester University in 1973. Such was her fame during the Sixties that an Italian newspaper wrote: 'Ena Sharples is better known in Britain than its Prime Minister.'

COOPER, Tommy

Comedian/magician, b. 19 March 1922, Caerphilly, South Wales, d. 15 April 1984. A man with a craggy, mobile face and a manic expression, he developed a unique act – a bungling magician whose every trick went hopelessly wrong, bringing him close to nervous despair. In fact, he was an accomplished magician and a member of the exclusive Magic Circle, as well as a stand-up comic. His childhood was spent in Exeter and Southampton, from where he joined the Horse Guards for seven years. Soon after he left the Army in 1947, he turned professional as an entertainer, doing cabaret work, and making his TV debut on Christmas Eve that year. Appearances at the Windmill Theatre in London, in summer seasons, pantomimes, and scores of TV programmes followed. In 1954, he appeared in Las Vegas and, in later years, did TV shows that were seen in Europe and Australia. He performed before royalty at Buckingham Palace and Windsor Castle, and in several Royal Variety shows in London and Glasgow. A much-loved comedian, he was regarded as the 'comic's comic', such was his esteem among fellow-entertainers. He died at the end of his act on the stage of Her Majesty's Theatre, in London, at the close of a live televised performance. His red fez and famous catchphrase 'Just like that!' have become part of theatrical history. Tommy left a widow, Gwen, and two children.

UNFORGETTABLES

DAVIES, Rupert

Actor, b. 22 May 1916, Liverpool, d. 22 November 1976. Famous for his TV portrayal of Inspector Maigret, the amiable but shrewd French detective. At 16, he started an apprenticeship for the Merchant Navy, and at 22 was an observer in the Fleet Air Arm. Shot down in 1942 off the Dutch coast, during World War Two he was a prisoner-of-war in Germany, until 1945, during which time he became interested in acting. After 'demob' in 1946, he started work in television and made his stage debut in London in *Back Home*, an ex-POW show. Work in various repertory theatres followed, with a long spell at the Old Vic in, among other plays, *The Merry Wives of Windsor*, *Henry V* and *A Midsummer Night's Dream*. He also appeared in several films, including the *The Spy Who Came In From the Cold*, *Witchfinder General* and *Zeppelin*. In 1960, he played George Simenon's pipe-smoking detective *Maigret* on BBC television and stayed with the series for four years and 52 episodes. Although the role made him a star and he was subsequently a busy actor, he was never able to shake off the Maigret image. In 1963, he was named Actor of the Year and, in 1964, Pipeman of the Year. Rupert left a widow and two sons.

DORS, Diana

Actress, b. 23 October 1931, Swindon, Wiltshire, d. 4 May 1984. A much-loved personality who achieved intial fame and notoriety as a sex symbol, but who ultimately became a serious character actress and a national institution. Stagestruck as a schoolgirl, she studied at RADA and, at 16, was under contract to the Rank Organisation. The same year she appeared in the first of her many films, *Shop At Sly Corner*. By the age of 25, she was Britain's highest-paid actress and its answer to Marilyn Monroe. Among her films were *Holiday Camp*, *The Last Page*, *A Kid For Two Farthings*, *The Weak and the Wicked*, *Baby Love* and *Theatre of Blood*. It was in *Yield to the Night*, in 1956, that she earned praise as a dramatic actress. She also filmed, less successfully, in Hollywood, Italy and Spain. On TV, she starred in *A Nice Little Business*, *Queenie's Castle* and *Just William*, appeared in *Celebrity Squares* and *The Two Ronnies*. She wrote several books, including her memoirs, *Behind Closed Doors* and *For Adults Only*. Towards the end of her life, shadowed by ill-health, she continued working on TV and did a spell as an agony aunt for TV-am. Diana was married three times: to Dennis Hamilton, who died; American comedian Dickie Dawson, from whom she was divorced; and, finally to actor Alan Lake, who survived her death but committed suicide five months later. Three sons survive – two from her second marriage, one from her third.

GORDON, Noele

Actress/singer, b. 25 December 1923, East Ham, London, d. 14 April 1985. The 'Queen of the Soaps', she played Meg Mortimer, owner of the *Crossroads* motel, 3521 times. Educated at Ilford Convent School, she trained at RADA, then went into rep in Edinburgh and Birmingham, before reaching London. She appeared in the stage hits *Black Velvet*, *Let's Face It*, *Diamond Lil* (with Mae West) and her first major success, *Brigadoon*, in which she gave 1000 performances between 1949 and 1951. She visited the US to study TV and came back to join ATV, the newly founded Midlands ITV company, in 1955 as an adviser on women's programmes. She subsequently became a familiar face on TV in such programmes as *Week-End*, *Fancy That*, *Tea With Noele Gordon* and *Midland Profile*. She joined *Crossroads* when it began in 1964, as Meg Richardson, owner of the motel, and stayed with the serial for 17 years. During this time, she was eight times voted Favourite Female Personality on TV in the *TVTimes* Top 10 Awards. When she was sacked from the serial in 1981, to the outrage of millions of fans, she returned to the theatre and musical comedy in a successful production of *Gypsy* at the Haymarket, Leicester, and a London production of *Call Me Madam*. In her youth, she had been chosen as a model by John Logie Baird when making his early experiments in colour TV. Noele never married.

GREENE, Richard

Actor/producer, b. 25 August 1918, Plymouth, d. 1 June 1985. A Hollywood film star who became television's definitive Robin Hood in the Fifties. Educated at Cardinal Vaughan School, at 18 he joined the Brandon Thomas Repertory Company in Scotland. Four years later, when touring in *French Without Tears*, he was seen by a Hollywood talent scout and starred opposite Loretta Young in *Four Men and a Prayer*. By 1940, he was established. Among his films were *My Lucky Star, Kentucky, The Little Princess, The Hound of the Baskervilles* and *Stanley and Livingstone*. He joined the Army at the outbreak of the war and was medically discharged five years later. In 1945, he made his London stage debut in *The Desert Rats*. The following year, he went to Hollywood and eventually made more than 40 films, both there and in Britain. Among these were *Forever Amber, Lorna Doone, Desert Hawke, Black Castle, Bandits of Corsica* and *Captain Scarlett*. In 1955, a decline in his career was arrested by starring in ITV's *The Adventures of Robin Hood*. The series ran for four years and 143 episodes, and was re-run in the early Sixties. He also starred in the spin-off film *Sword of Sherwood Forest*. Later that decade, he went into semi-retirement. After an operation for a brain tumour in 1983, he worked no more. Richard's first marriage, to actress Patricia Medina, was dissolved; his second was to Beatrice Summers.

HANDL, Irene

Actress/novelist, b. 27 December 1901, London, d. 29 November 1987. One of Britain's best-loved comedy actresses – her eccentric cockney characters were unique – she entered showbusiness at the late age of 36. She trained at the Embassy School of Acting and was an immediate hit in the West End success *George and Margaret* in 1937. Two years later, she had a small role in a film and, during the next 25 years, created a gallery of marvellous cameo performances in such memorable successes as *The Belles of St Trinian's, Brothers-in-Law* and *I'm All Right Jack*, with Peter Sellers. At 64, she published her first novel, *The Sioux*, following it with a second in 1973, *The Gold Tip Pfitzer* – both critically acclaimed books. Television brought her added fame when she starred with Wilfred Pickles in *For the Love of Ada*. Among other TV series she appeared in were *Metal Mickey, Supergran* and *In Sickness and In Health*. She never married. Right up until the end of her life, she continued to work in films, TV and even pantomimes. Irene said of her work: 'My loveable old girls make a lot of people happy and I appreciate it.' We all did.

HENDERSON, Dickie, OBE

Comedian/dancer, b. 30 October 1922, London, d. 22 September 1985. A versatile, all-round entertainer who was a popular television star of the Fifties and early Sixties. Privately educated in Hollywood and Britain, he made his debut at the age of 10 in Noel Coward's film *Cavalcade*, while touring the US with his famous father, music-hall entertainer Dick Henderson. He returned to Britain and, at 16, made his theatrical debut as an 'eccentric dancer'. He was in the Army during the war, after which he played in revues and pantomimes. In 1953, he made his first TV appearance in *Face the Music*, followed by the Arthur Askey series *Before Your Very Eyes*. He compered *Sunday Night at the Palladium* and then starred for 12 years in *The Dickie Henderson Show*, a domestic comedy series, with June Laverick as his wife. He made numerous appearances on TV, toured the US, Australia, Canada and Hong Kong, and appeared in eight Royal Variety shows. His theatre work included a year in the West End hit musical *Wish You Were Here*, and 20 months in *Teahouse of the August Moon*. In 1980, Dickie was made an OBE for his services to the theatre and charity. His first wife, Dixie Rose, with whom he had two children, died in 1969; his second marriage was to Gwynneth.

UNFORGETTABLES

HOBLEY, McDonald

Announcer/compere/actor, b. 1917, Port Stanley, Falklands, d. 30 July 1987. He was the first post-war announcer for the reopening of the BBC television service. Educated at an English prep school, then in South America and, finally, at Brighton College. After college, in 1936, he joined the company at Brighton's Theatre Royal. He also appeared in Cambridge and Bath, and toured in J B Priestley's *Time and the Conways*. At the outbreak of war, he joined the Royal Artillery, serving on Louis Mountbatten's staff and, finally, as an announcer for South Eastern Asia Command radio in Ceylon (now Sri Lanka). He left the Army in 1946 and was the only one of 281 applicants to be selected as the BBC's sole male continuity announcer. In 1954, he was voted TV Personality of the Year. He was also the chairman of the radio series *Does the Team Think?* In 1956, he left the BBC to join ITV as a commentator until 1959, when his contract ended and he returned to the theatre. He appeared in various plays and pantomimes with repertory companies, and in London's West End with a run in *No Sex Please, We're British*. McDonald was married three times.

JACKSON, Gordon, OBE

Actor, b. 19 December 1923, Glasgow, d. 14 January 1990. A gifted actor who won fame with his television portrayal of the meticulous butler Hudson in *Upstairs, Downstairs* which ran for six years from 1970, and was seen throughout the world. Educated at Hillhead High School, he left at 15 to join Rolls-Royce and train to become an engineering draughtsman. While still at school, as an amateur actor, he broadcast on the BBC in radio plays. At 17, Ealing Studios cast him as a soldier in *The Foreman Went To France*. More film roles followed, until he abandoned draughtsmanship to become a full-time actor. For 10 years, he worked in repertory at Glasgow, Worthing and Perth, finally making his London debut in 1951 in *Seagulls Over Sorrento*. Four years later, he was Ishmael in Orson Welles's London stage production of *Moby Dick*, subsequently playing leading supporting roles in *Macbeth, Hamlet, Hedda Gabler* and *Twelfth Night*, and the title role in *Noah* at Chichester Festival Theatre. He appeared in many films, including, *Whisky Galore, The Great Escape, The Ipcress File, The Prime of Miss Jean Brodie, Tunes of Glory* and *The Shooting Party*. His other TV work included *The Soldier's Tale, A Town Like Alice* and the long-running series *The Professionals*. He was made an OBE in 1979. Gordon was married to actress Rona Anderson and had two sons.

JACQUES, Hattie

Actress/comedienne, b. 7 February 1924, Sandgate, Kent, d. 6 October 1980. A versatile actress and a comic personality, she made her professional debut at the age of 20 at the Players' Theatre, London. It was here that she succeeded in the role she considered her favourite – as the Fairy Queen in pantomime – and frequently returned to in later years to write, produce and appear in the Players' late-night revues and pantomimes. She did a 1947–8 tour with the Old Vic, and became a well known radio voice when she joined the celebrated *ITMA* team in 1948 as Sophie Tuckshop, the greedy schoolgirl. She went on to create further memorable characters in other radio successes, *Educating Archie* and *Hancock's Half-Hour*. For 20 years, she enjoyed a comedy partnership with Eric Sykes, as screen brother and sister, and was a regular member of the *Carry On* team, appearing in 14 of the films. Other films included *Nicholas Nickleby, The Pickwick Papers* and *Make Mine Mink*. She was also a singer, playing Titipu in the BBC's version of *The Mikado* (1967) and the TV musical version of *Pickwick* (1969). Her marriage to actor John Le Mesurier was dissolved in 1965 and she never remarried. They had two sons. In private life, she was a shy person, sensitive about her ample proportions. Hattie once said: 'When you're my size, you're conditioned from childhood to people making jokes against you. You have to make them laugh with you, not at you.'

JAMES, Sid

Actor, b. May 1913, Johannesburg, South Africa, d. 26 April 1976. A much-loved comic actor with a 'lived-in' face and an infectious chuckle. Until he was 25, he did various jobs – coal-heaver, stevedore, boxer, dancer and skating instructor. He joined the South African Army in 1939, serving with an entertainments unit. Demobbed in 1946, he came to Britain and spent several years in rep, including the Old Vic. Plays included musicals *Kiss Me Kate, Guys and Dolls* and *The Solid Gold Cadillac*. He also appeared in more than 250 films, including *The Lavender Hill Mob, Too Many Crooks, The Deep Blue Sea, Trapeze!* and most of the *Carry On* productions. Already a well known face, it was his partnership with Tony Hancock that was to make him a household name. *Hancock's Half-Hour* ran for five years on BBC radio and nearly three years on TV. After the duo split up, James starred in several TV comedy series, *East End, West End, George and the Dragon, Citizen James* and *Bless This House*. He was back on the stage, starring in *The Mating Season* at the Empire Theatre in Sunderland, when he collapsed during the performance and died. Sid was twice married: to dancer Meg Williams, with whom he had a daughter; and to actress Valerie Ashton, with whom he had a son and a daughter.

KINNEAR, Roy

Actor, b. 8 January 1934, Wigan, d. 20 September 1988 while filming in Spain. One of the most popular and well-loved character actors in films and TV, his roles ranged from classics to broad comedy, from Shakespeare to pantomime. Short, fat and bald, he once said: 'I see my characters as short, fat and bald – and that's the way I play them.' With an engaging grin and a breathless, anxious manner, he had the qualities of a clown, exploiting his physique to create a unique niche for himself playing cockney rogues and vagabonds. Educated at George Heriot's School, Edinburgh, he went straight to RADA at 17, breaking his time there to do National Service in the Army. He first appeared in rep at Newquay in 1955, and four years later joined Joan Littlewood's Theatre Workshop, appearing in *Make Me An Offer* and *Sparrers Can't Sing*. In the Sixties, he won national celebrity in TV's *That Was the Week That Was*, subsequently appearing in many TV plays and series, and starring in the TV series *Inside George Webley*. Among notable theatre roles were Sancho in *The Travails of Sancho Panza* at the National, 1969, Pishchik in *The Cherry Orchard*, 1985, and a revival of *A Man For All Seasons* at the Savoy, 1987. His numerous films included *Help!, The Three Musketeers*, and *One of Our Dinosaurs Is Missing*. He was married to Carmel and had three children.

LOWE, Arthur

Actor, b. 22 September 1915, Hayfield, Derbyshire, d. 15 April 1982. A celebrated character actor best known for his portrayal as the pompous Captain Mainwaring in the TV comedy series *Dad's Army*. He left school at 16, joined the cavalry during World War Two and, while serving in Palestine, acquired the taste for acting. After the war, he took a course at RADA, then joined a rep company in Manchester. His West End stage debut was in 1950, after which he had leading roles in the musicals *Call Me Madam, Pal Joey* and *The Pajama Game*, and in John Osborne's play *Inadmissable Evidence*. He first appeared on TV in 1951, but it was his role as the irascible Leonard Swindley in *Coronation Street*, which was to last for six years, that made his name. He appeared in several films during his career, including *Kind Hearts and Coronets, The Ruling Class, O Lucky Man, No Sex Please, We're British* and a big-screen version of *Dad's Army*. Among his other TV work was his role as Mr Micawber in *David Copperfield*, and Father Duddleswell in the comedy series *Bless Me, Father*. He collapsed in his dressing room while appearing in the comedy *Home at Seven* with his actress wife, Joan Cooper, and died in Birmingham General Hospital. A kindly, modest man, he never considered himself a star. Arthur was married for 34 years and had one son and a stepson.

UNFORGETTABLES

McANALLY, Ray

Actor, b. 13 March 1926, Buncrana, Co Donegal, d. 15 July 1989. A fine character actor who achieved international fame nearer the end of his career through films, but who was long revered as one of Ireland's leading theatre players. Throughout his life, McAnally nourished a passionate commitment to Irish theatre in general and Dublin's Abbey Theatre in particular. Educated at the National School at Moville, Donegal, and St Eunan's College, Letterkenney, he studied for the priesthood at St Patrick's College, Maynooth, Co Kildare. At 21, he joined the Abbey Theatre and appeared in more than 200 plays, including works by O'Casey, Shaw, Synge and Yates. He made his London debut in 1962, at the Arts Theatre in *A Cheap Bunch of Nice Flowers*, and won critical respect two years later in *Who's Afraid of Virginia Woolf?* He played *Macbeth* at the Abbey in 1971, the first Shakespeare performed there for 30 years, appeared at Chichester and the Aldwych for the Royal Shakespeare Company and was directing, acting and teaching at the Abbey in the Eighties. His film career started in 1958 and included *Billy Budd*, *The Mission* (Best Supporting Actor Oscar), *White Mischief* and his last film, *Venus Peter*. His TV successes included *A Perfect Spy*, 1987 (BAFTA Best Actor), and *A Very British Coup*, 1988 (BAFTA Best Actor).

MORECAMBE, Eric, OBE

Comedian, b. 14 May 1926, Morecambe, Lancashire, d. 28 May 1984. Half the double act – with Ernie Wise – that became one of television's most inventive comedy partnerships. Born John Eric Bartholomew, he adopted the name of his birthplace. At 15, already a singer and dancer, he joined Bryan Michie's *Youth Takes a Bow*, in which he met his future partner, Ernest Wiseman. Following National Service, chance reunited them in 1947, when Morecambe joined Lord John Sanger's Circus and found himself a 'feed' to the resident comic, Wise. They finally broke into BBC radio through *Workers' Playtime* and eventually had their own series *You're Only Young Once*. In 1954, their first TV series, *Running Wild*, flopped, but they returned seven years later with *The Morecambe and Wise Show* and thereafter enjoyed phenomenal success. They also made three films, *The Intelligence Men*, *That Riviera Touch* and *The Magnificent Two*. He and Wise wrote their biography, *Eric and Ernie*, in 1978, and Morecambe wrote two further books – a novel, *Mr Lonely*, and a children's book, *The Reluctant Vampire*. In 1976, he was made an OBE and Freeman of the City of London, and in 1977 he received an honorary doctorate from Lancaster University. Eric was married for 31 years to Joan Bartlett, a former dancer, and they had three children: a daughter and two sons (one of them adopted).

NEGUS, Arthur, OBE

Antiques expert/presenter, b. 29 March 1903, Reading, Berkshire, d. 5 April 1985. Son of a cabinet maker, he was educated at Reading School. At 17, when his father died, he took over as a dealer in antiques and continued the business for 20 years. During World War Two – when he was a War Reserve Policeman – the business was destroyed in an air raid. In 1946, he joined Knowles & Co, a Gloucestershire firm of fine art auctioneers, as an appraiser, becoming a partner in 1972. His experience and expertise, coupled with a warm and cheerful manner, made him a television natural to host *Going For a Song*, which ran for 10 years from 1965. Radio and other TV series followed, including *Pride of Place*, *Collector's World*, the long-running *The Antiques Road Show*, and finally, in 1984, *Arthur Negus Enjoys*. He wrote two books, *Going For a Song: English Furniture* (1969) and *A Life Among Antiques* (1982). Arthur was made a Freeman of the City of London in 1976, and an OBE in 1982. He was married for 59 years to Irene Amy Hollett, and they had two daughters.

NICHOLS, Dandy

Actress, b. 1907, Hammersmith, London, d. 6 February 1986. Celebrated as the down-trodden wife of Alf Garnett in *Till Death Us Do Part*. Christened Daisy, she was a stage-struck child playing truant to see John Gielgud at the Old Vic in his first *Hamlet*. For 12 years, she was a secretary in a shoe-polish factory, learning her craft in the evenings at drama, diction and fencing classes at St Pancras. Spotted by a producer, she joined his repertory company in Cambridge, adopting the childhood nickname Dandy for the stage. During World War Two, she returned to office work for two years and did a six-week tour with the services entertainment organisation ENSA. In 1945, she returned to acting and rapidly became a character actress, specialising in comedy roles. She subsequently appeared in more than 60 films, including *Hue and Cry, The Deep Blue Sea, The Knack, Doctor Doolittle* and *Yield to the Night* with Diana Dors. In 1957, she was the first to join ATV's twice-weekly soap *Emergency–Ward 10*. She was chosen to play Else in the BBC's *Till Death Us Do Part* in 1964 and remained until 1973, when she tired of the role. She returned to continue as Else in the spin-off series *In Sickness and In Health*. In later years, she also scored critical success in several plays, notably Harold Pinter's *The Birthday Party, The Clandestine Marriage, Plunder* and *Home*, the latter both in London and New York. Dandy's only marriage was dissolved.

NIXON, David

Magician/entertainer, b. 29 December 1919, London, d. 1 December 1978. Celebrated as the amiable TV magician and *What's My Line?* panellist in the Fifties and Sixties. Started conjuring as a boy, making his first professional appearance in 1941, entertaining servicemen. After the war, he teamed up with Norman Wisdom in variety and concert parties. In 1953, he came to television through joining the panel of *What's My Line?* and was subsequently in demand for many shows, including *My Wildest Dream, Home and Dry, It's Magic, The David Nixon Show, Comedy Bandbox, Candid Camera* and *Now For Nixon*. He spent 37 years as an entertainer, making four round-the-world cabaret tours, worked regularly in pantomime and appeared before royalty. A leading member of the Grand Order of Water Rats, he was accorded the honour of being King Rat in 1967 and 1977. David was married three times: his last to Vivienne Nichols, with whom he had a son and a daughter.

Lord OLIVIER, Laurence

Actor/director/manager, b. 22 May 1907, Dorking, Surrey, d. 15 July 1989, Steyning, West Sussex. The greatest actor of his generation, whose astonishing achievements and versatility embraced practically all the great heroic roles in the classical theatre, as well as a range of diverse characters in many memorable films. He was founder director of the National Theatre (1963–73) and first to bring Shakespeare successfully to the screen, both as actor and director. At 10, in a school production of *Julius Caesar*, he was seen by the famous actress Ellen Terry, who wrote: 'The small boy who played Brutus is already a great actor'. He joined Birmingham rep in 1926 and did seasons at the Old Vic (later as a co-director) and with the Shakespeare Memorial Company. He was acclaimed for roles in *Romeo and Juliet, Hamlet, Henry V, Titus Andronicus* and *Othello*. Other theatrical successes ranged from *Uncle Vanya* to *The Entertainer*. He starred in the Hollywood film *Beau Geste* in 1929, with memorable matinee-idol roles in *Wuthering Heights, Rebecca* and *Lady Hamilton*. Olivier's masterpieces of Shakespeare on film were *Henry V* (Oscar), *Hamlet* (Oscar), and *Richard III*. His TV successes included *Brideshead Revisited, A Voyage Round My Father, The Ebony Tower* and *King Lear*. He was knighted in 1947 and created a baronet in 1970. Lord Oliver and his third wife, actress Joan Plowright, had three children in addition to a son from his second marriage, to actress Vivien Leigh.

UNFORGETTABLES

PHOENIX, Pat

Actress, b. 26 November 1924, Galway, Ireland, d. 18 September 1986. An actress who created a legendary character in Britain's longest-running television soap, *Coronation Street*. Raised in Manchester, she started her career in 1939 with the BBC in a radio play, and the following year in *Children's Hour*. Soon after leaving school, she joined Manchester Arts Theatre Company, and for several years was in provincial rep throughout the north of England. In the early Fifties, she joined Joan Littlewood's celebrated Theatre Workshop. Her theatre roles included the plays *Suddenly Last Summer, The Miracle Worker, Gaslight* and *My Cousin Rachel*. In 1960, when her career was at a low ebb, she landed the role with which she was to become identified for the rest of her life, as *Coronation Street*'s Elsie Tanner. She appeared in the first episode and stayed, except for a two-year break, until 1983. After the *Street*, she toured theatres, did radio phone-ins, chat-shows and appeared on TV-am. She also starred in a comedy series for TV, *Constant Hot Water*, in which she played a seaside landlady. She wrote two autobiographies, *All My Burning Bridges* (1974) and *Love, Curiosity, Freckles and Doubt* (1983). Pat was married three times, her last to actor Anthony Booth, shortly before her death. She had no children.

QUAYLE, Sir Anthony, CBE

Actor/producer, b. 7 September 1913, Ainsdale, Lancashire, d. 20 October 1989. One of the theatre's 'greats', with a career that ranged from the classics and Shakespeare to film and television. Educated at Rugby, he trained for the theatre at RADA, making his professional debut in 1931 at the 'Q' Theatre as Richard Coeur de Lion and Will Scarlett in *Robin Hood*. In 1934, he played Guildenstern in John Gielgud's *Hamlet* and, from then on, began to appear in classics with the Old Vic, both at home and abroad. An Army staff officer during the war, he fought behind the enemy lines with Albanian partisans. Demobilised as a major in 1945, he returned to the theatre in *The Rivals* (with Edith Evans). In 1946, he directed *Crime and Punishment* (with John Gielgud and Edith Evans) and played Enobarbus in *Antony and Cleopatra*. He joined the Shakespeare company at Stratford-upon-Avon and led from 1947 to 1956 as its director. He played Aaron in *Titus Andronicus* (with Laurence Olivier as Titus) to critical acclaim in London, New York and Europe. Among his many successes were *Long Day's Journey Into Night, Galileo, Sleuth* and *King Lear*. In 1983, he formed the Compass Theatre and toured the provinces with distinguished productions. His many films included Olivier's *Hamlet, The Guns of Navarone, Ice Cold In Alex* and *Lawrence of Arabia*. Made a CBE in 1952 and knighted in 1985, Anthony left a second wife and two daughters.

ROSSITER, Leonard

Actor, b. 21 October 1926, Liverpool, d. 5 October 1984. A versatile actor whose work ranged from classical and modern theatre to films and popular television. Unable to afford to go to university, he worked in an insurance office until he was 27, when he joined Preston rep. Four years later, he landed a role in the successful musical *Free As Air*. He moved to the Bristol Old Vic in 1959, and subsequently appeared in many films, including *A Kind of Loving, Billy Liar, This Sporting Life, Oliver!, King Rat* and *2001 – A Space Odyssey*. His work in television included many plays and series, with a long spell in *Z-Cars*, and in the theatre several notable critical successes, such as *The Resistable Rise of Arturo Ui, The Caretaker, Semi-Detached* and *Rules of the Game*. In the Seventies, his role as the lascivious landlord Rigsby in the long-running comedy series *Rising Damp* made him nationally famous, consolidated by another starring role, in *The Fall and Rise of Reginald Perrin*, from 1976 to 1980, in which he created another memorable character. He also starred in a film version of *Rising Damp* in 1980. His commercials for Cinzano in the Eighties, with Joan Collins, were comic masterpieces. Leonard died during a performance of *Loot* at the Lyric Theatre in the West End of London. He was married to the actress Gillian Raine and had a daughter.

SILVERS, Phil

Comedian/actor, b. 11 May 1912, Brooklyn, New York, d. 1 November 1985. Internationally renowned for his comic genius as the loveable, wise-cracking, ever-on-the-make *Sgt Bilko*. Christened Philip Silversmith, he made his professional debut in showbusiness at the age of 11 as a 'breakdown' singer, entertaining cinema audiences when the projector failed. Two years later, he was a boy tenor in vaudeville. At 17, having appeared in two-reeler films, he joined Minsky's Burlesque troupe and toured for five years. His feature film debut was in *Hit Parade*, in 1940, followed by a succession of supporting roles in numerous musicals and light comedies throughout the next 20 years, including *You're In the Army Now*, *Roxie Hart*, *Cover Girl*, *Something For the Boys* and *It's a Mad Mad Mad Mad World*. In 1950, the TV series *You'll Never Get Rich* launched him in the role of *Sgt Bilko*, stationed at a fictional army camp in Fort Baxter, Kansas. The show ran for four years and has been repeated on and off ever since. Although he enjoyed subsequent success in both theatre and films, including *A Funny Thing Happened on the Way to the Forum*, the Sgt Bilko character overshowed all else that he did. Phil was married for 30 years to former television hostess Evelyn, and had four daughters.

TROUGHTON, Patrick

Actor, b. 25 March 1920, d. 28 March 1987. A versatile actor, both in the theatre and television, who became widely known for his portrayal of *Doctor Who*. Educated at London's Mill Hill School, he was trained at the Swiss Cottage School of acting, where he won a scholarship to Leighton Rollin's Studio for Actors at Long Island, New York. At the outbreak of World War Two, he hitched a lift back home in a ship that was sunk by a mine off the English coast. He survived to serve in the Royal Navy for the rest of the war, attaining the rank of commander. Demobbed in 1946, he joined Bristol Old Vic, working in Shakespearean productions. In 1950, at the Gateway Theatre, he played Hitler in *Eva Braun*. His television career started in 1948, embracing a vast range of work that included *The Six Wives of Henry VIII*, *A Family at War*, *Doctor Finlay's Casebook*, *Colditz* and *Churchill's People*. He appeared in many films, including *Frankenstein*, *Doomwatch*, *Sinbad and the Eye of the Tiger* and *The Omen*. But his real fame was the result of a three-year stint in BBC's *Doctor Who*, when he became the second actor to play the eccentric Time Lord. He collapsed and died in Columbus, Georgia, while making a personal appearance to fans at a *Doctor Who* convention. Patrick was married three times and left a widow and four sons, two daughters, a stepson and a stepdaughter. Son David follows in his acting footsteps.

WARNER, Jack, OBE

Actor/comedian, b. 24 October 1896, London, d. 24 May 1981. Renowned for 21 years on TV as the likeable, kindly 'copper on the beat' George *Dixon of Dock Green*. Christened John Waters, he was educated at Coopers' Company School and London University. He joined the RAF during World War One and was awarded the Meritorious Service Medal in 1918. At 30, he joined his famous music-hall sisters, Elsie and Doris Waters (Gert and Daisy), in variety and rapidly became successful as a stand-up comedian. During World War Two, he became known to millions through BBC Radio's *Garrison Theatre*, and then the long-running and popular *The Hugget* family series, with Kathleen Harrison as his wife. After this, he appeared in more than 50 films, including *Hue and Cry*, *The Captive Heart*, *Holiday Camp*, *It Always Rains on Sunday*, *The Final Test*, *Carve Her Name With Pride* and *The Blue Lamp*, in which he played a policeman, George Dixon, who was shot dead by a criminal (Dirk Bogarde). Six years later, in 1956, the character was resuscitated by writer, Ted Willis and *Dixon of Dock Green* was born. Warner played the role until his retirement in 1976. He was made an OBE in 1965 and an honorary DLitt by City University in 1975, the year he published his autobiography *Jack of All Trades*. Jack was married to Molly for 46 years.

USEFUL ADDRESSES

TV COMPANIES

BBC

Headquarters:
Broadcasting House, Portland Place
London W1A 1AA
Tel: 071-580 4468

Television:
Television Centre, Wood Lane
London W12 7RJ
Tel:081-743 8000

IBA Offices

Headquarters:
70 Brompton Road,
London SW3 1EY
Tel: 071-584 7011

Northern Ireland:
Royston House
34 Upper Queen Street
Belfast BT1 6HG
Tel: (0232) 248733

Scotland:
123 Blythswood Street
Glasgow G2 4AN
Tel: 041-226 4436

Wales & West of England:
Elgin House, 106 St Mary Street
Cardiff CF1 1PA
Tel: (0222) 384541/2/3

8th Floor, The Colston Centre
Colston Avenue
Bristol BS1 4UB
Tel: (0272) 213672

East of England:
24 Castle Meadow
Norwich NR1 3DH
Tel: (0603) 623533

Midlands:
Lyndon House
62 Hagley Road, Edgbaston
Birmingham B16 8PE
Tel: 021-454 1068

10/11 Poultry
Nottingham NG1 2HW
Tel: (0602) 585105

North-East England, The Borders, Isle of Man:
3 Collingwood Street
Newcastle upon Tyne NE1 1JS
Tel: 091-261 0148/091-232 3710

49 Botchergate, Carlisle CA1 1RQ
Tel: (0228) 25004

North-West England:
Television House
Mount Street
Manchester M2 5WT
Tel: 061-834 2707

South of England and Channel Islands:
Castle Chambers
Lansdowne Hill
Southampton SO1 0EQ
Tel: (0703) 331344/5

Ground Floor, Lyndean House
Albion Place
Maidstone ME14 5DZ
Tel: (0622) 761176/7

Royal London House
153 Armada Way
Plymouth PL1 1HY
Tel: (0752) 663031/662490

Yorkshire:
Dudley House, Albion Street
Leeds LS2 8PN
Tel: (0532) 441091/2

Regional ITV companies

Anglia Television:
Anglia House, Norwich NR1 3JG
Tel: (0603) 615151

Brook House, 113 Park Lane
London W1Y 4DX
Tel: 071-408 2288

Border Television:
Television Centre
Carlisle CA1 3NT
Tel: (0228) 25101

18 Clerkenwell Close
London EC1R 0AA
Tel: 071-253 3737

Central Television:
(West Midlands)
Central House, Broad Street
Birmingham B1 2JP
Tel: 021-643 9898

(East Midlands)
Television Centre
Nottingham NG7 2NA
Tel: (0602) 863322

35–38 Portman Square
London W1A 2HZ
Tel: 071-486 6688

46 Charlotte Street
London W1P 1LX
Tel: 071-637 4602

Channel Television:
The Television Centre
St Helier, Jersey
Channel Islands
Tel: (0534) 59446

The Television Centre
St George's Place
St Peter Port, Guernsey
Channel Islands
Tel: (0481) 23451

Grampian Television:
Queen's Cross
Aberdeen AB9 2XJ
Tel: (0224) 646464

Albany House
68 Albany Road
West Ferry
Dundee DD5 1NW
Tel: (0382) 739363

23/25 Huntly Street
Inverness IV3 5PR
Tel: (0463) 242624

6 Manor Place
Edinburgh EH3 7DD
Tel: 031-226 3926

29 Glasshouse Street
London W1R 5RG
Tel: 071-439 3141

Granada Television:
Granada Television Centre
Manchester M60 9EA
Tel: 061-832 7211

Albert Dock
Liverpool L3 4AA
Tel: 051-709 9393

36 Golden Square
London W1R 4AH
Tel: 071-734 8080

HTV Wales:
Television Centre
Culverhouse Cross
Cardiff CF5 6XJ
Tel: (0222) 590590

HTV West:
Television Centre
Bath Road
Bristol BS4 3HG
Tel: (0272) 778366

LWT:
South Bank Television Centre
London SE1 9LT
Tel: 071-261 3434

Scottish Television:
Cowcaddens
Glasgow G2 3PR
Tel: 041-332 9999

The Gateway
Edinburgh EH7 4AH
Tel: 031-557 4554

7 Adelaide Street
London WC2N 4LZ
Tel: 071-836 1500

Suite 306, Sunlight House
Quay Street, Manchester M3 3JY
Tel: 061-834 7621

Thames Television:
Thames Television House
306-316 Euston Road
London NW1 3BB
Tel: 071-387 9494

149 Tottenham Court Road
London W1P 9LL
Tel: 071-388 5199

Teddington Lock
Teddington
Middlesex TW11 9NT
Tel: 081-977 3252

TSW (Television South-West)
Derry's Cross, Plymouth
Devon PL1 2SP
Tel: (0752) 663322

Bowater House
68 Knightsbridge
London SW1X 7NN
Tel: 071-589 9755

The Colston Centre
Colston Street, Bristol BS1 4UX
Tel: (0272) 21131

TVS (Television South):
Television Centre
Southampton SO9 5HZ
Tel: (0703) 634211

Television Centre
Vinters Park
Maidstone ME14 5NZ
Tel: (0622) 691111

Spenser House
60–61 Buckingham Gate
London SW1E 6AJ
Tel: 071-828 9898

Tyne Tees Television:
Television Centre, City Road
Newcastle upon Tyne NE1 2AL
Tel: 091-261 0181

151 Bloomsbury Square
London WC1A 2LJ
Tel: 071-405 8474

Ulster Television:
Havelock House
Ormeau Road
Belfast BT7 1EB
Tel: (0232) 328122

6 York Street
London W1H 1FA
Tel: 071-486 5211

Yorkshire Television:
Television Centre
Leeds LS3 1JS
Tel: (0532) 438283

Television House
32 Bedford Row
London WC1R 4HE
Tel: 071-242 1666

Other ITV companies

Independent Television News:
ITN House
48 Wells Street
London W1P 4DE
Tel: 071-637 2424

TV-am:
Breakfast Television Centre
Hawley Crescent
London NW1 8EF
Tel: 071-267 4300/01-267 4377

Independent Television Association:
Knighton House
56 Mortimer Street
London W1N 8AN
Tel: 071-636 6866

Independent Television Publications:
247 Tottenham Court Road
London W1P 0AU
Tel: 071-323 3222

Channel Four

Channel Four Television:
60 Charlotte Street
London W1P 2AX
Tel: 071-631 4444

Brookside Productions/ Mersey Television:
43 Brookside
West Derby
Liverpool L12 0BA
Tel: 051-259 1602

AGENTS

AIM (Associated International Management)
5 Denmark Street
London WC2H 8LP
Tel: 071-836 2001

Susan Angel Associates
First Floor
12 D'Arblay Street
London W1V 3FP
Tel: 071-439 3086

Arlington Enterprises
1/3 Charlotte Street
London W1P 1HD
Tel: 071-580 0702

A.R.T. Casting
2 Mount Pleasant
Liverpool L3 5RY
Tel: 051-708 7669/
051-708 7791

The Artists Agency
10000 Santa Monica Boulevard
Suite 305
Los Angeles
California 90067
Tel: (0101) 213 277 7779

A.T.S. Casting
26 St Michael's Road
Leeds LS6 3AW
Tel: (0532) 304300

Aza Artists
652 Finchley Road
London NW11 7NT
Tel: 081-458 7288

George Bartram Associates
Stonewood House
5 Commercial Street
Birmingham B1 1RS
Tel: 021-643 9346

Julian Belfrage Associates
60 St James's Street
London SW1A 1LE
Tel: 071-491 4400

Nina Blatt
The Coach House
1A Larpent Avenue
London SW15 6UP
Tel: 081-788 5602

Michelle Braidman
10/11 Lower John Street
London W1R 3PE
Tel: 071-437 0817

USEFUL ADDRESSES

Barry Brown Management
47 West Square
London SE11 4SP
Tel: 071-582 6622

Curtis Brown
162–168 Regent Street
London W1R 5TB
Tel: 071-437 9700

Darryl Brown
1 Dorset Road
London SW19 3EY
Tel: 081-540 3968

Peter Browne Management
13 St Martin's Road
London SW9 0SP
Tel: 071-737 3444

Brownjohn and King Management
100 Fellows Road
London NW3
Tel: 071-722 1149

The Brunskill Management
Suite 8A
169 Queen's Gate
London SW7 5EH
Tel: 071-581 3388/
071-584 8060

Barry Burnett Organisation
Suite 42–43
Grafton House
2–3 Golden Square
London W1R 3AD
Tel: 071-437 7048/
071-734 6118

CCA Personal Management
4 Court Lodge
48 Sloane Square
London SW1W 8AT
Tel: 071-730 8857

CDA
Apartment 20
47 Courtfield Road
London SW7 4DB
Tel: 071-370 0708

Roger Carey Management
64 Thornton Avenue
Chiswick
London W4 1QQ
Tel: 081-995 4477

Peter Charlesworth
Second Floor
68 Old Brompton Road
London SW7 3LQ
Tel: 071-581 2478

Chatto and Linnit
Prince of Wales Theatre
Coventry Street
London W1V 7FE
Tel: 071-930 6677

Jeremy Conway
Eagle House
109 Jermyn Street
London SW1 6HB
Tel: 071-839 2121

Vernon Conway
19 London Street
London W2 1HL
Tel: 071-262 5506

Lou Coulson
37 Berwick Street
London W1V 3RF
Tel: 071-734 9633

Crouch Salmon Associates
59 Frith Street
London W1V 5TA
Tel: 071-734 2167

Daly Gagan Associates
68 Old Brompton Road
London SW7 3LQ
Tel: 071-581 0121

Larry Dalzell Associates
Suite 12
17 Broad Court
London WC2B 5QN
Tel: 071-379 0875

Isobel Davie
37 Hill Street
London W1X 8JY
Tel: 071-493 0343

Hazel De Leon
19 Gloucester Place Mews
London W1 3PN
Tel: 071-486 5438

Felix De Wolfe
Manfield House
376–378 The Strand
London WC2R 0LR
Tel: 071-379 5767

Direct Line Personal Management
CHEL
Room 35
26 Roundhay Road
Leeds LS7
Tel: (0532) 444991

Bryan Drew
Mezzanine
Quadrant House

80–82 Regent Street
London W1R 6AU
Tel: 071-437 2293

Jean Drysdale Management
Still Waters
Trolvercroft
Penpol
Feock
Nr Truro
Cornwall

Joyce Edwards
275 Kennington Road
London SE1 6BY
Tel: 071-735 5736

Ellison Combe Associates
17 Richmond Hill
Richmond-upon-Thames
Surrey TW10 6RE
Tel: 081-940 7863

Clifford Elson Publicity
1 Richmond Mews
London W1V 5AG
Tel: 071-437 4822

June Epstein Associates
Flat 1
62 Compayne Gardens
London NW6 3RY
Tel: 071-328 0864/0684

Essanay
2 Conduit Street
London W1R 9TG
Tel: 071-409 3526

Evans & Reiss
221 New Kings Road
London SW6 4XE
Tel: 071-384 1843

Jacque Evans Management
54 Lisson Street
London NW1 6ST
Tel: 071-402 3248

Kate Feast Management
43A Princess Road
London NW1 8JS
Tel: 071-586 5502

Aida Foster
33 Abbey Lodge
Park Road
London NW8 7RJ
Tel: 071-262 2181

Jill Foster
19A Queen's Gate Terrace
London SW7 5PR
Tel: 071-581 0084

Patrick Freeman Management
4 Cromwell Grove
London W6 7RG
Tel: 071-602 4035

French's
26 Binney Street
London W1Y 1YN
Tel: 071-629 4159

Kerry Gardner Management
16 Kensington High Street
London W8 5NP
Tel: 071-937 4478

Noel Gay Organisation
24 Denmark Street
London WC2H 8NJ
Tel: 071-836 3941/071-240 0451

Eric Glass
28 Berkeley Square
London W1X 6HD
Tel: 071-629 7162

Goodwin Associates
12 Rabbit Row
Kensington Church Street
London W8 4DX
Tel: 071-229 8805

Jimmy Grafton Management
9 Orme Court
London W2 4RL
Tel: 071-221 9364

David Graham Management
London House
271–273 King Street
London W6 9LZ
Tel: 081-741 8011

Joan Gray Personal Management
29 Sunbury Court Island
Sunbury-on-Thames
Middlesex TW16 5PP
Tel: 081-979 1789

Plunkett Greene
4 Ovington Gardens
London SW3 1LS
Tel: 071-584 0688

Green & Underwood
2 Conduit Street
London W1R 9TG
Tel: 071-493 0308

Sandra Griffin Management
Richmond Bridge House
417–421 Richmond Road
Twickenham
Middlesex TW1 2EX
Tel: 081-892 3637

Jo Gurnett Personal Management
2 New King's Road
London SW6 4SA
Tel: 071-736 7828

Louis Hammond Management
Golden House
29 Gt Pulteney Street
London W1R 3DD
Tel: 071-734 1931

Hamper-Neafsey Associates
4 Gt Queen Street
London WC2B 5DG
Tel: 071-734 1827/071-404 5255

Roger Hancock
Greener House
66–68 Haymarket
London SW1Y 4AW
Tel: 071-839 6753

Harbour & Coffey
9 Blenheim Street
London W1Y 9LE
Tel: 071-499 5548

The Bagenal Harvey Organisation
141–143 Drury Lane
London WC2B 5TB
Tel: 071-379 4625

Hatton & Baker
18 Jermyn Street
London SW1Y 6HN
Tel: 071-439 2971

Duncan Heath Associates
Paramount House
162 Wardour Street
London W1V 3AT
Tel: 071-439 1471

Hobson's
64 Thornton Avenue
London W4 1QQ
Tel: 081-995 3628

Hope and Lyne
108 Leonard Street
London EC2A 4RH
Tel: 071-739 6200

Howes & Prior
66 Berkeley House
Hay Hill
London W1X 7LH
Tel: 071-493 7570

Mike Hughes Entertainments
Prince of Wales Theatre
Coventry Street
London W1V 7FE
Tel: 071-930 9161

Hutton Management
200 Fulham Road
London SW10 9PN
Tel: 071-352 4825

Inter-City Casting
383 Corn Exchange
Manchester M4 3DH
Tel: 061-832 8848

International Artistes
Mezzanine Floor
235 Regent Street
London W1R 8AX
Tel: 071-439 8401

ICM
388–396 Oxford Street
London W1 9HE
Tel: 071-629 8080

8899 Beverly Boulevard
Los Angeles
California 90048
Tel: (0101) 212 556 5600

IMG
The Pier House
Strand on the Green
London W4 3NN
Tel: 081-994 1444

Carole James Management
2 Water Lane House
Water Lane
Richmond-upon-Thames
Surrey TW9 1TJ
Tel: 081-940 8154

Joy Jameson
219 The Plaza
535 Kings Road
London SW10 0SZ
Tel: 071-351 3971

Joseph and Wagg
Studio One
2 Tunstall Road
London SW9 8BN
Tel: 071-738 3026

J Y Publicity
100 Ebury Street
London SW1W 9QD
Tel: 071-730 9009

Rolf Kruger Management
22–23 Morley House
314–322 Regent Street
London W1R 8RY
Tel: 071-580 9432

LWA
61–63 Beak Street
London W1R 3LF
Tel: 071-434 3944

USEFUL ADDRESSES

Michael Ladkin Personal Management
2A Warwick Place North
London SW1V 1QW
Tel: 071-834 6627

Tessa Le Bars Management
18 Queen Anne Street
London W1M 9LB
Tel: 071-636 3191

Jane Lehrer Associates
Third Floor
17 Nottingham Street
London W1M 3RD
Tel: 071-486 0888

Bernard Lee Management
Moorcroft Lodge
Farleigh Common
Warlingham
Surrey CR3 0PE
Tel: (0883) 625667

L'Epine Smith & Carney Associates
10 Wyndham Place
London W1H 1AS
Tel: 071-724 0739

Tony Lewis Entertainments
235–241 Regent Street
London W1R 8TL
Tel: 071-734 2285

London Management
235–241 Regent Street
London W1A 2JT
Tel: 071-493 1610

MLR
200 Fulham Road
London SW10 9PN
Tel: 071-351 5442

MPC Artists and Management
Hammer House
113–117 Wardour Street
London W1V 3TD
Tel: 071-434 1861

Julia Macdermot
14 Leamore Street
London W6 0JZ
Tel: 081-741 0269

McCartt-Oreck Barrett
10390 Santa Monica Boulevard
Suite 310
Los Angeles
California 90025
Tel: (0101) 213 553 2600

Ken McReddie
91 Regent Street
London W1R 7TB
Tel: 071-439 1456

John Mahoney Management
Lower Ground Floor
94 Gloucester Place
London W1H 3DA
Tel: 071-486 2947

Hazel Malone Management
Suite 29
London House
271–273 King Street
London W6 9LZ
Tel: 081-741 0707

Markham & Froggatt
Julian House
4 Windmill Street
London W1
Tel: 071-636 4412

Marmont Management
Langham House
302–308 Regent Street
London W1R 5AL
Tel: 071-637 3183

Billy Marsh Associates
19 Denmark Street
London WC2H 8NA
Tel: 071-379 4004

Marina Martin Management
6A Danbury Street
London N1 8JU
Tel: 071-359 3646

Nigel Martin-Smith Personal Management
Half Moon Chambers
Chapel Walks
Manchester M2 1HN
Tel: 061-832 8259

Mayer Management
Suite 44
Grafton House
2–3 Golden Square
London W1R 3AD
Tel: 071-434 1242

Miller Management
82 Broom Park
Teddington
Middlesex TW11 9RR
Tel: 081-943 1292

Morgan & Goodman
1 Old Compton Street
London W1V 5PH
Tel: 071-437 1383

William Morris Agency
31–32 Soho Square
London W1V 5DG
Tel: 071-434 2191

151 El Camino Drive
Beverly Hills
California 90212
Tel: (0101) 213 274 7451

Dee O'Reilly Management
112 Gunnersbury Avenue
London W5 4HB
Tel: 081-993 7441

PBAM
First Floor
37 Marshall Street
London W1V 1WL
Tel: 071-734 8346

PBJ Management
47 Dean Street
London W1V 5HL
Tel: 071-434 0672

PVA Management
22–23 Gayfere Street
London SW1P 3HP
Tel: 071-233 0599

Al Parker
55 Park Lane
London W1Y 3LB
Tel: 071-499 4232

Peters Fraser & Dunlop
Fifth Floor
The Chambers
Chelsea Harbour
Lots Road
London SW10 0XF
Tel: 071-376 7676

Peter Prichard
118 Beaufort Street
London SW3 6BU
Tel: 071-352 6417

Prime Performers
The Studio
5 Kidderpore Avenue
London NW3 7SX
Tel: 071-431 0211

Douglas Rae Management
28 Charing Cross Road
London WC2H 0DB
Tel: 071-836 3903

Margaret Ramsay
14A Goodwins Court
St Martin's Lane
London WC2N 4LL
Tel: 071-240 0691/071-836 7403

Joan Reddin
Hazel Cottage
Wheeler End Common
Lane End
Buckinghamshire HP14 3NL
Tel: (0494) 882729

John Redway & Associates
16 Berners Street
London W1P 3DD
Tel: 071-637 1612

John Reid Enterprises
32 Galena Road
London W6 0CT
Tel: 081-741 9933

Stella Richards Management
42 Hazlebury Road
London SW6 2ND
Tel: 071-736 7786

Saraband Associates
265 Liverpool Road
London N1 1LX
Tel: 071-609 5313

Anna Scher Theatre Management
70–72 Barnsbury Road
London N1 0ES
Tel: 071-278 2101

James Sharkey Associates
Third Floor Suite
15 Golden Square
London W1R 3AG
Tel: 071-434 3801

Philip Shaw Associates
Suite 204
Garden Studios
11–15 Betterton Street
London WC2H 9BP
Tel: 071-379 0344

Neville Shulman
4 St George's House
15 Hanover Square
London W1R 9AJ
Tel: 071-486 6363

Spotlight Casting Directory
7 Leicester Place
London WC2H 7BP
Tel: 071-437 7631

Annette Stone Associates
9 Newburgh Street
London W1V 1LH
Tel: 071-734 0626

The Richard Stone Partnership
25 Whitehall
London SW1A 2BS
Tel: 071-839 6421

Talent Artists
37 Hill Street
London W1X 8JY
Tel: 071-493 0343

Ruth Tarko Agency
50–52 Cecil Street
Hillhead
Glasgow G12 8RJ
Tel: 041-339 8037/041-334 0555

David White Associates
2 Ormond Road
Richmond-upon-Thames
Surrey TW10 6TH
Tel: 081-940 8300

Michael Whitehall
125 Gloucester Road
London SW7 4TE
Tel: 071-244 8466

David Wilkinson Associates
24 Denmark Street
London WC2H 8NJ
Tel: 071-240 0451

Dave Winslett Entertainments
4 Cliff End
Purley
Surrey CR2 1BN
Tel: 081-668 0531

Writers and Artists Agency
11726 San Vicente Boulevard
Suite 300
Los Angeles
California 90049
Tel: (0101) 213 820 2240

April Young
The Clockhouse
6 St Catherine's Mews
Milner Street
London SW3 2PU
Tel: 071-584 1274

Young Casting Agency
7 Beaumont Gate
Glasgow G12 9EE
Tel: 041-334 2646/041-339 5180

Sonny Zahl Associates
57 Gt Cumberland Place
London W1H 7LJ
Tel: 071-724 3684/071-723 5699

FAN CLUBS

Send a stamped, self-addressed envelope
with all enquiries

The A-Team Appreciation Society
'Xanth'
11 Somercotes
Laindon
Basildon
Essex SS15 5TZ

Auf Wiedersehen, Pet
David Beavis
Heatherley Cheshire Home
Effingham Lane
Copthorne
West Sussex RH10 3HS

The Avengers
Stay Tuned
114 Dartmouth Street
Burslem
Stoke-on-Trent
Staffordshire ST6 1HE

Overseas club:
Stay Tuned
64 Southampton Road
Carole Park
Queensland 4300
Australia

Battlestar Galactica
'The Thirteenth Tribe'
c/o 19 Woodlands Road
Stanton
Burton-on-Trent
Staffordshire DE15 9TH

Beauty and the Beast UK Chamber
Sheila Waters
14 Judith Road
Kettering
Northamptonshire NN16 0NX

Crossroads: The Noele Gordon and Crossroads Appreciation Society
John Kavyo and Simon Cole
Flat 8
Harewood Apartments
9 Undercliff Road
Boscombe
Bournemouth BH5 1BL

The Emmerdale Club
PO Box 330
St Albans
Hertfordshire AL4 0LF

Garrison's Gorillas Appreciation Society
4 Hedera Road
Southampton SO3 6SF

Home and Away Fan Club
PO Box 12
Ripon
North Yorkshire HG4 3YN

USEFUL ADDRESSES

The Poldark Appreciation Society
PO Box 25
Charing
Kent TN27 0JZ

The Prisoner: Six of One
PO Box 60
Harrogate HG1 2TP

Prisoner: Cell Block H
Room 28
St James Chambers
St James Street
Derby DE1 1QZ

Randall and Hopkirk (Deceased)
Appreciation Society
10 Brook Avenue
Edgware
Middlesex HA8 9XF

The Saint Club
8 Beverley Road
Hampton Wick
Kingston-upon-Thames
Surrey KT1 4DZ

Scarecrow and Mrs King Fellowship
c/o Margaret Richardson
30 Kirkdale Green
Rye Hill
Newcastle upon Tyne NE4 6HU

The Sooty Fan Club
c/o Windhill Manor
Leeds Road, Shipley
West Yorkshire BD18 1BP

Take the High Road Fan Club
PO Box 25, Charing
Kent TN27 0JZ

The TV Enthusiasts Club
(News and views about
television)
64 Daisy Road
Brighouse
West Yorkshire HD6 3SX

'V'
The Freedom League
c/o 30 Borodin Close
Brighton Hill
Basingstoke
Hampshire RG22 4EN

Westerns
Laramie Trail
196 Whitehouse Common Road
Sutton Coldfield
West Midlands B75 6DN